Cyberpsychology

BPS Textbooks in Psychology

BPS Wiley presents a comprehensive and authoritative series covering everything a student needs in order to complete an undergraduate degree in psychology. Refreshingly written to consider more than North American research, this series is the first to give a truly international perspective. Written by the very best names in the field, the series offers an extensive range of titles from introductory level through to final year optional modules, and every text fully complies with the BPS syllabus in the topic. No other series bears the BPS seal of approval!

Many of the books are supported by a companion website, featuring additional resource materials for both instructors and students, designed to encourage critical thinking, and providing for all your course lecturing and testing needs.

For other titles in this series, please go to **http://psychsource.bps.org.uk**.

Cyberpsychology

The Study of Individuals, Society and Digital Technologies

MONICA THERESE WHITTY

UNIVERSITY OF WARWICK, UK

GARRY YOUNG

NOTTINGHAM TRENT UNIVERSITY, UK

The British Psychological Society

WILEY

This edition first published 2017 by the British Psychological Society and John Wiley & Sons, Ltd.
© 2017 John Wiley & Sons, Ltd.

Registered Office
John Wiley & Sons, Ltd, The Atrium, Southern Gate, Chichester, West Sussex, PO19 8SQ, UK

Editorial Offices
350 Main Street, Malden, MA 02148–5020, USA
9600 Garsington Road, Oxford, OX4 2DQ, UK
The Atrium, Southern Gate, Chichester, West Sussex, PO19 8SQ, UK

For details of our global editorial offices, for customer services, and for information about how to apply for permission to reuse the copyright material in this book please see our website at www.wiley.com/wiley-blackwell.

The right of Monica Therese Whitty and Garry Young to be identified as the authors of this work has been asserted in accordance with the UK Copyright, Designs and Patents Act 1988.

All rights reserved. No part of this publication may be reproduced, stored in a retrieval system, or transmitted, in any form or by any means, electronic, mechanical, photocopying, recording or otherwise, except as permitted by the UK Copyright, Designs and Patents Act 1988, without the prior permission of the publisher.

Wiley also publishes its books in a variety of electronic formats. Some content that appears in print may not be available in electronic books.

Designations used by companies to distinguish their products are often claimed as trademarks. All brand names and product names used in this book are trade names, service marks, trademarks or registered trademarks of their respective owners. The publisher is not associated with any product or vendor mentioned in this book.

Limit of Liability/Disclaimer of Warranty: While the publisher and authors have used their best efforts in preparing this book, they make no representations or warranties with respect to the accuracy or completeness of the contents of this book and specifically disclaim any implied warranties of merchantability or fitness for a particular purpose. It is sold on the understanding that the publisher is not engaged in rendering professional services and neither the publisher nor the author shall be liable for damages arising herefrom. If professional advice or other expert assistance is required, the services of a competent professional should be sought.

Library of Congress Cataloging-in-Publication Data

Names: Whitty, Monica Therese, 1969– author. | Young, Garry, 1966– author.
Title: Cyberpsychology : the study of individuals, society and digital technologies / Monica Whitty, Garry Young.
Description: Hoboken : Wiley, 2017. | Includes bibliographical references and index.
Identifiers: LCCN 2016014408 | ISBN 9780470975626 (pbk.) | ISBN 9781118321126 (epub)
Subjects: LCSH: Internet users–Psychology. | Internet–Psychological aspects. | Internet–Social aspects. | Virtual reality–Moral and ethical aspects. | Cyberspace–Psychological aspects. | Computer crimes.
Classification: LCC HM851 .W4556 2016 | DDC 302.23/1–dc23
LC record available at https://lccn.loc.gov/2016014408

A catalogue record for this book is available from the British Library.

Cover image: Mina De La O / Gettyimages

Set in 11/12.5pt Dante by SPi Global, Pondicherry, India

1 2017

The British Psychological Society's free Research Digest e-mail service rounds up the latest research and relates it to your syllabus in a user-friendly way. To subscribe go to **www.researchdigest.org.uk** or send a blank e-mail to **subscriberd@lists.bps.org.uk**.

Brief Contents

List of Tables, Figures and Boxes   x

Chapter 1   Introduction   1

Chapter 2   The 'Self' in Cyberspace   9

Chapter 3   Online Relationships   23

Chapter 4   Online Dating   39

Chapter 5   Online Sexual Activities   51

Chapter 6   Internet Infidelity   62

Chapter 7   Children's and Teens' Use of Digital Technologies   73

Chapter 8   Online Education   86

Chapter 9   Leisure and Entertainment   101

Chapter 10   Online Gaming and Gambling   114

Chapter 11   Online Deception   128

Chapter 12   Online Crimes: Scams, Fraud and Illegal Downloads   141

Chapter 13   Online Crimes: Cyberharassment, Hate Crimes and Cyberwarfare   156

Chapter 14   Online Crimes: Child Pornography and Paedophilia   170

Chapter 15   Online Support and Health Care   187

Chapter 16   Concluding Thoughts   200

References   203

Index   240

Contents

List of Tables, Figures and Boxes   x

Chapter 1   Introduction   1

Chapter 2   The 'Self' in Cyberspace   9
- **2.1** Defining the 'Self'   9
- **2.2** The self in cyberspace   13
- **2.3** Disembodied selves in cyberspace   13
- **2.4** The cyborg self   16
- **2.5** Goffman: Performing self online   17
- **2.6** Possible selves in cyberspace   18
- **2.7** Social identities in cyberspace   19
- **2.8** Visually anonymous?   20
- **2.9** Conclusions   21

Chapter 3   Online Relationships   23
- **3.1** Traditional relationships: Offline realm   23
- **3.2** Applying old theories to online relationships   25
- **3.3** New theories to explain online relating   27
- **3.4** A brief history of online relating   30
- **3.5** Contemporary online spaces   33
- **3.6** Interacting in various spaces   36
- **3.7** Future development in the field   37
- **3.8** Conclusions   37

Chapter 4   Online Dating   39
- **4.1** What is an online dating site?   39
- **4.2** Motivations for using an online dating site   40
- **4.3** Psychological characteristics of online daters   41
- **4.4** Comparing online dating sites with personal ads   42
- **4.5** Presenting oneself on an online dating site   43
- **4.6** Dating deception   44
- **4.7** A perfect match or a numbers game?   45
- **4.8** Stages in the online dating process   46
- **4.9** Conclusions   49

Chapter 5 Online Sexual Activities — 51

- 5.1 The beginnings of Internet sex — 51
- 5.2 The Triple A Engine — 52
- 5.3 Cybersex: Debilitating or liberating? — 53
- 5.4 Interactive sex entertainment — 54
- 5.5 Cybersex addiction — 54
- 5.6 The Internet as an enabler of risky offline sexual encounters — 55
- 5.7 The Internet and sexual health information — 56
- 5.8 Social support and exploring sexuality — 57
- 5.9 Teens and risky sexual online behaviour — 58
- 5.10 Teledildonics and the future of sex in cyberspace — 60
- 5.11 Conclusions — 60

Chapter 6 Internet Infidelity — 62

- 6.1 Defining Internet infidelity — 63
- 6.2 Unfaithful online sexual activities — 63
- 6.3 Virtual or real? — 65
- 6.4 Emotional infidelity — 65
- 6.5 Gender differences: Which is worse – sex or love? — 66
- 6.6 Qualitative differences between online and offline affairs — 68
- 6.7 Virtual affairs with an avatar — 70
- 6.8 Conclusions — 71

Chapter 7 Children's and Teens' Use of Digital Technologies — 73

- 7.1 Internet usage — 73
- 7.2 The digital divide — 74
- 7.3 Digital technologies: Harmful or empowering for young people? — 75
- 7.4 Illegal content and illegal activities — 76
- 7.5 Cyberbullying and cyberharassment — 77
- 7.6 Scams, children and teens — 79
- 7.7 Identity development — 80
- 7.8 Activism — 81
- 7.9 Radicalization — 82
- 7.10 Conclusions — 84

Chapter 8 Online Education — 86

- 8.1 Technology and learning — 86
- 8.2 E-learning — 87
- 8.3 E-learning versus face-to-face learning — 89
- 8.4 Synchronous and asynchronous communication within e-learning — 90
- 8.5 Media richness theory — 93

	8.6	Salmon's stage model of e-learning	95
	8.7	3-D learning environments	96
	8.8	Conclusions	99
Chapter 9	**Leisure and Entertainment**		**101**
	9.1	What is leisure and what motivates our pursuit of it?	101
	9.2	Online family leisure	103
	9.3	Older adults	103
	9.4	Technoference: Encroaching on leisure time within relationships	104
	9.5	Telecommunication	105
	9.6	Time and functional displacement effects	106
	9.7	Twitter	110
	9.8	Conclusions	112
Chapter 10	**Online Gaming and Gambling**		**114**
	10.1	Internet addiction	114
	10.2	Internet gambling addiction	116
	10.3	Internet gaming addiction	117
	10.4	Aggressive video games	118
	10.5	Transcending taboos: Video games	123
	10.6	Games for learning	124
	10.7	Conclusions	126
Chapter 11	**Online Deception**		**128**
	11.1	Defining deception	128
	11.2	Deception in cyberspace	129
	11.3	Do we lie more online?	133
	11.4	Detecting deception	137
	11.5	Conclusions	138
Chapter 12	**Online Crimes: Scams, Fraud and Illegal Downloads**		**141**
	12.1	Phishing	142
	12.2	Vishing	143
	12.3	Why are people tricked by phishing?	144
	12.4	Improving detection	146
	12.5	Mass-marketing fraud	146
	12.6	Awareness campaigns	149
	12.7	Cognitive and motivational errors	150
	12.8	What type of person tends to be susceptible to MMF?	151
	12.9	Stages involved in the online dating romance scam	152
	12.10	Illegal downloads	152
	12.11	Conclusions	154

Chapter 13	Online Crimes: Cyberharassment, Hate Crimes and Cyberwarfare	156
	13.1 Online harassment and stalking	156
	13.2 Cyberstalking and the law	158
	13.3 Psychologically profiling criminals and victims	159
	13.4 Hate crimes	160
	13.5 Cyberwarfare	162
	13.6 Surveillance and monitoring	165
	13.7 Conclusions	168
Chapter 14	Online Crimes: Child Pornography and Paedophilia	170
	14.1 The Internet and the increase in child pornography	171
	14.2 Child pornography and the law	172
	14.3 Pseudo-photographs	174
	14.4 Types of child pornography offenders	176
	14.5 Characteristics of child pornography offenders	179
	14.6 The relationship between child pornography and hands-on offending	180
	14.7 Theoretical approaches to child pornography offending	181
	14.8 Conclusions	185
Chapter 15	Online Support and Health Care	187
	15.1 The Internet and health	187
	15.2 Characteristics and motivations	188
	15.3 Online health searching and cyberchondria	189
	15.4 Social media, group forums and support sites	191
	15.5 E-therapy	193
	15.6 Assessing the effectiveness of e-therapies	196
	15.7 Immersive virtual environments as aids to treatment	197
	15.8 Conclusions	198
Chapter 16	Concluding Thoughts	200
References		203
Index		240

List of Tables, Figures and Boxes

TABLES

7.1	Opportunities and risks relating to young people's use of the Internet (adapted from Livingstone, 2009)	76
11.1	The feature-based model: ranking predictions of likelihood of lying (adapted from Hancock et al., 2004)	135
12.1	Errors in decision-making with respect to scams (identified by Lea et al. 2009a, p. 24)	150

FIGURES

8.1	Measures of learning performance (adapted from Sun & Cheng, 2007, p. 666)	94
10.1	The general aggression model's episodic processes (Anderson & Bushman, 2002, p. 34)	123
12.1	Example of a phishing email	143

BOXES

7.1	Young people's use of the Internet in the UK	74
7.2	Young people's use of the Internet in the US	74

1 Introduction

Digital technologies play important roles in both our everyday and working lives and will continue to increase in importance in the future. Given this importance it is no wonder that cyberpsychology has emerged as a new subdiscipline within psychology and is being taught in many mainstream psychology degrees as well as disciplines such as media and communications, philosophy, sociology, criminology and security studies. Well-regarded, high-impact journals have been available for some time that focus solely on cyberpsychology. Conferences have also been designed to focus on this topic and are growing in popularity. Cyberpsychology master's courses are sprouting up across the globe and the number of students drawn to these courses continues to increase – most likely because the Internet continues to grow and affect people's lives in new, challenging and exciting ways.

Cyberpsychology is the study of individuals, societies and digital technologies and the psychology of how these interact. Cyberpsychology applies psychological theory to explain how individuals interact in cyberspace and how these interactions might affect our offline lives. It offers a new way to define the self and society. In this book, we have attempted to cover the breadth and depth of cyberpsychology, although as the discipline expands it is likely to incorporate new and exciting areas and foci.

This book is intended as a textbook for both undergraduate and postgraduate students in psychology as well as other relevant degrees that incorporate psychology into their syllabuses. It aims to set out key theories and empirical research conducted within the field of cyberpsychology. It does so by also considering real-world problems and events, and considers how theories in this field might shed further light on our understanding of these issues. Moreover, it engages readers with novel and relevant issues – encouraging them to critically evaluate the current literature and to take their own personal stance on particular issues.

We begin the book by focusing on the complex issue of defining the 'Self' in cyberspace, and present the argument that the Internet has changed the way we view and understand the self. In Chapter 2, we start by considering traditional theories of the self – for example, trait theory, social identity theory, possible selves, a social constructionist approach and a postmodern view of the self. We follow this with a history of how the self has been understood in cyberspace. In this chapter we acknowledge Turkle's early work, which theorized that individuals could explore and gain new insights about identity within cyberspace. Other theorists who embraced these utopian views about the Internet are also mentioned in this chapter, with

Cyberpsychology: The Study of Individuals, Society and Digital Technologies, First Edition.
Monica Therese Whitty and Garry Young.
© 2017 John Wiley & Sons, Ltd. Published 2017 by John Wiley & Sons, Ltd.

particular reference to feminist theorists, such as Haraway. We note, however, that Turkle has in more recent times rejected her own earlier claims and now takes the opposite view, arguing that digital technologies can lead to a new sense of solitude. Gergen's theory on the saturated self is also highlighted here, as is his view that new technologies have led to a fragmentation of the self. We briefly outline the ways in which traditional theories of the self have been applied to how the self might be presented in cyberspace – for example, considering Goffman's 'performing self', the theory of 'possible selves' and social identity theory. We conclude the chapter by noting that there are few places where users can be visually anonymous, and we therefore suggest that theories of the self online need to consider differences between spaces where users are visually anonymous and those where they present images of themselves, as well as the choices they make to visually present themselves.

In Chapter 3, we set out some of the theories and classic studies that have examined online relationships – both between friends and romantic. We begin by setting out some of the well-known theories on relationship development that explain how relationships develop in the physical realm, such as social evolutionary theory, social penetration theory, exchange theory and equity theory. We then move on to examine how these theories might be used to explain the development of online relationships, and point out some of their shortcomings. Given these shortcomings, theories have been developed to explain the uniqueness of some relationships initiated and developed in cyberspace compared with the physical world. Theories such as the 'disinhibition effect', social presence theory, social information processing theory and hyperpersonal communication theory are outlined. We explain how these theories have emerged and how they have been applied to explain online relating. We also provide a brief history of online relating and detail some of the ways in which relating has changed as technology has developed – especially from a more textual space to a space with greater bandwidth and less visual anonymity.

Online dating has changed from a stigmatized method for finding a date to a popular matching method for people in many countries across a range of ages. Chapter 4 focuses specifically on this phenomenon, and picks up on some of the theories outlined in Chapter 3 to examine how relationship initiation and development differ from but also share commonalities with relationships formed in other places online and in the physical realm. We examine research that has found personality differences relating to use of online dating; for example, some studies have found that shy individuals are more likely to use dating sites compared with more socially confident individuals. We also explore the notion that the self is commodified on online dating sites and that how one is presented is, in part, dependent on which aspects are more likely to draw in desirable dates (this motivation sometimes leads to deception, where daters lie about certain aspects of themselves, such as height and weight). We also go through the stages involved in the online dating process, noting that a new wave of dating apps is changing users' experiences of this process.

In Chapter 5 we consider online sexual activities. We note that, even in the early days of the Internet, people engaged in cybersex, in the form of erotic textual communication. This chapter outlines some of the well-cited papers that consider why individuals partake in cybersex. The Triple A Engine, for example, is a model put forward by Cooper and his colleges to argue that the Internet's affordability, anonymity and accessibility initially led some individuals to be drawn to this space to engage in sexual activities. Cooper believed that some of these people became cybersex compulsives. This chapter further outlines some of the problems associated with cybersex as well as some of its liberating aspects. One of the problems, which continues to exist in contemporary times, is that the Internet enables risky offline sexual encounters, with research revealing correlations between locating sexual partners online and contracting sexually transmitted infections (STIs). Sexting, described in this chapter, is also an activity that is problematic and sometimes illegal. On the flip side, however, the Internet provides sexual health information, which is easy to access, without the perceived embarrassment of asking a doctor, thereby potentially preventing the transmission of sexual diseases.

As we discuss in Chapter 6, some people perceive Internet infidelity to be a genuine betrayal that can have real repercussions in couples' lives. We define Internet infidelity based on current theories and empirical findings. We examine the sexual and emotional aspects of relationship transgressions both online and offline. This chapter also presents a critical examination of the theories that explain why men and women become jealous in the physical world (e.g., social evolutionary theory and the social cognitive approach) and whether these theories can be applied to explain jealousy about seemingly equivalent activities in cyberspace. Although there is a dearth of research available on Internet infidelity, the chapter points out some possible qualitative differences between online and offline affairs. Online affairs, for example, are potentially easier to split off from people's everyday lives – making it easier for people engaging in an affair to rationalize that it is not a relationship transgression. We also consider whether having cybersex with an avatar might constitute 'real' betrayal. Here, we provide some real-life examples in which people have felt hurt and betrayed by their partners' cybersex activities in *Second Life*.

There has been much talk over the years about the digital divide. Some discuss this with respect to a divide between social classes, while others consider differences between ages (e.g., digital natives vs. digital immigrants). Chapter 7 focuses on digital natives – children's and teens' use of digital technologies. It does not, however, simply address the ease with which young people have appropriated digital technologies into their lives. In addition, it considers the issues young people have had to deal with since before there was an Internet (e.g., identity, sexuality, activism) and how these issues are dealt with in cyberspace. We examine here whether the use of digital technologies might be harmful or empowering for young people and detail empirical findings that support both views. A balanced view is provided, pointing out both the risks and the opportunities. We examine the types of illegal content young people might be exposed to and the kinds of illegal activities some young people engage in. We also ask whether, for some youth, exposure to illegal content might be the start of a slippery slope. Although we examine cyberharassment in Chapter 13, in this chapter, we pay some attention to how this behaviour can affect young people. This chapter also outlines how criminals target young people in order to scam them as well as how their identity might be stolen to then be used to scam others (e.g., the grandparents scam). Finally, the chapter addresses the very real concern of radicalization of youth via the Internet.

As far back as 1913, Thomas Edison predicted that new technology would be at the forefront of education. As Chapter 8 illustrates, Edison was probably correct in his prediction, but most likely in ways that he did not imagine. We begin the chapter by focusing on e-learning and compare this with face-to-face learning, noting the advantages e-learning has to offer. We also comment on the features used in e-learning that might have a detrimental effect on students' learning performance. When comparing e-learning with face-to-face learning, we find that different types of learning might benefit from different teaching practices. For example, researchers have found that students prefer face-to-face discussions when engaged with difficult tasks and computer-mediated learning for simple tasks. In this chapter, as we have done in other chapters, we compare and contrast synchronous and asynchronous communication. We highlight the advantages of both with respect to e-learning. We also point out the necessary conditions for successful e-learning, including cognitive presence, social presence and teaching presence. In addition, we introduce the reader to media richness theory: a theory that has been applied to a number of settings, including educational. We set out, according to this theory, when it is best to use e-learning practices. Salmon's stage model is also looked at in this chapter, together with applications of this model to *Second Life*. Indeed, *Second Life* and other 3-D learning environments have become popular spaces for educators to use as learning environments, and in this chapter we take a look at some of the studies that have evaluated learning in these environments.

In Chapter 9 we move the focus from education to the pursuit of leisure and entertainment. Does the Internet free up time in which to pursue leisure activities? Does it provide new forms of entertainment? This chapter examines these questions and many more. We begin the chapter by operationalizing leisure, pointing out the different forms of leisure, such as serious and casual pastimes, and how, in the past, families might have more often joined together to play a board game at home. In contrast to this more traditional view, when we think of online games, we often image a teenager in a locked bedroom playing games in isolation or hooked up with other teenagers in their own bedrooms. Researchers, however, have found that online games can also help family members to keep in touch. Moreover, and as the reader will learn, one of the main functions of the Internet for older users is the pursuit of leisure activities, such as engaging in virtual hobbies (e.g., constructing family trees). Importantly, this chapter consults the literature on how much time we spend online for leisure and entertainment and how this compares with time spent on entertainment in the physical world. It examines the displacement and the engagement hypotheses. Readers will probably not be surprised to learn that many people multitask entertainment in both realms (e.g., playing an online video game while watching the television). The chapter does question, however, how psychologically healthy it is to combine these tasks. In the final section of this chapter we consider how Twitter has been used as a source of entertainment, as well as the impact it has had on the perceived relationship between those who follow celebrities and the celebrity tweeters themselves.

Chapter 10 considers entertainment in more detail by focusing on gaming and gambling. We begin by examining online gaming and gambling addictions. It has been speculated, for instance, that Internet gambling is potentially more likely to lead to addiction than gambling offline. Certain features of online gambling, such as access, privacy, anonymity and a better game experience, might increase the risk of developing problems. The addition of 'Internet gaming disorder' in the latest *Diagnostic and Statistical Manual of Mental Disorders* (DSM) is considered here together with some of the research linking online gaming problems with other psychological problems (e.g., attention deficit hyperactivity disorder (ADHD), sleep deprivation, substance abuse). This chapter also examines the theories and empirical evidence that address whether video games might lead to violent behaviour. Some of these theories include social learning theory, script theory, the frustration–aggression hypothesis, the cognitive neoassociation model and the general aggression model. We provide a critique of each of these theories and give details of studies that have attempted to find evidence for a link between aggressive behaviour and playing aggressive video games. We conclude, however, that the research findings are, at best, weak. Nevertheless, although violent videos games may have little to zero impact on aggressive behaviour, there still might be reason to feel some concern for people who play video games with certain content – that is, content considered taboo in the physical world (such as rape, torture or cannibalism). In this chapter we consider the available literature that investigates this issue, which suggests that some people might not be able to cope psychologically with engaging with this material in a game. Although much of the focus of this chapter is on the negatives of playing video games, we note that there are also many positives. For starters, video games are fun and enjoyed by many. Second, video games are increasing in popularity as educational tools, and in a range of settings. We conclude the chapter by considering some of the ways in which games might be used to teach new skills as well as attitudes.

In earlier chapters, we examine how people self-disclose more about themselves online (becoming hyperhonest). In contrast, in Chapter 11, we examine whether people are more deceptive in cyberspace compared to in the physical realm. Online, users can potentially deceive a greater number of people in novel ways. We begin this chapter by defining deception and move on to consider the types of deceptions evident in cyberspace: identity-based deception and message-based deception. Case studies on the 'Munchausen by Internet' phenomenon are provided in order to give examples of identity-based deception. (Munchausen's syndrome is a psychological condition where someone lies about being ill or induces symptoms of illness in themselves.) Munchausen by Internet is therefore a psychological condition, and some believe it ought to be formally recognized in the DSM. The Internet might afford us more opportunities to lie, but do we actually lie more on the Internet? This chapter examines the empirical evidence that addresses this question and elucidates some interesting conclusions. The current research suggests that people, in the main, lie more on the telephone. The chapter presents the features-based model, which explains this finding. We present studies that support this model but also point out that the model is not always supported when a distinction is made between spontaneous and planned lies. We also examine research that has attempted to detect deception – both offline and in cyber realms. Although much research is still needed, computer scientists, in particular, are starting to detect criminals who hide behind multiple identities.

Chapter 12 focuses on deception carried out by criminals including criminal acts such as phishing, mass-marketing fraud (MMF) and illegal downloads of online material. We begin the chapter by focusing on phishing, explaining how it works and the numbers of people who are tricked by this scam. The chapter also considers spear phishing, which is similar to phishing but involves a targeted attack rather than a random hack. Research has been conducted using real phishing emails to investigate why users respond to these emails. It has been found, for example, that paying attention to visceral triggers increases the likelihood of responding. Personality has also been found to play a role in predicting who is more likely to respond to a phishing email. This chapter considers the training programmes that have been developed to help end users detect phishing emails and the evaluation of these programmes. As the reader will note, there is still a great need to develop more effective training programmes. This chapter also considers another type of scam, that of MMF, which is a type of fraud that exploits mass communication techniques (e.g., bulk mailing, email, instant messaging, social networking sites (SNSs)) to con people out of money. We provide examples and data on the number of victims of this fraud. We provide a detailed account of the stages involved in the online dating romance scam. As with phishing attacks, personality has been found to predict the sorts of person who are more likely to respond to MMFs; however, the profiles potentially differ according to the specific fraud. The sorts of cognitive and motivation errors that victims are likely to make are also noted here. We point out that the harm caused by these types of scams can be both financial and psychological. Prevention and detection of MMF is difficult, as this chapter explains, and awareness campaigns have yet to be properly evaluated. Finally, we examine illegal downloads of online material, such as music and video. We comment on how individuals who engage in these activities often do not recognize their actions as criminal. Approaches to preventing this form of criminal behaviour are discussed, including encouraging individuals to think differently about purchasing materials such as videos and music in the future.

In Chapter 13 we continue focusing on the topic of online crimes by examining cyberharassment, hate crimes and cyberwarfare. We begin the chapter by considering online harassment and online stalking (a form of harassment). We operationalize these terms and discuss some of the problems with inconsistencies in the law across different countries. According to the literature, the Internet has afforded new opportunities to cyberstalk both individuals and organizations. Additionally, cyberstalking can, of course, accompany stalking and harassment in the physical realm. This chapter outlines some of the main distinctions between stalker and cyberstalking profiles, while noting that the research is fairly scant. It then moves on to consider hate crimes more broadly and examines how they might be carried out in cyberspace. We provide examples of hate crimes as well as extremists groups that have an online presence in order to recruit members to their groups. We also consider cyberwarfare – another topic with a scarcity of available research. We note here that governments and society have yet to properly codify and sanction a body of norms to govern state action in cyberspace. We also highlight some of the features of cyberwar that set it apart from traditional warfare. These features, we suggest, need to be considered as scholars and governments rethink the rules of war with respect to cyberwarfare. One way to detect and counteract cyberattacks is via surveillance and monitoring. Although surveillance may be employed with good intentions, it nonetheless impinges on innocent civilians' privacy. Unsurprisingly, then, there has been much upset voiced by citizens about governments 'spying' on their online activities. We conclude this chapter by considering some of the current debates regarding surveillance and monitoring.

Chapter 14 continues to focus on online crimes, this time with a focus on child pornography and paedophilia. We acknowledge the increase in child pornography since the advent of the Internet and offer some reasons for this increase. The chapter also, importantly, provides a summary of legislation around child pornography in the UK and the US, and highlights some of the differences in this legalization. This comparison is made in order to elucidate the problems that can arise when law enforcement has to deal with this crime across borders; the comparison also points out some of the issues surrounding the application of the law to more recent phenomena, such as sexting. The psychological disorders associated with certain types of paedophilia are outlined, as is the role the Internet plays in these disorders. We also explain the differences between paedophiles who view child pornography and those who collect it, breaking down the types of collectors into the following categories: closet collector, isolated collector, cottage collector and commercial collector. This chapter summarizes the research that has considered the profile of the child pornography offender, although we note that many studies contend that a typical child pornography offender profile does not exist. The relationship between those who view child pornography and those who commit hands-on offences is considered with respect to the slippery slope hypothesis. In the final sections of this chapter we examine theoretical models that have been specifically developed or applied from other fields to explain why someone becomes a paedophile, considering, for example, courtship disorder theory, social learning theory, Finkelhor's precondition model, the pathways model and the integrated theory of sexual offending.

The focus in Chapter 15 moves from online crimes to online support and health care. We begin the chapter by highlighting figures that demonstrate the shift from obtaining health-related information in the physical world, via doctors and specialist services, to searching for sources online. We explicate the research that suggests that individuals who have just been diagnosed with a medical condition or who are seeking to help others cope with their medical problems are the most likely to search for health-related information on the Internet. We acknowledge here the benefits of obtaining health-related information from the Internet but also point out some of the problems associated with this activity. Some patients, for instance, feel more anxious after reading information about their particular illnesses. In addition, we note a specific problem associated with Internet searches for health-related information, that of 'cyberchondria'. Cyberchondria is construed not only as a form of reassurance-seeking but also as a manifestation of health anxiety and hypochondriasis. In this chapter we also consider the utility of online health forums, presenting evidence to suggest both the positive and negative effects of engaging in such forums. We also focus on e-therapy, operationalizing the term and examining the research on the benefits and drawbacks of this form of therapy. The disinhibition effect is revisited in this chapter in the context of the problems it might cause for some individuals in therapy. Although there has been some research on the evaluation of the effectiveness of e-therapies (some of which we summarize here), we note that more research is needed and that currently the findings are mixed. We conclude this chapter by considering immersive virtual environments and how they have been employed as tools in the treatment of a range of psychological problems. We provide examples of various psychological problems that could potentially be treated in these environments, such a phobias and post-traumatic stress disorder.

Our final chapter is a wrap up of the book. In Chapter 16, we remind the reader of some of the main issues discussed in the book and point to the current gaps in the literature. We remind the reader that it is important to understand that, as the Internet evolves, the way we behave online may also change, although some aspects will remain the same. We question whether the Internet has brought about a new world with new psychological issues, opportunities and challenges, and how much of our psychology remains the same.

2 The 'Self' in Cyberspace

Ever since the beginnings of the Internet, how the self has been constructed and understood in cyberspace has been an area of concern. Are we different people online from the people we are offline, or does the Internet provide us with new opportunities to gain greater insights about ourselves? Do the selves we create in cyberspace transcend to other spaces? This chapter provides an overview of some of the key psychological theories and research that have examined the self in cyberspace. It is recognized in this chapter that scholars operationalize the self in various ways. We are not promoting one theory over another but rather highlighting some of the more influential work carried out in the field.

2.1 DEFINING THE 'SELF'

There have been many theories put forth to explain the concept of 'Self'. Philosophers and theologians were the first to try to define the self. Psychologists often use the terms 'self' and 'identity' interchangeably, although many would argue that these are separate concepts (e.g., Owens, 2006). Although it is beyond the scope of this book to set out the competing psychological theories about the self and identity, before examining the self in cyberspace, it is worthwhile to consider some of these original theories.

As far back as the 1890s, psychologists have attempted to define what they mean by the 'self'. William James (1892/1963), one of the pioneers in psychology, made a distinction between two aspects of the self: the self as subject, or the 'I', and the self as object, or the 'me'. The 'looking-glass self' was a concept developed by Cooley (1902) to describe the concept that a person's self grows out of society's interpersonal interactions and the perceptions of others. For Cooley, there is no self without society.

2.1.1 Trait theory and the self

Trait psychologists have argued that the self contains specific traits that are evolved, heritable and universal across cultures (MacDonald, 1998; McCrae, 2000). These theorists assume that traits are fairly stable over time, that individuals have different traits and that traits influence behaviour. Cattell (1946), for example, proposed a two-tiered personality structure with 16 primary factors (warmth, reasoning, emotional stability, dominance, liveliness, rule-consciousness, social boldness, sensitivity, vigilance, abstractedness, privateness, apprehension, openness to change, self-reliance, perfectionism and tension) and five secondary factors (extroversion, anxiety, tough-mindedness, independence and self-control). Goldberg (1990) proposed that there are five personality factors: openness to experience, conscientiousness, extroversion, agreeableness and neuroticism.

2.1.2   Identity: 'Who am I'?

Identity is essentially about 'who I am'. Erikson (1950, 1968) was one of the first psychologists to explicitly examine the notion of identity. According to Erikson, identity comprises a consistent set of attitudes and values about oneself. He argued that in achieving identity one must develop some specific ideology: a set of personal values and goals. In forming an identity, he believed, the individual is able to shift their thinking from a here-and-now orientation to include a past and a future orientation. Erikson drew from psychodynamic theory to argue that 'identity formation' is a developmental task that adolescents must achieve. He believed that every adolescent is confronted with a crisis of identity formation, and that identity formation is the most valuable accomplishment of adolescence. Marcia (1980, 1991) extended Erikson's work to consider the processes involved in achieving identity. According to Marcia, there are four paths that adolescents can take: identity diffusion, foreclosure, moratorium and identity achievement. Unlike Erikson, Marcia believed that the developmental task of 'identity' is constantly being re-formed as individuals vacillate through phases of achievement and moratorium throughout most of their lives.

Not all psychologists would agree with Erikson's understanding of identity. Akin to Marcia, many believe that identity is not a task confined to adolescence. For McAdams (1993), identity is the 'personal myths' or stories individuals construct about themselves to bring together the different parts of themselves and their lives into a purposeful and convincing whole.

2.1.3   Social identity

Not all psychologists would agree that identity is concerned with an individual's identity; some would argue instead that identity is more about group membership or 'social identity'. Tajfel and Turner developed social identity theory to explain people's tendencies to categories themselves into groups in order to gain a greater sense of self-worth (see, e.g., Tajfel, 1979; Tajfel & Turner, 1979; Turner, 1975). According to this theory, identity is made up of both social and personal identities. Social identity is defined as membership of specific social groups (such as an activity group) or wider social categories (e.g., nationality or gender). Groups, according to these theorists, give individuals a sense of belonging to the social world. People divide the world into 'us' (in-group) and 'them' (out-group). When a social identity is salient, individuals compare their attitudes and behaviours to those of other group members. According to social identity theory, the in-group will discriminate against the out-group in order to enhance its self-worth. Researchers have proposed that social identity concerns can motivate individuals to rate in-group members more positively than out-group members (e.g., Abrams & Hogg, 1988).

The social identity model of deindividuation effects (SIDE) was developed to expand upon social identity theory and self-categorization theory (Lea & Spears, 1991; Reicher, 1984; Spears & Lea, 1994). This theory conceptualizes self-construal as flexible and situation-specific. As Lea, Spears and de Groot (2001) explain, 'a person's behavior in any situation can be placed along a continuum ranging from entirely personal (conforming to personal standards) to entirely group-based (conforming to salient group norms and standards)' (p. 527). According to SIDE theory, when people are 'visually anonymous', their personal identities become less important and social identities become salient. There is a shift from personal identity to group identity, thus promoting behaviour that is normative to the group. Visual anonymity is said to encourage depersonalization because it reduces the interpersonal basis for social comparison, self-awareness and self-presentation. When this happens, individuals see and present themselves less as unique individuals and more in terms of their similarity to the perceived prototypical attributes of the salient social group (i.e., stereotyping). In turn, the anonymity of others means that they will be also be perceived for their group attributes rather than as unique individuals. 'In short, SIDE proposes that depersonalized perceptions of self and others increase attraction toward group members and that this process is stimulated by the dearth of individuating cues in visually anonymous interactions' (Lea et al., 2001, p. 528).

2.1.4 Possible selves

In attempting to understand the 'self', psychologists have debated over whether there is one unitary, measurable self or whether there are multiple aspects. The theory of 'possible selves' contends that people do not simply understand themselves as a person in the present moment but also hold cognitive representations of their future selves (Markus & Nurius, 1986, 1987). According to Markus and Nurius (1986, 1987), the self-concept contains: the 'expected self' (the person you believe you can realistically become), the 'hoped-for self' (the person you hope to become) and the 'feared self' (the self you do not desire to become).

Higgins (1987, 1989) made a clearer distinction between these aspects of self. He proposed three aspects of self: the 'actual self' (your representation of the attributes that you or another believe you actually possess), the 'ideal self' (your representation of the attributions that you or another believe you would ideally like to possess), and the 'ought-to self' (your representation of the attributions that you or another believe you ought to possess). Higgins developed 'self-discrepancy theory' to explain that individuals are guided by the aim of becoming closer to two different end states: their ideal self and their ought-to self. The 'ideal self-regulatory system' focuses on the absence or presence of positive outcomes, whereas the 'ought self-regulatory system' focuses on the absence or presence of negative outcomes. Higgins also argued that individuals who have a large discrepancy between these different selves are more likely to be psychologically unhealthy (e.g., depressed, anxious or have low self-esteem).

2.1.5 The self as actor

Goffman (1959/1997) took a very different approach to understanding the self and identity. He developed a dramaturgical analysis of social relations and interactions in everyday life. Goffman saw people as actors. He described the self as both a performer and a character. According to Goffman, the 'self-as-performer' is not merely a social product but also has a basic motivational core. In contrast, the 'self-as-character' represents an individual's unique humanity. It is this part of the self that is a social product—that is, it is performed outwardly in social life. The 'self-as-character' is one's inner self.

In Goffman's theory, individuals need to present themselves as acceptable persons to others. He argued that individuals are strategic in their impression formation. In particular, Goffman was interested in distinguishing between expressions 'given' (e.g., spoken communication) and expressions 'given off' (e.g., nonverbal cues) in a face-to-face interaction.

Goffman contended that individuals often perform an idealized view of the situation. He stated, 'when the individual presents himself before others, his performance will tend to incorporate and exemplify the officially accredited values of the society' (1959/1997, p. 101). Therefore, he believed that part of individuals' strategy is to present themselves as acceptable people to others. According to Goffman, 'the impressions that the others give tend to be treated as claims and promises they have implicitly made, and claims and promises tend to have a moral character' (p. 21).

2.1.6 The postmodern self

The postmodern movement is complex and diverse; however, in the main, postmodern theorists would agree that human knowledge is subjective. Knowledge is relative and fallible and there is no absolute truth. Postmodern scholars see truth as situational, and it is impossible to separate the observer from the observed. To understand a person, it is necessary to understand their social context, which includes culture and language.

According to postmodern theorists, therefore, the self is fragmented and situational. They would contend that there is no unitary knowable self. Gergen (1991), for example, has argued that the postmodern culture has made the category of 'self' redundant. He has stated that the media 'furnishes us with a multiplicity of incoherent and unrelated languages of the self' (p. 6). We will return to consider Gergen in more detail later in this chapter.

2.2 THE SELF IN CYBERSPACE

So why consider the self or identity in cyberspace? Is there anything different about this space compared to other mediums to suggest that the self might be expressed or understood in different ways? Many scholars have believed, even in the early days of the Internet, that cyberspace affords unique opportunities for expressing the self.

As already noted, in the 1990s the Internet looked very different from how it looks today. It was more texted-based, was slower and had fewer people inhabiting its space. In some ways, it was easier than it is today on the Internet to hide and pretend to be someone or something else – or, as Peter Steiner illustrated in a famous *New Yorker* cartoon in 1993, 'On the Internet, nobody knows you're a dog.' The anonymous nature of the Internet, some scholars argued, provided opportunities for people to be 'disembodied' – that is, to create and experience an online identity that was no longer dependent on or constrained by their physical appearance.

2.3 DISEMBODIED SELVES IN CYBERSPACE

Sherry Turkle (1995) was one of the first theorists to consider this idea of disembodiment and selves in cyberspace. She is famous for naming the computer a 'second self' and argued that the Internet provided people with the opportunity to 're-invent' themselves. In her early work, Turkle (1995) studied the interactions that took place in virtual environments, such as MUDs (multiple-user dungeons or multiuser domains) and MOOs (multiple object oriented). Drawing from psychodynamic theory, she argued that cyberspace provided opportunities for individuals to play with identity. Turkle held the view that cyberspace can be a liberating space for individuals and could be a place where people can discover a deeper truth about themselves. She wrote: 'As players participate they become authors not only of text but of themselves, constructing new selves through social interaction' (p. 12).

Turkle believed that the Internet provided psychologists with a radical new lens through which to consider identity. She took a postmodern view of the self, arguing that people can have multiple selves rather than a unitary, continuous self:

> I am not implying that MUDs or computer bulletin boards are causally implicated in the dramatic increase of people who exhibit symptoms of multiple personality disorder (MPD), or that people on MUDs have MPD, or that MUDing is like having MPD. What I am saying is that the many manifestations of multiplicity in our culture, including the adoption of online personae, are contributing to a general reconsideration of traditional, unitary notions of identity. (Turkle, 1995, p. 260)

It is important to understand that Turkle did not believe there was a complete schism between online and offline selves. In the virtual space, some of her participants experimented with identities they hoped to 'become' in their everyday lives. For example, she described the experience of a participant named Gordon:

> On MUDs, Gordon has experimented with many characters, but they all have something in common. Each has qualities that Gordon is trying to develop in himself. He describes one current character as 'an avatar of me. He is like me, but more effusive, more apt to be flowery and romantic with a sort of tongue-in-cheek attitude toward the whole thing'. (Turkle, 1995, p. 190)

Turkle believed that, in Gordon's case, experimentation online was psychologically healthy as it provided him with a new way to see himself, which could lead to a higher quality of everyday life.

Although Turkle did believe that this disconnection with 'physical' bodies in cyberspace created new opportunities to experience the self, she also found that complete separation between offline and online selves was not always psychologically healthy. She wrote:

> Sometimes such experiences can facilitate self-knowledge and personal growth, and sometimes not. MUDs can be places where people blossom or places where they get stuck, caught in self-contained worlds where things are simpler than in real life, and where, if all else fails, you can retire your character and simply start a real life with another. (Turkle, 1995, p. 185)

Turkle provided a case study of a man who described himself as being too immersed in MUDs. Stewart spent too much time constructing a life in a MUD that was more expansive that the one he lived in physical reality. Turkle described this self as his ideal self, the self he wished to be in his 'real life'. Stewart self-consciously used MUDs as a place to experiment with new ways of being and hoped that by doing so he might change as a person in his real life. He felt that the online environment was a safe space to do so. However, Turkle argued that Stewart's online persona was too far removed from his real self. Online he was very social, the life of the party. However, in the rest of his life he was very socially anxious. Engaging in MUDs highlighted to Stewart the self he wished to be but could not be. This led him to spend many hours in MUDs, preferring this space over his real world. Turkle argued, therefore, that, in considering how psychologically beneficial playing MUDs can be for a person, one needs to consider how similar the person's online characters are to their 'real' self.

2.3.1 Criticisms of Turkle's early work

Turkle's work is important because it provided psychologists with a new way of thinking about online identities. Moreover, it challenged early scholars' views that the Internet was an impersonal medium, where people could only relate in a shallow, illusory and hostile manner (Kiesler, Siegel & McGuire, 1984; Sproull & Kiesler, 1986; Stoll, 1995). Despite these strengths, there are some problems with her work.

Turkle's early notions of identity in cyberspace were based on her research on MUDs and MOOs. In these spaces, individuals were expected to assume the roles of characters. These places were designed to be playful and fun. Players were expected to be someone other than themselves (Whitty, 2007a; Whitty & Carr, 2003; Wynn & Katz, 1997) and so we might expect people to play out different selves in such spaces. Does her theory hold in other less playful spaces, such as email or a political blog? The Internet is not a homogenous space, and so we cannot develop a one-theory-fits-all approach.

What of this notion of disembodiment? Can people completely separate themselves from their physical bodies to create a utopian self? Others have concurred with Turkle's view. Clark (1997), for instance, proposed that in 'the virtual environment, we can exist in either a disembodied or a cyberspatial form' (p. 86). Rollman, Krug and Parente (2000) wrote, 'by eliminating time, distance, and body, the architects of the Internet have created an unhindered medium that connects the mind and spirit' (p. 161). Feminist scholars, such as Haraway (1991) and Plant (1992), argued that the Internet provides real opportunities to create postmodern selves. They were hopeful that individuals could escape the sorts of gendered expectations placed on people in everyday life. For example, Klein (1999) wrote:

> In postmodern and cyberthinking, the categories of 'women' and 'men' (or young and old or white and black) have lost any meaning[;] ... it is up to the individual to be whatever s/he desires – including donning the body/ies s/he wishes to appear in, at a given time – some sort of an eternal fancy dress ball, one might think. (p. 202)

Not all scholars agree, however, that individuals can be completely disembodied in cyberspace. Researchers, for instance, have found that complex gender information can be transmitted via text, with certain linguistic cues distinguishing men's conversations from women's (Lea & Spears, 1995). Thomson and Murachver (2001) found that women are more likely to make references to emotional and personal information online. Moreover, these researchers found that participants in their experimental study were able to identify the gender of the person they were communicating with online. Whitty (2003a) has argued that 'although we do not have physical, tangible bodies in cyberspace, we do nevertheless have bodies' (p. 344). She also makes the point that we have embodied responses to our online encounters. Whitty contends that research on how individuals flirt, engage in sexual activities, and develop and maintain online relationships demonstrates the importance of the body (Whitty 2003a; Whitty & Carr, 2006).

Turkle (2011), herself, has changed her original views about cyberspace. She no longer believes that cyberspace holds the utopian promise she hoped for in the 1990s. She now believes that the Internet is too accessible and too much a part of people's lives, making individuals feel overwhelmed and depleted. Virtual worlds, she argues, offer richer, better lives than reality. In her more recent work she contends that the Internet can lead to a new sense of solitude. She writes:

> Technology is seductive when what it offers meets our human vulnerabilities. And as it turns out, we are very vulnerable indeed. We are lonely but fearful of intimacy. Digital connections and the social robot may offer the illusion of companionship without the demands of friendship. Our networked life allows us to hide from each other, even as we are tethered to each other. (Turkle, 2011, p. 6)

2.3.2 The saturated self

Gergen (2000) took a similar view to Turkle's current position. He argued that, in postmodern times, the self has become saturated with too many identities. This, he maintained, is due to modern communication technologies. Digital technologies have caused problems for the 'modern self'. He has argued that the self has become increasingly fragmented.

According to Gergen (2000), seven technologies began this process of social saturation: rail, post, automobile, telephone, radio, motion pictures and commercial publishing; 'each brought people into increasingly close proximity, exposed them to an increasing range of others, and fostered a range of relationships that could never have occurred before' (p. 53). He has theorized that, in more recent times, a second or high-tech phase in the technology of social saturation has emerged, which includes air transportation, television and electronic communication. Consequently, not only are we developing more relationships than before but also the pace at which these relationships unfold is quicker than it has ever been. Moreover, Gergen (2000) pointed out that these relationships are both actual and imaginary. An example of imaginary relationships, he contends, is the downloading of pornographic images from the Internet. He has commented that, 'as the traditional individual is thrust into an ever-widening array of relationships, he or she begins increasingly to sense the self as a strategic manipulator. Caught in often contradictory or incoherent activities, one grows anguished over the violation of one's sense of identity' (p. 17).

2.4 THE CYBORG SELF

As already mentioned in this chapter, Donna Haraway (1991) argued that, in the early days of the World Wide Web, cyberspace provided real opportunities to create postmodern selves. She believed that women, in particular, could escape gender roles. She named her theory 'cyborg feminism'. She wrote:

> A cyborg is a cybernetic organism, a hybrid of a machine and organism, a creature of social reality as well as a creature of fiction. Social reality is lived social relations, our

most important political construction, a world-changing in fiction. The international women's movements have constructed 'women's experience', as well as uncovered or discovered this crucial collective object. This experience is a fiction and fact of the most crucial, political kind. Liberation rests on the construction of the consciousness, the imaginative apprehension, of oppression, and so of possibility. The cyborg is a matter of fiction and lived experience that changes what counts as women's experience in the late twentieth century. (p. 149)

Haraway used the cyborg metaphor to represent the political play of identity. Our bodies, she believed, could be changed by technology, which could thereby change our lives dramatically. Her view is similar, in some ways, to that expressed in Turkle's early work. However, even Turkle herself found little evidence for the breaking away of gender roles. Some of the same criticisms directed towards Turkle can therefore be applied to Haraway's work. There has been little evidence to suggest that technology has afforded women opportunities to escape gender in the way Haraway imagined.

2.5 GOFFMAN: PERFORMING SELF ONLINE

Goffman was not around when the World Wide Web was first being researched by academics; however, many have applied his theories to cyberspace. Those who have applied Goffman's theory have been interested in how the self is performed online and how individuals manage the impressions of themselves that they give out. For example, an early study of academic webpages found that most presentations were 'paper-text-like' and that academics were not performing new presentations of the self (Miller & Arnold, 2000). However, these researchers were examining the Internet in the 1990s – a time when users were limited in the amount of bandwidth and resources available to create personal webpages.

More recent research has taken a very different view. Tufekci (2008), for example, has argued that many of the activities that take place on SNSs can be understood by applying Goffman's theory of the self. She wrote: 'users engage in impression management by adjusting their profiles, linking to their friends, displaying their likes and dislikes, joining groups, and otherwise adjusting the situated appearance of their profiles' (p. 547). Others have made a similar argument, stating: 'Facebook is a multi-audience identity production site. The control users have over the privacy settings of their accounts enables them to partition their Facebook pages into many "back" and "front" regions (Goffman, 1959[/1997]), whereby staging different identity shows for different audiences' (Zhao, Grasmuck & Martin, 2008, p. 1832). Goffman's work has been popular among those who have studied online dating sites. We consider his work further in Chapter 4.

> **SUGGESTED ACTIVITY**
>
> Have a look at one of your SNS profiles. Does it present who you 'really' are? Does it present a certain version of your 'self', and if so which parts of yourself does it represent? Which theories presented in this chapter could be applied to explain the presentation of your self on your profile?

2.6 POSSIBLE SELVES IN CYBERSPACE

A number of studies have considered how Higgins' 'possible selves' theory might apply to online presentations of self. Manago, Graham, Greenfield and Salimkhan (2008), in a focus group study, found that different participants chose to present different parts of themselves on their Myspace profile. They claimed that 'profiles can represent the authentic self, selected aspects of the multifaceted self, the idealized self, or experiments with possible selves' (p. 51).

Bessière, Seay and Kiesler (2007) carried out one of the more interesting studies using Higgins' theory. These researchers suggested that MMORPGs (massively multiplayer online role-playing games) could be ideal environments for individuals to create characters that reflect their ideal selves. They stressed that it is the anonymity of this space that facilitates these presentations of self. They predicted, first, that players would view their character as being more akin to their ideal self than they believed themselves to be. Second, they hypothesized that individuals who scored lower on measures of psychological well-being would be more likely to create characters closer to their ideal self and less like their actual self compared with those who scored high on measures of psychological well-being. This is in line with Higgins' self-discrepancy theory, described above. Bessière et al. employed the Big Five Personality Inventory, which assesses individuals on the following traits: conscientiousness, extroversion, neuroticism, agreeableness and openness. In a unique approach, they asked individuals to rate their *World of Warcraft* character on how similar its traits were to those of their actual and ideal selves. Bessière et al. found some support for their hypotheses. In the main, participants rated their character in *World of Warcraft* as being more conscientious and extroverted and less neurotic than they were themselves. This was more likely for those who were depressed or had lower self-esteem. Those who scored higher on psychological well-being measures were less likely to rate their character as being better than themselves.

2.6.1 Real me

As a variant of 'possible selves theory', John Bargh and Katelyn McKenna claim to have drawn from Roger's (1961/2004) theory of the self to explain how people present themselves online (see Bargh, McKenna & Fitzsimons, 2002; McKenna, Green &

Gleason, 2002; McKenna, Green & Smith, 2001). They used the term 'Real Me' to mean the traits or characteristics that an individual possesses and would like to possess but is typically unable to express to most people. It is a construct that refers to the aspects of a person's inner core (or who they 'really are'). Bargh and McKenna argued that, because cyberspace is anonymous, in that environment it is easier to express oneself to unknown individuals as the traditional gating features evident in face-to-face interactions are absent.

McKenna et al. (2002) developed the Real Me scale, which consists of four questions. The first two require a yes/no response. First, participants are asked whether they reveal more about themselves to people they know on the Internet than to people they know in real life ('non-Net friends'). Second, they are asked whether there are aspects that their Internet friend know about them that they feel they could not share in 'real life' with non-Net friends. The following two questions ask participants to rate on a seven-point scale the extent to which their family and friends would be surprised if they were to read the participants' emails and newsgroup postings.

Bargh et al. (2002), in contrast, opted to measure the Real Me by other means. They measured the Real Me by asking participants to list a maximum of 10 traits or other characteristics that they possessed and would like to express but typically felt unable to express. As in the McKenna et al. (2002) study, the assumption is that the Real Me is known to participants.

Being able to express one's Real Me, Bargh and McKenna believed, could have important implications for relationship development. We will consider these authors' work on the Real Me and relationship progression in cyberspace in more detail in Chapter 3.

2.7 SOCIAL IDENTITIES IN CYBERSPACE

The expanded model of social identity theory, known as SIDE theory, explained earlier in this chapter, has been applied to explain online identities and behaviours. One of the premises of SIDE theory is that social identity becomes salient in visually anonymous environments, so it is an obvious theory to apply to interactions in cyberspace. Researchers believe they have found evidence for the impact of group influence and social norms in anonymous computer-mediated communication (CMC) environments.

In an early experiment on CMC, Spears, Lea and Lee (1990) manipulated the salience of group identity versus personal identity. In the condition in which group identity was salient, the researchers told the participants that the study was about the communication styles of psychology students as a group. In the condition in which personal identity was salient, they told the participants that they were studying individual differences in communication styles. Half of the groups communicated via terminals in separate rooms (making them visually anonymous) and the other half communicated in the same room, where they could see each other. Throughout the study, the researchers provided feedback about the progressive participant norm relating to the discussion topics. As predicted, they found that groups polarized in the direction of the group norms when group identity was salient, and this tendency was stronger in the condition where participants were visually anonymous. Of course, one of the criticisms that can be made here is that, given this was a lab-based study, we do not know whether we would obtain the same findings in naturally occurring groups.

In another example of a lab-based study, Cress (2005) examined online social loafing, again drawing from SIDE theory. Participants completed a social value orientation test in order to ascertain whether they were more individualist or more prosocial. They were then required to participate in a synchronous working team, consisting of six members who were all working in different rooms from one another. This task was a social dilemma: the more team mates contributed, the more they earned as individuals; however, the more the individuals contributed to the group, the less they earned. In the experiment, half of the participants worked with a shared database displaying photographs of the members and the other half did not see member portraits. As expected, the study found that participants who scored high on the prosocial scale perceived the group norm to be more salient than did individualist-type people. Second, it was found that anonymity moderated the effect of social value orientation on cooperative behaviour. When presented with member portraits, those who were more prosocial increased in social loafing, which is analogous to the predictions of SIDE theory.

2.8 VISUALLY ANONYMOUS?

Of course, today, there are fewer places online where people can be visually anonymous than there were in the early days of the Internet, as users enjoy displaying pictures of themselves and viewing other people's pictures (e.g., on SNSs, online dating sites, blogs, chat rooms and so forth). This does not mean that individuals are no longer experimental or strategic in the ways they present themselves (as we will see Chapter 4, on online dating); however, it does mean we have to develop new theories to understand the evolving Internet. When we display our physical selves online, what is of interest is how we present those selves – which photographs, for example, we choose to display and what interpretations of our identity are made by users who view our online profiles. We might ask, as Turkle did in her earlier work, whether we are more likely to manipulate and play with a presentation of self online than offline, through the images we choose to present. As the Internet changes and develops, much more rigorous research is needed in order to test out and develop new theories about the self. In the future, there may be far fewer opportunities to express oneself online compared with on a visually anonymous Internet.

2.9 CONCLUSIONS

This chapter has summarized some of the key theories on the self and identity and has examined how they have been applied to explain online presentations of self. Some theories have accounted for multiple selves and how the Internet has afforded more possibilities for experimenting with presentations of self. Some scholars have posited that people can be strategic with their presentation of self, a point we revisit in the following chapters. However, we need to read these theories in the context of an understanding of how the Internet was constructed at the time of the research. In the early days, people were more likely to be visually anonymous than they are today. Given the differences between the early and current digital technologies, we might also expect different presentations dependent on the space at that time. When you read through the literature, you will note that the physical world is often referred to as the 'real' world, suggesting that presence in an online environment is 'not real'. As the reader, you might want to question whether how you behave in online spaces is 'unreal' or whether it is simply another expression of yourself. Moreover, online and offline spaces are becoming more seamless as people combine social networking usage in real time with activities taking place in the physical realm (e.g., sharing photographs and videos of what you are currently doing and asking friends to comment on these at the same time). Future theories on the self and identity might need to rethink understanding face-to-face and cyberspace as binary oppositions.

In Chapter 3 we revisit some of the notions posited here about a visually anonymous Internet and the opportunities it afforded individuals when initiating and developing relationships online. As in this chapter, you will learn that there are many different positions taken by scholars as to the healthy and unhealthy aspects of interacting in digital spaces.

DISCUSSION QUESTIONS

1. Do you present yourself differently in different online spaces? In what ways are you different and in what ways are you consistent? Why do you think this is?
2. Do you agree with Turkle's early view that the Internet is a utopian playing field?
3. Do you agree with Gergen's view that the 'self is under siege'?
4. Can you suggest ways to apply Goffman's theory to explain self-presentations in cyberspace?
5. Is there an ideal space in which to present the 'ideal self'?

SUGGESTED READINGS

Bargh, J. A., McKenna, K. Y. A. & Fitzsimons, G. M. (2002). Can you see the Real Me? Activation and expression of the 'true self' on the Internet. *Journal of Social Issues, 58,* 33–48.

Bessière, K., Seay, F., & Kiesler, S. (2007). The ideal elf: Identity exploration in *World of Warcraft. CyberPsychology & Behavior, 10*(4), 530–535.

Gergen, K. J. (1991). *The saturated self.* New York, NY: Basic Books.

Goffman, E. (1959/1997). In the presentation of self in everyday life. In C. Lemert & A. Branaman (Eds.), *The Goffman reader* (pp. 21–26). Cambridge, MA: Blackwell.

Haraway, D. (1991). *Symians, cyborgs and women: The reinvention of nature.* London, UK: Free Association.

Lea, M., & Spears, R. & de Groot, D. (2001). Knowing me, knowing you: Anonymity effects on social identity processes within groups. *Personality and Social Psychology Bulletin, 27*(5), 526–537.

Turkle, S. (1995). *Life on the screen: Identity in the age of the Internet.* London, UK: Weidenfeld & Nicolson.

Turkle, S. (2011). *Alone together: Why we expect more from technology and less from each other.* New York, NY: Basic Books.

3 Online Relationships

Although the Internet was not originally designed to be a social space, it did not take long for users to start appropriating it in social ways. Much of what we do online is social, and research has demonstrated that psychologically healthy relationships can be formed and maintained online. As outlined in this chapter, scholars have also learnt that these relationships are not always the same as their offline counterparts (sometimes they are closer or more intimate and sometimes they are more transitory). This chapter begins with a brief overview of some of the main theories developed prior to the advent of the Internet to explain relationship formation. It is important to consider these theories with regard to explaining the initiation, development and maintenance of relationships formed on the Internet; however, it has also been necessary to develop new theories to explain some of the observed differences in the ways people relate online compared with in more traditional spaces.

3.1 TRADITIONAL RELATIONSHIPS: OFFLINE REALM

What comes to mind when you think about how a 'traditional' offline romantic relationship develops from initiation to commitment? How you imagine these trajectories is quite possibly different from the way your parents' relationship developed, which is again different from the development of other romantic relationships in other cultures as well as in the distant past. It is important to be mindful of this point as you read the literature on relationship formation.

Romantic attraction is a fairly new motivator for bringing couples together (see Whitty & Carr, 2006). In early nineteenth-century Europe, marriages were often arranged (Murstein, 1974; Rice, 1996) and in current times some cultures still have arranged marriages. Courtship was very formal in the late nineteenth and early twentieth centuries, and families still had a say in whom their children would marry (Cate & Lloyd, 1992). It was not until the mid-twentieth century, in Westernized cultures, that courtship became more informal and the peer group established the rules of dating (Mongeau, Hale, Johnson & Hillis, 1993). The sexual revolution of the 1960s in Westernized culture changed courting for both men and women, bringing

Cyberpsychology: The Study of Individuals, Society and Digital Technologies, First Edition.
Monica Therese Whitty and Garry Young.
© 2017 John Wiley & Sons, Ltd. Published 2017 by John Wiley & Sons, Ltd.

about the sort of courtship you might have imagined when you thought about how your parents met. This time period brought about more choice for individuals; marriage was no longer necessary for a couple to represent their commitment, and cohabitating became a popular choice.

It is important to note that many theories about romantic relationships are based on specifically Western norms of the 1960s onwards. Below we summarize some of the theories that aim to explain how and why romantic relationships develop.

3.1.1 Social evolutionary theory

In brief, social evolutionary theory explains that, through natural selection, humans have inherited certain traits and emotional reactions. Humans have evolved to value certain qualities in the opposite sex. When it comes to forming romantic relationships, the more an individual possesses certain characteristics, the more likely they are to attract others of the opposite sex (Buss, 1987). According to this theory, women are more attracted to men who can provide for their offspring. Men, in contrast, are attracted to women who are fertile and thus reproductively valuable. Numerous studies on attraction have found support for this theory, finding that men seek out women who are physically attractive and that women are more romantically interested in men who have high socioeconomic status (see, e.g., Buss & Barnes, 1986; Greenless & McGrew, 1994; Kenrick, Sadalla, Groth & Trost, 1990; Townsend & Wasserman, 1997).

3.1.2 Social penetration theory

In contrast, social penetration theory considers the development of romantic relationships (and can also be applied to friendships). The theory was proposed by Altman and Taylor (1973) and has been modified by others (e.g., Morton, Alexander, & Altman, 1976). According to this theory, relationships move from less intimate to more intimate involvement over time. The process has been described using an onion analogy, arguing that people self-disclose deeper and deeper aspects about themselves as a relationship progresses. This theory discusses the depth and breadth of relationship formation. Depth represents dimensions that start at the surface and move to the central, core aspects of personality. Breadth refers to information about a broad range of topics, such as one's family, career and so forth. According to social penetration theory, in the early phases of relationship development, one moves with caution, discussing less intimate topics and checking the conversations for signs of reciprocity. Gradually one feels safer and conveys other aspects of oneself.

3.1.3 Exchange and equity theories

Exchange and equity theories have examined the types of choices individuals make when selecting a romantic partner. Exchange theory explains relationships in terms of rewards and costs. Thibaut and Kelley (1959) developed the first of these theories, arguing that, whatever our feelings are for someone (no matter how pure and admirable our motives might seem), individuals pursue relationships with others only so long as those relationships are satisfying in terms of the overall rewards and costs. According to exchange theory, individuals try to maximize their profits; that is, the rewards should outweigh the costs. These theorists also argued that, in order to predict how satisfied an individual is likely to be with a given relationship, it is necessary to take their expectations into account. For instance, individuals develop expectations about relationships based on their past relationships and observations of relationship outcomes with other people similar to themselves. Therefore, for them to be satisfied with a relationship, the outcomes must match or exceed these comparison levels. Like exchange theory, equity theory suggests that individuals in personal relationships try to maximize their outcomes. Advocates of this theory argue that, when individuals find themselves in inequitable relationships, they experience distress, and the degree of distress increases in proportion to the perceived inequity. When individuals experience such distress, they will attempt to restore equity.

In contrast to Thibaut and Kelley's (1959) theory, which states that the information individuals use to generate comparison levels comes from their own past experiences and/or from observations of similar others, equity theory focuses on the relative contributions and outcomes of the partners. Therefore, the relevant information for deciding what is fair in the relationship comes from within the relationship. Those who make more of a contribution should expect to get more out of it; those who put in less should expect less from the relationship. There is also a fair amount of research to support these theories. Harrison and Saeed (1977), for example, performed a content analysis of 800 heterosexual personal ads. They found complementary but gendered differences between what individuals offered of themselves and what they hoped for in a potential partner. In other words, they found that individuals sought out others of about equal attractiveness to themselves and that, if they sought out someone more attractive, they typically offered some other quality in return (e.g., social status and wealth) to balance out the difference.

3.2 APPLYING OLD THEORIES TO ONLINE RELATIONSHIPS

New theories have been developed to explain how people initiate, develop and maintain relationships in cyberspace and how those relationships progress to offline spaces. Before outlining these new theories, however, this chapter considers how some of the above theories have been applied to explain online relationships.

3.2.1 Social evolutionary theory

Some of the gender differences that social evolutionary theory predicts in attraction to the opposite sex are evident online. Dawson and McIntosh (2006), for example, found that in online personal ads men were more likely to write ads that emphasized wealth while women were more likely to place emphasis on physical attributes. With respect to online dating (a topic we consider in more detail in Chapter 4), researchers have found that women are more likely to go to greater efforts to have an attractive photograph representing themselves on their profile (Whitty, 2008a; Whitty & Carr, 2006). Moreover, women, more than men, lie about their looks or use outdated photographs, while men are more likely to exaggerate or lie about their social status. Whitty and Buchanan (2010), in their study of online dating screen names, found that men more than women were attracted to screen names that indicated physical attractiveness, and women more than men were attracted to screen names that indicated intelligence or were neutral. Similarly, men were more motivated than women to contact screen names that indicated physical attractiveness, and women were more motivated than men to contact screen names that indicated intellectual characteristics.

3.2.2 Social penetration theory

Researchers have found that, when individuals are online, they are likely to self-disclose depth and breadth aspects about themselves more quickly than they might face to face (e.g., Joinson, 2001). Given that self-disclosure can be different online compared with traditional settings, new theories have been developed to explain this type of relating (see the sections Disinhibition Effect and Hyperpersonal Theory later in this chapter). It is important, however, to understand, as this chapter demonstrates, that one theory cannot be applied to explain the whole of online communications; for example, as will be demonstrated in Chapter 4, social penetration theory cannot be applied to explain relationships initiated from an online dating site (Whitty, 2008a).

3.2.3 Exchange theory and equity theory

Researchers have described the characteristics online daters look for in others as an exhaustive shopping list (Whitty, 2008a; Whitty & Carr, 2006). These researchers have argued that, on online dating sites, people treat themselves and others as commodities. Exchange theory and equity theory can be applied here to explain the seeking out of a balance between attractive qualities (e.g., looks, hobbies, personality) in others and oneself. We will examine these notions further in Chapter 4.

SUGGESTED ACTIVITY

Think about the last romantic relationship you formed. How were digital technologies used to initiate and develop this relationship? Were some easier to flirt in than others?

3.3 NEW THEORIES TO EXPLAIN ONLINE RELATING

Despite the utility of the above theories, scholars have learnt that how people interact and relate online can sometimes be very different from how they interact and relate in more traditional spaces. Given this difference in relating, new theories have been devised to explain some of the unique interactions that take place in some online spaces. This chapter now considers these theories.

3.3.1 Disinhibition effect

Researchers have found that, in some online spaces, individuals are more likely to open up about aspects of themselves in cyberspace and act out behaviours they might not otherwise manifest in traditional face-to-face settings (Joinson, 2001). This is known as the 'disinhibition effect' (Suler, 2004). Suler (2004) describes this as a double-edged sword, as some people reveal secret emotions, fears and wishes or show unusual acts of kindness and generosity, which Suler refers to as 'benign disinhibition'. Barak, Boniel-Nissim and Suler (2008) found that, because of the online disinhibition effect, individuals are able to open up more in online support groups. This, they argue, fosters personal empowerment, control, self-confidence, and improved feelings. In contrast, there are times when people are ruder, more critical, angry or threatening than they typically are face to face. This Suler (2004) calls 'toxic disinhibition'. Cyberharassment is an example of this type of toxic disinhibition (we examine this topic in more detail in Chapter 13).

3.3.2 Social presence theory

Social presence theory was one of the first theories to be applied to online settings. Notably, this theory was first devised when individuals were communicating online exclusively via textual exchanges. The theory posits that social presence is the feeling one has that other individuals are involved in a communication exchange. Since online communication involves fewer nonverbal cues (such as facial expression, posture, dress and so forth) and auditory cues in comparison to face-to-face communication, it has been said to be extremely low in social presence (Hiltz, Johnson & Turoff, 1986). According to this theory, as social presence declines, communication becomes more impersonal. In contrast, when more information is available about how one physically looks, this leads to greater positive regard. Hence, given that there is less social presence online compared with on other media, online communication has been said to be less personal and intimate. The problem with this theory, with regards to online relationships, is that genuine and intimate relationships form online.

Given the evidence contradicts what this theory predicts, other theories have subsequently emerged to explain how real relationships are formed via text in online environments.

3.3.3 Social information processing theory

Walther (1995) criticized the early theories, such as social presence theory. While he still subscribed to the reduced social cues view, he believed that many of these studies did not account adequately for time. Given the shortcomings of previous research, Walther and his colleagues sought to develop a more thorough understanding of the exchanges that take place in online environments. In doing so, Walther came up with the 'social information processing theory'. This theory proposes that the main difference between face-to-face communication and CMC is the pace at which relationships develop in each space, rather than the capability to develop relationships. Walther argued that, although CMC may be more aggressive at first, with time this dissipates. Walther (1992, 1995, 1996) stressed in this theory that many of the differences between online relationships and face-to-face relationships diminish over time, and, although restricted bandwidth may limit the rate of information exchange, this problem can be alleviated by allowing longer and/or more frequent communication.

3.3.4 Hyperpersonal communication

Walther extended his social information processing theory to develop a hyperpersonal communication framework. This theory posits that 'CMC users sometimes experience intimacy, affection, and interpersonal assessments of their partners that exceed those occurring in parallel face-to-face activities or alternative CMC contexts' (Walther, Slovacek & Tidwell, 2001, p. 109). Walther (1996) argues that people use the technical capacities of the Internet to assist in impression development. According to this theory, receivers idealize partners because of the messages they receive, which they believe demonstrate similarities between themselves and their online partner as well as the latter's highly desirable character. In contrast, senders exploit technology to selectively self-present aspects about themselves that the other is assumed to deem socially desirable. The features of CMC allow individuals to be strategic in their presentation of self and the CMC environment creates a space where the outside world is filtered out and cognitive resources are instead employed to focus on the online communications. As Walther (2007) explains, 'The CMC channel facilitates editing, discretion, and convenience, and the ability to tune out environmental distractions and re-allocate cognitive resources in order to further enhance one's message composition' (p. 2539). Walther argues that, once this cycle of communication has begun, 'CMC may create dynamic feedback loops wherein the exaggerated expectancies are confirmed and reciprocated through mutual interaction via the bias-prone communication processes' (p. 2539).

Researchers have found support for this theory in both dyads and groups. In a study by Hancock and Dunham (2001), for example, participants were assigned to either a text-based conversation condition or a face-to-face dyadic interaction. In this study, 80 participants rated their partner's personality profile on breadth and intensity. They found, just as the hyperpersonal theory would predict, that impressions formed in the CMC environment were less detailed but more intense than those formed face to face. In more recent research, Jiang, Bazarova and Hancock (2013) found that partners' initial self-disclosures via text-based CMC were more intimate than disclosures made face to face. The communications that followed via CMC continued to be higher in intimacy.

3.3.5 *Real Me*

As outlined in Chapter 2, in the early 2000s researchers (e.g., Bargh, McKenna & Fitzsimons, 2002; McKenna & Bargh, 2000; McKenna, Green & Gleason, 2002) proposed that the Internet was the ideal space to present what Rogers termed the 'real self'. They replaced the term with the idea of the 'Real Me', understanding this term to be equivalent to Rogers' (1951/2003, 1961/2004) 'real self'. They use the term 'Real Me' to mean the traits or characteristics that an individual possesses and would like to but is typically unable to express to most people. It is a construct that refers to the aspects of a person's inner core (or who they 'really are'). The researchers argued that this was because cyberspace was anonymous and that it is easier to express oneself to unknown individuals where the traditional gating features evident in face-to-face interactions are absent.

In Chapter 2 we highlighted how McKenna et al. (2002) went about developing the Real Me scale. As a reminder, the Real Me scale consists of four questions. The first two require a yes/no response. First, participants are asked whether they reveal more about themselves to people they know on the Internet than to people they know in real life ('non-Net friends'). Second, they are asked whether there are aspects that their Internet friends knew about them that they feel they could not share in 'real life' with non-Net friends. The following two questions ask participants to rate on a seven-point scale the extent to which their family and friends would be surprised if they were to read the participants' emails and newsgroup postings. The study provided clear evidence for their theory.

These researchers employed an additional method to measure the Real Me. Bargh et al. (2002) asked participants to list a maximum of 10 traits that they believed they possessed and expressed to others in social settings (actual self) and a maximum of 10 traits they possessed and would like to express but typically felt unable to express (true self). They also created a reaction-time self-description task, where words appeared on a computer screen every few seconds and participants were asked to press keys signifying 'yes' and 'no' as quickly as possible to determine whether the word described them or not. In the experiments that used the reaction-time task, the researchers found that the true-self concept was more accessible in memory during Internet interactions and the actual self was more accessible during face-to-face interactions. In their final study they again found that participants were more likely to express their true-self qualities to their partners over the Internet compared to in face-to-face interactions.

With regard to online relationships, these researchers have argued that some individuals are able to develop more intimate relationships online, given that many feel more comfortable opening up about themselves in this space – and self-disclosure brings people closer together. They believe this is especially the case for those who are shy and socially anxious.

3.4 A BRIEF HISTORY OF ONLINE RELATING

It is almost impossible to imagine that less than 15 years ago most online romantic activities involved purely textual exchanges. New ways needed to be found to overcome the lack of nonverbal cues in online interactions (e.g., in the form of emoticons). It is important to understand the history of how the Internet looked around the turn of the millennium. In this section we outline some of the online spaces that emerged where online relationships began to be initiated and to form.

3.4.1 Bulletin board systems: Line-by-line relationships

Bulletin board systems were an especially popular space in the early days of the Internet, and many were quite sexual in nature. They were a precursor to the World Wide Web; however, they looked very different from spaces currently available on the Internet. They were typically single-line systems, which meant that only one user could be online at a time. Individuals could only communicate using text. Even in the early days, they were social spaces where people met, had discussions, published articles, downloaded software and perhaps managed to play games. A systems operator would sometimes censor the messages on these sites, but in the main they were fairly liberal. Users could leave both public and private messages. Some bulletin board systems were especially designed for people to meet others who shared their sexual interests and to live out their sexual desires online or offline (as we will see in Chapter 5).

3.4.2 MUDs and MOOs: A place for real relationship formation

MUDs and MOOs were text-based online virtual systems in which multiple users are connected at one time. These were spaces where interactive role-playing games (very similar to the table-top game *Dungeons and Dragons*) could be played. MUDs and

MOOs were a form of synchronous communication. Participants took on a chosen character and communicated with other characters online.

In the early days, researchers were divided over whether real friendships and romantic relationships could actually form in these spaces. The empirical work suggested that they did and sometimes moved successfully from these spaces to the offline world. Parks and Roberts (1998), for instance, examined relationships developed in MOOs and found that most of the participants they surveyed (93.6%) formed at least one ongoing personal relationship during their time on MOOs. A variety of kinds of relationships were identified, including close friendships (40.6%), friendships (26.3%) and romantic relationships (26.3%). Parks and Roberts (1998) concluded that 'the formation of personal relationships on MOOs can be seen as the norm rather than the exception' (p. 529). Interestingly, the majority of the online relationships were with members of the opposite sex. This finding was consistent across ages and relationship status. As Parks and Roberts point out, this result is quite different from 'real life', where same-sex friendships are far more common than cross-sex friendships.

Utz (2000) examined the interactions that take place in MUDs. In her study, she found that 76.7% of her respondents reported forming a relationship online that developed offline. Of these, 24.5% were reported to be romantic. In addition, Utz found that, with time, people do learn how to 'verbalize nonverbal cues'. The MUDders she surveyed typically used emoticons to denote feelings and emotions.

3.4.3 Chat rooms: Less means more

Chat rooms involve synchronous communication or, according to Whitty, Buchanan, Joinson and Meredith (2012), 'near synchronous' communication. Most chat rooms have a particular theme, although this is not necessary. When a user enters a chat room, they can type a message that will be visible to all other individuals. Hundreds of people can be in the same virtual room at the same time typing messages to the group. Chat rooms are similar to instant messaging, except with more than two people. Sometimes these rooms are moderated. Chat rooms were very popular in the early days of the Internet and were text-only. In more recent times individuals often represent themselves as an avatar. Moreover, individuals share photographs and videos and use webcams.

In the past, researchers found that romantic relationships and friendships were initiated and developed in chat rooms. Whitty and Gavin (2001), for instance, learnt from interviewing 60 Internet users that ideals that are important in traditional relationships, such as trust, honesty and commitment, are just as important in relationships formed in these spaces. Rather than finding evidence of less 'real' or less satisfying relationships online, Whitty and Gavin found that some of the participants in their study reported that their relationships seemed to work better solely on the Internet.

Whitty and Gavin also found that chat room users reported feeling less self-conscious and less aware of being socially evaluated, which in turn allowed them to reveal intimate details about themselves while maintaining distance and personal space. Ironically, many of the male participants believed that by disguising their identity they could be more emotionally honest and open.

3.4.4 Discussion groups and Usenet newsgroups: A place for the 'Real Me'

A discussion group or Usenet newsgroup is a continuous public discussion about a particular topic. This is a form of asynchronous communication. Sometimes these groups are moderated. They were very popular in the early days of the Internet. These groups still exist today and are often still in text-based form only, although pictures and video can also be posted. With regard to personal relationships, Parks and Floyd (1996) found in their research on newsgroups that almost two thirds of their sample (60.7%) admitted to forming a personal relationship with someone they had met for the first time in a newsgroup. Of these, 7.9% stated that the relationship was romantic. They found that women were more likely than men to have formed a personal relationship online. It is also noteworthy that those who participated in more newsgroups were more likely to have developed personal relationships. Parks and Floyd also found that many of the relationships that began online also moved to interactions in other channels, including, for some, face to face.

As explained earlier in this chapter, McKenna et al. (2002) were interested in what they refer to as the 'Real Me', which they define as traits or characteristics that individuals possess and would like to express but are usually unable to demonstrate to others. In this study the authors were interested in learning whether individuals who are better able to disclose their Real Me online than offline are more equipped to form close relationships online and then take these relationships offline successfully. The authors randomly selected 20 Usenet newsgroups to include in their study. Over a three-week period, questionnaires were emailed to every fifth poster in each of the newsgroups (excluding spam). The first study found that, when people conveyed their Real Me online, they developed strong Internet relationships and took these relationships offline. Two years after this initial study, 354 of the 568 participants were emailed a follow-up survey (the remainder of the sample had email addresses that were no longer valid). In line with the researchers' prediction, these relationships remained relatively stable and durable over the two-year period. McKenna et al. (2002) concluded from this research that

> rather than turning to the Internet as a way of hiding from real life and from forming real relationships, individuals use it as a means not only of maintaining ties with existing family and friends but also of forming close and meaningful new relationships in a relatively nonthreatening environment. The Internet may also be helpful for those who have difficulty forging relationships in face-to-face situations because of shyness, social anxiety, or a lack of social skills. (p. 30)

3.5 CONTEMPORARY ONLINE SPACES

In modern times, the Internet has become a more popular place for couples to meet. Dutton, Helsper, Whitty, Buckwalter and Lee (2008) sampled married couples in Australia, Spain and the UK and found that 9% of married couples in Australia 6% in the UK and 5% in Spain had first met their partner online. The largest proportion of married couples that met online ranged from 26 to 55 years old. Of interest was the finding that using CMC is likely to introduce people to others whom they likely would not have met through other means; that is, the Internet opens people up to more diversity in their choice of partner, for example by introducing individuals with greater differences in age or education but with more similar interested and values. In more recent research on the same project (Oxford Internet Institute, 2011), researchers found that, in a pan-European study that also included Australia, Brazil, Japan and the US, 15% of married couples had met their partner online. The most common places included online dating sites, followed by chat rooms and then SNSs. Other places included a personal website, an online community, an online gaming site and being directly contacted via email or instant messaging.

The modes of CMC previously discussed in this chapter mainly employed text-based exchanges. However, today, many spaces are not visually anonymous. The features of the space might affect how we interact with one another and how we perceive each other. Walther et al. (2001) evaluated the timing of presenting a physical image of oneself online in short-term and long-term virtual international groups. They found that seeing a photograph of members of the virtual group prior to and during computer conferencing had a positive effect on intimacy/affection and social attractiveness for short-term, unacquainted groups. Virtual groups who saw photographs after having known each other for some time experienced less affection and social attraction once the photograph was introduced compared with long-term users who never saw each other's photographs.

In a more recent trend, we often link up online with people who we already know offline. Subrahmanyam and Greenfield (2008), for example, found that adolescents use electronic communication, such as instant messaging, email, text messaging, blogs and SNSs, to reinforce existing relationships, both with friends and romantic partners. Moreover, they contend that adolescents are increasingly integrating these tools into their offline worlds. For example, SNSs are used to garner information about new people they meet in their offline world. This section next turns to consider more contemporary online spaces and the ways in which relationships are developed within these spaces (one of these spaces, online dating sites, will be examined in detail in Chapter 4).

3.5.1 *MMORPGs: Still a very social space*

Earlier in this chapter, we wrote about MUDs and MOOs. MMORPGs have largely taken over from these earlier spaces. In MMORPGs, players take on the role of a fictional character, typically in a fantasy world, and have agency over many of their character's actions. MMORPGs differ from MUDS and MOOS in that they are not solely text-based; they also have sophisticated graphics. In addition to playing the game, individuals can write text to one another and be social in these spaces. The worlds created in these games continue to evolve even when the player is absent from the game – examples include *EverQuest*, the *Final Fantasy* series, *World of Warcraft* and, more recently, *Warhammer*. The popularity of these games continues to grow. More recently, the nature of this interaction with some MMORPGs has become more 'adult' based. *Age of Conan*, *Requiem: Bloodymare*, *2Moons* and *Warhammer*, for example, provide increased opportunities for extreme violence and more graphic depictions of violent outcomes.

Researchers have found that players are still drawn to these games, in part, for their social element. Yee (2006) has identified five motivations for why individuals play MMORPGs, including achievement, relationships, immersion, escapism and manipulation. In his work he found that male players are more likely to be driven by the achievement and motivation factors, while female players are more likely to be driven by the relationships factor. He also found that players developed meaningful relationships with others they met in MMORPGs. Interestingly, Yee (2001) found that 60% of male players and 75% of female players believed that some of their *EverQuest* friendships were comparable with or better than their offline friendships. He also found that 3% of male players and 15% of female players formed offline relationships (i.e., married, dating or engaged to) with someone they first met in Norrath (the realm depicted in *EverQuest*).

Second Life is another example of a MMORPG. It is an online virtual world developed by Linden Lab and was launched in 2003. *Second Life* users, known as residents, interact with each other through avatars. Unlike other MMORPGs, there is no game objective. Instead residents meet other residents, explore and help to create the virtual environment. Participants can socialize, participate in individual and group activities, and create and trade virtual property. Romantic relationships and friendships have been known to be initiated and develop in *Second Life*. Gilbert, Murphy and Avalos (2011) surveyed 199 participants who had been involved in intimate relationships in *Second Life*. They found that the majority of participants viewed their *Second Life* relationships as real rather than as a form of game-playing.

3.5.2 Social networking sites: Face-to-face and virtual friends

Boyd and Ellison (2007) define SNSs

> as web-based services that allow individuals to (1) construct a public or semi-public profile within a bounded system, (2) articulate a list of other users with whom they share a connection, and (3) view and traverse their list of connections and those made by others within the system. The nature and nomenclature of these connections may vary from site to site.

Friendster, which emerged in 2002, was one of the first mainstream SNSs, and was followed by Myspace and LinkedIn. Facebook was launched in 2004 and is currently the largest SNS in the world.

Research into SNSs has found that adolescents and young adults use these sites to strengthen various aspects of their offline connections (Pempek, Yermolayeva & Calvert, 2009; Subrahmanyam, Reich, Waechter & Espinoza, 2008). (We will consider adolescents and online relationships further in Chapter 7.) However, researchers have found that SNSs are also being used to find new friends (Raacke & Bonds-Raacke, 2008). Interestingly, Pempek et al. (2009) found that Facebook users spend more time observing content than posting content.

Researchers have found that there are specific social benefits derived from being a member of an SNS (Ellison, Steinfield & Lampe, 2007, 2011; Steinfield, Ellison & Lampe, 2008). Ellison et al. (2007), for instance, found a strong association between use of Facebook and three types of social capital: bridging social capital, bonding social capital and maintained social capital, the strongest relationship being with bridging social capital. Moreover, it was found that Facebook usage might have greater benefits for users with low self-esteem and low life satisfaction.

Not all experiences on SNSs are positive. Muise, Christofides & Desmarais (2009) found that increased Facebook use significantly predicted Facebook-related jealousy. Utz and Beukeboom (2011) examined SNS jealousy and SNS relationship happiness and the consequences of SNS use for romantic relationships. Overall, they found that participants experienced more happiness than jealousy in reaction to their partner's activities on SNSs. However, individuals low in self-esteem experienced more jealously related to SNSs than those high in self-esteem. Self-esteem also moderated the effects of SNS use and the need for popularity on SNS-related jealousy and SNS-related relationship happiness.

How you present yourself on an SNS can have implications. Tong, Van der Heide, Langwell and Walther (2008), for example, examined the relationship between the number of friends on a Facebook profile and observers' ratings of attractiveness and extroversion. The study found a curvilinear relationship between the number of friends on an individual's SNS and the individual's social attractiveness. In the condition where the profile indicated the fewest friends (102), ratings of social attractiveness were the lowest and the highest ratings were for the profile that had approximately 300 friends. However, any profile that had more than 300 friends declined to a level approaching the profile with 102 friends. Furthermore, these authors found that individuals with profiles that had more friends were more likely to be judged as extroverted; however, the greatest degree of extroversion was associated with a moderate number of friends and declined with large numbers of friends. Therefore, individuals with profiles that had the largest number of friends were more likely to be judged as introverted.

Getting to know a person through a SNS can be potentially different from knowing someone via other online spaces or in face-to-face interactions. Antheunis, Valkenburg and Peter (2010), for example, looked at the uncertainty reduction process in initial online interactions on a Dutch SNS. They found that participants used three types of uncertainty reduction strategies: passive, active and interactive.

Passive strategies were the most commonly used, followed by interactive and active strategies. Importantly, these authors point out that,

> In contrast to text-based CMC environments, social network sites have more auditory and visual cues available and are relatively open systems. Apparently, this allows CMC participants not only to use interactive [uncertainty reduction strategies] (i.e., direct questioning and self-disclosure), but also to observe their target persons (passive strategy), or to ask other participants for information about the target persons (active strategy). (p. 106)

These researchers, however, also found that, although the passive strategy was the most frequently used, the interactive strategy was the only one that reduced the information seeker's level of uncertainty. As is to be expected, they also found that a low level of uncertainty led to social attraction. More importantly, however, they found that the relationship between level of uncertainty and social attraction is not direct but is rather moderated by the perceived valence of the information (i.e., the extent to which an individual perceives the information of the target person to be positive or negative, regardless of its credibility or quality).

3.6 INTERACTING IN VARIOUS SPACES

As discussed in Chapter 2, scholars need to be more cognisant of the fact that people communicate and develop and maintain friendships and romantic relationships across various spaces. No longer can researchers refer to the offline realm as the 'real world'. As also discussed in Chapter 2, this means that individuals may well have multiple presentations of self across multiple spaces. What implications might this have for relationship maintenance?

De Andrea and Walther (2011) examined the above question by investigating the ways in which observers explain discrepancies between Facebook self-portrayals and impressions formed through other interpersonal interactions. Participants were easily able to identify online self-presentations that were misleading among both friends and acquaintances; however, they rated online self-presentations of acquaintances to be more misleading than friends' presentations. Moreover, misleading presentations of self were more likely to lead to judgements of untrustworthiness and hypocrisy when an acquaintance made the misleading presentation. Although acquaintances were given harsher judgements, friends were not let off the hook. Friends who posted dishonest self-portrayals were rated as untrustworthy (with the friend, rather than the act, being judged as immoral and dishonourable) and hypocritical. The results of this study suggests that individuals are unforgiving of discrepancies between online and offline self-presentations.

3.7 FUTURE DEVELOPMENT IN THE FIELD

As already acknowledged in this chapter, the Internet will continue to grow and new fads will arise, and so it is difficult to confidently predict what psychologists will be researching with regard to relationships in the future. No doubt connection speeds will become quicker and there will be even more bandwidth available. Most scholars, to date, have considered the differences between online spaces and offline spaces when it comes to initiating, developing and maintaining relationships. However, the reality is that individuals use a variety of media together with traditional communication. When getting to know someone in the early days of a relationship, no longer is it typically the case that individuals get to know each other in one space online, switching between media until they finally meet face to face. Instead, individuals incorporate various media into their relationship formation and development. New research about relationships needs to take these changes in media usage into account.

3.8 CONCLUSIONS

The world has changed very quickly since the 1990s. However, as this chapter has pointed out, not everything we do when it comes to forming relationships is completely different from how it was before the advent of the Internet. New theories have been developed to explain online relating; however, many of the theories developed to explain traditional forms of dating and relationship development still provide a useful lens. New theories have found that sometimes the relationships people form online are closer and more intense (hyperpersonal) compared with those formed face to face. Researchers are also looking into the difference between knowing someone visually online compared with being visually anonymous. Moreover, studies have found that individuals are unforgiving when there is a lack of consistency in self-presentation across different spaces. In the future, psychologists might not use the binary view of online and offline relationships that many scholars currently take. Moreover, in considerations of relationship development, we would recommend that scholars take into account the features of each space and the unique rules govern those spaces.

In Chapter 4, we look at one type of online space in more detail, considering environments where individuals seek out potential romantic partners – online dating. As in this chapter, you will learn that there are problems with self-presentation on these sites, which sometimes makes it difficult for daters to decide whether they want to know more about a particular person. Nonetheless, many people do successfully form relationships after meeting on these sites.

DISCUSSION QUESTIONS

1. Do you have any friends who you exclusively interact with on an SNS? Are these any different from the ones you know face to face?
2. Consider Walther's hyperpersonal theory. Have you ever formed relationships online that felt closer than your face-to-face relationships?
3. Consider McKenna's notion of the Real Me. Have you found it is easier to self-disclose your true self online?
4. How do you envisage the future when it comes to meeting friends and romantic partners via digital technologies?

SUGGESTED READINGS

De Andrea, D. C. & Walther, J. B. (2011). Attributions for inconsistences between online and offline self-presentations. *Communication Research, 38*(6), 805–825.

Ellison, N. B., Steinfield, C. & Lampe, C. (2007). The benefits of Facebook 'friends': Exploring the relationship between college students' use of online social networks and social capital. *Journal of Computer-Mediated Communication, 12*, 1143–1168.

Joinson, A. N. (2001). Self-disclosure in computer-mediated communication: The role of self-awareness and visual anonymity. *European Journal of Social Psychology, 31*, 177–192.

McKenna, K. Y. A., Green, A. S. & Gleason, M. E. (2002). Relationship formation on the Internet: What's the big attraction? *Journal of Social Issues, 58*, 9–31.

Tong, S. T., Van der Heide, B., Langwell, L. & Walther, J. B. (2008). Too much of a good thing? The relationship between number of friends and interpersonal impressions on Facebook. *Journal of Computer-Mediated Communication, 13*, 531–549.

Walther, J. B. (2007). Selective self-presentation in computer-mediated communication: Hyperpersonal dimensions of technology, language and cognition. *Computers in Human Behavior, 23*, 2538–2557.

Whitty, M. T. & Carr, A. N. (2006). *Cyberspace romance: The psychology of online relationships.* Basingstoke, UK: Palgrave Macmillan.

4 Online Dating

In Chapter 3, we learnt that increasingly people are meeting their partners online – in particular on online dating sites. We have stressed in this book that there is no one theory that fits all when it comes to the Internet. Instead, we need to consider the various spaces online, how they are constructed and the norms that govern their spaces. In this chapter, you will learn that the hyperpersonal relationships observed in other spaces online do not apply to those formed on online dating sites. Moreover, there are various strategies people use to find a partner on these sites, and relationships progress through different stages from those of relationships formed in other online spaces as well as those formed in more traditional face-to-face settings.

4.1 WHAT IS AN ONLINE DATING SITE?

Online dating sites started appearing in the 1980s, though these were in a fairly primitive form compared to how we know them today. As Whitty and Carr (2006) explain:

> Online dating sites began appearing in the 1980s and are still increasing in popularity as an alternative or addition to offline dating. Similar to newspaper personals (but with much more information), individuals construct a profile, describing themselves and often providing photographs of themselves and sometimes sound bites and video. Users typically have to pay to use this service and once they identify a person whose profile they like, online contact is made through the system to gauge whether the other individual might also be interested. From there, individuals typically organize to meet face-to-face. (p. 4)

In the early days, online dating was stigmatized and researchers found that shy people were gravitating to these sites to find a mate (Scharlott & Christ, 1995). In the 1980s, these sites were largely text-based with limited space for individuals to create a dating profile in the hope of attracting others. Currently, many online dating sites attempt to effectively match users. These dating sites are continuing to work on refining tools to match the most suitable people with each other. Online daters are often expected to complete personality tests, as well as surveys on their interests and what aspects they are looking for in a partner. From there, matches are often given compatibility

Cyberpsychology: The Study of Individuals, Society and Digital Technologies, First Edition.
Monica Therese Whitty and Garry Young.
© 2017 John Wiley & Sons, Ltd. Published 2017 by John Wiley & Sons, Ltd.

ratings. Other sites allow clients to find their own matches; on these sites, users must work through a plethora of profiles to make their choice. In addition to the generic online dating sites, such as e-Harmony, Parship and Match.com, there are also more specialized online dating sites, which gather like-minded individuals together. There are, for example, sites designed specifically for Christians, Jews, vegans, goths, emos, vegetarians and prisoners. Sites such as these are similar to social groups that one might join in the hope of finding another who shares the same values or interests.

> **SUGGESTED ACTIVITY**
>
> Have a look at some online dating sites that are open to the public to freely view. What are your observations regarding how people present themselves on these sites? Are there any clear gender differences? Which presentations do you believe will be more successful at leading to a serious relationship?

4.2 MOTIVATIONS FOR USING AN ONLINE DATING SITE

So why choose to find a partner via an online dating site? Research, to date, has reported social and personality reasons for choosing online dating as a way to find a match. Brym and Lenton (2001), for example, have hypothesized a number of reasons, including:

- given that career and time pressures are increasing, people are looking for more efficient ways of meeting others for intimate relationships;
- single people are more mobile due to demands of the job market, so it is more difficult for them to meet people face to face for dating; and
- workplace romance is on the decline due to growing sensitivity about sexual harassment – hence, alternatives dating approaches are needed.

Albright (2007) argues that the appeal is the large pool of people available in an environment that enhances romantic projections. Whitty and Carr (2006) found that participants gave a number of reasons for using an online dating site, including:

- because it was an alternative to the pubs and clubs scene;
- because they were shy or reserved;
- because they felt they had no other option;
- because it was convenient; and
- because of the privacy it affords.

4.3 PSYCHOLOGICAL CHARACTERISTICS OF ONLINE DATERS

One of the reasons given in the previous section for using an online dating site is that individuals may feel shy or reserved. Currently, however, research findings on the personality make-up of online daters is mixed. When considering the available studies on the characteristics of online daters, we need to be mindful that the numbers of people using online dating sites have increased dramatically, and so we might expect the psychological profiles of online daters to have changed; therefore, we may no longer find that the majority of online daters are shy.

Poley and Luo (2012) quite rightly point out that over the years there have been two competing hypotheses with regard to the types of people who are drawn to online dating: the social compensation hypothesis (SCH) and the rich-get-richer hypothesis (RGRH). The SCH contends that individuals high in dating or social anxiety and low in social competence (who typically experience difficulties forming relationships in more traditional face-to-face settings) will use online dating to compensate for deficits they encounter offline. In contrast, the RGRH argues that people low in social anxiety and high in social competence will be more likely to use online dating; given that these people already have good social and dating skills, they ought to be able to transfer these skills to the Internet and be more competent than their less competent counterparts.

In earlier research on online dating, there was strong support for the SCH hypothesis. McKenna and colleagues (2002; see Chapter 3 for a description of their work), for example, found that socially anxious people were more likely to reveal their 'true' self online and develop successful romantic relationships with people they met on the Internet. Whitty and Buchanan (2009) examined the characteristics of individuals who were more likely to engage in speed dating and online dating and looked at the types of people who are more likely to prefer these forms of dating. As the SCH would predict, they found that individuals who scored high on shyness were more likely to have tried online dating and were more likely to consider using it in the future. The opposite, however, was found in Valkenburg and Peter's (2007) research. They found that Dutch people low in dating anxiety used online dating more than those high in dating anxiety. Admittedly, the studies measured slightly different constructs: one measured shyness while the other measured dating anxiety. More recently, Poley and Luo (2012) found that those high in anxiety and lacking social skills reported a significantly greater use of face-to-face dating as well as a preference for face-to-face dating. However, they did not find evidence for the RGRH, given that social competence and incompetence dimensions had little bearing on actual and preferred face-to-face and online dating behaviours. The dating arena is a constantly changing playing field, and we need to bear this in mind when considering the discrepancies in the results found on the types of people who are drawn to online dating and the potential for those types to change in the future.

4.4 COMPARING ONLINE DATING SITES WITH PERSONAL ADS

Do online dating sites compare with other matching methods or are they unique tools? If they are unique, new theories need to be delineated to explain relationship formation in these spaces.

In Chapter 3 we outlined theories about traditional relationships and examined their utility in explaining online relationships. We learnt that, although the theories were of some use, new theories are essential in explaining some of the differences between how individuals initiate and maintain relationships that start online. Perhaps the best comparison that can be made with online dating and previous forms of matchmaking involves newspaper personal ads and video dating.

Psychologists have been interested in examining how individuals present themselves in newspaper ads (which still exist today). Cameron, Oskamp and Sparks (1977), for instance, found from their analysis of 347 heterosexual ads appearing in *Singles News Register* that the pattern of offers and requests was 'reminiscent of a heterosexual stock market' (p. 27). In other words, the self is commodified. Individuals were much more likely to present self-descriptions that included favourable traits (e.g., warmth, friendliness and sincerity) than unfavourable traits: 85% of the personal ads described attractive traits, with just 3% of men and 6% of women describing negative qualities.

Distinct gender differences in self-presentation and qualities sought after by men and women have been identified in these personal ads. Cameron et al. (1977), for example, found that personality traits were emphasized by women more than men. In their sample, appearance was also stressed by women (67%) more than men (35%). In contrast, 38% of men compared to 12% of women wrote that appearance characteristics were desirable in a potential partner. Occupation was mentioned by men (46%) more than women (20%). In contrast, women (24%) were more likely to specify the desired occupation of the prospective partner than men (3%). In Smith, Waldorf, and Trembath's (1990) analysis of 514 singles ads, it was found that physical attractiveness was most frequently sought by men (57%) compared to women (26%). Moreover, requests for a thin partner were made by a third of men compared to a mere 2% of women. Koestner and Wheeler (1988) found that men wrote that they had expressive traits (e.g., a good communicator) and sought instrumental traits (e.g., a liking for outdoor activities). In contrast, women offered instrument characteristics and sought expressive ones.

Gonzales and Meyers (1993) found in their analysis of personal ads that many of the advertisers described themselves as the 'ideal' man or woman. At first glance this might seem a little over the top; however, it is arguably a sensible strategy for men and women to highlight certain traits over others. If one is to attract a potential partner, in the first place one needs to advertise attractive wares over ones that might seem unattractive or mediocre.

Clients who video date are presented with written information and video clips of their potential dates. The video-dating service typically selects potential partners it considers to be good matches for their client. The client is then presented with demographic information, self-descriptions and photographs of prospective dates followed by a videotaped interview. The client then decides which of these potential dates they are interested in. The individuals selected are then contacted to decide whether, in turn, they are interested in meeting this individual.

As with previous research on attraction, it has been found with regard to video dating that men are mostly attracted to good-looking women and that women desire men with high social status (Green, Buchanan and Heuer, 1984). Again, this is what evolutionary theory would predict. Riggio and Woll (1984), in contrast, found that the more popular male video daters were the ones who were physically attractive, good actors and expressive. Popular women were those who were physically attractive. Exchange theory might better explain the male daters here, in that they might be trying to maximize the qualities they have to offer.

Woll and Young (1989) were interested in the relationship and self-presentational goals of video-dating clients, the strategies those clients employed in obtaining these goals and the images they chose to present to others. These theorists suggest that the video daters hoped that by presenting a realistic picture of themselves they would, in turn, be successful at attracting the ideal partner. Despite this apparently sensible strategy, Woll and Young (1989) point out that these same video daters were dissatisfied with the people who had been selecting them, perceiving a discrepancy between their ideal partner and the person who was realistically interested in their profile.

Online dating, personal ads and video dating are similar in many ways (see Whitty, 2007b). One obvious similarity between these dating methods is that individuals have time to craft a presentation of themselves prior to any meeting. This is very different from more traditional forms of dating, where individuals typically meet face to face and conversation is therefore more spontaneous (e.g., in pubs and clubs or at work). Moreover, with each of these forms of matchmaking a dater has more control over impression formation than they would otherwise face to face (Whitty, 2007b). There are also some obvious differences that it is worthwhile to note. With newspaper ads, often the person who contacts the advertiser is not someone who has constructed the personal ad themselves. Another clear difference is that more visual information is available for video daters and online daters. Researchers have specifically examined presentation of self on online dating sites, which this chapter now turns to examine.

4.5 PRESENTING ONESELF ON AN ONLINE DATING SITE

As with individuals who construct personal ads, online daters claim to go to great efforts in constructing attractive profiles (see Ellison, Heino & Gibbs, 2006; Whitty, 2008a, 2008b, 2008c; Whitty & Carr, 2006). Whitty (2007b, 2008a) has argued that, as with newspaper ads, online daters are driven to 'commodify' themselves – ensuring they are presenting a self that others will feel compelled to 'buy' into. This parallels Cameron et al.'s (1977) claim, mentioned earlier, that newspapers ads are 'reminiscent of a heterosexual stock market' (p. 27). One of Whitty's (2008a) participants describes this process of 'selling himself':

> The other thing for me personally is I'm great at writing trade manuals for someone, but when it comes to writing about yourself and trying to sell yourself it's a very different story. I don't know whether that's more of a male trait than a female trait. It depends how good you want to try selling yourself too isn't it? (Wayne) (p. 1714)

Some of the characteristics that researchers have found online daters consider important to present include their looks, interests, activities, personality, humour, occupation, intelligence, uniqueness, and hopes and dreams (see Whitty & Carr, 2006, for an exhaustive list and percentages). Whitty (2008a) found that online daters were more likely to present numerous positive characteristics rather than just a few. If you revisit exchange theory (see Chapter 3), you will note that this theory posits that individuals look to maximize rewards when it comes to deciding upon an appropriate relationship. Hence, it would seem a sensible strategy to outline as many positive characteristics as possible, so as to appear a highly rewarding option. After all, one has to appear a more rewarding choice than the many other available profiles.

Chapter 3 also outlined social evolutionary theory. According to this theory, men are attracted to women who are fertile and reproductively valuable and women are attracted to men who have high socioeconomic status. In a study by Sears-Robert Alterovitz and Mendelsohn (2011) on online dating profiles, it was found that evolutionary predictions about partner preferences held true for men throughout the life span. Men were more likely to seek out younger women, and this was increasingly so as they grew older. Moreover, they were more likely to offer more status information in their profiles than women. The theory, however, did not hold true for older women. Women at any age sought status-related information more than did men; however, throughout the life span, women did not offer physical attractiveness more often than men. In addition, women over 75 years sought out younger men than themselves.

As with the previous research on personal ads and video dating, researchers have found that individuals are very strategic with how they present themselves on an online dating site. Whitty (2007b, 2008a) found that online daters are savvy enough to know that simply presenting an attractive self is not enough. Instead daters also have to present a self that appears to be honest and authentic. Whitty (2007b) named this the BAR theory, whereby, to successfully attract a mate, online daters need to construct profiles that present a balance between an 'attractive' and a 'real' self.

4.6 DATING DECEPTION

A challenge for online daters is determining whether a profile contains honest or misleading information. In 1983, Austrom and Hanel (cited in Ahuvia & Adelman, 1992) found in their research that no outright lies were told in personal ads, but there was evidence of exaggeration and selective truth telling. Whitty (2008a; Whitty & Carr, 2006) found that, when online daters misrepresented themselves on their profiles, they understood these as embellishments, but when others did so they were often deemed untrustworthy or lacking in self-awareness; either way, if the person did not match up to their profile, they usually did not make it to the second date.

Toma and Hancock (2012) examined deceptions in online dating profiles and found that deceptive profiles are detectable only by computerized linguistic analyses. Human judges found it much more difficult to detect deception based on the written component and instead needed to rely on linguistic cues unrelated to profile deception. The more dishonest profiles contained significantly shorter self-descriptions. This is in contrast to research that has examined deception in synchronous environments, where liars have been found to use more words in conversation. Emotion-related cues, first-person-singular pronouns and negation terms were all evident in deceptive profiles. Contrary to what was expected, negative emotion terms were not more likely to be present in deceptive profiles, and Toma and Hancock suggest this is because the asynchronous environment allows one to be more strategic in the employment of these words.

Researchers have drawn from Goffman's (1959/1997) theory to explain online daters' presentations of self in cyberspace (e.g., Ellison et al., 2006; Whitty, 2008a; Whitty & Carr, 2006) and the deceptions evident in profiles. Whitty (2008a) argues that online dating sites provide little opportunity to witness expressions 'given off' in the way that Goffman describes. She states that:

> Possible ways to 'read between the lines' or look for the expressions 'given off' is evident when participants skeptically viewed clichéd profiles. Moreover, online daters checked to see if their date matched up to their profile when they meet [sic] face-to-face. In Goffman's terms they are able to see how well the 'real character' matches up to the performance. When there is a discrepancy, as Goffman would predict, the online daters … judge their dates as immoral, believing they had an obligation to match the impressions created in their profile. (p. 1720)

4.7 A PERFECT MATCH OR A NUMBERS GAME?

As demonstrated in this chapter, online daters are strategic in the way they present themselves in their profiles; however, they are also strategic in the way they use dating sites. Whitty (2008a, 2008b) found that those daters who raised their expectations online compared with their offline expectations reported being unhappy with their matches and were potentially less likely to be successful at finding a partner. Whitty contends that many online daters become fussier, especially when they can see so many choices available to them. As described earlier, most online daters only describe their favourable traits, and consequently these sites consist of a sea of attractive available dates. Exchange theory again might help to explain these results. As explained in the previous chapter, Thibaut and Kelley (1959) argued that individuals developed expectations about relationships based on their comparisons with their own relationships and other people's relationships. There is a greater pool of 'hypothetical comparisons' that can be made by online daters. Perhaps unrealistic comparisons are being made, leaving online daters dissatisfied with what they are attracting.

Gender-defined strategies have also been observed by researchers (see Whitty, 2008a, 2008b; Whitty & Carr, 2006). Many of the women in Whitty's research reported spending copious amounts of time constructing a profile and reading through others' profiles to find their ideal match, while many of the men played a 'numbers game'; that is, they contacted many individuals hoping that someone would respond. The numbers game strategy was described by one of the male online daters in the following way.

> That is the smorgasbord approach. I guess it comes back to what I was saying before in that life is a numbers game. If you go to a dance then a barn dance is a numbers game and the purpose of that is, of course, is for the girls to met [sic] a guy but this is a similar thing [the online dating site] without the music in the sense that you can see, you can get an understanding of and get an appreciation of the individual before a move is made in a way that you can't do in a pub or a club or for that matter, even at dance. So the shot gun approach is a reasonably sophisticated manner. (Alan) (Whitty & Carr, 2006, p. 138)

In an interesting experimental study by Yang and Chiou (2010), it was found that participants did not all use the search options available on an online dating site in the most productive ways. The authors divided their sample into 'maximizers' (i.e., seeks the best by exhaustive searchers) and 'satisfiers'. They found that, when maximizers' cognitive resources are reduced by conducting more searches, they are less likely to ignore irrelevant information, and they thereby pay attention to attributes that were not pertinent to their original preferences. Yang and Chiou (2010) state that:

> Identifying the best from a large dataset of considerations becomes increasingly difficult, compelling maximizers to rely on external rather than internal standards to evaluate and select outcomes. Furthermore, the inevitability of trade-offs among attractive options intensifies the sting of passing up one attractive alternative when choosing a more attractive one. (p. 209)

4.8 STAGES IN THE ONLINE DATING PROCESS

There are arguably different phases involved in the development of a relationship with someone one has met on an online dating site compared with the stages involved in developing a relationship with someone one has met in other spaces online or in the physical realm. Whitty (2008c) has drawn from Givens' (1978) work on a traditional model of courtship to devise the five phases involved in online dating.

In Givens' five-stage model, the phases are attention (where women typically attempt to gain the attention of the opposite sex by displaying nonverbal signals); recognition (flirting behaviour consisting of pouting, primping, eyebrow flashes etc.); interaction (where conversation is initiated, typically by the male); sexual arousal; and finally resolution. Other scholars have also created models for the phases involved in formal matchmaking, such as personal ads, video dating and computer matchmaking. Ahuvia and Adelman (1992), for example, devised the SMI model (searching, matching and interacting). They parallel matchmaking services with basic market functions. For instance, in the marketplace 'searching' is initially required; that is, gaining information essential for exchange (in regard to matchmaking, this means searching for information about a potential other). Second, 'matching' is required to bring together compatible exchange partners (in regard to matchmaking, this means bringing together two singles who seem well matched). Finally, 'interacting' is when the couple physically meet.

In Whitty's model of the online dating process, she contends that Internet dating does include the three phases highlighted by Abuvia and Adelman; however, these phases do not necessarily fit neatly into the sequential order they propose. Matching, for instance, can happen at two points. First the site might suggest matches from a specific formula devised to 'scientifically' match individuals and then the client might search through the site's choices to decide whom they believe is an appropriate match. Alternatively, the client might begin by searching through the sea of profiles until they find profiles that are suitable matches. Next, contact is made on the site initially to indicate interest in another and the other has to reciprocate mutual interest. From there the two potential partners begin to interact and decide whether they wish to progress the relationship further. Whitty's model is delineated in the following sections.

4.8.1 Phase 1: The attention phase

During the attention phase, a person will try to attract someone of the opposite sex by displaying subtle nonverbal signals online. With online dating, one does not have an immediate target with whom to interact. Instead, individuals display signs of attractiveness by selecting an attractive photograph to represent themselves. In the main, profiles that do not show a photograph are overlooked (Whitty & Carr, 2006).

During this attention phase, another unique way online daters might go about attracting others to their profile is via the name they use to represent themselves (what is commonly referred to as a 'screen name'). Some use very flirtatious names (e.g., Imcute or Bubbly) while others select names that reflect their personal identity or interests (e.g., Mountainclimber). Others might select a nonflirtatious name (e.g., Jt28 or Smith48). Whitty and Buchanan (2010) found that certain screen names are deemed more attractive than others, and that men and women are motivated to make contact with individuals with different types of screen names. For example, it was found that men more than women were attracted to and motivated to contact screen names that indicated physical attractiveness (e.g., Hottie or Greatbody) and that women more than men were attracted to screen names that demonstrated intelligence (e.g., Wellread or Welleducated). Overall, less flirtatious names were perceived by the majority of people as less attractive.

4.8.2   Phase 2: The recognition phase

As with offline courting, the second phase of online dating requires more flirtation and some recognition. Online dating sites have attempted to mimic this step in the construction of their websites. Rather than immediately emailing a member of the site that the client finds attractive, instead, online daters are often given the option to virtually flirt; that is, many sites give the option to send a 'form' note via the site, often referred to as a 'wink' or a 'kiss'. Akin to flirting offline, this can appear less intrusive and more subtle than a more detailed email introducing oneself and asking for the person to, in turn, self-disclose.

4.8.3   Phase 3: The interaction phase

Similar to offline, the next phase in the online dating courting process involves interaction. This of course takes place online. It might initially take place through an exchange of emails via the site, a site's instant messaging service, personal email accounts, or an off-site instant messaging programme. It might then move to the telephone (usually mobile phone) or SMS texting. As with courting offline, this stage can also be flirtatious. Although the traditional physical offline cues are not present, substitutes can be found for these nonverbal cues. Typically, this third phase is relatively short. While some flirtation and self-disclosure take place for online daters during the interaction, this phase is more about verifying information and setting up the face-to-face meeting (or one or both of the pair decide to drop out of the process). Given that a profile already provides a curriculum vitae about the individual, additional information about the person does not need to be disclosed. Hence, during this phase, if the pair feels comfortable enough, they move to setting up a face-to-face date.

4.8.4   Phase 4: The face-to-face meeting

The fourth phase is roughly equivalent to Givens' fourth stage, referred to as the 'sexual arousal' stage. For online daters, the first date very much determines whether there will be any further dates. This meeting is different from a 'traditional' first date, where sexual attraction has already been established and the couple plan to spend a romantic evening together. Instead, it is a meeting where the pair test out physical chemistry and see how well their date matches up with their profile. For safety reasons, the meeting usually takes place in a public space (e.g., cafe shop, bar) and is likely scheduled to last for a restricted amount of time (so that individuals can make a quick escape if the interaction does not run smoothly). Some devise contingency plans, so that if the meeting works out well it will continue on to a proper date (e.g., dinner). Given fears that individuals will not live up to their profiles, some online daters are savvy enough to check out their date from a vantage point and, if the date does not turn out to look exactly how the individual had hoped (e.g., if the photo is a few years old or the date is somewhat different in size than described), then the person might not go through with the date (sometimes politely calling the other's mobile with an excuse as to why they could not make it).

4.8.5 Phase 5: Resolution

As with Givens' five stages of courting, resolution is the final stage of the online dating courting process. After the first meeting, individuals usually know whether they are sexually attracted to and whether they want to learn more about their date. If they are still uncertain, they might set up a few more dates; however, they will generally do so while checking out other options on the site. If they are confident that they are interested in moving forward, they will typically take themselves off the site. Problems arise between couples if expectations are not met and one of the pair is discovered to be still actively using the site when the other has taken themselves off.

4.9 CONCLUSIONS

Since around the turn of the millennium, online dating has moved from a stigmatized activity used by relatively few people to a very popular matchmaking tool, used by both young and old individuals. As this chapter illustrates, it is difficult to categorize the types of people who gravitate to online dating, and this is possibly because the type of person has changed over the years. It will also continue to change. Dating apps, such as Tinder, are changing the way some people do online dating; physical hook-ups may be solely for the purpose of having sex rather than moving towards a meaningful relationship.

The current research on online dating has elucidated that there are certain skills involved in crafting a profile as well as making contact with others on the site. It is not easy for people to pick up on deception cues from profiles, although research has found that some daters do embellish the truth about themselves on their profiles. The consequence of misrepresentations is usually that the courtship process does not move beyond the first date. Researchers believe that some strategies online daters employ will not lead to success (e.g., maximizing options from large datasets of considerations). Online dating sites do differ from traditional face-to-face methods as well as other online spaces with regard to how relationships begin and progress.

DISCUSSION QUESTIONS

1. Consider Goffman's theory and how it might be applied to explain how people present themselves on an online dating site.
2. In what ways do you think people might deceive others on online dating sites compared with other places (both face to face and online)?
3. Have you or has anyone you've known developed a romantic relationship with someone they met on an online dating site? How did this relationship progress? Does it fit with the stage theory presented in this chapter?
4. What aspects do you think it would be important to include in an online dating profile if you were to create one? Which theories would best explain your choices?

SUGGESTED READINGS

Poley, M. E. M. & Luo, S. (2012). Social compensation or rich-get-richer? The role of social competence in college students' use of the Internet to find a partner. *Computers in Human Behavior, 28,* 414–419.

Toma, C. L. & Hancock, J. T. (2012). What lies beneath: The linguistic traces of deception in online dating profiles. *Journal of Communication, 62,* 78–97.

Valkenburg, P. M. & Peter, J. (2007). Who visits online dating sites? Exploring some characteristics of online daters. *CyberPsychology & Behavior, 10*(6), 849–852.

Whitty, M. T. (2008). Revealing the 'real' me, searching for the 'actual' you': Presentations of self on an Internet dating site. *Computers in Human Behavior, 24,* 1707–1723.

Yang, M. L. & Chiou, W. B. (2010). Looking online for the best romantic partner reduces decision quality: The moderating role of choice-making strategies. *Cyberpsychology, Behavior, and Social Networking, 13*(2), 207–210.

5 Online Sexual Activities

Humans will find a sexual use for almost any new media. The Internet is no exception. Prior to the Internet, 'Polaroid sex' and of course video existed. Each of these media have been used for the production of both commercial and amateur pornography. What is unique to the Internet is that it has opened up opportunities for more interactive sexual encounters and exploration. This includes both the sexual activities that take place in cyberspace and those online sexual activities that the Internet enables. Psychologists have questioned whether it is healthy to partake in online sexual activities, with some scholars arguing that some individuals can be addicted to online sex. Others, in contrast, have argued that the Internet opens up new ways to explore sexuality in a potentially safe environment. As the preceding chapters have pointed out, the Internet will continue to open up new opportunities for new interactions, and this also applies to online sex and erotica. For example, teledildonics and virtual reality will most likely continue to be developed to create new sexual experiences. This chapter examines the literature on the psychology of online sexual activities and considers whether they are liberating or debilitating. It does so by considering a range of activities. Importantly, though, while it is undeniably important to consider the issue of online paedophilia, this will be postponed until Chapter 14.

5.1   THE BEGINNINGS OF INTERNET SEX

People have been engaging in sexual activities on the Internet since its inception. Although, at first, individuals were limited to textual exchanges, many found no difficulties with 'erotic talk'. This is nicely illustrated in Carol Parker's (1997) book *The Joy of Cybersex*:

GERSH   I press against you …
GEEKGIRL and I rub my belly to slick my hand with oil
GERSH   pushing against you … hot … Can't take my eyes off you … Watching you arch …

Cyberpsychology: The Study of Individuals, Society and Digital Technologies, First Edition.
Monica Therese Whitty and Garry Young.
© 2017 John Wiley & Sons, Ltd. Published 2017 by John Wiley & Sons, Ltd.

GEEKGIRL	Stroking lightly up your thigh with one hand ... stroking my breast with the other as my nipples harden under your gaze ... sigh
GERSH	my hand dips down and strokes between your legs ... just a touch ...
GEEKGIRL	my legs part a little ... hips moving slowly
GERSH	Deeper this time ... I can feel you ... wet ... warm ... mmmmhhhh

Scholars have attempted to categorise some of the various types of sexual activities that take place online. 'Hot chat', for example, has been defined as 'two or more individuals engag[ing] in discourses which move beyond light-hearted flirting' (Whitty & Carr, 2006, p. 21). In contrast, 'cybersex' is 'generally understood to be synchronous communication in cyberspace where two or more individuals engage in discourses about sexual fantasies' (Whitty & Carr, 2006, p. 21).

As mentioned in Chapter 3, bulletin board systems were an especially popular space in the early days of the Internet and many of these systems were sexual in nature. Some were designed for people to meet others who shared their sexual interests and to enable them to live out their sexual desires online and/or offline. Social scientists have examined these sites and the people who inhabit them (e.g., Wysocki, 1998; Wysocki & Thalken, 2007). Wysocki (1998) was interested in seeing whether online sex was a replacement for face-to-face relationships or whether instead it enhanced them. She investigated her research question by interviewing participants using a bulletin board called the 'Pleasure Pit'. In her study, she identified five main reasons for using sexually explicitly bulletin boards, including anonymity, time constraints in one's personal life, the ability to share sexual fantasies with other people, the desire to participate in online sexual activity and the desire to find people with similar sexual interests to meet face to face. Notably, Wysocki also found that many of the people she interviewed did not reveal to their offline partners that they were using the Internet as a sexual outlet.

5.2 THE TRIPLE A ENGINE

In a similar way, as described in the preceding chapters, in the early days of the Internet, scholars were divided in their views over whether the Internet is a healthy space to explore and learn about sexuality or whether engaging in online activities leads to psychologically problematic behaviours. Al Cooper and his colleagues wrote at length about the problems and joys cyberspace has to offer individuals – especially when it comes to sex. Cooper, Scherer and Marcus (2002) stated that 'the Internet can equally threaten or aid a healthy, sex-positive, emotionally satisfying sex life' (p. 210). Cooper (1998) developed what he named the 'Triple A Engine' to explain how the Internet can be a potent medium for sexual activity. He pointed out that it is easy to 'access' the Internet, that it is 'affordable' and that one can be 'anonymous' online. Given these aspects of the Internet, sexual activities online are available at any time, cost little or nothing, and can be used anonymously, allowing users to safety engage in sexual activities without people knowing their 'true' identities. However, these theorists argued that the seductive appeal of the Internet could also lead to problematic behaviours. Cooper, Delmonico and Burg (2000), for example, found a small proportion of individuals whose online sexual behaviour was clearly compulsive. They also found that both women and gay men were more highly represented than heterosexual men in the group of individuals they identified to be cybersex compulsives.

5.3 CYBERSEX: DEBILITATING OR LIBERATING?

Cybersex has been around since the early days of the Internet. The extract earlier in this chapter written between Gersh and geekgirl is an example of cybersex. A definition of cybersex was offered earlier in this chapter; however, there are many ways in which individuals can engage in sexual discourses in cyberspace. This might be by themselves or with others – either physically or virtually present. Shaughnessy, Byers and Thornton (2011) asked 292 students to define cybersex. Consistent with previous definitions, their participants defined it as an interactive online sexual activity and most described it as taking place in real time. Thirty-six per cent of their sample stated that cybersex is a 'describing activity' – that is, an activity that involves describing sexual activities, having sex and sexual acts. Twenty-five per cent stated that it involved self-stimulation, and 21% stated that it involved arousal. Thirteen per cent stated that it involved visual stimuli – which is an advance on the early understandings of cybersex, given that participants then were mostly limited to textual exchanges.

Problems associated with cybersex include cybersex addiction (detailed later in this chapter) and infidelity (see Chapter 6 for a detailed discussion). However, is there anything positive about engaging in cybersex? Whitty (2008d) has suggested that cybersex is potentially a liberating activity, especially for those who wish to explore sexuality. Adams, Oye and Parker (2003) argue that the Internet offers a liberating space for older people. They state: 'Without a doubt, sexual expression on the Internet has a facilitative potential for older adults. For example, individuals can find a sense of "normalcy" about their sexual interests when finding others with similar pursuits' (p. 413). In a study of MMORPG players, Valkyrie (2011) found that the participants she interviewed reported mixed views on cybersex. Sometimes it was perceived as harassment from women players. Others felt that it added another dimension to their virtual world experience, as explained by 'Beck':

> Leveling Drg is a drag. Lots of time LFP [looking for party], and well, I had to keep myself entertained somehow. There was another Drg that I knew. She was good fun to talk to, and I started by talking to her about Drg, and this that and the other. Eventually,

it just turned into cyber sex (laughs). So yeah, that's about it really that went on for a few months. It was good fun, and very distracting ... its cyber sex, it's all about how vivid your imagination can be and trying to tune into the other persons at the same time. (p. 89)

5.4 INTERACTIVE SEX ENTERTAINMENT

As already highlighted, cyberspace has provided a new space for a range of interactive sexual activities. As in the past, pornography can be either amateur or professionally created. However, the Internet has provided a new space for more interactive sex entertainment. To date, little research has focused on any of the potential psychological benefits of interactive sex entertainment, despite these forms of entertainment having been around for well over a decade. An example of this is CU-SeeMe, which was videoconferencing software used by many as an interactive sex entertainment site. In more recent times, we have seen sites such as Chatroulette, where strangers are randomly paired to engage in web-based conversations. They can opt to use voice, webcam and/or text. On this site, strangers continue to chat until one decides to move on to the next stranger. Bilton (2010), in the *New York Times*, describes his experience using the website:

At one moment I was sitting in the living room with my wife, and on entering the site, we were siphoned into a dimly lit room with a man who told us he was in Russia. Moments later we were watching a woman dance half-naked in a kitchen in Turkey, and then we stared in shock at a gaggle of laughing college students in a dorm room somewhere. With each click of the mouse we were transported into a stranger's life – then whisked along to another jarring encounter.

After five minutes, we disconnected and sat in silence, disturbed by the rawness of some of what we had seen ... [Another time, we] clicked Next and there were three naked men in Amsterdam dancing to Rick Astley music ... Then a man told us he was in jail ... It's very strange, and not just because you are parachuting into someone else's life (and they yours), a kind of invited crasher. It is also the eerie thrill of true randomness – who, or what, will show up next? (p. 1)

5.5 CYBERSEX ADDICTION

Researchers have spent some time examining the negative aspects of engaging in online sexual behaviours. Cybsersex addiction is a topic that has received much focus from researchers (see, e.g., Griffiths, 2000a, 2000b, 2001). Addiction to sexual activities can include a range of activities, such as cybersex and viewing pornography. As mentioned earlier in this chapter, Cooper, Delmonico and Burg (2000) found a small proportion of individuals whose online sexual behaviour was clearly compulsive. They also found that both women and gay men were more highly represented than heterosexual men in the group of individuals they identified to be cybersex compulsives. Daneback, Ross and Månsson (2006) found that online sexual compulsives are more likely to be men who are in a relationship, are bisexual and have a sexually transmitted infection. Schneider (2000) has argued that cybersex addiction is a major contributing factor to separation and divorce. Moreover, Schneider's study found that about half (52%) of cybersex users had lost interest in relational sex. More recently, Brand et al. (2011), in a study of 89 heterosexual male participants, found that those participants who experienced greater subjective sexual arousal from watching Internet pornographic pictures reported more problems in their daily life. These individuals were also more likely to be addicted to cybersex. Corley and Hook (2012), in a study that examined self-identified female sex and love addicts, found that these women were more likely to engage in hypersexual Internet behaviours compared with nonaddicts.

5.6 THE INTERNET AS AN ENABLER OF RISKY OFFLINE SEXUAL ENCOUNTERS

Cyberspace not only opens up new ways to perform sex but has also created new opportunities to locate individuals to engage in sexual activities in the physical world. With the existence of websites such as Gaydar and apps such as Badoo, Grindr and Hornet, it should come as no surprise to learn that cyberspace has become a popular place to hook up for sex, especially for anonymous sex between men (Gass, Hoff, Stephenson & Sullivan, 2012). Malu, Challenor, Theobald and Barton (2004), in a sample of British participants, found that the use of the Internet to seek sexual partners was more prevalent for men who have sex with men (47%), compared with men who have sex with women (14%) and women who have sex with men (7%). Sex workers, in particular, have noted that the Internet has played a dramatic role in increasing opportunities for commercial sex encounters (Parsons, Koken & Bimbi, 2004). Liau, Millett and Marks (2006) found from an offline survey on men who have sex with men that 40% of their participants located their sexual partners via the Internet.

The number of people using the Internet to locate sexual partners is a concern, given that there has been found to be a correlation between locating sexual partners online and contracting STIs, including HIV. Involvement in anonymous sex between men who find each other online, for example, is associated with greater involvement in HIV-related risky practices (Kakietek, Sullivan & Heffelfinger, 2011; Klein, 2012).

Lee, Tam, Mak and Wong (2011), in a study of 77 Chinese HIV-infected men, found that over half (58%) of their sample had found partners via the Internet a year prior to their infections.

The above studies suggest that simply using the Internet to find partners leads to a higher risk of engaging in unsafe sexual practices. However, scholars have found that there are other factors we need to consider. For example, researchers have argued there may be cohort effects, with the older generation of men who have sex with men being potentially more likely to engage in sexually risky behaviours compared with the younger generation (Kubicek, Carpineto, McDavitt, Weiss & Kipke, 2011). Garofalo, Herrick, Mustanski and Donenberg (2007) have found evidence to support this notion. In their sample of 270 young men who have sex with men, they found that 68% of their sample had used the Internet to locate a sexual partner. Of these, 48% were successful at finding a partner, and about half of those individuals (53%) used condoms consistently. Coleman et al. (2010) found in a sample of 2,716 men who have sex with men that those who scored higher on compulsive sexual behaviour were more likely to engage in unprotected anal intercourse.

Not all researchers, however, have found a direct relationship between locating sexual partners online and engaging in unsafe sex practices. In a study that focused on male sex workers, Parsons et al. (2004) found that some male escorts felt that the Internet had given them more control over the sexual requests made by their clients. Moreover, they stated that it gave them an opportunity to educate their clients about safe sex practices. One of the male escorts they interviewed had the following to say:

> When I was younger, I worked out of an escort service, and I would have sex with people, and I used to do things that I didn't want to do. And I hated that. And that made me feel bad about it, and that made me feel like a whore. And so, when I started doing this [advertising on the Internet independently], even though I sort of am a whore, I said, I'm going to arrange so that I don't feel like a whore. So I don't do anything I don't want to do. Anything, I don't want to do ... I don't have unsafe sex. They'll say 'Do you do bareback,' and I say 'No.' That's it, you know. That's all they want to hear. But I don't want to lie, and I try and give 'em a little lecture ... I'm also thirty-six. I mean, I say over the phone I'm thirty-two, but I'm thirty-six. I think a lot of these young kids, these 21-year-olds, they didn't see the generation before them die of AIDS. (p. 1030)

5.7 THE INTERNET AND SEXUAL HEALTH INFORMATION

Although the evidence is fairly clear about the increase in sexual risks associated with those who seek partners via the Internet, on the other side of the coin is the utility of the Internet for providing sexual health information, which in turn could prevent sexual risks. Malu et al. (2004) found that those who used the Internet to locate sexual partners were also more likely to use the Internet to access sexual health information.

Research has found that the Internet provides a unique opportunity for men who have sex with men to learn about sexual health and relationships (Brown, Maycock & Burns, 2005). Kubicek et al. (2011) found, in a sample of 526 young men, that the Internet was an important venue for these young men not only to locate sexual partners but also to obtain information about sexual behaviour and health. They contend that the Internet has provided a new space for many young men to learn about health information as well as share their stories (we will examine, in detail, the use of the Internet for health in Chapter 15). Many of the men in their sample spent time getting to know their potential sexual partners online first, prior to meeting offline. The authors conclude that 'providers hoping to initiate online intervention programs should be aware of how young men are accessing the Internet and for what purposes in order to most effectively reach their target populations' (p. 812). Others too have found that the Internet is useful for individuals to learn about sexual health information, such as HIV prevention (Mustanski, Lyons & Garcia, 2011). Hooper, Rosser, Horvath, Oakes and Danilenko (2008) found that the majority of men who have sex with men in their sample accessed the Internet for sexual health information (86% for psychical sexual health; 69% for HIV prevention).

Researchers have found that women sex workers can and are willing to participate in online HIV/STI prevention intervention programmes (Hong, Li, Fang, Lin & Zhang, 2011). In a sample of 1,022 female sex workers, Hong et al. found that 40% of their sample had searched online for HIV/STI information and about two thirds of their sample were willing to participate in online HIV/STI prevention programmes.

Although the Internet is an appropriate space to provide sexual health information and research has found that some individuals are willing to use the Internet to learn more about sexual health, as will be discussed in more detail in Chapter 15, not all of this information is credible. For example, in a meta-analysis, Eysenbach, Powell, Kuss and Sa (2002) found that 70% of the 79 studies reviewed concluded that much of the health information available online is inaccurate, out of date or incomplete. Lindley, Friendman and Struble (2012) found that not all sexual health sites available to lesbians cover all the information they need.

5.8 SOCIAL SUPPORT AND EXPLORING SEXUALITY

The Internet can also provide support to those coping with their sexuality. There is a wealth of literature produced on the types of support the Internet can provide for individuals with sexual issues or for those who wish to learn more about sexuality.

Adolescence is a time of identity exploration, and one of the domains of identity is sexuality (Erikson, 1964; Marcia, 1966). As will be discussed in more detail in Chapter 7, the Internet has provided new opportunities for adolescents to explore sexual identity. Subrahmanyam, Smahel and Greenfield (2006) examined a large sample of conversations in both monitored and unmonitored teen chat rooms. In their study they found that 5% of the conversations were sexual. Participants who claimed to be female produced more implicit sexual communication, and participants who identified as male produced more explicit sexual communication. Suzuki and Calzo (2004) found that sexual health was a popular topic on bulletin boards. They argued that, for teens, 'bulletin boards proved to be a valuable forum of personal opinions, actionable suggestions, concrete information, and emotional support and allowed teens to candidly discuss sensitive topics, such as sexuality and interpersonal relations' (p. 685).

Since the early days of research into the Internet, researchers have found that the Internet is potentially a safe space for individuals, in particular adolescents, to 'come out'. McKenna and Bargh (1998) found that individuals of all ages (15–62 years, $M = 34$ years) with marginalized sexualities felt comfortable expressing their sexuality as well as coming out online. Moreover, the acceptance they received in these online groups gave them the confidence to come out offline to friends and family. Bond, Hefner and Drogos (2009) found, in a small sample of 56 self-identifying LGB participants, that the majority of participants reported using media more than face-to-face communication as a means of gathering information during the coming out process. This was more likely to be the case for younger than older participants. Interestingly, the authors found that participants who used media more during the coming out process were less open with their families regarding their sexuality. Furthermore, there was no relationship found between feeling lonely or having low self-esteem and media use. More recently, Mustanski et al. (2011) found in a sample of 329 young men (18–24 years) that participants reported the Internet provided support during the coming out process as well as support for those who received homophobic messages.

SUGGESTED ACTIVITY

Have a look at some of the sexual health information available online. Do you think individuals your own age would be more or less inclined to seek out this information online compared with asking a doctor or visiting a health clinic? Why do you think this?

5.9 TEENS AND RISKY SEXUAL ONLINE BEHAVIOUR

Although cyberspace can offer a safe space for adolescents to explore their marginalized sexuality and come out, the risks involved with engaging in online sexual practices cannot be ignored. During the 2010s a new behaviour, known as sexting, has caused a multitude of problems for teenagers. Sexting is the use of a mobile or similar electronic device to distribute sexually explicit images. Teenagers might send these pictures of themselves to a friend or partner only to learn that the image has subsequently been distributed to their social network. Moreover, the images could potentially be sent to a paedophile.

Lenhart (2009), in the US, found that 4% of mobile-phone-owning teens aged 12–17 years said they had sent sexually suggestive nude or nearly nude images of themselves to someone else via text messaging. She also found that 15% of mobile-phone-owning teens aged 12–17 years said they had received sexually suggestive nude or nearly nude images of someone they know via text messaging on their mobile phone. Furthermore, older teens were much more likely to send and receive these images: 8% of 17-year-olds with mobile phones had sent a sexually provocative image by text and 30% had received a nude or nearly nude image on their phone.

Lenhart also found that teenagers who pay their own phone bills are more likely to send 'sexts': 17% of teens who paid for all of the costs associated with their mobile phones had sent sexually suggestive images via text, whereas just 3% of teens who did not pay for, or only paid for a portion of the cost of, their mobile phone had sent these images. Moreover, the focus groups she ran revealed that there are three main scenarios for sexting: (1) exchange of images solely between two romantic partners, (2) exchanges between partners that are shared with others outside the relationship and (3) exchanges between people who are not yet in a relationship but where at least one person hopes to be in a relationship (we examine sexting again in Chapter 14, in relation to under-18 nudity and the law).

The types of risky online sexual behaviours adolescents decide to engage in are, in part, determined by peer norms (Baumgartner, Valkenburg & Peter, 2011). Baumgarter et al. (2011) focused on four kinds of sexual online behaviour: searching for someone on the Internet with whom to talk about sex; searching for someone on the Internet with whom to have sex; sending a photo or video in which one is partly naked to someone one only knows online; and sending an address or telephone number online to someone one only knows online. The authors found that descriptive as well as injunctive peer norms predicted whether an adolescent engaged in risky sexual online behaviour. Descriptive norms, however, were found to be stronger. The researchers conclude that 'perceived behaviour of peers may be more important in the explanation of adolescents' risky sexual online behaviour than what adolescents perceive their peers approve of' (p. 757). Despite the influence of peer norms found in the above study, interestingly, the same researchers found in a previous study that adolescents did not take more online sexual risks than adults (Baumgartner, Valkenburg & Peter, 2010).

Being exposed to sexually explicit online material can, however, influence adolescents' attitudes towards sex. Peter and Valkenburg (2006) found from the Dutch participants they surveyed that exposure to sexually explicit online material is related to more recreational attitudes towards sex. This relationship was, however, influenced by the adolescents' gender and mediated by the extent to which they perceived online material as realistic.

5.10 TELEDILDONICS AND THE FUTURE OF SEX IN CYBERSPACE

As argued already in this book, online relating and sexuality will most likely change in the future. Cyberspace will continue to evolve and attract new users. One of the potential new developments is teledildonics, which involves the integration of the physical world (i.e., the use of sex toys) and cyberspace. Often, in these types of interactions, another person or group of people manipulate the sex toys remotely. Currently, smartphones have apps to link to these devices, which include KissPhone, LovePalz and VIVI vibrator. Once activated, all provide a sensation that is meant to feel like the physical body. The KissPhone, for example, has been described as follows: 'The KissPhone is designed for remote kissing. It has a mouth which you kiss – it subsequently measures the pressure, percussion speed, temperature, and sucking force of your mouth, transmits those same parameters to the remote user's Kissphone where it recreates your kiss for your teleparamour' (Halon, 2009). How these will be developed in the future is yet to be seen, and the psychological impact of engaging with these devices is yet to be realized.

5.11 CONCLUSIONS

As with online relationships, people were engaging in online sexual activities even when the Internet existed only as a textual medium. As this chapter illustrates, there are both positive and negative aspects to engaging in online sexual activities. Although, at present, the research suggests that people who locate sexual partners online are more at risk of engaging in offline risky sexual practices, this might not be the case in the future. The Internet can be used to promote safe sex practices and it can be constructed in such a way as to provide a safe space, especially for young people, to explore and learn about sexuality. The dark side of online sexual activities, however, cannot be ignored. As will be covered in greater depth in forthcoming chapters, some people are addicted to online activities, including cybersex, and some engage in sexual activities to cheat on their partner. The future of online sexual activities is unknown. There is the potential to develop more interactive devices, such as Teledildonics, but the psychological impact of such devices and how they might affect people's relationships has yet to be researched.

DISCUSSION QUESTIONS

1. Is the Triple A Engine still of use to explain why people engage in online sexual activities?
2. How would you define cybersex?
3. Is the Internet a positive or negative space to engage in online sexual behaviours?
4. Do you believe that engaging in online interactive pornographic games, such as Chatroulette, is a psychologically healthy or unhealthy thing to do?
5. Considering the theoretical and empirical literature, what does it mean to be addicted to online sexual behaviours?
6. How do you perceive the future of sex in cyberspace?

SUGGESTED READINGS

Baumgartner, S. E., Valkenburg, P. M. & Peter, J. (2011). The influence of descriptive and injunctive peer norms on adolescents' risky sexual online behaviour. *Cyberpsychology, Behavior, and Social Networking, 14*(12), 753–758.

Brand, M., Laier, C., Pawlikowski, M., Schachtle, U., Scholer, T. & Alstotter-Gleich, C. (2011). Watching pornographic pictures on the Internet: Role of sexual arousal ratings and psychological-psychiatric symptoms for using sex sites excessively. *Cyberpsychology, Behavior, and Social Networking, 14*(6), 371–377.

Cooper, A., Delmonico, D. L. & Burg, R. (2000). Cybersex users, abusers, and compulsives: New findings and implications. *Sexual Addiction & Compulsivity: The Journal of Treatment and Prevention, 7*, 5–29.

McKenna, K. Y. A. & Bargh, J. A. (1998). Coming out in the age of the Internet: Identity 'demarginalization' through virtual group participation. *Journal of Personality and Social Psychology, 75*(3), 681–694.

Parsons, J. T., Koken, J. A. & Bimbi, D. S. (2004). The use of the Internet by gay and bisexual male escorts: Sex workers as sex educators. *AIDS Care, 16*(8), 1021–1035.

Wysocki, D. K. (1998). Let your fingers to do the talking: Sex on an adult chat-line. *Sexualities, 1*, 425–452.

6 Internet Infidelity

The company behind Ashley Madison, a popular online dating service marketed to people trying to cheat on their spouses, said on Monday that the site had been breached by hackers who may have obtained personal data about the service's millions of members.

The group of hackers behind the attack, going by the name Impact Team, said they had stolen information on the 37 million members of Ashley Madison. To prevent the data from being released, the hackers said, the company needed to shut down the site entirely.

The hackers promised to release the real names, passwords and financial transactions of members if Ashley Madison did not meet that demand. The hackers have leaked some information online already, but that data did not appear to be the bulk of what was collected. (Grandoni, 2015)

The above extract from a news article emphasizes how Internet-enabled cheating is a big business. Cyberspace has created new opportunities to cheat on one's partner, and in many ways has made it easier to carry out an affair (both online and offline). The research on Internet infidelity has examined the types of online sexual activities that might be considered unfaithful and which ones might cause the most upset for people. This chapter questions whether all online sexual behaviour, including cybersex with an avatar, might be considered acts of betrayal. We also examine other forms of relationship transgression, such as emotional betrayal. How men and women differ on their understandings of infidelity are examined through the lens of theories such as social evolutionary and social cognitive theories. However, as the reader will note, researchers need to gain a more in-depth understanding of betrayals that might take place online in order to develop theories that incorporate relationship transgressions that take place in the physical and cyber realms – especially given the importance and frequent usage of digital technologies in many people's lives.

Cyberpsychology: The Study of Individuals, Society and Digital Technologies, First Edition.
Monica Therese Whitty and Garry Young.
© 2017 John Wiley & Sons, Ltd. Published 2017 by John Wiley & Sons, Ltd.

6.1 DEFINING INTERNET INFIDELITY

For a number of years, scholars debated whether or not Internet infidelity was a real phenomenon (e.g., Cooper, 2002; Maheu & Subotnik, 2001; Whitty, 2003b; Young, 1998). These days there is general agreement that people can and do cheat on their partners on the Internet. There are, however, conflicting views on which behaviours might be considered unfaithful.

Internet infidelity has been operationalized in a number of ways. Shaw (1997) defined Internet infidelity as 'behaviorally different from other kinds of infidelity; however, the contributing factors and results are similar when we consider how it affects the way partners relate' (p. 29). A more specific definition has been offered by Young, Griffin-Shelley, Cooper, O'Mara and Buchanan (2000), who stated that a cyberaffair is 'a romantic and/or sexual relationship that is initiated via online contact and maintained predominantly through electronic conversations that occur through email and in virtual communities such as chat rooms, interactive games, or newsgroups' (p. 60). In contrast, Maheu and Subotnik (2001) provide a generic definition of infidelity: 'Infidelity happens when two people have a commitment and that commitment is broken – regardless of where, how or with whom it happens. Infidelity is the breaking of a promise with a real person, whether the sexual stimulation is derived from the virtual or the real world' (p. 101).

As already highlighted in this book, the Internet will continue to evolve, and so a statement about the specific spaces online in which individuals might cheat (e.g., email, SNSs) is difficult to include in any definition of Internet infidelity. The definition of Internet infidelity offered here is as follows:

> Internet infidelity occurs when the rules of the relationship are broken by acting inappropriately in an emotional and/or a sexual manner with at least one person other than one's partner. The rules might differ for different couples, but there are some fundamental rules that are often unspoken and are typical expectations of most committed relationships. The Internet might be the exclusive, main or partial space where the inappropriate emotional or sexual interactions take place.

6.2 UNFAITHFUL ONLINE SEXUAL ACTIVITIES

As with offline infidelity, the types of behaviours that are considered unfaithful online are classified as emotional and/or sexual. However, there is a range of sexual and emotional activities that one can engage in and not all of these are necessarily considered to be unfaithful by all individuals.

6.2.1 Cybersex

Chapter 5 considered cybersex and offered a definition, stating that cybersex is 'generally understood to be synchronous communication in cyberspace where two or more individuals engage in discourses about sexual fantasies' (Whitty & Carr, 2006, p. 21). It was also pointed out that there are various understandings about what cybersex entails but, in the main, individuals see it as a descriptive, interactive activity that sexually arouses individuals and might contain a visual element. Previous research has consistently found that cybersex is perceived as an act of infidelity (Mileham, 2007; Parker & Wampler, 2003; Whitty, 2003b, 2005). This is not limited to studies that ask participants whether they would be upset if they learnt that their partner was engaging in such activities. Mileham (2007), for example, interviewed 76 men and 10 women whom she had recruited from Yahoo's 'Married and Flirting' and MSN's 'Married but Flirting' chat rooms. Married people inhabit these sites and engage in cyberflirting and cybersex and sometimes arrange to meet offline. She found that some of these participants acknowledged that online activities could be perceived as unfaithful.

6.2.2 Other online sexual activities

Chapter 5 outlined a host of online sexual activities, not all of which have been considered by researchers of Internet infidelity. In addition to cybersex, Parker and Wampler (2003) identified a range of other online sexual interactions that participants believed to be unfaithful, including interacting in adult chat rooms and becoming a member of an adult website. More recently, Schneider, Weiss and Samenow (2012) identified a range of online sexual activities that individuals considered to be unfaithful, including viewing pornography alone, sexual chatting and viewing porn, and sexual chatting and then meeting up with the person with whom they were chatting. These cyber activities might take place via computers and/or smartphones.

6.2.3 Pornography

Viewing pornography is not considered by the majority of participants surveyed by the research to be an unfaithful act (although it is often still upsetting for individuals to learn their partner has been viewing pornography). Parker and Wampler (2003) found that visiting adult chat rooms but not interacting, and visiting various adult websites were also not considered to be relationship transgressions. It has been suggested that viewing pornography is less likely to be understood as a relationship transgression because it is a passive act, which often does not involve interacting with another. Moreover, there is no real possibility of it leading to interaction with the person being watched.

> **SUGGESTED ACTIVITY**
>
> Which online sexual activities would you be upset with your partner engaging in? Are there some online sexual activities that would not bother you? Do you think your views are similar to those of others?

6.3 VIRTUAL OR REAL?

Why are online sexual activities considered by the majority to be unfaithful acts given that these activities are only *virtual*? According to Whitty (2003b, 2005, 2011), the answer lies with research conducted on more traditional relationship transgressions. Previous research into infidelity has found that 'mental exclusivity' is as important as 'sexual exclusivity' (Yarab & Allgeier, 1998). Roscoe, Cavanaugh and Kennedy (1988), for example, found that undergraduates believed that engaging in sexual interactions such as kissing, flirting and petting with someone other than their partner ought to be considered unfaithful. Yarab, Sensibaugh and Allgeier (1998) revealed an array of unfaithful sexual behaviours in addition to sexual intercourse, including passionately kissing, sexual fantasies, sexual attraction and flirting. Yarab and Allgeier (1998) found that, when considering sexual fantasies, the greater the threat of the sexual fantasy to the current relationship, the more likely the fantasy was to be rated as unfaithful. For instance, fantasizing about a partner's best friend was considered by most to be a greater threat, and therefore more unfaithful, than fantasizing about a movie star.

Returning to the question, empirical research suggests that it is the sexual desire for another that is the act of betrayal. Hence, displays of that sexual desire as well as fantasizing about the object of one's desire can be upsetting for one's partner. But this desire needs to be seen as potentially mutual and obtainable. Therefore, if one has sexual fantasies about Brad Pitt or a male gigolo, one's partner is far less likely to be concerned than if one fantasizes about having sex with their best friend or a stranger they have cybersex with online.

6.4 EMOTIONAL INFIDELITY

The research on offline infidelity has identified that not all infidelity is sexual – it can be emotional. Emotional infidelity is understood to be falling in love with another individual other than one's partner, or sharing intimate and/or secret details about oneself with someone one is attracted to, other than one's partner. Emotional infidelity has been found to be equally upsetting whether it takes place online or offline. This finding makes sense in light of the research summarized in Chapter 3 on online relationships – where such relationships, for some, are understood to be as intimate and emotionally fulfilling as offline relationships. Emotional infidelity is illustrated in the extract below, which is from a study where participants were required to complete a story following a cue about Internet infidelity (Whitty, 2005):

> 'It is cheating,' she said rather calmly.
>
> 'No, I'm not cheating. It's not like I'm bonking her anyway. You're the one I'm with and, like I said, I have *NO* intentions of meeting her.' He hopped into bed.
>
> 'It's "emotional" cheating,' she said, getting annoyed.
>
> 'How so?' he asked, amusement showing in his eyes.
>
> 'Cheating isn't necessarily physical. That's one side of it. …' He pulled the sheets over himself and rolled over. 'Well … I know you have not met her *yet*, that's why, but I'm still a little annoyed, Mark.' She sat on the edge of the bed.
>
> 'Don't be mad. You're the one I love. So *how* is it emotional cheating?' He sat up.
>
> 'You're keeping stuff from me. Relationships are about trust! How can I trust you if you keep stuff from me about the "Internet girl"?' (pp. 62–63)

6.5 GENDER DIFFERENCES: WHICH IS WORSE – SEX OR LOVE?

Overall, it seems that men and women do not differ in how much or how regularly they experience jealousy or upset in regard to traditional forms of infidelity (Buss, 2000). Nonetheless, some researchers have found that men and women differ in the 'weighting given to the cues that trigger jealousy' (Buss, 2000, p. 46). As Buss (2000) explains: 'men are predicted to give more weight to cues of sexual infidelity, whereas women are predicted to give more weight to cues of long-term diversion of investment, such as, emotional involvement with another person' (p. 46). This he explains through an evolutionary lens. According to this theory, through natural selection the human species has inherited certain traits and emotional reactions. Researchers, such as Buss, contend that ancestral men faced a grave threat from cuckoldry – being uncertain about the paternity of their partner's children. Consequently, men are more likely to respond with more intense jealousy to sexual infidelity than women. Ancestral women, on the other hand, faced the risk that an unfaithful male partner might divert his resources to another woman and her children. Therefore, women have developed an innate jealousy towards emotional infidelity (the assumption being that the man will expend resources on the 'other woman' he is in love with).

Research on offline infidelity has found that, when forced to choose whether sexual or emotional infidelity is most upsetting, women, more than men, rate extradyadic emotional behaviour as more upsetting (Shackelford & Buss, 1996).

Some have found this result even when participants are not forced to decide. For example, Roscoe et al. (1988) asked participants to list what behaviours they believed were relationship transgressions. In this study, men were more likely to state that a sexual encounter with a different partner was an exemplar of infidelity. In contrast, women were more likely to state that spending time with another and keeping secrets from a partner were acts of infidelity. It is, however, noteworthy that both men and women report extradyadic sexual behaviour to be more unacceptable and a greater betrayal than extradyadic emotional behaviour (Shackelford & Buss, 1996).

Not all theorists agree with evolutionary theorists' accounts of infidelity. DeSteno, Bartlett, Braverman and Salovey (2002), for example, have argued that the methodology Buss and his colleagues used to test their claims was not sound. One reason for this is because the same results are not always found when different methodologies are employed to test this hypothesis. Buss and his colleagues' findings have been supported via forced-choice questions, asking participants to choose whether they believe sexual or emotional infidelity is worse. Gender differences, however, are typically not obtained when participants are asked to rate how upset they would feel as a result of each of these scenarios.

Alternative theories have been developed to explain jealousy and upset experienced as a result of betrayal. Some theorists have contended that existing gender differences need not reflect innate modules. Instead, they might be better explained by a social cognitive approach or by developmental theories (e.g., DeSteno & Salovey, 1996; Harris, 2004; Harris & Christenfeld, 1996). Proponents of these theories believe it is crucial to understand what men and women read into their partners' infidelity. This has been named the 'double-shot hypothesis' (DeSteno & Salovey, 1996) or the 'two-for-one hypothesis' (Harris & Christenfeld, 1996), both of which essentially state that men feel doubly upset when thinking about their female partner having sex with another man, as the male partner holds the belief that this most likely means she is in love with the other man. Hence, sexual infidelity implies emotional infidelity. Women, in contrast, think that men can have sex without being in love and so do not believe that sexual infidelity implies emotional infidelity. Instead, women get the double hit if they believe their male partner is in love with another woman. This is because they believe that emotional infidelity implies sexual infidelity. Men, however, do not assume that their female partner is having sex with another man with whom she is in love. Therefore, he does not experience any additional upset from this thought.

To test out their claims, Harris and Christenfeld (1996) asked their participants to think of a serious romantic relationship they had been involved in and to imagine that this partner had been engaging in sexual intercourse with someone else. On a five-point Likert scale, participants had to rate the likelihood that their partner was in love with the person with whom they had just engaged in sex. In addition, they were again asked to think of a serious romantic relationship they had been involved in and to imagine that their partner was in love with someone else. On a five-point Likert scale, participants had to rate the likelihood that their partner was having sex with the person with whom they were in love. As predicted, they found that men were more likely to say that their partner was in love with the person with whom they were having sex, and women were more likely to say that their partner was having sex with the person with whom they had fallen in love.

6.5.1 Gender differences on the Internet

The gender differences with regard to Internet infidelity are mixed, and not as clear-cut as the research on traditional infidelity. Consistent with previous research on offline infidelity, in a story-writing task, Whitty (2005) found that women, more than men, mentioned emotional betrayal in their stories of cyberinfidelities. Also, in line with previous research on offline betrayal (e.g., Amato & Previti, 2003; Paul & Galloway, 1994), she found that women were more likely than men to write that they would end their relationship if they found out their partner was having an affair on the Internet. Moreover, the women in Whitty's (2005) study were more likely than the men to talk about the time and distancing from the relationship the infidelity caused.

Interestingly, when asked to rate scenarios, any gender differences have been found to occur in the opposite direction from what traditional theories of infidelity would predict. Parker and Wampler's (2003) study, which considered online sexual activities, found that women viewed these activities more seriously than men did. Whitty's (2003b) study found that women were more likely than men to believe that sexual acts were an act of betrayal. Whitty and Quigly (2008) considered whether the double-shot hypothesis or the two-for-one hypothesis applied to attitudes towards cyberinfidelities. Their research did not find any gender differences or any support for these hypotheses. Moreover, they found that participants were much less likely to believe that cybersex implied love or that online love implied cybersex than they were to believe that sexual intercourse implied love or that love implied sexual intercourse. They argue that this could be for a number of reasons. First, given that previous research has found that most people have not engaged in online sexual activities, making connections between love and cybersex does not come easily. Second, given that cybersex is qualitatively different from sexual intercourse, although individuals might still perceive it as a relationship transgression, they do not necessarily link it with love in the same way they would offline relationship transgressions.

6.6 QUALITATIVE DIFFERENCES BETWEEN ONLINE AND OFFLINE AFFAIRS

There is a dearth of research available on differences between online and offline affairs. However, from what we know about online relationships, we might theorize two differences. The first is that online relationships might have a more seductive appeal than offline relationships, given that we know that 'hyperpersonal' relationships can form online. The second is that online affairs might be psychologically easier to engage in given that the virtual world is theoretically easy to 'split off' from people's everyday lives.

6.6.1   Idealizing online relationships

Chapter 3 points out that relationships developed online can sometimes be 'hyperpersonal' (Walther, 1996, 2007; Walther, Slovacek & Tidwell, 2001). Given the hyperintimacy that can be achieved during CMC, there is the danger that these relationships, while they remain online, might appear more appealing and enticing, leading to idealization. Because of certain features of CMC, individuals can be strategic in their self-presentations, creating a more likeable person than perhaps they are more commonly perceived to be in other spaces. The reactions one receives to this well-crafted, likeable self could potentially be more appealing than the responses one receives to a more mundane self of everyday life. Moreover, if the individual that person is communicating with is employing the same strategy, they too might seem a more likeable person than people known in one's everyday life. It has been argued that this seductive appeal of online relating could therefore easily lead to an online affair (Whitty, 2010; Whitty & Carr, 2005).

6.6.2   Object relations: Splitting

Melanie Klein's work on splitting is also useful in explaining the appeal of online relationships (Whitty & Carr, 2005, 2006). She believed that splitting was one of the most primitive or basic defence mechanisms against anxiety. According to Klein (1986), the ego prevents the bad part of the object from contaminating the good part of the object by splitting it off and disowning a part of itself. An infant in its relationship with its mother's breast conceives the breast as both a good and a bad object. The breast gratifies and frustrates, and the infant will simultaneously project both love and hate onto it. On the one hand, the infant idealizes this good object but, on the other hand, the bad object is seen as terrifying, frustrating and a persecutor threatening to destroy both the infant and the good object. The infant projects love and idealizes the good object but goes beyond mere projection in trying to induce in the mother feelings towards the bad object for which she must take responsibility (i.e., a process of projective identification). This stage of development Klein termed the 'paranoid-schizoid position'. The infant may, as another defence mechanism for this less developed ego, seek to deny the reality of the persecutory object. While in our normal development we pass through this phase, this primitive defence against anxiety is a regressive reaction that, in a sense of always being available to us, is never transcended. The good objects in the developed superego come to represent the fantasized ego ideal and thus 'the possibility of a return to narcissism' (Schwartz, 1990, p. 18).

In line with Klein's object relations theory, it might be useful to understand the individual with whom one is having an online affair to be the good object. Given that the interactions that take place in cyberspace can often be seen as separate from the outside world (Whitty & Carr, 2006), it is potentially easier to split an online affair off from the rest of the individual's world. The online relationship can potentially cater to an unfettered, impotent fantasy that it is difficult to measure up to in reality. Hence, the online affair can potentially lead to a narcissistic withdrawal.

It has been argued that offline infidelity occurs because there are problems in one's relationship or because of certain personality characteristics (see Fitness, 2001). Buss and Shackelford (1997) have identified some key reasons why people betray their partners, including complaints that one's partner sexualizes others, exhibits high levels of jealousy and possessiveness, is condescending, withholds sex or abuses alcohol. These are perhaps the same reasons individuals are motivated to initiate online affairs. However, drawing from Klein's theory, it has been argued that online affairs are perhaps easier to maintain than offline affairs – that the online relationship can become idealized through the process of splitting, while simultaneously denying the bad aspects of the person one is having the affair with and at the same time the bad aspects in oneself. It is possibly easier to idealize an individual online (the good object) when one can more easily filter out the potential negative aspects of the relationship (the bad object). The relationship can be turned on or off at one's leisure and the communication content, to some extent, can be more easily controlled. Moreover, the Internet does provide an environment where it is easier to construct a more positive view of the self and to avoid presenting the negative aspects of the self. In contrast, it is not so easy to indulge in one's fantasies of perfection in an offline affair, as one still has to deal with the real person. Given the nature of these affairs as psychologically different from offline affairs, it is argued later in this chapter that therapy needs to take into account these differences; however, before considering treatment approaches, it is important to examine exactly what is understood to be Internet infidelity.

6.7 VIRTUAL AFFAIRS WITH AN AVATAR

This chapter has examined the many types of relationship transgressions that can take place online. We have focused on studies that have examined transgressions that occur between real people online. However, what of engaging in online sexual acts in a game or virtual world using an avatar? Would couples perceive such an act as an act of betrayal? Although little research has been conducted in order to answer this question, anecdotal evidence might go some way to helping begin to think about whether a virtual affair using an avatar is a 'real' relationship transgression.

Morris (2008) reported the story of an English couple who divorced because of the husband's alter ego's hot chatting with another woman in *Second Life*. *Second Life* is a MMORPG where individuals create their own avatars (personas) and interact in a fantasy world. Morris wrote that the couple initially met online, after which their avatars become partners in *Second Life* – that is, until Amy Taylor (aka Laura Skye in *Second Life*) caught her husband, David Pollard (aka Dave Barmy in *Second Life*), having cybersex with a prostitute in *Second Life*. As Morris reports:

> Horrified, Taylor ended the online relationship between Skye and Barmy but stayed with Pollard in real life.
>
> It was then that fact and fiction really began to collide. Taylor decided to test Dave Barmy – and thus Pollard's loyalty – by turning to a virtual female private eye called Markie Macdonald. A 'honey trap' was set up in which an alluring avatar chatted Barmy up. He passed the test with flying colours, talking about Laura Skye all night. Barmy and Skye got back together in cyberspace, marrying in a ceremony held in a pretty tropical grove. In real life at their flat in Cornwall, Taylor wept as she watched the service, and in 2005 – real life again – the couple married in the less glamorous surroundings of the St. Austell registry office. But Taylor sensed something was wrong and eventually found Dave Barmy chatting affectionately to a woman who was not Laura Skye. She found it even more disturbing than his earlier tryst, as there seemed genuine affection in it and – in real life – she filed for divorce.

Despite the fact that avatars were involved, in this scenario there were still real people interacting behind them. Moreover, as was highlighted earlier in this chapter, emotional betrayal can be just as upsetting as sexual betrayal. This might account for Taylor's upset. However, although Taylor, in this scenario, obviously believed that her husband had cheated on her, we still need to consider whether the majority of people would see things in the same light. In her case the two lived intense lives together in a fantasy world (considered to be a game). Perhaps Taylor found it difficult to separate play from reality.

In one of the few studies that have examined infidelity in *Second Life*, Gilbert, Murphy and Avalos (2011) surveyed 199 participants who had been involved in an intimate relationship in *Second Life*. They found that the majority of participants viewed their *Second Life* relationships as real rather than as a form of game-playing. However, not all their findings presented these relationships in glowing terms. A portion of their participants believed that their virtual relationship was deemed a threat to their real-life relationship with the potential for 'detrimental effects rising as the couple progressively adds non-immersive digital and physical channels of communication to the original 3D relationship' (p. 2039). This study suggests that, for some, developing a romantic relationship with an avatar in a game could be understood as an act of infidelity.

6.8 CONCLUSIONS

There is much we still need to learn about Internet infidelity. We also need to be mindful of the changing nature of the Internet. Web 2.0 brought about a much more interactive Internet (using applications to increase interactivity), and it will continue to develop in increasingly sophisticated ways. Today, individuals often use digital technologies for social purposes, which could potentially result in a large proportion of relationship transgressions being initiated and/or conducted online. The question of whether romantic and/or sexual relationships that develop in more playful areas of the Internet might be construed as relationship transgressions is yet to be properly examined. Affairs are potentially easy to initiate and maintain because of digital technologies, and these technologies must surely play a significant role in most forms of infidelity. How partners deal with such affairs if they wish to continue their relationships also requires further investigation.

DISCUSSION QUESTIONS

1. Why do you think that individuals often believe cybersex is as much of a betrayal as sexual intercourse?
2. Why do you think that individuals believe that learning that one's partner has been viewing pornography is not as upsetting as learning they have engaged in cybersex with a stranger online?
3. How useful do you think socioevolutionary theory is in explaining Internet infidelities?
4. Consider the application of Klein's theory on splitting to explaining online affairs. Is this a useful theory to explain a virtual affair?
5. Do you believe that having an affair with an avatar in a game is a relationship transgression? Draw from theories in psychology to explain your answer.
6. How do you envisage the future with regard to infidelities in cyberspace?

SUGGESTED READINGS

DeSteno, D. & Salovey, P. (1996). Evolutionary origins of sex differences in jealousy? Questioning the 'fitness' of the model. *Psychological Science, 7*, 367–371.

Gilbert, R. L., Murphy, N. A. & Avalos, C. (2011). Realism, idealization, and potential impact of 3D virtual relationships. *Computers in Human Behavior, 27*(5), 2039–2046.

Hertlein, K. M. & Piercy, F. P. (2008). Therapists' assessment and treatment of Internet infidelity cases. *Journal of Marital and Family Therapy, 34*(4), 481–497.

Roscoe, B., Cavanaugh, L. & Kennedy, D. (1988). Dating infidelity: Behaviors, reasons, and consequences. *Adolescence, 23*, 35–43.

Whitty, M. T. (2003). Pushing the wrong buttons: Men's and women's attitudes towards online and offline infidelity. *CyberPsychology & Behavior, 6*(6), 569–579.

Whitty, M. T. (2005). The 'realness' of cyber-cheating: Men and women's representations of unfaithful Internet relationships. *Social Science Computer Review, 23*(1), 57–67.

7 Children's and Teens' Use of Digital Technologies

Children and teens, compared to adults, have in some ways a very different understanding and experience of digital technologies. While adults have known a world before the Internet, children and adolescents have grown up with a range of digital technologies used to educate them, for them to build friendships and with which they learn about their identities. This chapter examines some of the ways in which young people use the Internet and some of the opportunities it might present to these users as well as the potential risks. We discuss the digital divide between young and older people, which makes it difficult for parents to advise young people in an informed way about the potential dangers they might encounter in cyberspace. The Identity Development section examines how the Internet has changed the way young people form an identity, providing new ways for them to reflect and think about the self as well as presenting new challenges for identity formation.

7.1 INTERNET USAGE

In 2011, the Oxford Internet Survey reported that young people used the Internet more than older people (Dutton & Blank, 2011). It found that almost all 14-to-17-year-olds used the Internet. Childwise (2010) reported that 90% of UK children use the Internet, the average child doing so more than five times a week and for an average of two hours a day. Box 7.1 details the statistics that Livingstone (2006) compiled about young people in the UK, and Box 7.2 outlines the statistics about youth in the US highlighted in a report by the Pew Research Center.

Cyberpsychology: The Study of Individuals, Society and Digital Technologies, First Edition.
Monica Therese Whitty and Garry Young.
© 2017 John Wiley & Sons, Ltd. Published 2017 by John Wiley & Sons, Ltd.

> **BOX 7.1 YOUNG PEOPLE'S USE OF THE INTERNET IN THE UK**
>
> Livingstone (2006) found that:
>
> - 98% of children and young people had used the Internet.
> - 75% of 9-to-19-year-olds had accessed the Internet from a computer at home.
> - 92% of 9-to-19-year-olds had accessed the Internet from a computer at school.
> - 36% of children and young people lived in homes with more than one computer.
> - 24% of children and young people lived in a house with broadband access.
> - 19% of children and young people had Internet access in their bedroom.

> **BOX 7.2 YOUNG PEOPLE'S USE OF THE INTERNET IN THE US**
>
> The Pew Internet (2009) trends data showed that:
>
> - 88% of 12-to-13-year-olds used the Internet.
> - 95% of 1-to-17-year-olds accessed the Internet.
> - 73% of teen Internet users used a SNS.
> - 52% of young people used the Internet to get information.
> - 48% of young people used the Internet to shop.
> - 38% of young people used the Internet to share stories, photos or videos.
> - 31% of young people looked for health information online and 17% used the Internet to access information about health issues such as drug use and sexual health.
> - 14% of young people had created a blog.

7.2 THE DIGITAL DIVIDE

Researchers have suggested that, despite the rapid take-up of the Internet by young people, there are inequalities in children's and young people's access to the Internet. Livingstone and Helsper (2007) found that boys, older children and middle-class children all benefit from more frequent and better-quality Internet usage than that enjoyed by girls, younger children and working-class children. Similarly, researchers found that, in a US sample, African American children from lower-income households and children whose parents had a high-school diploma or less were less likely to use a computer at home than white children and children from higher-income families (Brodie et al., 2000).

Wei and Hindman (2011) point out that the concern about the digital divide ought not to be about access or how much individuals use the Internet but rather about how they use it. These authors found that children from higher socioeconomic groups are more likely to use the Internet for informational purposes than those from lower socio-economic groups. Similarly, Wood and Howley (2012) found in a sample of Ohio schools that most students had access to computers and the Internet. The differences lay in the number of available laptops that could be brought into the classroom, in access to computer labs, in adequacy of software and in speeds and reliability of Internet connections. For each of these variables, the differences typically favoured the more affluent suburban schools. However, not all researchers have found that it is the type of school that determines the extent of the digital divide between young people. In a study that spanned many countries, Zhong (2011) found the availability of ICT facilities, rather than the type of school, was a significant predictor of students' self-reported digital skills. They also found that it was important to consider the home environment. Adolescents' access to ICTs in the home, their socioeconomic background and their history of using ICTs were positively associated with self-reported digital skills. In addition, they found that boys reported more sophisticated digital skills than girls.

7.3 DIGITAL TECHNOLOGIES: HARMFUL OR EMPOWERING FOR YOUNG PEOPLE?

There are mixed opinions as to whether children ought to be online, and parents are often concerned about what their children are doing. This is partly to do with the divide between parents' and children's knowledge of the Internet and partly to do with perceptions about young people's behaviour online. Livingstone (2009) argues that there is a polarized view about children online. She states:

> Children are seen as vulnerable, undergoing a crucial but fragile process of cognitive and social development to which the Internet tends to pose a risk by introducing potential harms into the social conditions for development, justifying in turn a protectionist regulatory environment.

The contrasting view is that children are seen as

> competent and creative agents in their own right whose media savvy skills tend to be underestimated by the adults around them, the consequence being that society may fail to provide a sufficiently rich environment for them. (p. 16)

Table 7.1 Opportunities and risks relating to young people's use of the Internet (adapted from Livingstone, 2009)

Potential opportunities	Potential risks
Access to global information	Illegal content
Educational resources	Grooming by paedophiles
Social networking among friends	Encountering extreme or sexual violence
Entertainment, games and fun	Other harmful offensive content
User-generated content creation	Racist/hate material and activities
Civic and political participation	Advertising and stealth marketing
Privacy for identity expression	Biased information or misinformation
Community involvement/activism	Abuse of personal information
Technology expertise and literacy	Cyberbullying/harassment
Career advancement/employment	Gambling, phishing, financial scams
Personal/health/sexual advice	Self-harm
Specialist groups and fan forums	Invasions/abuse of privacy
Shared experience with distant others	Exposure to illegal activities

The reality is that the Internet provides great opportunities for young people but equally presents many risks (summarized in Table 7.1). As shown in the table, there are many opportunities young people can gain from the use of digital technologies and so it is reasonable to argue that, in order to protect young people from risks online, the solution is not to create a general ban against using the Internet. Instead, parents need to be aware of the risks and of the kinds of support they need to be offering children (Livingstone, 2009). This chapter now turns to consider in more detail some of the kinds of risks young people might be facing (some of these topics, however, are also dealt with in other chapters).

7.4 ILLEGAL CONTENT AND ILLEGAL ACTIVITIES

The Internet has a range of content that parents would rather not have exposed to their children. The fear, of course, is that exposure to such content might be the start of a slippery slope to engaging in such activities and/or that the child is too young to understand the content. Research has yet to be conducted to help ascertain the real effects of young people's exposure to illegal content; however, initial research has found that young people are exposed to all kinds of illegal content. For example, despite the antidrug campaigns available online, young people tend to be exposed to drug-related and prodrug websites (Belenko et al., 2009). The National Survey of Parents and Youth, conducted in the United States with a sample of 7,145 participants, found that, in terms of their viewing of prodrug and antidrug websites, approximately 10.4% of 12-to-18-year-olds had been exposed to drug-related websites, 5.4% had only viewed websites that communicated antidrug messages, 1.7% only viewed prodrug websites and 3.2% had visited both types of sites (NAHDAP, 2004). Interestingly, viewing prodrug websites was related to marijuana use.

Young people who engage in online illegal activities can have differing viewpoints about some online crimes compared with offline crimes. Jambon and Smetana (2012) found that the majority of US college students have illegally downloaded music. Wingrove, Korpas and Weisz (2011) sampled 172 youths at a US midwestern university and found that there was a large amount of support for illegally downloading music. In comparison to shoplifting, the 'participants indicated lesser endorsement for deterrence, social influence, personal morality, and obligation to obey the law as reasons to comply with music piracy laws' (p. 271–272). Jambon and Smetana found that youths also understood downloading music as a different type of crime from more traditional crimes (such as theft in the physical world), arguing that it was moral to do so because they perceived the music industry to be immoral and because music is too highly priced. Bonner and O'Higgins (2010), in contrast, found that the young people they studied believed that downloading music was immoral but nonetheless chose to download music. They argued that their participants morally disengaged from the act, believing that downloading music is a reality of the modern world.

As has been highlighted in this book, not all cultures or social groups have access to or use the Internet in the same way. School children in Nigeria, a country renowned for engaging in online crimes, have been found to be the perpetrators of cybercrimes (Amosun & Ige, 2009). School children in Amosun and Ige's study found that the majority of the school-aged children they surveyed (69%) had stolen another person's name and social security number to purchase goods and services. In addition, these participants admitted to sending computer program viruses to crash servers, sending emails to solicit foreign currency, stealing people's identities and watching online pornographic films depicting children. Participants in such crimes are known as 'Yahoo Boyz'.

7.5 CYBERBULLYING AND CYBERHARASSMENT

Cyberbullying is becoming an increasing concern. There are plenty of news stories that elucidate the horrors of cyberbullying, such as the following:

> The alleged cyberbully – a girl who used to go to Orono High with the victim but now attends a high school in southern Maine – was arrested and charged with the offenses on Nov. 1 by Veazie police Sgt. Keith Emery.

'I've handled harassment calls for 24 years and have never seen threats as violent, disgusting and vulgar as these,' Emery said last month of the anonymous posts, which began appearing on the victim's Tumblr blog account in late September.

'They started out telling the girl she was ugly, a whore, slut, et cetera. As the messages continued through October, they got threatening,' the sergeant said. 'Just very vulgar and horrific threats. There were dozens of these types of messages.'

Emery said last month that the suspect, whose name was withheld because of her age, confessed after she was interviewed at the Veazie police station in October. The terrorizing charge was elevated to felony status because the threats prompted the victim and her family to evacuate their home on several occasions, he said. (Gagnon, 2012)

Cyberbullying is defined as intended and repeated harm caused by communication via the use of computers, mobile phones and other electronic devices. It can involve the expression of malicious or cruel sentiments to another person, and/or the posting of humiliating or embarrassing information about someone in a public online space. It might also involve more than one person conducting the bullying and more than one person becoming a victim of the bully or bullies. Bennett, Guran, Ramos and Margolin (2011) noted four methods of cyberbullying: direct hostility, intrusiveness, public humiliation and exclusion. Sexting, as described in Chapter 5, is sometimes used as a form of bullying, in which bullies post compromising photographs or videos of the victim on websites and SNSs, with the intention to humiliate the victim, often offering disparaging remarks.

As we learnt in Chapter 3, online relationships can sometimes be very detached from the physical world, and cyberbullying is a good example of a toxic form of the disinhibition effect. Alvarez (2012) claims: 'The potential for anonymity and the lack of empathy on behalf of the bully are in fact considered to be among the most injurious aspects of cyberbullying' (p. 1206).

Children and adolescents are being bullied online, especially in SNSs, and then have to deal with the aftermath in the playground. Internet bullying peaks in middle school and declines in high school (Williams & Guerra, 2007). Unfortunately, cyberbullying appears to be underreported, with studies finding that 28–50% of victims do not tell anyone about their victimization and that less than one third tell their parents (Bennett et al., 2011; Slonje & Smith, 2008; Wolak, Mitchell & Finkelhor, 2006). Boys are more likely to be the cyberbullies and girls more likely to be the victims (Bennett et al., 2011; Wang, Iannotti & Nansel, 2009). Raskauskas and Stoltz (2007) found that being a victim of bullying on the Internet or via text messages was related to being a bully at school. Loneliness has also been found to be a predictor of cybervictimization (Sahin, 2012). Barlett and Gentile (2012), in a longitudinal study of university students, found that positive attitudes towards anonymity and strength (i.e., the view that the only way for weaker people to acquire strength is to get even with bullies in an online environment) significantly predicted attitudes towards cyberbullying. Moreover, they found that positive attitudes towards cyberbullying, strength and anonymity all significantly predicted engaging in cyberbullying behaviour.

The psychological harm caused by cyberbullying can be quite severe, causing young people to feel frustrated, angry and sad. Bullied children have been known to refuse to go to school, to have become chronically ill, to have run away and even to have attempted suicide (Hinduja & Patchin, 2007). Parris, Varjas, Meyers and Cutts (2012) identified two coping forms for high-school children: reactive coping (avoiding the bullying situation) and preventative coping (talking in person and increased security and awareness). They also found that a group of students felt unable to cope with being cyberbullied. At this stage, psychologists need to further research prevention strategies for cyberbullying as well as how to support victims.

> **SUGGESTED ACTIVITY**
>
> As a youth, did you know anyone who was cyberbullied or were you a victim yourself? How did it affect them or you, and how did they or you cope with being victimized?

7.6 SCAMS, CHILDREN AND TEENS

In Chapter 12 we will learn more about online scams; however, it is important to note that adults are not the only victims of fraud. Fraudsters are also targeting teenagers. Fraudsters lure young people onto websites promising them free goods, including video-game systems, iPods and so forth. The information the teenagers give out, such as email addresses and personal information, can then be sold to marketers and potentially be used for identity theft.

Teenagers are also having their identities stolen so that their grandparents can be defrauded. In a fairly recently emerging type of fraud, teenagers' identities are being stolen from spaces such as SNSs to use in what is known as the 'grandparents scam' or the 'emergency scam'. In this scam, a fraudster using the stolen identity pretends to be the teenager in a distressing emergency situation and contacts teenagers' grandparents seeking assistance in the form of money. The false narrative might be about the teenager having had their wallet stolen or even needing bail to get out of jail. In each situation, the fraudster posing as the teenager asks that the grandparent should act quickly and not tell the parents.

Of course the Internet does not offer a completely bleak picture for children and adolescents; instead, it can offer many opportunities. Some of these opportunities are summarized in the next two sections of this chapter, in which we consider issues such as identity development and activism.

7.7 IDENTITY DEVELOPMENT

Chapter 2 outlined a number of theories about the self and the self in cyberspace. We summarized theories on adolescent development and identity achievement, such as the work of Erikson and Marcia. Here we examine, in a little more detail, empirical work on the utility of the Internet when it comes to identity development for adolescents.

There has been much research that demonstrates that cyberspace is a rich and safe environment for adolescents to explore and experiment with identity (Rheingold, 1993; Stern, 2004; Valkenburg & Peter, 2008). Online identity experimentation can involve pretending to be someone else online (Valkenburg & Peter, 2008) or changing some aspects of one's offline identity in one's presentation of oneself online (Whitty & Gavin, 2001). Lenhart, Rainie and Lewis (2001) found that, in the US, almost 25% of adolescents who used instant messaging pretended to be someone else. Valkenburg, Schouten and Peter (2005) found that Dutch boys and girls do not differ in the frequency in which they experiment with identity, but do differ in the sorts of identities they select.

There are a number of advantages to experimenting with identity online. In a study by Valkenburg and Peter (2008) that surveyed 1,158 Dutch adolescents between 10 and 17 years of age, it was found that those adolescents who experimented more frequently with their identity online (i.e., pretending to be someone else when communicating online) were also more likely to communicate with people online from varied ages and cultural backgrounds. These online identity experiments were found to have an indirect positive effect on adolescents' social competence.

In addition to the advantages the Internet provides adolescents, digital technologies have been found to be a useful resource for personal growth and reaffirming identity. In a qualitative study consisting of in-depth interviews with immigrant adolescents from the Soviet Union residing in Israel, it was found that the Internet provided a space for these young people to develop and strengthen their identity (Elias & Lemish, 2009). For example, the participants below had the following to say:

> Sometimes I feel worthless, as if Russians are not as good as Israelis. So I try to be better than them in school, in general knowledge. I am proud of the fact that I am a good student, that I know lots of things ... Thanks to the internet, I always have something to say. (Anna, 12, five years in Israel)

> I prefer professional websites that explain how to build internet sites. I also like to redesign computer games. I even changed my cellphone. I've downloaded a program from the internet and put it into my phone. As a result I don't have the Hebrew and the Arabic languages in my cellphone, but only the Russian and the Ukrainian. What does it give me? A feeling of power! (Andrei, 15, 1.5 years in Israel) (p. 541)

Similarly, Whitty and Gavin (2001) found that young people felt freer to express themselves online. For example, two participants had the following to say:

> They all think I'm a six foot tall tanned lifesaver. I tell them certain things that are true, but other things are bull****. I mean, I can get away with it so why not? What they

don't know won't hurt them. I will admit that I am pretty sly when it comes to smooth talking certain ladies on the Net and if it means lying to get to second base then go for it. (22-year-old male)

You can never be sure that anyone you talk to on the Net is telling the truth so there's very little trust. That can work both ways because you're free to be whatever you like, which means you're not intimidated by what people think. (17-year-old male) (p. 629)

> **SUGGESTED ACTIVITY**
>
> Have you ever disguised aspects of your identity or pretended to be someone else online? If so, was this a positive or negative experience for you?

7.8 ACTIVISM

There are numerous spaces online where individuals might engage in political activities. Political engagement online can either be expressive or involve acquiring information. Expressive behaviour can include writing blog posts, writing political statuses on Facebook, uploading political videos and sharing political opinions. Informational behaviour might include reading political blog posts (Macafee & de Simone, 2012). Social media has been said to afford individuals new ways to exchange information and to self-present and self-express their political views (Macafee & de Simone, 2012).

Researchers have asked whether civic 'online participation' might invigorate democracy and/or whether the Internet motivates young people, in particular, to engage with politics. Before moving on to consider the research, it is worthwhile to consider Haythornthwaite and Wellman's (2002) assertion that the Internet does not function on its own but rather is embedded in real life. In other words, what we do online is real life. The findings about how politically active young people are online are mixed. In the main, however, the findings suggest that the Internet does not promote greater interest and participation in politics by young people.

Online exposure to campaign information has been found to positively affect young people's political efficacy, knowledge and/or participation (Kenski & Stroud, 2006). Some researchers have found that those who use the Internet more frequently to gain information are also more likely to regularly engage in civic activities (Pasek, Kenski, Romer & Jamieson, 2006). However, others have found no relationship between the two (Scheufele & Nisbet, 2002).

When considering online participation, it is important also to consider participation in the physical world – to examine how these might be similar or different. Hirzalla and Van Zoonen (2011), for instance, have surveyed young Dutch people about their online and offline civic activities. They found that young people's offline and online participation correlated. Moreover, they argued that the term 'online participation' is too broad a concept and that instead researchers should consider various functions and forms of online participation. Macafee and Simone (2012) found that expressive use of social media incited offline behaviour but that informational use did not. Calenda and Meijer (2015) concluded from surveying 2,163 students in Italy, the Netherlands and Spain that the Internet can reinvigorate political participation but does not trigger a shift from 'old' to 'new' politics.

7.9 RADICALIZATION

Police are urgently trying to trace Shamima Begum, 15, Kadiza Sultana, 16, and Amira Abase, 15, after they flew to Istanbul from Gatwick airport on Tuesday. It is believed they have fled to Syria to join Islamic State.

Reports have emerged that at least one of the girls had been in contact with Aqsa Mahmood, who left her Glasgow home in November 2013 after becoming radicalized.

The former foreign secretary, William Hague, said it was unrealistic for the security services to find everything. Now the Commons leader, Hague praised the work of the security services, telling *Pienaar's Politics* on BBC Radio 5 Live: 'It's unrealistic to expect that every single thing is found and remember that we've spent the last couple of years being heavily criticised for having so much surveillance.' (*The Guardian*, 2015).

This concern about radicalization has been echoed by various groups, including the UK Safer Internet Centre, which put out the following notice in November 2014:

The UK Safer Internet Centre is taking the unusual step of publishing this special bulletin to all Local Safeguarding Children Boards [LSCBs] due to the unprecedented online threats posed to children across the UK from radicalization and extremism. This action follows discussions with colleagues at Home Office and [the Department for Education] and in the same way that the Government have raised the threat level, this bulletin aims to mirror this heightening of concern particularly with regards to children.

The threats we are seeing take many forms, not only the high profile incidents of those travelling to countries such as Syria and Iraq to fight, but on a much broader perspective also. The internet, in particular social media, is being used as a channel, not only to promote and engage, but also as Robert Hannigan (Director of GCHQ) recently suggested, as a command structure. Often this promotion glorifies violence, attracting and influencing many people including children and in the extreme cases, radicalizing them. Research concludes that children can be trusting and not necessarily appreciate bias that can lead to them being drawn into these groups and adopt these extremist views, and in viewing this shocking and extreme content may become normalized to it.

This threat is not just from groups, such as Islamic State, but from 'far right' groups also.

We are perhaps more familiar with this 'grooming' process and the risks posed to children by older young people and adults who form relationships with children to ultimately abuse them – the process is similar and exploits the same vulnerabilities.

It is for this reason that we are calling on all LSCBs to:

- Consider and discuss the threats from radicalization and extremism for their children
- Include the conclusions in your Strategies and Action Plans, ensuring that addressing Radicalization is effectively embedded in safeguarding practice and that PREVENT coordinators are engaged and signposted
- Consider how the threat of Radicalization through the Internet and Social Media is being addressed
- Review how the above points are being addressed within your member agencies and their success/effectiveness
- Review esafety education in the light of these widening and extreme risks. (UK Safer Internet Centre, 2014)

Stories such as the one reported by *The Guardian* (above) and concerns raised by many groups in society are becoming increasingly common. Much more research is needed, however, into understanding how young people are radicalized, the role of the Internet with regard to radicalization and how to prevent this radicalization. Online radicalization might be achieved via various methods. These include speeches, graphics, training manuals, slides, blogs, podcasts, tutorials on building bombs, tutorials on how to sneak into Iraq, tutorials on setting off improvised explosive devices, fundraising effects and video games (which children and adolescents are encouraged to play pretending to be a warrior killing US soldiers) (Wright, 2008).

Researchers at RAND Europe tested the following five hypotheses by conducting interviews with 15 extremists:

1. The Internet creates more opportunities to become radicalized.
2. The Internet acts as an 'echo chamber': a place where individuals find their ideas supported and echoed by other like-minded individuals.
3. The Internet accelerates the process of radicalization.
4. The Internet allows radicalization to occur without physical contact.
5. The Internet increases opportunities for self-radicalization.

They found support for the first two hypotheses but not for the last three. They argue the case that, although the Internet facilitates the radicalization of individuals, it is not the sole driver of the process (RAND Europe, 2015).

Neumann (2013), who is an expert in cyberconflict and terrorism, makes the poignant point that removing content from the Internet is the least desirable and least effective approach to counteracting online terrorism. Instead, he contends, governments should spend more time and resources on reducing the demand for radicalization and violent extremist messages (e.g., by educating young people to question the messages they see online as well as by discrediting, countering and confronting extremist narratives). The best approach, Neumann believes, to counteracting radicalization is to exploit violent extremists' online communication by gaining intelligence and gathering evidence in a comprehensive and systematic fashion.

In his paper, Neumann summarizes six processes and dynamics that explain how online radicalization works. First, he contends, being immersed in extremist content (e.g., discourses about martyrdom and death and videos of suicide operations and beheadings) for extended periods of time is likely to desensitize a person. Drawing from Pyszczynski et al. (2006), he argues that 'constant exposure to discourses about martyrdom and death – combined with videos of suicide operations and beheadings – can produce "mortality salience," an overpowering sense of one's own mortality, which increases support for suicide operations and other, often excessively brutal, terrorist tactics' (p. 435). Second, emotionally charged videos from conflict zones (e.g., atrocities by Western troops, such a torture and rape) can lead to 'moral outrage'. Third, when people spend too much time in virtual communities, online spaces starts to function as 'criminogenic environments' – that is, environments where deviant and extreme behaviours are learnt and absorbed and extreme ideas become normalized, especially given that the other individuals that people are spending time with hold similar extreme views. Fourth is an effect already mentioned in this book, the 'disinhibition effect', where groups and individuals are less likely to abide by social rules and more likely to become hostile online. This is thought to occur in online spaces where individuals are anonymous. Fifth, as also previously mentioned in this book, individuals can often feel distressed and depressed when there is a large discrepancy between their actual and ideal selves. Individuals who play online role-playing games and choose a character that is close to their ideal self can start to feel increasingly anxious and depressed. Neumann theorizes that those individuals who play a character who is violent, over time, might wish to live out their pro-violent selves. Finally, the Internet can link up people with similar interests (in this case, extremists) who might never have met had there been no Internet. Neumann's points are interesting, and future research in this area might benefit from considering whether these six processes and dynamics do explain why individuals become radicalized on the Internet.

7.10 CONCLUSIONS

Although the Internet is no longer a new medium, it was nonetheless not in existence when many adults were young. Of course, this was also previously the case for other types of media, such as television and radio. However, as our earlier chapters have pointed out, the Internet has opened up new ways to relate, exist and express oneself. Young people are bound to have different experiences from those of the older generation, and the generation after them may also experience technology differently as it continues to evolve and become a part of people's everyday lives. This chapter has raised some pertinent points about some of the issues that concern young people in relation to the Internet, including identity formation, harassment and bullying, criminal activities that are cyberenabled and cyberdependent, engaging in politics, and online radicalization. The research raises important questions about the ways in which young people need to be educated and made aware of how to engage online in safety and in psychologically beneficial ways.

DISCUSSION QUESTIONS

1. What do you think are the risks and benefits for young people of using digital technologies?
2. Do you think it is immoral to download music or films from the Internet illegally? Would you ever do this? Why, or why not?
3. In what ways do you think young people develop identities by interacting online?
4. Do you think we would all have the same identities we have now if there were no Internet? Do you think you might be have been different? Why is that?
5. Does the Internet help you learn and engage with politics? Why is this?
6. What is your view on young people and online radicalization?

SUGGESTED READINGS

Bartlett, C. P. & Gentile, D. A. (2012). Attacking others online: The formation of cyberbullying in late adolescence. *Psychology of Popular Media Culture*, 1(2), 123–135.

Bonner, S. & Higgins, E. (2010). Music piracy: Ethical perspectives. *Management Decision*, 48(9), 1341–1354.

Hirzalla, F. & Van Zoonen, L. (2011). Beyond the online/offline divide: How youth's online and offline civic activities converge. *Social Science Computer Review*, 29(4), 481–498.

Livingstone, S. & Helsper, E. (2007) Gradations in digital inclusion: Children, young people and the digital divide. *New Media & Society*, 9(4), 671–696.

Neumann, P. R. (2013). Options and strategies for countering online racialization in the United States. *Studies in Conflict & Terrorism*, 36, 431–459.

8 Online Education

In Chapter 7 we examined young people's experiences of digital technologies. In this chapter, we focus on another important issue relating to young people: education. More specifically, we examine here how digital technologies have changed the ways in which people learn and how online tools might be best used in educational settings. The aim of this chapter is to discuss online education in relation to questions such as: How does online learning differ from more traditional correspondence/distance learning, particularly in relation to student and tutor tasks and experience? What technical and pedagogical challenges does online education have to overcome when presented within an integrated education system, not only in terms of meeting student learning goals but also in terms of enhancing students' overall experience? Although many of the issues raised here are relevant to all forms of education directed at all age groups, the focus of the discussion will be on higher education.

8.1 TECHNOLOGY AND LEARNING

In 1913, when cinematography was still in its infancy, Thomas Edison predicted that this new technology would be at the forefront of education, to the point where books would become obsolete in schools because every branch of human knowledge would soon be taught through the medium of motion pictures (Tamim, Bernard, Borokhovski, Abrami & Schmid, 2011). In contrast to the world envisaged by Edison, and as Tamim et al. (2011) point out, 'the effect of analog visual media on schooling, including video, has been modest' (p. 4). Nevertheless, some hundred years later, at least with regard to higher education and to digital rather than analogue technology, online education is fast becoming a viable alternative to traditional university learning (Petrakou, 2010). In fact, according to Robinson and Hullinger (2008), there has been 'no change in higher education more sweeping than the transformation brought about by the advent of the Internet and Web' (p. 101). This is because the 'Internet and related technologies have increased the opportunity for learning through the elimination of time and place constraints and the availability of flexible and innovative channels for interaction'

Cyberpsychology: The Study of Individuals, Society and Digital Technologies, First Edition.
Monica Therese Whitty and Garry Young.
© 2017 John Wiley & Sons, Ltd. Published 2017 by John Wiley & Sons, Ltd.

(p. 107; see also Burgstahler, 2000; Chickering & Ehrmann, 1996). As a consequence, educational communication can now take place pretty much anytime and anyplace, and can involve anyone (Aggarwal & Bento, 2000; Pittinsky, 2003).

Based on the results of a 2007 survey (Allen & Seaman, 2007), it was found that approximately 20% of US college students were enrolled on courses taught completely online (which equates to approximately 3.5 million students). These researchers also showed that enrolment for online courses was around six times that for the equivalent educational courses taught in more traditional environments, thereby making online learning the 'fastest growing instructional modality in higher education' (Shea & Bidjerano, 2009, p. 543). Given this growing trend, and using figures taken from the US National Center for Education Statistics (again, published in 2007), it was estimated that by 2016 there would be a record numbers of college enrolments taking place in the US and, of these, an increasing number will be from nontraditional students who will have enrolled on online courses (Shea & Bidjerano, 2009). In support of this growing trend, Allen and Seaman (2014) reported that in the US, as of 2012, approximately 7.1 million students had taken at least one online higher education course and that some form of online course was available in 94.5% of higher education institutions. Furthermore, Allen and Seaman (2013) note how nearly 70% of US chief academic officers consider online learning to be of utmost importance to the long-term recruitment strategy of their institution (see also Linder, Fontaine-Rainen & Behling, 2015).

Many higher education institutions also provide 'blended courses' that offer a mixture of traditional face-to-face teaching and online learning. The integration of online technology is fast becoming a ubiquitous feature of higher education teaching and learning (Mayadas, Bourne & Bacsich, 2009). More recently, 'massive open online courses' (MOOCs) have started to appear in ever increasing numbers. To anyone with Internet access, MOOCs are freely accessible university-standard courses geared towards large students numbers (Boxall, 2012).

8.2 E-LEARNING

E-learning refers to electronically (and digitally) supported learning and teaching. Since the turn of the century, e-learning has become increasingly prevalent within higher education institutions (Koutsabasis, Stavrakis, Spyrou & Darzentas, 2011) and blended learning common practice (Gikandi, Morrow & Davis, 2011; Sharpe, Benfield, Roberts & Francis, 2006). (Blended learning refers to the integration of traditional face-to-face teaching with online educational content: namely, material that students can access online in order to prepare for or supplement face-to-face teaching.) Brown (2006), using findings from the International Data Corporation, estimated that by 2008 the e-learning market would be worth somewhere between $21 and $28 billion. E-learning is facilitated through the use of multimedia CD-ROMs or virtual learning environments (e.g., the software Blackboard) where teaching material – including lecture slides, notes, assessment details and discussion boards, as well as links to readings, websites, blogs and podcasts – may be posted for students to access before, during or after face-to-face contact, or even as an alternative to it. As Larreamendy-Joerns and Leinhardt (2006) have observed, a seismic shift is occurring in the educational landscape, out of which is emerging two phenomena in online education: (1) the merger of online and more traditional teaching and learning (blending) and (2) the increasing availability of online distance learning courses (particularly in the US). Online assessment and feedback are also becoming the norm within higher education, including blended learning.

E-learning, in one form or another, constitutes a mediated environment. Mediated environments incorporate communication technology as a means of creating a virtual space in which learners can interact. Within this mediated environment, learners share an aspect of themselves (as described below, they have some form of 'presence'), although the aspect they share may vary in accordance with the technology available. It may be, for example, that they share what they write on a discussion board or within an online chat room, or it may be that they share some aspect of themselves in the form of an avatar (Childs, 2010).

Given that such technology requires a critical mass of users to adopt and use it for it to be effective, e-learning brings with it its own organizational challenges, which relate to its 24/7 availability. Among these are levels and types of support, and (seemingly necessary) changes in the current system of work and cooperation among teachers, students and administration (Koutsabasis et al., 2011), some of which are considered in more detail below. More recently, with advances in technology mobility, mobile learning (m-learning) is further reinforcing the idea that learning can occur anytime and anywhere through the use of smartphones, webpads and tablet PCs, for example (Lan & Sie, 2010).

The increased use of mobile devices within the education setting highlights one of the key features of e-learning: namely, its ability to integrate within an online programme a variety of media, from basic text through to pictures, audio, animation and video (Sun & Cheng, 2007). Together, these create multimedia instructional materials that are designed to promote the educational interests of the learner (Gillani & Relan, 1997; Vichuda, Ramamurthy & Haseman, 2001) to the extent that computers are having a significant impact on the nature of teaching and learning (Dede, 1996; Kozma, 1994). In contrast, however, research evidence suggests that multimedia educational material does not necessarily significantly increase students' understanding of course content (Sun & Cheng, 2007). Moreover, there is some evidence to suggest that some multimedia elements within course content may have a detrimental effect on students' learning performance (Bartscha & Cobern, 2003; Rieber, 1996). Such findings support Clark's (1994) famous and contrasting claim that media have no more of an effect on learning than a grocery truck has on the nutritional value of the produce it brings to market, and therefore it is the pedagogical content that is of importance, not the medium by which it is delivered. In light of these contrasting comments, let us consider how online education compares with more traditional face-to-face teaching and learning.

> **SUGGESTED ACTIVITY**
>
> Think about your own education. How has e-learning been integrated into your own learning and/or how your tutor delivers the material to you?

8.3 E-LEARNING VERSUS FACE-TO-FACE LEARNING

How effective is e-learning compared to traditional face-to-face contact at achieving the same learning outcomes? Robinson and Hullinger (2008) state that studies that measure the effectiveness of e-learning tend to fall into three broad categories: student outcomes in terms of educational achievement (which focus on test scores and grades); student attitudes towards learning; and the level of overall student satisfaction with online learning. These authors go on to claim that research findings support the view that online (e-learning) and face-to-face teaching meet the same learning outcomes (e.g., Palloff & Pratt, 2001). Importantly, they add that research should focus not on the extent to which online and face-to-face education is the same, or on how we can replicate face-to-face teaching online, but, rather, on what is done well within these online learning environments.

An and Frick (2006), following a survey of 105 US university students, reported that these students generally preferred face-to-face discussions (whether with a tutor or among peers) when engaging in difficult tasks or tasks that required (or would be aided by) immediate clarification, or when they needed to generate new ideas or engage in collaborative thinking. For the majority of these students, CMC was preferred for simple tasks only. An and Frick proffer a caveat, however, insofar as the findings are based on student *perceptions* (of what they feel is good for them; of their preferences) and not on independent measures of what actually constitutes effective learning. Liu, Liao and Pratt (2009) likewise note that sociopsychological factors may influence users to select or hold a preference for a particular medium owing to their perceived satisfaction with that medium rather than its more effective information processing capabilities.

Having said that, what is done well should not be based simply on how e-learning students' grades (for example) compare to those of students engaged in face-to-face teaching and learning but on the *quality* of the learning experience as a whole (Robinson & Hullinger, 2008). One way to assess the overall quality of student engagement is the effort the student makes – in terms of an investment of time and energy – to study a subject; to practice, obtain and act on feedback; as well as to analyse and solve problems (see Kuh, 2003; Wilbur, 1998). Importantly, then, while it remains the responsibility of the student to engage in academic activities, it is the responsibility of the educational institute to 'create purposeful course designs that promote interaction, participation, and communication in the online learning environment' (Robinson & Hullinger, 2008, p. 107).

According to Knight (2007), with reference to the UK Open University, the view that online courses are less successful than more traditional educational routes and have lower retention rates is rapidly becoming out of date, as is the view that online courses require IT competences beyond those of most people returning to education. In reality, it is much more likely that online courses demand 'no more of their students than they are regularly capable of in their day-to-day lives' (p. 95). Thus, the related view that online tutoring is less satisfactory is equally likely to be outdated, thereby failing to 'reflect the rapidly changing nature of society's relationship with new technology' (p. 95). That said, for Liu et al. (2009), the learner's attitude towards e-learning will likely be dependent on factors such as their present level of technical competence (see also Seyal & Pijpers, 2004) and the appropriateness of the adopted technology (media) to the educational task. Depending on how these factors present themselves at any given time, learners who are required to use different levels of media technology might adopt different acceptance behaviours and so express different levels of satisfaction. In fact, rather than a lack of familiarity and competence with IT, for Knight (2007), appropriate workload and relevance of the course to student needs are more likely to be factors influencing retention. In addition, Knight holds that retention rates and student satisfaction are more likely to be attributed to the degree 'to which they feel comfortable with the academic environments, which may be very different from the employment and social environments to which they are accustomed' (Yorke, 2004, p. 24).

Wood, Solomon and Allan (2008) suggest that, in response to the demands of the 'millennial generation' (which approximates to those born between 1984 and 1992), educational institutions will likely have to reconsider how they deliver e-learning. Because of the technology the millennial generation has grown up with, according to Ferrell and Ferrell (2002), its members are much more receptive to technology-based pedagogical experiences and, Childress and Braswell (2006) inform us, thrive within online environments. Typically, this generation of undergraduate students is highly engaged with modern communication technologies such as Facebook, blogs and YouTube (Wood et al., 2008).

8.4 SYNCHRONOUS AND ASYNCHRONOUS COMMUNICATION WITHIN E-LEARNING

Internet-based e-learning platforms and CMC are either synchronous or asynchronous. Both are extensively used within blended learning programmes as well as exclusively online education courses. In the case of asynchronous e-learning, students are able to interact with other students and instructors/tutors (although not in real time, of course) and engage with various educational material in a manner that enables them to plan their learning schedule (Koutsabasis et al., 2011). Thus, for Petrakou (2010), asynchronous communication affords students greater flexibility and so increases their sense of control over the learning process. A further advantage of asynchronous communication is that the teacher and students do not need to assemble at the same time (Mayadas et al., 2009; see also Harasim, 1990); it is time and place independent (An & Frick, 2006). In addition, according to An and Frick (2006), through the use of asynchronous communication, students

- can study in a place that is convenient and at a time that better fits their schedules, thereby enabling a degree of self-pace and control over their learning (see also Vrasidas & McIsaac, 2000), although this may reduce the amount of student-to-student interaction (see also Murphy, Rodriquez-Manzanares & Barbour, 2011);
- have more time to analyse, reflect on and respond (in an informed and thoughtful way) to study content (see also Garrison, Anderson & Archer, 2000); and
- engage in more social learning (rather than individual correspondence learning) in which they are able to interact online with other students as well as their tutor(s) (see also Sutton, 2001).

An and Frick (2006) also note that asynchronous e-learning affords a more comfortable environment for those who perform less well in face-to-face discussion, where exchanges require more spontaneity. This may especially be the case for students whose first language is not the same as the language used within the institution and/or for those who are shy (see also Berge & Collins, 1993; Leasure, Davis & Thievon, 2000).

8.4.1 The importance of presence

Garrison, Anderson and Archer (2000) argue that successful e-learning requires three things: cognitive presence, social presence and teaching presence. Cognitive presence is a measure of the extent to which communication within an online exchange is perceived to be meaningful and the extent to which this meaningfulness is sustained. Social presence signifies the extent to which those involved in the communication are able to represent themselves as actual people, such that their 'personalities' can be expressed within the online environment. Teaching presence is indicative of the way in which the tutor is able to craft the educational experience, both as a facilitator of learning and through input on the design, structure, content and presentation of the teaching material (de Freitas & Neumann, 2009). In relation to this last point, it is interesting to note that 3-D virtual environments such as *Second Life* (which we will discuss in more detail later in this chapter) are being used to enable pre-service teachers to practice teaching (see Cheong, 2010, for a study on how such virtual teaching has had a positive impact on pre-service teachers' personal teaching expectancy).

Asynchronous e-learning can, however, have a detrimental effect on learners who feel isolated, and may even have contributed to this condition to begin with, owing to the fact that such communication – with its lack of immediacy – makes it difficult for students to interact quickly and so feel connected to their tutor and fellow students. This can result in increased drop-out rates (Schullo et al. cited in de Freitas & Neumann, 2009, p. 987; see also Bernard et al., 2004). In fact, Hrastinski (2008) found when studying post-secondary-level e-learning classes in the US that, while asynchronous educational interaction better enabled students to reflect on their learning, synchronous communication increased student motivation to engage with the course.

One of the benefits of synchronous communication with respect to online learning is that it enables immediate feedback. Petrakou (2010) reports that students experience less isolation and therefore more integration within a course when engaged in synchronous communication with their tutor (see also Hrastinski, 2006). The immediacy of the feedback also decreased ambiguity and facilitated social relations with other students, including the exchange of less complex information than was found in asynchronous exchanges (Murphy et al., 2011). Thus, Murphy et al. note, although a synchronous component within the e-learning programme may not be central to any instructional aspect of the course (i.e., to the conveying of direct instructions), it may be of benefit in terms of facilitating more general communication and support, and so for the more social integration of students into the online community.

Keskitalo, Pyykkö and Ruokamo (2011), therefore, conclude that strong scaffolding and support are needed within e-learning environments. Scaffolding plays a critical role in Vygotsky's (1978) 'zone of proximal development' and is provided by a more capable expert, teacher or peer who helps learners to perform a task they would not normally be able to accomplish if working independently. This approach advances the students' learning from the current level of understanding to a point where support is no longer required (De Smet, Van Keer & Valcke, 2008). Moreover, according to Neville (1999), it appears that scaffolding in the form of peer support has a beneficial effect on student motivation.

In short, asynchronous communication affords a degree of learning flexibility and facilitates more reflexive and thoughtful student–student and student–tutor communication, which is on par with more traditional interactions. It also seems to be preferred (compared to face-to-face exchanges) by those students who have more experience and/or training in computers (Tallent-Runnels et al. (2006). This finding is compatible with An and Frick (2006)'s finding that efficiency and convenience were important factors for students when assessing satisfaction with teaching and learning. Students who found face-to-face interactions to be faster, more convenient and thus more efficient preferred this type of communication; the same was found for those who perceived CMC to be more efficient. A similar relationship was found among distance education coordinators (working for the Open University in Israel) whose choice of preferred distance learning media for the course they were coordinating was related to their prior skill level with the technology requirements of the preferred media (Caspi & Gorsky, 2005).

8.4.2 Cognitive presence

Importantly, while it may be the case that asynchronous communication affords greater flexibility and so a higher degree of personal control over one's studies, for DeSmet, Van Keer and Valcke (2008), such control can lead to difficulties in organizing one's learning. Computer-mediated communication may be burdensome for tutors to use and overwhelming for students to digest (An & Frick, 2006). Imagine, for example, receiving a series of lengthy emails on a regular basis. A prerequisite for successful e-learning, then, is the learner's ability to discern structure within the asynchronous (or synchronous, for that matter) communication that has pedagogic import (Laurillard, 1998). Irrespective of the medium and therefore the level of technology involved, for Johnson and Johnson (1996), a clearly defined and definable structure within the communication is a requirement for learning. Schellens and Valcke (2006) found that interactions within asynchronous discussion groups became more intense and more task focused, and achieved a high degree of knowledge exchange in smaller and average-sized groups (n = 8–10 and 11–13, respectively) compared to larger groups (n = 15–18), in which discussion was much less focused.

> **SUGGESTED ACTIVITY**
>
> How much do you engage in asynchronous communication during your time spent studying? What are the advantages and disadvantages of this? Other than face-to-face discussion with your tutor and peers, do you communicate with them online synchronously? If so, how do you find this? If not, would you like to be able to do so, perhaps making it an integrated part of the course?

8.5 MEDIA RICHNESS THEORY

According to media richness theory, effective communication is a product of the fitness of the medium in relation to the nature of the communication task (Daft & Lengel, 1986; Trevino, Lengel & Daft, 1987). Communication richness or leanness is therefore held to be an objective property of the communication medium measured as the extent to which it enables (or facilitates) shared meaning and understanding within a time interval. Whether media are considered rich or lean is established by the following criteria (based on Daft, Lengel & Trevino, 1987; cited in Sun & Cheng, 2007, p. 664):

1. *Capacity for immediate feedback*: The medium facilitates quick convergence on a common interpretation.
2. *Capacity to transmit multiple cues*: An array of cues, including physical presence, voice inflections, body gestures, words, numbers and graphic symbols facilitate

conveyance of interpretation and meaning, rather than simply information or data.
3. *Language variety*: Numbers and formulas provide greater precision, but natural language conveys a broader set of concepts and ideas.
4. *Capacity of the medium to have a personal focus*: This refers either to the conveyance of emotions and feelings or to the ability of the medium to be tailored to the specific needs and perspectives of the receiver.

Media richness theory postulates that learners will benefit from richer communication media when the course content is equivocal (more ambiguous and open to interpretation). Conversely, where the material is unequivocal (e.g., a mathematical formula), less rich media should suffice and in fact be more direct. Whether this results in learners adopting media whose richness correlates with levels of equivocality is not always straightforward (see Dennis & Kinney, 1998, for discussion on varied findings), and in some cases the richness may be a distraction from learning (e.g., Matarazzo & Sellen, 2000).

Sun and Cheng (2007) applied media richness theory to e-learning based on two orthogonal measures: learning score (objective indicator) and student satisfaction when using a particular medium (subjective indicator). Together these constitute a measure of a particular medium's learning performance (see Figure 8.1).

In accordance with media richness theory and their hypotheses, Sun and Cheng (2007) found that using high-richness multimedia materials to convey course content with a high degree of uncertainly and equivocality had a positive effect on both learning score and learning satisfaction. On the other hand, those materials that were much more unequivocal were better suited to regular text-based communication and, therefore, using high-richness media to promote learning performance for more numerical and/or fact-based content was far less effective.

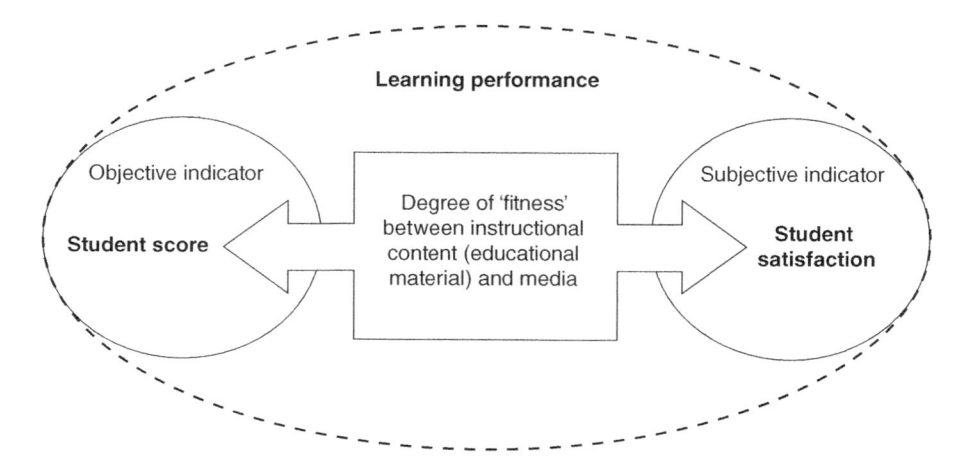

Figure 8.1 *Measures of learning performance (adapted from Sun & Cheng, 2007, p. 666)*

Liu et al. (2009) found that the most media-rich communication – incorporating text, audio and video – always generated higher levels of what they refer to as 'perceived usefulness' (on the part of the learner) compared to material communicated in the form of text with an audio accompaniment or in the form of audio–video presentations. Liu et al. thus concluded that educational content communicated via rich media is more likely to result in higher user acceptance because it stimulates higher perceived usefulness.

8.6 SALMON'S STAGE MODEL OF E-LEARNING

Salmon (2004) devised a five-stage model for online teaching and learning in which students must develop and master a number of technical skills. For successful e-learning, at stage 1, learners must be both willing and able to remotely access the educational material and engage in online communication. Stage 2 is characterized by online socialization. Here, students must establish their online identity and be willing and able to find fellow students with whom to interact online. Information exchange occurs at stage 3, whereby students exchange relevant course information and undertake course-related learning tasks. Salmon also notes that stages 1–3 are characterized by mutual student support to enable each learner to achieve personal goals. At stage 4, rather than a simple exchange of information, task-related discussion occurs that is much more collaborative in nature, allowing students to tackle more complex educational tasks online. At stage 5, personal reflection and more sophisticated individual learning take place as students explore the online system with a view to furthering their own personal goals (including developing transferable skills and establishing how to apply their online experiences to other learning). The learner may initially interact with only a small number of other students (stage 1), but this number increases as they enter stages 2–4. By the time they reach stage 5, however, it is likely that students will be engaging in more individual learning pursuits.

Salmon, Nie and Edirisingha (2010) applied Salmon's five-stage model to educational courses presented in *Second Life*. They found that the model applied to this learning environment equally as well as to other environments, although they did note slight variations in some of the stages. Stage 1 was characterized by a greater number of initial technical difficulties than might be expected with traditional text-based e-learning: for example, having to download the software, create one's avatar and learn how to manipulate it. They did note that the 3-D environment and use of an avatar facilitated stage 2: student online identity and socialization. Information exchange and knowledge construction (stages 3 and 4) were also much more characteristic of face-to-face dialogues – owing to the presence of avatars and the synchronous nature of exchanges – rather than those typically found when using more text-based (and asynchronous) communication.

8.7 3-D LEARNING ENVIRONMENTS

3-D virtual worlds are among the more interesting technological advances that have been applied to teaching and learning since the turn of the century. Dickey (2003) describes these (broadly construed) as networked, desktop virtual reality, which typically provides three important features: 'the illusion of 3D space, avatars that serve as visual representations of users, and an interactive chat environment for users to communicate with one another' (p. 105). Within an educational setting, they provide, for geographically distant learners, 'an accessible means of creating a rich and compelling 3D context for situating learning' (p. 105) as well as communicative tools and Web integration to support discourse and collaboration. 3-D environments therefore offer possibilities for teaching and learning that are distinct from both face-to-face environments and other forms of e-learning (Savin-Baden et al., 2010). Recall Chapter 2, where we discussed how social presence signifies the extent to which those involved in the communication are able to represent themselves as actual people, such that their 'personalities' can be expressed within the online environment (de Freitas & Neumann, 2009; Garrison, Anderson & Archer, 2000). This is possible during asynchronous communication, although synchronous communication seems to facilitate social presence more. Enabling more informal – less task-oriented – communication between students further supports students' needs (Hrastinski, 2006).

Kirriemuir (2010) reports that, by the early summer of 2009, e-learning within virtual worlds had been noted in over 80% of UK universities and that, in some instances, the use of this provision was prevalent across a number of different departments and groups within the same institution. Kirriemuir also reports an overall positive view of this technology, even from those who had initially experienced technical problems – and, specifically with regard to *Second Life*, comments on its successful use in many UK universities (most notably, the Open University).

Petrakou (2010) carried out an ethnographic study on an English-language course run in the virtual world of *Second Life*. Students would attend classes in *Second Life* as their avatar and engage with the tutor, who was also present in this 3-D world in avatar form. Petrakou observed that students socialized much as they would in traditional education settings; they began to get to know each other as they navigated their way around the new environment and asked about each other's lives outside *Second Life*. Petrakou also asked the students to comment on their assessed presentation, which they had to deliver in *Second Life* to their tutor and peers, who, like them, were present as avatars. Students commented on how it was difficult to interpret the audience's reaction to the presentation, given that it was not possible to gauge whether the audience was engaged or bored. One student said: 'It becomes more like talking to a wall, and the focus is shifted from the audience towards how you yourself sound' (Petrakou, 2010, pp. 1023–24). This was seen to have both advantages and disadvantages: on the one hand, one is not disturbed or distracted by the audience but, on the other hand, there is an absence of presenter–audience interaction.

The 3-D setting also meant that students tended to disburse across the virtual environment when engaged in small group tasks, so as not to disturb others, much as one might expect if located in a nonvirtual classroom. One aspect of the e-learning that was much more unique to teaching in this environment was the fact that the tutor avatar would fly above the students, so as not to disturb them, when monitoring their task discussions. Interruptions were made only when corrections were needed or to provide feedback.

Petrakou described the course in *Second Life* as a mixture of synchronous and asynchronous exchanges. Synchronous communication did occur, and was indeed required during group tasks performed in *Second Life*, but also occurred when students were having a break from the specifics of the course. This allowed students to meet in the guise of their avatars *almost* face to face. Students could also carry out some work, including group tasks, asynchronously outside *Second Life*. As Petrakou notes, a website and a course blog formed part of the learning environment, and were included to support asynchronous communication and exchanges of information in between the (synchronous) sessions.

When reporting on how students behaved at the start of the course, Petrakou recollects that the large number of students present during the course launch meant that spoken communication was quite difficult. This is because the teacher and students all talked at the same time, and so it was a challenge to identify who was speaking at any given moment. Yet, as the course progressed, Petrakou observed adaptations occurring and was thus able to draw the following conclusion (in a manner consistent with Gaimster, 2008): 'It seems that in the beginning students [relied] on their conception of real world conditions also in the virtual environment. However, when the students [became] better acquainted with the environment, new norms and rules for social interaction [emerged]' (Petrakou, 2010, p. 1026). As such, by adapting to the technology, the students 'did not interact with computers; they interacted through computers with each other' (Barab, Thomas & Merrill, 2001, p. 136).

8.7.1 Evaluating 3-D learning environments

When evaluating the role of *Second Life* as a teaching and learning medium, Keskitalo, Pyykkö & Ruokamo (2011) note several authors (Edirisingha, Nie, Pluciennik & Young, 2009; Holmberg & Huvila, 2008; Omale, Hung, Luetkehans & Cooke-Plagwitz, 2009; Salmon, 2009; Warburton, 2009) who claim that the value of virtual worlds lies in their capacity to provide a greater sense of social presence and belonging when compared with more traditional text-based e-learning environments, where, according to Löfström and Nevgi (2007), students may feel more isolated and lonely. Arguably, then, 3-D environments should be seen as part of an ongoing transition away from a more traditional emphasis on content (even within other e-learning platforms) towards provisions that facilitate interpersonal relationships, to the extent that students are persuaded to feel not so much that they are simply using such virtual technology but that they actually *reside in* that virtual space (Jarmon, Traphagan, Mayrath & Trivedi, 2009; Kalyuga, 2007; White & Le Cornu, 2010).

Keskitalo et al. (2011) refer to findings (e.g., Holmberg & Huvila, 2008; Mayrath, Sanchez, Traphagan, Heikes & Trivedi, 2007; Omale et al., 2009) that attribute the success of *Second Life* – in sustaining the interest and motivation of learners – to its appearance and to the fact that it affords avatar-based interactions in a shared space that permits synchronous communication. In addition, Keskitalo et al. note that students prefer group work when in *Second Life* (Jarmon & Sanchez, 2008; Mayrath et al., 2007) and that participating in discussions seems to be facilitated compared to in other, more traditional educational environments, with more direct and spontaneous tutor–student and student–student communication (Edirisingha et al., 2009; Holmberg & Huvila, 2008; Omale et al., 2009).

Keskitalo et al. (2011) do, however, note contradictory results of students' collaborations. Some findings indicate that student learning communities are not always easy to find and, even if found, that participation can be difficult (Jones, Morales & Knezek, 2005; Warburton, 2009), particularly for those with less technical skills or experience. Keskitalo et al. (2011) therefore point to certain issues that educators must consider while planning to use *Second Life* as a medium for e-learning, such as the time it takes to get acquainted with the virtual environment and with the control of one's avatar (Delwiche, 2006; Mayrath et al., 2007; Ondrejka, 2008; Salmon, 2009; Warburton, 2009).

Hay and Pymm (2011) also report, based on anecdotal evidence from students less familiar with 3-D virtual environments, that initiating their learning (reminiscent of Salmon's stage 1) can be quite time consuming, especially if the distance learner does not have the time to play around with the technology, thereby limiting social presence, interaction and knowledge exchange (Salmon's stages 1–4). Moreover, for some students, the virtual environment may be so overwhelming that the technology acts as a distraction rather than as a facilitator of learning (Omale et al., 2009). Therefore, from the perspective of the learner, 'this highlights the need for educators to ensure that the use of a virtual world is a carefully considered and integrated part of a subject, rather than merely using it as an "add on"' (Hay & Pymm, 2011, p. 200). Similarly, Keskitalo et al. (2011) argue that *Second Life* 'must be used in a pedagogically appropriate way, and students' activities must be well structured in order to promote meaningful learning and meet learning goals' (p. 17). Furthermore, Mathews, Andrews and Luck (2012) state:

> Clearly, educators need to ensure that incorporating a virtual world learning environment into a course can be justified not just from the subject-discipline perspective, but that such an addition also provides meaningful opportunities for learning. They must also be mindful of the time and effort that might be involved for students when engaging in these experiences ... Importantly, dealing with technological issues in managing the students' experiences in the virtual world should not overshadow the teaching and learning objectives identified for the activity. (p. 20)

According to Savin-Baden (2008), it is widely acknowledged that 3-D virtual learning environments foster much educational potential, especially with regard to social interaction. Hemmi, Bayne and Land (2009), for their part, however, offer a caveat, when commenting on the issue of 'honesty' (with regard to avatar presentation of oneself), suggesting that 'alternative' constructions of identity may be viewed negatively by some students: as being deceitful and even morally wrong.

8.8 CONCLUSIONS

In conclusion, as this chapter highlights, it would seem that e-learning, particularly when presented exclusively online, provides educational opportunities for a greater number of people and offers increased flexibility and personal control over one's learning. However, e-learning is also changing the way in which higher education delivers content to students enrolled on more traditional courses (e.g., in the form of blended learning). Such innovation requires changes to be made in how teachers prepare their classes, of course, thereby requiring continued professional development. In addition, it requires changes in how students interact with their peers and their tutors, at least if it is to enhance their wider educational experience. Nevertheless, through continued advancements in technology, it seems reasonable to declare that e-learning is making a valuable contribution to the quality of higher education and to the need for inclusivity and widening participation.

DISCUSSION QUESTIONS

1. Media richness theory holds that learners will benefit from richer communication media when the course content is equivocal (more ambiguous and open to interpretation) than when the material is unequivocal (e.g., a mathematical formula). To what extent does media richness theory match your learning experience?
2. Consider Salmon's model of e-learning and its five stages. Do any of the stages relate to your experience of education (whether online or exclusively face to face)? In other words, did you enter into and pass through the stages described by the model?
3. If engaged in learning in a virtual 3-D environment such as *Second Life*, what advantages and/or disadvantages would you say there are to holding classes in such a space? In addition, would it make a difference to you how your tutor's avatar appeared? In other words, how much would you want their avatar to have the appearance of a teacher (whatever that might be), and why?

SUGGESTED READINGS

Bayne, S. & Land, R. (2012). *Education in cyberspace*. London, UK: Routledge.

Childress, M. D. & Braswell, R. (2006). Using massively multiplayer online role-playing games for online learning. *Distance Education, 27*(2), 187–196.

Petrakou, A. (2010). Interacting through avatars: Virtual worlds as a context for online education. *Computers & Education, 54*, 1020–1027.

Savin-Baden, M. (2008). From cognitive capability to social reform? Shifting perceptions of learning in immersive virtual worlds. *ALT-J, 16*(3), 151–161.

Starkey, L. (2012). *Teaching and learning in the digital age*. London, UK: Routledge.

9 Leisure and Entertainment

Have new digital technologies freed up more time to pursuit leisure activities or have they simply created more work for the average user? Many daily errands that used to take up time in the form of travelling, lining up in queues and communicating with others can now be carried out online (e.g., banking, shopping). Arguably, this should help to free up more time to pursue leisure activities, but has it? More than this, the Internet provides a means by which we can pursue our leisure interests – so much so that, for Rojek (1994), the Internet is a space in which to re-imagine leisure, a claim supported by the fact that, in 2006, nearly 40% of those surveyed in the US reported leisurely surfing the Internet as part of their daily routine (Fallows, 2006).

This chapter considers some of the above questions and examines how the Internet and related technologies have affected our pursuit of leisure. We begin by discussing what is meant by 'leisure' and what motivates our pursuit of it, using selective examples as illustrations. The chapter then moves on to consider the changing nature of telecommunications and its relationship to leisure. We also focus on the impact of the Internet on more traditional forms of telecommunications, paying particular attention to the 'displacement' and 'engagement' hypotheses. Finally, we discuss Twitter and its use by celebrities, as well as the impact this has on the perceived relationship between those who follow celebrity tweets and the celebrity tweeters themselves.

9.1 WHAT IS LEISURE AND WHAT MOTIVATES OUR PURSUIT OF IT?

Before considering how digital technologies might have changed the ways in which we use our leisure time, it is important to operationalize what we mean by leisure. For Bregha (1985), leisure is the most precious expression of our freedom. More specifically, though, it can be divided into two broad areas: serious pursuits and casual pastimes. Leisure, as a serious pursuit, typically involves commitment, effort and perseverance (e.g., joining an amateur dramatics society or being part of a Sunday football league), whereas leisure in the form of a casual pastime is characteristically short-lived, much more spontaneous and requires little or no training (Stebbins,

Cyberpsychology: The Study of Individuals, Society and Digital Technologies, First Edition.
Monica Therese Whitty and Garry Young.
© 2017 John Wiley & Sons, Ltd. Published 2017 by John Wiley & Sons, Ltd.

2007). According to Nimrod (2010), casual leisure consists of the following types of activity:

- play (e.g., dabbling in the arts, but not in any committed way as is characteristic of serious leisure);
- relaxation;
- passive entertainment (e.g., watching television);
- active entertainment (e.g., party games);
- sociable conversation;
- sensory stimulation;
- casual volunteering;
- aerobic activity (e.g., walking, dancing).

One motivation for people engaging in leisure activities (even casually) is the attainment of a specific physical or psychological goal – for example, swimming in order to keep fit, or to look sporty and/or to increase one's self-esteem (Manfredo, Driver & Tarrant, 1996). In addition, some people pursue certain leisure activities for their experiential quality – for example, travelling in order to experience foreign cultures and customs (Manfredo et al., 1996). Compatible with each of these is Ryan and Gledon's (1998) description of four motivations that act as determinants of the level of satisfaction gained from the pursuit of leisure interests. The first is intellectual stimulation (e.g., acquiring new knowledge or discovering new ideas: say, from different cultures). The second is more social: building or strengthening relations. The third is the pursuit of personal challenges: competing to prove you can do it or to establish how good you are at something. Finally, there is the idea that some of us are motivated by the need to avoid or reduce overly stimulating life situations.

Each of the motivational components described above is compatible with the use of new media in our leisure pursuits. As Harris (2005; see also Brown, 2008) notes, the Internet blurs the boundaries between traditionally separate activities, shifting leisure towards virtual spaces and away from what Rowe (2006) calls a 'leisure landscape once characterized by the physical transport of people' (p. 324). Consequently, whatever we take leisure to be, or whatever our motivation for pursuing a particular leisure interest, the Internet has afforded many new opportunities for engaging in casual leisure activities, some of which are considered below.

SUGGESTED ACTIVITY

Consider the leisure activities you pursue online. How would you categorize them according to the categories of leisure described earlier in this chapter? Are all these activities pursued exclusively online? If so, what are they and why do you think they are exclusive to the Internet?

9.2 ONLINE FAMILY LEISURE

There is limited research on online leisure activities involving families. Social network games are online games played via social network sites (e.g., Facebook). These differ from MMORPGs insofar as they typically involve nonsimultaneous, turn-taking forms of gameplay (e.g., *Farmville*, a game in which one is able to create, build and nourish the farm of one's dreams, and *Castleville*, in which one can create one's own fantasy kingdom). Boudreau and Consalvo (2014) were interested in whether this form of casual leisure pursuit was used as a means of keeping in touch with family members and, if so, what type of communication it facilitated. In other words, do family members use the game as a topic of conversation (a shared interest, so to speak) or do they use the game to keep in touch with each other? Through the use of both online questionnaires and interviews (via email and Skype), Boudreau and Consalvo (2014) found that

> even though the goal of social network gameplay among family members may not have been initially intended as a way to keep in touch with each other, through the act of play, family members often felt more obligated to continue playing solely for the purpose of supporting each other over other friend dynamics. By drawing on pre-existing, familial connections, players were able to extend the life of their gameplay. Moreover, topics surrounding gameplay often extended into alternative subjects of communication through both on- and offline interactions, broadening the scope of familial interactions. (p. 1128)

This view is compatible with the sentiment expressed on the Playfish website (a UK-based company that designs social networking games), which in 2009 stated:

> We create games that let you play together with real-world friends and family using the infrastructure built by social networks. This is in some ways a return to the roots of games. You play with the same people you would play cards, board games or go bowling with in the real world. Sharing the game experience with friends makes it more compelling and fun. (cited in Rossi, 2009, p. 2)

The primary aim of social networking games is not, then, the mastering of gaming skills as a means of increasing one's status within the game, as often the skillset required to play these games is quite low. Instead, game advancement is often achieved through recruitment (Rossi, 2009). As Wei, Yang, Adamic, de Araújo and Rekhi (2010) note, 'engagement in a social game is closely tied with the ability to recruit friends' (p. 1).

9.3 OLDER ADULTS

The literature on online entertainment often focuses on young people; however, there are some interesting studies that examine how older people might use the Internet for entertainment and leisure activities. According to Nimrod (2014), the pursuit of leisure is one of the main functions of the Internet for older users (Loges & Jung, 2001), with older adults (those 65 years of age or over; see Fox, 2004) using the Internet to pursue a number of different leisure activities, such as researching and constructing family trees, compiling photo albums, playing games and engaging in virtual hobbies (Opalinski, 2001). Moreover, seniors' online communities (forums that explicitly target seniors) provide a unique form of casual leisure for older adults (Nimrod, 2010). Nimrod (2011) concludes that such communities provide older adults with 'a unique form of casual leisure that involves play, active entertainment and sociable conversation' (p. 228). In fact, one of the main social appeals of these communities is explained by the fact that the members are of similar ages but from different places, including different countries (Nimrod, 2014), which is made possible by their online status. In addition:

> The communities seem to serve as a stage for discussing every possible subject, ranging from very *private* subjects, such as problematic relationships or fear of death, to *public* subjects such as global warming or politics. Subjects range from very *serious* (e.g., employees' exploitation) to very *casual* (e.g., jokes), and although some of them are *exclusive* for seniors (e.g., ageing, retirement rights), many of them are *general*. With more positive than negative but overall a pretty balanced tone, it seems that the communities also enable expressing a wide range of emotions, ranging from very *negative* (e.g., sadness, anger, grief) to very *positive* (e.g., happiness and playfulness). (Nimrod, 2010, p. 389; emphasis in original)

For those members who were less socially active within these online communities – what Nimrod (2010) refers to as 'lurkers' – their activity and, it would seem, their enjoyment can best be described as encapsulating a form of passive entertainment, similar to watching television.

9.4 TECHNOFERENCE: ENCROACHING ON LEISURE TIME WITHIN RELATIONSHIPS

In Chapter 2 we looked at how relationships are initiated and developed in online spaces. Couples, of course, can also use digital technologies to maintain contact when they are physically apart (e.g., on work assignments). Internet technology can help those in intimate relationships to feel closer to each other when apart and so more 'connected' (Coyne, Stockdale, Busby, Iverson & Grant, 2011). Importantly, however, the same technology, when not being used to help keep couples connected, may be perceived as interfering in their relationship (e.g., during their joint leisure-time activities). McDaniel and Coyne (2014) use the term 'technoference' to describe intrusions or interruptions of this kind. McDaniel and Coyne found that higher instances of perceived technoference were negatively correlated with relational and/or personal well-being. Specifically, those who perceived more technoference typically reported more frequent conflict over technology use, lower levels of relationship and life satisfaction, and more depressive symptoms.

9.5 TELECOMMUNICATION

To understand further the impact the Internet has had on our leisure pursuits, we need to consider more traditional (pre-Internet) media and the extent to which the Internet has displaced these media in our pursuit of new forms of (or even well-established) leisure activities. We will begin by examining various forms of telecommunication.

Historically, the different forms of telecommunication divide into two types. The first traces its origins to the telegraph but is best exemplified by the telephone. The formatting of this type of communication allows for interaction – sending and receiving messages targeted at particular individuals – that lacks any centralized control. This type of telecommunication is often thought of as augmenting face-to-face communication by enabling, for example, faster communication over greater distances. Telecommunication of the other type, however, is centralized, is not targeted at individuals and is not typically interactive. Characteristic forms of telecommunication formatted in this way are radio, cinema and, more commonly, television.

For Kayany and Yelsma (2000), the two distinct 'connectivity' functions of the Internet are (1) online media, whereby computers or other portable devices act as new agents for information similar to the more traditional media devices such as television and radio, and (2) CMC, which enables synchronous communication (which rivals the telephone) as well as asynchronous communication (such as email, blogs or message boards) that acts to replace postal communication. The Internet therefore fits both of the traditional 'types' of telecommunication: it augments face-to-face (targeted) communication, yet it can also be used for mass broadcasts, which simply require the 'would-be' recipient to tune in (access the web address) to receive the published information (Robinson, Kestnbaum, Neustadtl & Alvarez, 2000). In fact, as a result, the Internet has become a powerful tool enabling instantaneous use of these two broad types of telecommunication around the world.

It has been found that leisure time spent on the Internet does not necessarily replace all the time we might use on other types of entertainment in the physical world (e.g., watching television, listening to the radio). Kayany and Yelsma (2000) argue that modern households are technologically complex environments, insofar as they often consist of multiple television sets, radios, mobile telephones, computers and gaming consoles: what Silverstone (1991) refers to as a domestic sociotechnical system. In support of this claim, Berger (2006) reported that the average American spends 9.2 hours each day using consumer media. Rideout, Foehr and Roberts (2010) similarly report that US children and adolescents spend approximately 53 hours a week (roughly 7.5 hours per day) watching television and films, reading newspapers and magazines, listening to music, playing computer games and using the Internet. In fact, if one were to focus solely on watching television and, in doing so, include accessing television through the Internet and mobile phones, viewing time in the US is on par with the number of hours taken up with full-time employment (Comstock & Scharrer, 2007). In the UK, Ofcom (2014) announced that 83% of adults go online using any type of device in any location. They also reported that 42% of adults claimed that the media activity they would miss the most would be watching television, followed by using their smartphone (22%) and then going online via their PC/laptop (15%). Within the 16–24-year age group, however, missing one's smartphone increased to 47%, whereas watching television dropped to a mere 13%. In fact, 71% of 16-to-24-year-olds reported watching television online using any device, and, in a survey in the United States reported by Cha (2013), the Internet was considered by adults to be a more essential medium than television. Cha also went on to note how revenue from television advertising declined by 21.2% in the United States between 2008 and 2009, whereas online advertising revenue grew by 8.3% over roughly the same period: an increase purportedly due to the popularity of online videos.

Given that entertainment/leisure and information are the two functions of online media (Kraut et al., 1998), the integration of this technology by family members may well set the parameters of the domestic environment in which the modern family interact, helping to define the characteristics of the particular domestic sociotechnical system. Any changes to this system – brought about, say, by the introduction of some form of new (in this case, online) media – will typically result in a period of integration involving a reorganization of the role/function and relationship to the family (say, in terms of importance) of old media. The integration of one of these online devices will often displace other activities, including face-to-face communication. As a consequence, there may occur a time and/or functional displacement effect as the new medium is integrated into the household.

9.6 TIME AND FUNCTIONAL DISPLACEMENT EFFECTS

Given that each of us has only a finite amount of time to spend interacting with media devices, how much we can engage with one particular media activity – whether it be a newspaper, the radio, television or the Internet – is limited. If one assumes a zero-sum relationship between media appliances, then, where a new media activity is introduced, a zero-sum relationship would predict a deficit in one or more of the other existing activities. A zero-sum relationship is one in which a gain in the time spent on one device (the television, say) necessitates a deficit in the time taken up with another (the radio), with no change in the overall amount of engagement.

To illustrate, where a person still engages with media devices overall for four hours a day, listening to the radio has been displaced wholly or in part by watching television. Where once the individual listened to the radio for four hours a day, she now listens for only one hour; the remaining three hours are taken up with watching the television. In media research, the 'displacement hypothesis' (Neuman, 1991) predicts just such a symmetrical (increase–decrease) relationship (Kayany & Yelsma, 2000), in which an increase in the use of one piece of media technology and its associated activity leads to a decrease in the use of another: the former displacing the latter, as the above example of radio and television use illustrates.

Himmelweit, Oppenheim and Vince (1958) were, however, among the first to argue that displacement of old media by new is more likely to occur when the old and new serve the same *function*. Wishing to be entertained by a drama, for example, can be achieved via the radio or television: each serves the same function in this respect. But, for many, being entertained by a television drama is likely to displace radio drama. Following this, Kayany and Yelsma (2000) have argued more recently that, where new media exist in the same functional niche as older media, each competes with the other to meet the needs of the population. Functional displacement occurs, then, when a new medium better satisfies a need within the population that was once satisfied by older media. Historically, this has been shown to be the case with the onset of television. Time spent watching television displaced time spent engaging with other media, such as radio, the cinema and fiction (McQuail, 1994; Robinson, 1972; Weiss, 1969; Wright, 1986). As a relatively new form of technology, is the Internet displacing time spent on other more traditional media such that these activities are no longer pursued to the same degree (e.g., watching television and films, speaking on the telephone)? Or does the Internet simply provide a more modern means of accessing and therefore continuing to pursue these activities (e.g., watching television and films online, communicating via Skype)?

Neuman (1991) claims that any displacement effect depends on four principles:

1. *Functional similarity*: Where two devices enable a similar activity (essentially have the same function) but one is less efficient at enabling this activity, the less efficient device risks being displaced (e.g., cartoons replace comic books for children).
2. *Physical and psychological proximity*: Where two activities occur in a similar space (physical element) but one is less satisfying (psychological element), the less satisfying risks being displaced (i.e., where television, homework and chores are equally accessible to children, many would rather engage in the first activity).
3. *Marginal fringe activities*: These activities are more likely to be displaced but structured activities are not (e.g., free play is more likely to be displaced by new media but homework is not).
4. *Transformation*: Activities, including the devices that promote these activities, that fail to adapt to meet new needs and challenges risk being displaced (i.e., older media such as radio needed to adapt to survive alongside television by becoming more specialized – for example, by putting on programmes (such as jazz or classical concerts) that appealed to certain groups not catered to by television).

Given these four principles, the functional equivalence hypothesis would predict that a medium as popular as the Internet should replace media existing in the same functional niche (Robinson, 2011). This prediction was supported by the findings of surveys carried out by Cole et al. (2001) and Nie and Erbring (2002). In addition, James, Wotring and Forrest (1995) reported a negative correlation between time spent on computer bulletin boards and time spent on other media, such as television, the telephone and books. More recently, Lee, Tan and Hameed (2006) were interested in the relationship between Internet use and three traditional media activities: television viewing, radio listening and newspaper reading. They conjectured that, if one were to apply the four displacement principles above, one could predict that television would be the primary casualty of increased Internet use. This is because the Internet, like television, 'entertains and informs; but ... also allows for interactivity, interpersonal relationship, and asynchronicity. Moreover, television and the Internet often share the same physical space and are in direct competition for attention. If they are not in the same room, they are still within the household' (Lee et al., 2006, p. 304). Lee et al. also speculated that, compared to television, newspapers should possess greater longevity, owing to, as they put it, their 'credibility and portability' (p. 304). These authors also considered radio to be relatively safe from the likelihood of displacement, owing to 'its compatib[ilty] with many activities, such as driving, cooking, jogging, and even surfing the Internet' (p. 304) After all, it is not uncommon for a consumer to listen to traditional radio at the same time as using the Internet to read blogs, for example (Cha, 2013).

Lee et al. did, therefore, acknowledge that displacement was not inevitable, as things are more complicated than the hypothesis suggests, even when acknowledging functional equivalence (Anderson, 2008; Gershuny, 2003). In particular, the 'engagement hypothesis' predicts a positive relationship between two activities such that one – the Internet (in this instance) – could in fact promote more traditional media activities (Lee & Kuo, 2001; Mutz, Roberts & Van Vuuren, 1993). As they state: 'after reading an article in the newspaper, we may become curious and decide to find out more by surfing the Internet. As such, time spent on one activity may actually stimulate another' (Lee et al., 2006, p. 305; see also Robinson, Barth & Kohut, 1997; Robinson et al., 2000; Robinson & Kestnbaum, 1999; Vyas, Singh & Bhabhra, 2007). In contrast to the evidence supporting a displacement effect, other studies have found that, when new, functionally equivalent, media were introduced (CMC, for example), a complementary – or symbiotic or supplemental – relationship between these and print media emerged (Dimmick, Kline & Stafford, 2000; Lin, 2001; Robinson et al., 1997; Schramm, Lyle & Parker, 1961).

In line with their view of the Internet as a time-management tool, Lee et al. (2006) also claimed that the Internet's efficiency can create more time to do other things (Nie & Hillygus, 2002), which might include engaging with other media. In fact, Kayany and Yelsma (2000) reported a correlation between the amount of time participants spent online and their rating of the importance of online media for information and entertainment. Lee et al. (2006)'s study likewise found that the use of traditional media (television, radio and newspapers) was in fact positively correlated – meaning that the more one engaged in one of these activities, the more likely one was to engage in one or more of the others – and so did not find support for the Internet displacing any of these media. In fact, for Robinson et al. (2000), the use of a personal computer or the Internet may be more akin to how we use time-enhancing home appliances such as the telephone than time-displacing technologies such as the television. In other words, and in keeping with the findings of a meta-analysis of various US national surveys by Robinson (2011), one might wish to conclude that the Internet has become a powerful medium of communication and entertainment, but not at the expense of decreased use of other (older) media – although, that said, as a demographic, teens and young adults are reportedly migrating from more traditional mass media to SNSs (Li & Bernoff, 2011; Solis, 2011).

> **SUGGESTED ACTIVITY**
>
> Think about how you use your Internet devices in the pursuit of leisure. Do you use them in a functionally equivalent way to more traditional media (e.g., television, radio, newspapers)?

Psychologists and health professionals have started to question how healthy it is to multitask in the manner it appears we are, even when that multitasking involves combining leisure activities. This is illustrated in the extract below, in an article in *The Guardian* titled 'Why the Modern World Is Bad for Your Brain':

> Our smartphones have become Swiss army knife-like appliances that include a dictionary, calculator, web browser, email, Game Boy, appointment calendar, voice recorder, guitar tuner, weather forecaster, GPS, texter, tweeter, Facebook updater, and flashlight. They're more powerful and do more things than the most advanced computer at IBM corporate headquarters 30 years ago. And we use them all the time, part of a 21st-century mania for cramming everything we do into every single spare moment of downtime. We text while we're walking across the street, catch up on email while standing in a queue – and while having lunch with friends, we surreptitiously check to see what our other friends are doing. At the kitchen counter, cosy and secure in our domicile, we write our shopping lists on smartphones while we are listening to that wonderfully informative podcast on urban beekeeping.
>
> But there's a fly in the ointment. Although we think we're doing several things at once, multitasking, this is a powerful and diabolical illusion. Earl Miller, a neuroscientist at MIT and one of the world experts on divided attention, says that our brains are 'not wired to multitask well … When people think they're multitasking, they're actually just switching from one task to another very rapidly. And every time they do, there's a cognitive cost in doing so.' So we're not actually keeping a lot of balls in the air like an expert juggler; we're more like a bad amateur plate spinner, frantically switching from one task to another, ignoring the one that is not right in front of us but worried it will come crashing down any minute. Even though we think we're getting a lot done, ironically, multitasking makes us demonstrably less efficient.

Multitasking has been found to increase the production of the stress hormone cortisol as well as the fight-or-flight hormone adrenaline, which can overstimulate your brain and cause mental fog or scrambled thinking. Multitasking creates a dopamine-addiction feedback loop, effectively rewarding the brain for losing focus and for constantly searching for external stimulation. (Levitin, 2015)

In the final section of this chapter, we consider the role of Twitter (a popular SNS) in disseminating celebrity news to the public (among other things), and its impact as an entertainment device as well as the relationships celebrities and fans have with each other through this medium.

9.7 TWITTER

Twitter is a microblogging site that enables people to post – or 'tweet' –140-character texts to a network of others. The site was launched in 2006 and, by the end of 2010, was reported to have a user base in excess of 175 million (Hargittai & Litt, 2011). Messages range from spontaneous quips to reflective musings, from complaints to endorsements, and from the altogether mundane to breaking news (Marwick & boyd, 2010). In addition to their content, tweets can vary in terms of their target audience. Some tweets may be intended for individuals, with everyone else who 'follows' the tweet acting as an incidental audience; other tweets, in contrast, are used intentionally to disseminate information to a wider audience and, as such, should be viewed as marketing tools (Stever & Lawson, 2013). Unlike other SNSs, however, in which there is a greater level of reciprocity and sharing of access and information (e.g., Facebook, Myspace), Twitter does not require mutual following. Certainly, there is no technical need for reciprocity, and little in the way of social expectation of it either. Rather, the norm is for one's tweets to be followed by someone who one does not likewise follow (Greenwood, 2013). As Marwick and boyd (2010) observe, on Twitter, there is a disconnection between followers and followed (e.g., as of May 2016, the singer-songwriter John Mayer is followed by 785,000 users but follows only 80). Indeed, according to Jin and Phua (2014), the more followers one attracts on Twitter, the greater one's perceived social influence. For, as they go on to state,

> It is no coincidence that to be 'trending' (i.e., phrases or topics that are tagged at a greater rate than others) on Twitter at any given point in time is equivalent to having one's movie become a box-office hit or one's hit single rank on the Billboard chart; in other words, Twitter can be utilized as a form of social capital. (Jin & Phua, 2014, p. 182)

In May 2016, at the time of writing, pop music celebrities Katy Perry and Justin Bieber occupied the top two spots on the Twitter top 100 followers list, with nearly 89 million and just over 82 million followers, respectively. In fourth place was US president Barack Obama (over 75 million). The highest ranked sports person was Real Madrid's Cristiano Ronaldo (ranked 14th with over 42 million followers). By comparison, CNN

Breaking News, the *New York Times*, and BBC Breaking News had a much more modest 39 million, 28 million and 22 million followers, respectively (Twitter Counter, 2016).

Given the likelihood of this asymmetrical relationship, research suggests that one major motivation for Twitter use is interest in and perceived access to celebrities. For example, Hargittai and Litt (2011) found that, among the sample of young adults they surveyed, interest in celebrities and entertainment news more generally was a significant predictor of Twitter use. Twitter enables its users to accumulate 'weak ties' (Granovetter, 1973) or loose social connections that not only help to disseminate new information and novel ideas among those identified as 'followers' but also, in the case of those who 'follow' celebrities or other public figures, establish a connection that allows access to social resources that would perhaps be unavailable to the 'follower' offline (Jin & Phua, 2014).

From the point of view of the celebrity, then, Twitter provides a good medium for a personable chat with fans without having to grant access to private contact details. For Stever and Lawson (2013), the fact that Twitter allows a personable dialogue without obliging reciprocity is an important and attractive feature of the medium. They state that:

> Fans can send the celebrity personal messages without the celebrity needing to grant access to a personal page or site. The celebrity can reply in kind, again without having to join the fan's page or without forming any kind of formal connection with the fan. If a fan is inappropriate, the celebrity can 'block' that fan. A celebrity can read or not read 'Tweets' from fans as he or she chooses, and fans don't know if their messages are being read unless the celebrity replies. (p. 340)

The way celebrities communicate with fans on Twitter may make the fans' relationship with the celebrity seem more 'real', insofar as the celebrity is seen to be reaching out to them. Celebrities may, for example, tweet about their favourite things or things that they dislike, even to the point of providing quite trivial information not typically available or of interest elsewhere. This level of triviality and putative spontaneity may help to give the appearance of 'being there' with the celebrity: sharing the moment, as it were (Stever & Lawson, 2013). Some celebrities may also wish to use this medium as a way of expressing their views on particular topics – perhaps reacting to news events around the world – and, in doing so, acting (to a greater or lesser degree) as role models. Greenwood (2013) conjectures that engaging with famous people, even in the asymmetrical way characteristic of Twitter, may bestow on the follower of the celebrity a heighted sense of self-worth or social value. Such a relationship is characteristic of a 'parasocial interaction'.

The phenomenon of parasocial interaction (Horton & Wohl, 1956) describes the relationship between media users and celebrity figures (in this case), and is based on the idea that interaction between media users and celebrities (on Twitter, for example) can induce a parasocial relationship – an illusion of intimacy based on a one-sided and imaginative social rapport with a media figure (Rubin & McHugh, 1987) – whereby the users responds to the celebrity as though in a typical social relationship (Giles, 2002). Moreover, according to Greenwood (2013), Twitter encourages the enactment of what Marwick and boyd (2011) refer to as 'microcelebrity' among noncelebrity tweeters. This is believed to stem from the fact that *actual* celebrities have a social media presence on Twitter. Therefore, perhaps through an association based on the noncelebrity's use of or presence on the same medium as actual celebrities, these previously unknown individuals can acquire a kind of celebrity status (i.e., microcelebrity). Noncelebrity Twitter users are thus able to gain status and followers by marketing themselves and/or their thoughts as a type of attractive personal brand that is designed to appeal to the diverse population that make up Twitter's audience.

9.8 CONCLUSIONS

The Internet has left its mark on our pursuit of leisure, both in terms of enabling more time for leisure, owing to its use as a time-management tool, and in terms of transforming the way leisure and entertainment can be pursued. To support this general view, we began the chapter by operationalizing leisure: pointing out the various forms leisure can take, broadly divided into serious and casual pastime pursuits. We then discussed the ways in which the Internet, as a means of engaging in leisure, can be of benefit to various groups of people. We looked at, for example, research that shows that online games, played via social media, can help family members to keep in touch, and how one of the main functions of the Internet for older users is the pursuit of leisure activities, often through online forums designed especially for senior members of communities. We also considered the issue of how much time we spend online for leisure and entertainment and how this compares with time spent on entertainment in the physical world. We examined the displacement and the engagement hypotheses and learnt that, rather than one medium for the pursuit of leisure displacing another, many people multitask entertainment by using various media across both the Internet and other spaces. The chapter did question, however, how psychologically healthy it is to combine these tasks. In the final section we discussed how Twitter has been used as a source of entertainment, and how it has also had an impact on the relationship between fans and celebrities – perhaps facilitating what is known as a parasocial relationship on the part of the fan (or Twitter follower). We also considered how Twitter might enable noncelebrities to acquire a certain type of celebrity status.

DISCUSSION QUESTIONS

1. What impact have the Internet and related technologies had on the pursuit of leisure?
2. To what extent do the Internet and related technologies facilitate your personal relationships or impede them in a manner captured by the term 'technoference'?

3. What do the displacement and engagement hypotheses predict, and how might the Internet and related technologies be said to support or challenge them?
4. In what way might Twitter enable fans (or followers) to feel closer to a celebrity? In what sense might this be indicative of a parasocial relationship?

SUGGESTED READINGS

Berger, A. A. (2006). *Media and society: A critical perspective.* Lanham, MD: Rowman & Littlefield.

Comstock, G. & Scharrer, E. (2007). *Media and the American child.* San Diego, CA: Elsevier.

Robinson, J. P. (2011). IT use and leisure time displacement. *Information, Communication & Society, 14*(4), 495–509.

Stever, G. S. & Lawson, K. (2013). Twitter as a way for celebrities to communicate with fans: Implications for the study of parasocial interaction. *North American Journal of Psychology, 15*(2), 339–354.

10 Online Gaming and Gambling

In Chapter 9 we discussed how the Internet has changed how we spend our time on leisure and entertainment. In this chapter we focus, in more detail, on two forms of entertainment: games and gambling. Both these online activities have been the focus of numerous psychological studies. Some of the major concerns include addiction and whether playing aggressive games leads to aggressive behaviour. With respect to Internet addiction, the research to date suggests that some people have specific online problems, while others use the Internet to carry out established offline addictions (e.g., gambling, sexual addictions). Scholars have yet to agree on whether these should be classed as Internet addictions per se or as problematic behaviours. Researchers also fail to agree on the effects of playing video games. This chapter summarises some of the key research studies and provides an outline of some of the main theories that have been developed to examine the link between media and aggressive behaviour. It also examines the psychological impact of playing out taboo activities in video games. Finally, this chapter considers the types of skills one can acquire from playing games.

10.1 INTERNET ADDICTION

In the mid-1990s, Ivan coined the phrase 'Internet addiction disorder'; however, he did not originally treat the notion seriously. His message detailed symptoms such as fantasizing about the Internet and giving up on important social or occupational activities because of excessive Internet use. He intended his post to be a joke – a parody of addiction disorders. In spite of his intention, people took his notion seriously and as a consequence he received numerous emails from individuals claiming to suffer from Internet addiction disorder. Since this time, many scholars have conducted theoretical and empirical work on the topic – to investigate whether this is a real disorder as well as to devise treatment programmes for those with problematic behaviours associated with excessive Internet use.

In the late 1990s, Kimberly Young (1998) published a book entitled *Caught in the Net: How to Recognize the Signs of Internet Addiction and a Winning Strategy for Recovery*, which considered in detail the problem of Internet addiction. She reported numerous case studies that she believed were examples of Internet addiction. At this time, Young developed an instrument to diagnose Internet addiction, which was an adapted version of the criteria used in the *Diagnostic and Statistical Manual of Mental Disorders IV* for pathological gambling. Staying online for an average of 38 hours per week for recreational activity was deemed prima facie evidence of an Internet addiction (though in recent times this might be understood to be normal behaviour). In addition, Young identified five types of internet addiction, namely: cybersexual addiction to adult chat rooms; cyber-relationship addiction to online friendships or affairs; compulsions to engage in online gambling, auctions or forms of trading; compulsive Web surfing; and addiction to online game-playing or computer programming.

Young developed the ACE model to explain how 'accessibility', 'control' and 'escape' play significant roles in the development of Internet addiction (see, e.g., Young, Pistner, O'Mara & Buchanan, 1999). According to the ACE model, it is possible that a person looking for sexual kicks, or seeking out a place to gamble or play games, would be attracted to the Internet because of its unique qualities. The Internet, Young argued, allows some degree of escape from everyday life.

There are a number of problems with Young's work. First, the ACE model implies that the problem lies with the Internet, rather than with individuals who become addicted to it. Second, Griffiths (1999, 2000a, 2000b) has argued that many excessive users are not necessarily 'Internet addicts'. He states that, in many instances, a gambling addict, a sex addict and so forth are simply using the Internet as a place to engage in their addictive behaviours.

As an alternative to Young's diagnostic criteria, Griffiths (1998, 2000a, 2000b) argued that, when considering Internet addiction, researchers should consider the six traditional core components of addition: salience, mood modification, tolerance, withdrawal symptoms, conflict and relapse. However, Grohol (1998) has criticized Griffiths' suggestion for diagnosing Internet addiction, saying that 'any behavior can be viewed as addictive given such criteria, whether it be watching television, listening to the radio, ironing, going online, reading, sewing, or exercising' (p. 396).

The concept of Internet addiction has itself been criticized, with some arguing that it needs to be entirely abandoned (Starcevic, 2013). It might be argued, for instance, that the Internet is simply a medium to fuel other addictions (Griffiths, 2000a, 2000b). Starcevic has made the following emphatic argument:

> Although Internet addiction has become a widely used term, it is a misnomer and should be abandoned. This is because of the conceptual heterogeneity of the term and because being addicted to the 'delivery mechanism' or, more precisely, addiction to a medium, a means to an end or a vehicle for achieving something. Therefore, Internet addiction is as meaningful a term as 'casino addiction', which would denote addictive gambling in casinos (p. 17).

He continued this line of argument, stating the following:

> If it is assumed that addictive use of the Internet does exist, the addiction would actually pertain to the corresponding activities and not to the Internet itself. These activities are quite diverse and include gaming, gambling, viewing pornography and related

sexual behaviours, shopping, chatting, sending messages, etc. ... [A]lthough one can develop some of these other addiction only on the Internet ... that does not justify the term Internet addiction. (p. 17).

Starcevic's argument, together with those of others in the field (e.g., Griffiths, 2000a, 2000b), is an important one, but, as yet, much more research is needed to understand whether Internet addiction per se is a real disorder or whether the individual addictions that the Internet might enable should be the real focus of research investigations as well as treatment. This chapter now turns to consider two types of addictions that have been considered as potential types of online addiction: gambling and gaming.

10.2 INTERNET GAMBLING ADDICTION

Internet gambling is a popular activity and a form of gambling that could potentially be more problematic, for some people, than gambling conducted in the physical world. Griffiths (2003), for example, points out that there are a number of factors that make Internet gambling potentially seductive and/or addictive, including anonymity, convenience, escape, dissociation/immersion, accessibility, event frequency, interactivity, disinhibition, simulation and asociability. He has taken the view that these structural characteristics appear to be enhanced via technological innovation. Although there is no consensus on whether there ought to be a specific addiction labelled as Internet addiction, there is agreement that gambling online can be problematic for some individuals.

Researchers have also examined the profile of a person who is likely to have a gambling problem. The 2010 British Gambling Prevalence Survey found that individuals who used the Internet for multiple types of gambling were more likely be categorized as having a problem compared with those who engaged in fewer Internet gambling activities (Wardle, Moody, Griffiths, Orford & Volberg, 2011). MacKay and Hodgins (2012) found that cognitive distortions are a risk factor in online gambling. Gainsbury, Russell, Wood, Hing and Blaszczynski (2015) investigated whether Internet-disordered gamblers were a distinct group. They found that individuals vulnerable to developing a gambling problem are also likely to use Internet gambling and that the accessibility of this medium is likely to exacerbate gambling problems. They argued that certain features of Internet gambling (access, privacy, anonymity and better game experience) might increase the risk of developing problems. These features, they believe, enable longer engagement in sessions of immersive play without interruption and are also likely to be associated with poor physical health and disturbances in sleeping and eating patterns.

There have been a number of studies that have focused on adolescents with gambling problems. Olason et al. (2010), for example, found that adolescent

Internet gamblers were much more likely to experience problems than what are often termed 'land-based gamblers'. They also found that boys and older age groups were more likely to gamble on the Internet compared with girls and younger age groups. Potenza et al. (2011) examined correlates of at-risk problem Internet gambling in adolescents residing in the United States. They found that adolescents who gambled online were more likely to be classified as at-risk problem gamblers. These individuals were also more likely to be heavy users of alcohol as well as to report experiencing depression. Adolescent Internet gamblers were found to be less likely to have friends who gamble, compared with non-Internet gamblers, which these authors argue is consistent with the notion that online gambling is typically solitary in nature. Potenza et al. make the case that the accessibility of online casinos that are available 24 hours per day may influence the development of problematic gambling. They suggest that specific interventions, such as monitoring school computers and limiting access to gambling-related Internet sites, warrant consideration.

> **SUGGESTED ACTIVITY**
>
> Based on the current literature available on online gambling addiction, devise an intervention programme to prevent and deter individuals from engaging in excessive online gambling.

10.3 INTERNET GAMING ADDICTION

A mourning father has sent out a plea to other parents to protect their children from the dangers of playing computer games.

Blood clot victim, Chris Staniforth, 20, died after spending up to 12 hours at a time playing on his Xbox.

The gaming enthusiast suffered a blockage to his lungs when he developed deep vein thrombosis ... Chris' heartbroken father, David told The Sun, 'As a parent you think playing computer games can't do them any harm because you know what they are doing.

'Kids all over the country are playing these games for long periods – they don't realise it could kill them.'

(Twomey, 2011)

There are many stories in the news similar to the one reported above. Internet addiction was not formally recognized in DSM-IV-TR, but DSM-5 now includes 'Internet gaming disorder' in its research appendix. It was included in order to give credence to the problem as well as to encourage better science in achieving a clear aetiology and treatment programme for the disorder. As with online gambling problems, there have been studies dedicated to examining whether playing online games is problematic.

There is some evidence to suggest that there is a link between online gaming disorder and ADHD. Weinstein and Weizman (2012) claim that both video-game addiction and ADHD share a common mechanism of reward and sensitization, which is mainly mediated by dopamine, which might explain the link. They suggest that future studies should focus on the psychobiological mechanisms for both conditions and explore their commonalities further. Chen, Chen and Gau (2015) found that adolescents with ADHD-related symptoms reported a greater frequency in playing online games and less time engaging in homework. However, it should be pointed out that the research focused on students' reports only, rather than conducting a clinical assessment of these participants.

There have also been studies that have examined the relationship between Internet gaming disorder and substance abuse. Yen and Ko (2014), for example, have found comorbidity between Internet gaming disorder and nicotine dependence. In addition, they found that impulsivity could be the shared mechanism between behaviour and substance addition. Walther, Morgenstern and Hanewinkel (2012) found a relationship between tobacco, alcohol and cannabis use and problematic computer gaming. Moreover, they found that problematic computer gamblers were more likely than those without a problem to score high on the following measures: irritability/aggression, social anxiety, ADHD and low self-esteem. They did, however, find that problematic gamblers tended to be more similar to substance users than problematic computer gamers.

As with online gambling research, much more work is needed to help us understand what is currently referred to as Internet gaming disorder. At this point, it is difficult to make too many claims with confidence. Lam (2014), for instance, conducted a systematic review to examine the effect of problematic use of the Internet (for gaming purposes) on mental health: specifically, sleep problems among young people. Focusing, in particular, on the association between sleep problems and excessive online gaming use, Lam contends that, although there is some evidence to suggest a link, the studies are quite weak, often relying on poor methodologies. He suggests that much more research is needed on excessive online gaming use before psychologists will be able to develop a clear picture of individuals who are more prone to this disorder.

10.4 AGGRESSIVE VIDEO GAMES

In addition to considering problems associated with excessive use of video games, some scholars have emphatically argued that playing video games can lead to aggressive behaviour. This has also been an argument taken up by the media. Some news stories, for instance, have held the playing of violent video games to be the cause of violent acts carried out by young people, such as massacres. The following, for example, was written in the *Denver Post* (Human, 2007) to explain why (in the writer's opinion) two children from Columbine High School had massacred children in their school:

> Eric Harris and Dylan Klebold went on a killing rage at Columbine High School in 1999 because they were abruptly denied access to their computers, an Oregon psychiatrist says in a published study.
>
> The two young men relied on the virtual world of computer games to express their rage and to spend time, and cutting them off in 1998 sent them into crisis, said Jerald Block, a research and psychiatrist in Portland.
>
> 'Very soon thereafter- a couple of days – they started to plan the actual attack,' Block said.
>
> Block published his research in the current issue of the American Journal of Forensic Psychiatry, a peer-reviewed journal.
>
> The paper is likely to generate debate, said Cheryl Olson, co-director of the Center for Mental Health and Media at the Massachusetts General Hospital.
>
> 'Two-thirds of middle-school boys play M-rated games regularly,' Olson said. M-rated games contain intense violence or sexual content.
>
> 'They're not turning kids into killing machines,' Olson said. 'The evidence just isn't there.'
>
> Block sifted through thousands of pages of documents released by Columbine investigators and said he believes both Harris' and Klebold's parents banned them from their computers after the two were caught breaking into an electrician's van in 1998.
>
> Harris and Klebold had each previously been temporarily kept off computers at school or at home, and after each incident, Block said, the boys' writing or behaviour became more violent.
>
> Block said he worries about people immersing themselves so deeply and also about cutting them off cold-turkey.
>
> 'How do you pull them out, without triggering homicidal or suicidal behaviour?' he asked.

The above story is one of many that attempt to explain these boys' shocking actions. Perhaps onlookers can gain some solace from blaming the use of aggressive video games. In deciding for yourselves, however, whether the playing of video games or the withdrawal of permission to play these games explains why the boys shot their class mates, it might be worthwhile to consider that most children who play aggressive video games or are banned from playing their games do not commit murder. This chapter now turns to consider the psychological theories that have been applied to predict how individuals might change their behaviour as a consequence of playing aggressive video games.

10.4.1 Social learning theory

Before video games became popular and accessible, researchers were considering the effects of other forms of media on behaviour. One well-known piece of work considered the effects that watching violent television programmes, including cartoons, might have on children (Bandura, Ross & Rose, 1963). The theory used to frame this work is social learning theory, which most undergraduate students will find familiar. Albert Bandura developed this theory as a result of his interest in how observations of other people's behaviours might shape children's behaviours. Bandura argued that individuals acquire attitudes, emotional responses and new styles of behaviour by modelling and imitating others' behaviours; that is, we are not passive observers or recipients of external stimuli. In considering this body of work with respect to video games, some scholars have argued that playing video games that involve hitting or shooting another character might promote violent behaviour in the physical realm (e.g., Silvern & Williamson, 1987). Players are often given explicit rewards, such as points or virtual objects, for engaging in symbolic violent acts, which could potentially reinforce aggressive behaviours, according to this theory.

However, the body of work on media effects and violent behaviour has its critics. Cumberbatch, Jones and Lee (1988), for example, argue that the aggression that is witnessed might instead be understood as play fighting rather than 'authentic aggression', and as such experiments appear very artificial. Some suggest that children guess what is expected by the researcher and act accordingly (Borden, 1975). Ferguson (2010) argues that any modelling effects from these experiments appear to be small and short lasting. Social learning theory, in general, has been criticized for its generalizations in findings, with some researchers arguing that modelling is something that individuals can do, rather than something they necessarily do (Ferguson, 2010).

10.4.2 Script theory

Another theory developed to explain why a person behaves in a certain way is script theory. This theory has also been applied to explain aggressive behaviour. Script theory essentially purports that behaviours fall into certain patterns known as 'scripts' or knowledge structures. Individuals learn from society and their experiences appropriate ways to behave and ascribed meanings to these behaviours. Script theory has been applied, for example, to explain gendered behaviour, and how people behave in relationships. Children learn gender schemas early in life, based on society's ideas of what it means to be a male or female in a particular culture. They learn this via their observations of others, as well as from how others treat them. These schemas, it is argued, lead them to act in gendered ways. Applying this theory to aggressive behaviour, theorists have argued that those exposed to aggressive behaviours develop scripts indicating that this behaviour is normal and acceptable (Huesmann, 1988). If children play violent video games, scripts are developed that normalize aggressive behaviour.

10.4.3 Frustration–aggression hypothesis

The frustration–aggression hypothesis is another theory that is well known to many undergraduate psychology students. The theory, proposed by Dollard, Doob, Miller, Mowrer and Sears (1939), posits that frustration is a state that emerges when external factors interfere with a goal response. Frustration is said to lead to aggressive behaviours, which are then displaced. Take, for example, someone who has had a difficult day at work, unable to meet the targets they have been given. Given that it might be risky to show upset in the workplace, they might go home and take their anger or frustration out on their family. Applying this theory to violent video games, it might be argued that the build-up of frustration in the game and the heightened emotional arousal, due to the violence, might lead the gamer to displace their frustration into violent acts in the physical world. This theory has been broadly criticized as being too simplistic. Social learning theorists, in particular, have criticized this theory, arguing that frustrations typically only create a general emotional arousal and that it is important, instead, to examine how individuals respond to this arousal (Bandura, 1973).

10.4.4 Cognitive neoassociation model

The cognitive neoassociation model (Berkowitz, 1984) builds on the frustration–aggressive hypothesis in an attempt to explain aggressive behaviour. This model rejects the notion that behaviour is learnt (as proposed by theories such as the social learning theory, outlined above). Although he did not intend to dismiss the importance of learning, Berkowitz argued that media influences 'do not operate through observational learning only, if this concept is understood to refer to a relatively long-lasting acquisition of new knowledge or the adoption of a novel form of behavior. Some media affects are fairly transient ... as if the observed event had activated reactions or thoughts only for a relatively brief period' (p. 414).

In contrast to social learning theory, Berkowitz contends that it is problematic to argue that individuals imitate media, given that there are few opportunities to act out similar physical acts. He notes that, in most studies that have examined the link between observing aggression and committing aggressive acts, the aggression measured after the observation is typically physically different. According to the cognitive neoassociation model, thoughts, feelings and action tendencies are linked together in a person's memory, forming an 'associative network' (Collins & Loftus, 1975). Concepts that are primed are more accessible in memory. The model posits that individuals repeatedly exposed to a particular stimulus start to link and activate other similar thoughts (Berkowitz, 1984, 1990). When applying this model to explain media effects, it has been suggested that the media promotes actions. Playing a violent video game, therefore, can prime other semantically related thoughts, which increase the chance that the spectator will have other aggressive notions during this period (Anderson & Ford, 1986; Berkowitz, 1984). This process is believed to occur automatically, without conscious awareness. Exposure to any form of aggressive media can trigger aggressive feelings and bring to mind aggressive memories, beliefs and aggression-related skills. Giumetti and Markey (2007) provide the example of being exposed to an image of a gun in a game, which might evoke notions with similar meanings, such as shooting. This, in turn, might activate other semantically associated ideas, such as hurting someone. Being repeatedly exposed to similar stimuli (e.g., aggressive media) is said to strengthen the association. According to the theory, individuals who regularly play violent video games are therefore more likely to be aggressive individuals.

As with the previous theories, researchers have noted limitations of the cognitive neoassociation model. Sherry (2001) points out that, even if emotional responses are enhanced through watching violence in media, it should not necessarily follow that individuals will act more aggressively. Not all theorists, however, are completely against this theory. Instead, many well-known scholars in the field of video-games research have extended the model rather than rejecting it outright. Bushman (1995, 1996), for example, extended this model to include personal dispositions, which he believes makes some people more prone to the effects of priming than others. According to Bushman, individuals who are more dispositionally angry might possess a more developed cognitive–associative network of semantically related ideas about anger compared to those who are not. When such people are exposed to violent media, then, they will be more likely to become primed to act in an aggressive manner compared with people who do not have an angry disposition.

10.4.5 *General aggression model*

Given the dissatisfaction with many of the aforementioned theories, researchers have developed a more complex model in an attempt to explain and predict aggressive behaviour. This is referred to as the general aggression model (Anderson, 1997, 2004; Anderson & Bushman, 2002; Anderson & Dill, 2000; Bushman & Anderson, 2001). According to the model, both situational and dispositional variables interact to affect a person's internal state (see Figure 10.1). The internal state contains cognitions, affects and arousals, which all influence each other and have an effect on an individual's appraisal of an aggressive act. Once appraised, the individual then decides how to act next.

According to the general aggression model, violent video games have both short- and long-term effects. There has been more speculation on the long-term effects than empirical research. Researchers, however, claim to have obtained empirical findings to support some short-term effects. Anderson et al. (2003), in a review of the literature, found that many studies reported a number of short-term effects of playing video games, such as the increased likelihood of physically and verbally aggressive behaviour, and increased aggressive thoughts and emotions. Others have also found some short-term effects but have argued that these effects are smaller than those produced from watching violent television programmes (Sherry, 2001; see Young & Whitty, 2012, for a more detailed discussion).

Critiques of this theory have argued that the evidence to support the model is weak, at best (Cumberbatch, 2010; Ferguson, 2007; Sherry, 2001). Ferguson emphatically argues that there is no compelling support for either a correlational or

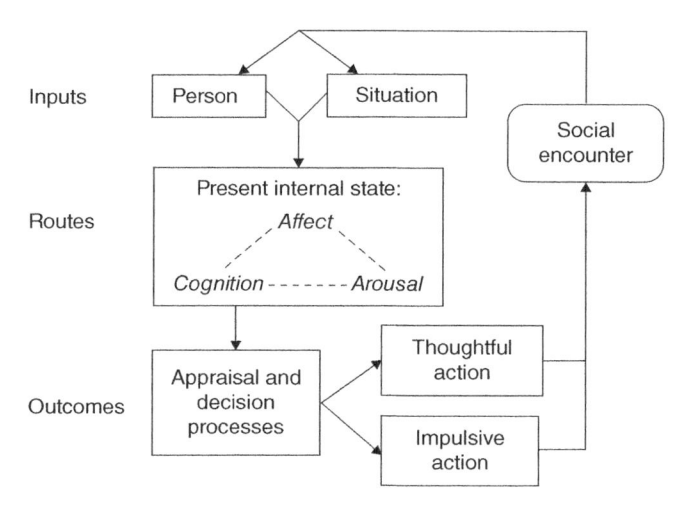

Figure 10.1 *The general aggression model's episodic processes (Anderson & Bushman, 2002, p. 34)*

causal relationship between violent game play and actual aggressive behaviour. Even when weak results have been obtained, researchers have argued that the tests to measure aggression lack face validity (Ferguson & Kilburn, 2009). Interestingly, in their own research, Ferguson and Rueda (2009) claim that playing violent video games can decrease hostile feelings and depression. Given these mixed results and problems with experimental designs, it is too early to make the claim (if it can ever be made at all) that playing violent video games causes aggressive behaviour. It would be fair to say that any claims that suggest that watching violent media can lead to mass killings (as suggested in an extract earlier in this chapter) are quite outlandish.

> **SUGGESTED ACTIVITY**
>
> Have you or your friends ever played violent video games? From your own subjective experience, do you think this changed or altered your behaviour or emotions? If so, in what ways? What might be the best way to measure this objectively?

10.5 TRANSCENDING TABOOS: VIDEO GAMES

In addition to aggressive acts, researchers have questioned where the limits should be (if anywhere) on the inclusion of acts that are considered taboo or criminal in the real world (Whitty, Young & Goodings, 2011; Young & Whitty, 2012). In addition to killing, some games include cannibalism (e.g., *Evil Dead*, *F.E.A.R.* and the *Resident Evil* series), rape (e.g., *Battle Raper*, *Phantasmagoria* and *RapeLay*) and incest (e.g., *The House of the Dead: Overkill*). Given that these acts are not able to cause the same form of harm as they do in the real world, researchers have been more concerned about the potential psychological harm that inclusion of these acts might cause (if any). Psychological harm might include stress or anxiety, shame, guilt or upset. The psychological harm might also be lessened or increased depending on how these acts are depicted, whether individuals are rewarded for carrying out the acts and whether the game involves interacting with other people (e.g., MMORPGs) or is single player. A study by Whitty et al. (2012) examined some of these concerns by focusing on how individuals played two different MMORPGs: *World of Warcraft* and *Sociolotron*. In *World of Warcraft*, players can engage in prohibited acts such as stealing, torture and killing. *Sociolotron* encourages individuals to engage in many actions that are considered taboo offline (e.g., torture, killing, rape, racist behaviour). The individuals reported that some acts were psychologically easier to play out than others and that the game offered them an escape from reality. Acts where there was no sanctioned equivalence (e.g., rape, paedophilia) were seen as worse than others, and players often described them as behaviours they could not psychologically cope with witnessing or playing out in a game. Sanctioned equivalence refers to an action, such as killing, for which there is a sanctioned – as in legal or authorized – equivalent. One may kill someone illegally in the case of murder, for example, but killing may also be sanctioned in the case of state-authorized execution or during combat, or in cases of self-defence. There is no sanctioned equivalent in the case of rape, paedophilia or incest (Young & Whitty, 2011).

The look of the game also appeared to make a difference in perceptions of particular acts; for example, some individuals believed they could cope with playing out rape with their characters in *Sociolotron* because the graphics were not very clear – clearer graphic depictions, they believed, would make the act appear more real to them, making it more difficult to play the game. The researchers also found that not all people experienced the games in the same way, suggesting that a proportion of individuals might not be psychologically harmed. This area of research might well be just as important to investigate as the question of whether playing violent videos games leads to increased aggressive behaviour.

> **SUGGESTED ACTIVITY**
>
> Consider the available video games that include taboo activities. Do you think any of these ought to be banned? Why do you think this?

10.6 GAMES FOR LEARNING

Much of what we have examined in this chapter has focused on the negative effects of playing online computer games; however, there are many positive reasons why someone might play these games. The obvious reason is that these games, for some, are an enjoyable leisure activity. Researchers have also found a number of positive effects associated with playing video games. Ferguson (2007), for example, found that playing violent video games was associated with improved visuospatial abilities. Given these results, accompanied by those of other studies, researchers started to reason that online computer games might actually develop useful skills (Subrahmanyam & Greenfield, 1994) and be used for educational and training purposes (Connolly, Boyle, MacArthur, Hainey & Boyle, 2012). Games that are specifically designed to improve or develop new skills are referred to as 'serious games', although computer games that have been developed just for entertainment purposes can also teach people new skills. Serious games have been formally defined as 'mental contest[s], played with a computer in accordance with specific rules, that [use] entertainment to further government or corporate training, education, health, public policy, and strategic communication objectives (Zyda, 2005, p. 26).

Models have been developed to categorize the types of skills individuals might learn from playing video games. Skills can include content understanding, collaboration and/or teamwork, problem-solving, communication and self-regulation, changing attitudes, improving knowledge, cognitive skills, motor skills, affective learning outcomes and communicative learning outcomes (O'Neil, Wainess & Baker, 2005; Wouters, Van der Spek & Van Oostendorp, 2009). In addition, video games can be designed with the intention to change motivations and affect – for example, towards exercise. Games have been designed to motivate people to learn subjects such as maths (Wijer, Jonker & Kerstens, 2008) and history (Huizenga, Admirall, Akkerman and ten Dam, 2008), although research has found that not all games achieve their objectives (Huizenga et al., 2008). Games have also been developed to assist individuals with intellectual and physical disabilities. Serious games, for example, have demonstrated great potential for people who are blind to develop work-based skills and to explore new spaces and reduce their reliance on guides (Evett, Battersby, Ridley & Brown, 2009; Brown et al., 2011).

Various workplaces and organizations have also developed games to teach and train staff. Various military organizations, for example, have developed serious games to train their officers and soldiers in skills such as strategies and tactics as well as cultural awareness, interpersonal communication, adaptability and rapport-building skills (Smith, 2010). It is common for government and corporations to train their staff. The game *It's A Deal!* was created for such purposes, to teach intercultural business communication between Spaniards and Britons in business settings (Guillen-Nieto & Aleson-Carbonell, 2012).

There is still much more research needed to determine how effective computer games are at imparting certain skills; however, the early research findings suggest some promise. Moreover, further research is needed to help us understand the various skills a game played in cyberspace might offer, compared with a stand-alone game (we note that this distinction is often missing in the literature). Some online video games, for instance, might be more effective at teaching team building and cooperation skills compared with their offline counterparts.

10.7 CONCLUSIONS

This chapter has focused on two forms of online entertainment: gambling and gaming. It began by examining whether individuals might be addicted to these activities because of the medium rather than the activity itself. Much more research is needed in this area. We have yet, for example, to arrive at a consensus on whether excessive online gambling and/or gaming can manifest as an addiction disorder and, if it does, how we might diagnose this problem. The DSM-5 included 'Internet gaming disorder' in its research appendix, in order to flag that this is a potential disorder that warrants further investigation. This chapter also examined the research on online gaming, focusing on the theories and empirical evidence on the relationships (if any) between playing violent video games and aggressive behaviour. This is another area of research that warrants further investigation. We added to the mix the notion that there might be other potential psychological harms from playing video games that include other taboo activities (e.g., rape, incest, paedophilia). The chapter concluded by focusing on the positive aspects of video games, pointing out that, in addition to their recreational value, researchers have also found that video games can be effective at imparting particular skills. The research on serious games, for instance, is a growing field, and to date has already offered many new ways to train and help individuals – spanning industry to those with physical disabilities. As video games become increasingly popular, we should be mindful of both their positive and their negative aspects.

DISCUSSION QUESTIONS

1. Do you agree with the literature that argues that violent video games can promote aggressive behaviour?
2. Can people really be addicted to the Internet?
3. Critically evaluate the research that examines online gaming addiction.
4. Should there be limits to the sorts of behaviours game designers include in their video games?
5. What features should researchers be focusing on in their evaluation of the effectiveness of serious games?

SUGGESTED READINGS

Anderson, C. A. & Bushman, B. J. (2002). Human aggression. *Annual Review of Psychology*, 53, 27–51.
Connolly, T. M., Boyle, E. A., MacArthur, E., Hainey, T. & Boyle, J. M. (2012). A systematic literature review of empirical evidence on computer games and serious games. *Computers & Education*, 59(2), 661–686.

Ferguson, C. J. (2010). Blazing angels or resident evil? Can violent video games be a force for good? *Review of General Psychology, 14*(2), 68–81.

Griffiths, M. (2003). Internet gambling: Issues, concerns, and recommendations. *CyberPsychology & Behavior, 6*(6), 557–568.

Potenza, M. N., Wareham, J. D., Steinberg, M. A., Rugle, L., Cavallo, A., Krishnan-Sarin, S. & Desai, R. A. (2011). Correlates of at-risk/problem Internet gambling in adolescents. *Journal of the American Academy of Child & Adolescent Psychiatry, 50*(2), 150–159.

Starcevic, V. (2013). Is Internet addiction a useful concept? *Australian & New Zealand Journal of Psychiatry, 47*(1), 16–19.

Young, G. & Whitty, M. T. (2012). *Transcending taboos: A moral and psychological examination of cyberspace.* Hove, UK: Routledge.

11 Online Deception

As already demonstrated in this book, in some ways we behave differently online from how we behave in the physical world. In Chapter 2 we examined whether individuals might explore and experience different identities in cyberspace from their identities offline. In Chapter 3, Chapter 4 and Chapter 5 we learnt that the ways in which people relate, develop friendships and develop romantic relationships in cyberspace can be somewhat different from the ways in which we form relationships in the physical world. We often self-disclose more online than we would face to face, and some people develop 'hyperpersonal' relationships in cyberspace. Paradoxically, although we might sometimes open up more about ourselves online, we also hold back or censor information. Moreover, some researchers have found that people can, or at least attempt to, be more deceptive in cyberspace than they are offline. Whitty and Joinson (2009) have named this phenomenon the 'truth/lies paradox'. Whitty and Joinson (2009) wrote:

> In many ways the Internet is a very different medium from, for example, the telephone and [face to face]. What makes this space unique is how we communicate within it. … [O]ften our communication is 'hyperhonest' and paradoxically is often 'hyperdishonest'. These two contrasting features should be of concern for scholars, web designers and of course the users of the Internet. (pp. 6–7)

This chapter examines the literature on online deception and examines in what ways individuals might be more or less deceptive in cyberspace than they are in the physical world.

11.1 DEFINING DECEPTION

Buller and Burgoon (1996) have defined deception as 'a message knowingly transmitted by a sender to foster a false belief or conclusion by the received' (p. 205). Bok (1989) defined deception as follows: 'When we undertake to deceive others intentionally, we communicate messages meant to mislead them, meant to make them believe what we ourselves do not believe. We can do so through gesture, through disguise, by means of action or inaction, even through silence' (p. 13). She made a distinction

Cyberpsychology: The Study of Individuals, Society and Digital Technologies, First Edition.
Monica Therese Whitty and Garry Young.
© 2017 John Wiley & Sons, Ltd. Published 2017 by John Wiley & Sons, Ltd.

between deception and lies, arguing that a lie is a form of deception and is essentially 'any intentionally deceptive message which is *stated*. Such statements are most often made verbally or in writing, but can of course also be conveyed via smoke signals, Morse code, sign language, and the like' (p. 13).

Bok reminds us that deceit is not a trivial matter. Over the centuries, philosophers have debated whether lying is an immoral act and if so whether all lies are immoral or only some types of lies under certain conditions. Bok (1989) has written: 'Deceit and violence – these are the two forms of deliberate assault on human beings. But deceit controls more subtly, for it works on belief as well as action' (p. 18). Bok writes about individuals who have been deceived, stating:

> Those who learn that they have been lied to in an important matter – say, the identity of their parents, the affection of their spouse, or the integrity of their government – are resentful, disappointed, and suspicious. The feel wronged; they are wary of new overtures. And they look back on their past beliefs and actions in the new light of the discovered lies. (p. 20)

Bok has also pointed out that deception can be disruptive for a society. In her view:

> A society, then, whose members were unable to distinguish truthful messages from deceptive ones, would collapse. But even before such a general collapse, individual choice and survival would be imperilled. The search for food and shelter could depend on no expectations from others. A warning that a well was poisoned or a plea for help in an accident would come to be ignored unless independent confirmation could be found. (p. 19)

A thorough investigation of all the individual and social consequence of deceit is beyond the scope of this book. Nonetheless, previous writings do demonstrate that lying is a serious matter and, if deceit is more prevalent online then it is a behaviour that warrants psychologists' and social scientists' attention.

11.2 DECEPTION IN CYBERSPACE

The Internet has provided us with a new platform on which to deceive. Online, individuals can potentially deceive a greater number of people. Moreover, cyberspace offers novel opportunities for deception not possible in face-to-face settings (Walther, 1996, 2007). The main reason why researchers believe that deception might be more prevalent online is because online communications and representations of the self are not physically connected to a person. Digital deception has been defined as 'the intentional control of information in a technologically mediated message to create a false belief in the receiver of the message' (Hancock, 2007, p. 209). We might not need a separate definition of deception that takes place in cyberspace compared with other media; however, it might be useful given that researchers have found that in some ways it (at least feels) easier to get away with some types of lies and that we can deceive in ways we are not able to in the physical world.

Researchers have attempted to categorize the types of deception that take place online. Utz (2005) argued that there are three types of deception: category deception (gender-switching), attractiveness deception and identity concealment. Although these distinctions are important, perhaps Hancock's (2007) categorization is more useful. Hancock argued that there are two different types of digital deception: identity- and message-based deception. Identity deception is the creation of a false identity or affiliation. This kind of deception might be easier to perform as well as to get away with in cyberspace than it is in the physical world. Message-based deception is deception based within the content of a communication between two or more people. Scholarly work has focused on both these forms of deception.

11.2.1 Identity-based deception

Individuals might disguise a range of identity-based information about themselves – for example, age, gender, race, sexual preference, health and physical attractiveness. Cyberspace offers more opportunities to manage identities and anonymity (or at least visual anonymity) than the 'real' world, and it may foster identity-based deception.

These days, most spaces online are not exclusively text-based. Nonetheless, in spaces where users can select an avatar to represent themselves, they still have the opportunity and freedom to manipulate their identity (Galanxhi & Nah, 2007). Moreover, users might not feel the same way about deception using an avatar as they do about deception in which they do not use an avatar. For example, Galanxhi and Nah (2007) found that, in online text-only chat spaces, deceivers felt greater anxiety than nondeceivers. However, in an avatar-based environment there was no significant difference experienced by deceivers and truth tellers. These authors reasoned that:

> In the text-only medium, anonymity can help protect the identity of deceivers, while in the avatar-supported medium, anonymity can be further increased by 'wearing a mask' to confuse or distract the recipient about one's identity. Hence, the mask (i.e., avatar) can increase the deceiver's perceived distance from its communication partner, thus lowering the deceiver's state anxiety level. (p. 778)

Of course, there are many reasons why a person might engage in identity-based deception: some may be malicious but others might be to protect the person (e.g., those who believe they hold a stigmatized identity). Bowker and Tuffin (2003) note:

> Within computer-mediated environments, people with disabilities may have much to gain as physical barriers to participation are broken down. Moreover, the online medium's capacity to conceal physical difference brings forth the opportunity for people with disabilities to access a social space for experiencing alternate subjectivities, which operate outside the stigma often associated with disabled identities.

Notably, not all online spaces promote deception – and, as stressed throughout this book, cyberspace ought not to be understood as a homogenous space. A good example of this is illustrated in Guillory and Hancock's (2012) study, which examined the effect of LinkedIn on identity deception. These authors focused on LinkedIn because research suggests that it is common for individuals to lie on curricula vitae. George, Marett and Tilly (2004), for example, found that about 90% of their sample lied on job applications. One obvious compelling motivation for doing so is to appear competent to a potential employer, thereby increasing one's chances of obtaining employment. However, Guillory and Hancock surmised that individuals might be less likely to lie on LinkedIn (an SNS designed for registered members to share details about their employment history, education and personal profile in order to establish networks of people known to them professionally) given that this is a public profile – as opposed to a traditional resume, which is often confidential. Therefore, the risk of being caught out by a lie on LinkedIn is higher than on traditional curricula vitae.

In the study by Guillory and Hancock (2012), undergraduate students aged between 18 and 22 years were randomly assigned to one of three conditions: writing a traditional offline word document resume, writing an online LinkedIn profile that was private, or writing a LinkedIn profile that was public. They were then asked to create a resume for a consultant position with a good salary and international office locations. Participants were asked to tailor resumes using their own information with the aim of appearing to be the most qualified candidate, and were told that the best-filled-in resume would win US$100. They were next told that the true purpose of the study was to detect deception and were asked to spend 15 minutes revealing and describing their deceptions. These were coded into verifiable information (e.g., responsibilities, abilities, skills) and unverifiable information (e.g., interests, hobbies). As predicted, Guillory and Hancock found that more verifiable lies tended to be present in traditional and private LinkedIn resumes and that public LinkedIn resumes contained more unverifiable lies. While Guillory and Hancock's work yields some interesting results, there are some obvious limitations to this work. Using undergraduate students provides a sample of individuals with a short employment history to embellish. Moreover, given that the participants were enrolled at university and that the university was known to the researchers, it is unlikely that the participants would lie about their university course and experience. This form of deception is commonly reported by organizations and so it would be of interest to carry out a similar study with different samples to determine whether the same findings are obtained.

11.2.2 Munchausen by Internet

Munchausen by Internet is an interesting example of identity-based deception. A review of the literature by Pulman and Taylor (2012) discusses the notion that the Internet has increased the frequency of occurrence of Munchausen syndrome (which is a psychological condition where someone lies about being ill or induces symptoms of illness in themselves). Munchausen syndrome tends to be chronic, and those with this syndrome become habitual liars (Doherty & Sheehan, 2010). It was

Feldman (2000) who first coined the phrase 'Munchausen by Internet' to describe an individual seeking attention by playing out a series of dramatic near-chronic illnesses and recoveries on the Internet. Pulman and Taylor argue that Munchausen by Internet should be formally recognized by the American Psychiatric Association in the DSM-5.

One classic example reported by Van Gelder (1991) is the case of 'Alex' and 'Joan'. Alex, who in reality was a middle-aged American psychiatrist, joined a chat room using the screen name 'Shrink Inc.' Given his original handle was neutral, the group did not realize he was a male and many assumed, mistakenly, that Alex was a woman. Alex realized that by pretending to be a woman he was able to generate vulnerability and intimacy with the woman online – far more so than in his profession offline. He reported being excited by this new opportunity to help people, and created a female character with the handle 'Talkin Lady', who eventually told the group that her real name was Joan Sue Greene and that she was a neuropsychologist in her late twenties. Joan was said to have been in a car accident with her boyfriend, who had died, and Joan herself was paralyzed and disfigured and had lost her ability to speak. Face-to-face meetings were therefore physically and emotionally challenging. The persona of Joan went through a number of changes from a woman suffering from depression and thoughts of suicide to a confident woman with many friends. Simultaneously, Alex was able to meet and engage in offline affairs with some of the chat room members via an introduction from his online persona, Joan. Alex eventually tried to kill off Joan with a terminal illness. It was at this point that the members discovered the deception – when they rang the hospital to send flowers to discover there was no such patient at the hospital. When members found out the truth about Joan/Alex, perhaps unsurprisingly, there was considerable outrage in the community. This case study provides a good example of Munchausen by Internet as well as a host of other deceptions. It also gives us insights into the motivations for these behaviours, including the ability to play with identity; being able to play out a caring and emphatic role that was possibly unachievable as a male; the ability to garner sympathy and intimacy from group members; and being able to achieve physical intimacy with group members offline.

Pulman and Taylor (2012) believe that social psychology offers a number of theories that can explain why Munchausen by Internet occurs. Some of these theories have been summarized earlier in this book. The 'disinhibition effect' (see Chapter 3), for example, suggests that Munchausen by Internet is more likely to occur online given that many spaces are asynchronous, thus providing an opportunity for individuals to be creative with their identity presentation, and anonymity can reduce end users' concern for other people's opinions. Other researchers argue that some Munchausen by Internet sufferers might be motivated by the simple pleasure they receive from deceiving others online. Whether Munchausen by Internet is formally recognized by DSM-5 might be a concern to some practitioners – but perhaps of greater interest is understanding in more detail the root cause.

11.2.3 *Message-based deception*

Message-based deception occurs when the identity of the communicants is known and the deception occurs within the content of the communication. This type of deception occurs more frequently than identity-based deception in face-to-face or mediated interactions. Examples might include blaming congested traffic for lateness when really you delayed your travel plans, or being ill when really you prefer not to take part in an event. As with identity-based deception, message-based deception does not always lead to negative outcomes. DePaulo, Wetzel, Sternglanz and Wilson (2003) argue that in many cases deception can lead to improved social cohesion and can protect privacy.

With regard to identity- and message-based deception, deceivers can, of course, simultaneously use both forms. Mass-marketing fraud is a good example of the use of both forms – where the deceiver takes on a different persona from their own and also uses message-based deception (e.g., geographic location, the reasons why they are requesting money). Mass-marketing fraud and other cybercrimes will be considered in Chapter 12 and Chapter 13, respectively.

11.3 DO WE LIE MORE ONLINE?

Do people actually lie more on the Internet? Caspi and Gorsky (2005) found that 73% of individuals believe that deception is widespread online, and some research supports this view. Although there might be more opportunity to lie online, and there is a general perception that people do lie more in cyberspace, it is important to undertake research to determine whether this really is the case. Early research suggested that individuals did lie on the Internet about specific aspects of themselves. Cornwell and Lundgren (2001), for example, found that participants were more likely to lie about their age and physical attributes to their online romantic partners than in face-to-face relationships. Whitty and Gavin (2001) found similar results, with participants believing that it was socially acceptable to lie in order to create opportunities for others to communicate with them online. They understood this type of lying to be 'white lies' that were not meant to be harmful or malicious. Moreover, the participants believed this type of deception was common online.

In more recent research, Naquin, Kutzberg and Belkin (2010) found that participants are more willing to lie when communicating via email than via pen and paper and felt more justified in doing so. Zimbler and Feldman (2011) examined deception in 15-minute conversations via email, instant messenger and face to face and found deception to be more evident in digital media compared to face to face. Although Naquin et al. and Zimbler and Feldman's research provides us with some interesting findings, these studies are nonetheless limited, given that they were conducted in the lab rather than in real life. In real life, individuals have a choice of media and communicate both with people known to them and with strangers.

More systematic research has examined the likelihood that someone might tell a lie over a range of media, including face to face and over the telephone. Such research has also drawn distinctions between the various types of media available online. For example, a text-only space might provide more opportunities for deception compared with a space where individuals are required to upload photographs and videos of themselves. This research is detailed below.

> **SUGGESTED ACTIVITY**
>
> Consider the various lies you have told over the past week – white and serious lies. Where did you say these lies and why did you choose that medium?

11.3.1 Theories to predict deception

There have been a number of theories developed to predict in which types of media individuals are more likely to lie. Supporters of the 'social distance theory' argue that, because lying makes individuals feel uncomfortable, they will choose leaner or less rich media in order to maintain social distance between themselves and the person they are lying to; that is, they will avoid media that contain cues that people believe will give away deceit (e.g., voice, body and language). Moreover, in less rich media, the deceiver has more control over the interaction – any unexpected questions can be thought about rather than being responded to immediately. If the social distance theory were supported by empirical research, we would find that people lie most in email, followed by instant messaging, followed by phone and then face to face. In contrast, the 'media richness theory' explains that, because lying is highly equivocal, individuals elect to lie more in rich media, which includes multiple cue systems, immediate feedback, natural language and message personalization. Hence, this theory predicts that individuals will lie more in face-to-face situations, followed by phone, instant messaging and then email.

Hancock (2007; Hancock, Curry, Goorha & Woodworth, 2005; Hancock, Thom-Santelli & Ritchie, 2004) and his colleagues have proposed an alternative theory, which they refer to as the 'feature-based model'. They devised this theory after testing for the two theories above and finding that they were not supported by their research. In their original study, they examined the lies of 28 students using a diary study that ran for seven days, in which the participants recorded all instances of lies (Hancock et al., 2004). The participants engaged in around six interactions a day and lied on average 1.6 times a day (26% of all social interactions included a lie). The most lies occurred during face-to-face interaction (n = 202, 1.03 per day), followed by telephone (n = 66, 0.35 per day), instant messaging (n = 27, 0.18 per day) and email (n = 9, 0.06 per day). The largest proportion of lies within a medium occurred on the telephone; the smallest proportion occurred via email. Interestingly, the more experience people had with email, the more lies they were likely to tell using that media (a relationship that was not found for instant messaging).

To explain their findings, Hancock et al. (2004) offered the feature-based theory (set out in Table 11.1 below). This theory sets out three dimensions that need to be considered when we examine deception, including whether the medium is synchronous, whether it is recordless and whether it is distributed (i.e., not co-present). The feature-based theory proposes that, the more synchronous and distributed but the less recordable a medium is, the more frequently lying should occur. One lies more in

Table 11.1 *The feature-based model: ranking predictions of likelihood of lying (adapted from Hancock et al., 2004)*

	Face to face	Phone	Instant messaging	Email	SNS	SMS
Media features						
Synchronous	x	x	x			
Recordless	x	x				
Distributed		x	x	x	x	x
Lying predictions						
Feature based	2	1	2	3	3	3

synchronous interactions, because the majority of lying is spontaneous and hence synchronous communication should present more opportunities to lie. In recorded communication, one is aware that the conversation is potentially kept or stored (e.g., in a saved email) and can be referred to in future conversations; hence, one is less likely to lie if one is aware that there is proof of the lie, which can be referred to later. In media where participants are not distributed, deception should be constrained to some degree as some lies can be immediately obvious (e.g., it could be difficult on a nondistributed medium to lie that one is writing a report when really one is playing a computer game).

Research since Hancock et al.'s (2004) study has found that the feature-based theory does not necessarily hold when considering the target of the lie and the type of lie being told. Whitty and Carville (2008), for example, asked 150 participants to rate on a Likert scale how likely they were to tell different types of lies across different media. They found that individuals were overall more likely to tell self-serving lies to people not well known to them. An example of a self-serving lie identified in the study is described as follows:

> You are having a [face-to-face] conversation with someone that you are 'close to' when they invite you to an event. You can think of something else you would rather spend your time doing so you tell them that you can't make it to the event, even though you can. (p. 1025)

These researchers argue that it is more risky and difficult to get away with telling a self-serving lie to individuals the liar feels close to – given that people close to us have more information about our day-to-day lives. For self-serving lies, individuals stated they were more likely to tell a lie in email, followed by phone and lastly face to face. This was the case regardless of whether the target was someone close or someone not well known to the liar. Such a finding supports the social distance theory. Whitty and Carville (2008) explain that self-serving lies are more likely to make the liar feel uncomfortable and apprehensive and so email is the ideal place to tell such as lie. When considering other-oriented lies, participants in this study were more likely to believe that they would tell these lies to individuals they felt close to. An example of an other-oriented lie was:

> You receive an email from a person you don't know well. Within the email they ask you if you think they look attractive. You don't think that they are attractive but you don't want to hurt their feelings so you email them back and tell them that they are attractive. (p. 1025)

Other-oriented lies are typically told to protect the feelings of the target of the lie. Given this, Whitty and Carville argue, one might feel more compelled to lie to a person close to oneself (than to someone not close) to protect their feelings rather than saying the truth, which could possibly cause them upset or distress. Participants in this study believed the type of medium would not influence the likelihood of them telling an other-oriented lie to someone close to them. Perhaps this is because the purpose of this type of lie is to maintain the integrity of the target, and one ought to be motivated to do this for someone one cares about in any type of medium. Such lies are not told to hurt people but are intended to make others feel better about themselves. The more one cares for another, surely the more motivated one is to utter such 'white lies'. In contrast, when it came to telling an other-oriented lie to individuals not well known to them, the participants claimed they would be less likely to tell the lie in email and most likely to tell the lie face to face. Again, this did not support the feature-based theory but instead supported the social distance theory. Whitty and Carville (2008) state:

> It is argued that people are more likely to talk aggressively in CMC ... than face-to-face because online there is a lack of social presence and less contextual cues. This is perhaps why this current study found that individuals were more likely to say a hurtful truth than an other-oriented lie to individuals not well-known to them in email. The social distance, in this particular case, motivates the person to tell unpleasant truths. (p. 1029)

One of the major criticisms directed at the above study is that it is based on hypothetical scenarios. It is difficult to ascertain from such a study whether people would lie in reality, and so we need to treat the results with caution. In order to feel confident that the results can be replicated, they need to be tested in the real world – in a diary study, perhaps, akin to Hancock and his colleagues' work.

Whitty et al. (2012) sought to replicate Hancock and colleagues' earlier work by drawing from a larger sample, examining a greater number of types of media and by distinguishing between spontaneous and planned lies. In their study, 76 individuals participated in a diary study and focused on six modes of communication: face-to-face, telephone, SNSs, instant messaging, email and text messaging (SMS). Based on Hancock and colleagues' findings, they hypothesized that more lies would be told via the telephone than face to face and via instant messaging, followed by SNS, email and SMS (see Table 11.1). Their hypothesis was only partially supported: participants were more likely to lie on the telephone, followed by face-to-face, with no significant differences found between face-to-face and instant messaging, as predicted. However, the data did not support the hypothesis that participants would lie more on instant messaging than on the other digital media, except with SMS, where, as predicted, participants lied more on instant messaging than SMS. This might be explained as follows: media features are not the only variable we need to consider when predicting deception, and/or other features might need to be considered within the model. The researchers add a further explanation: that instant messaging should perhaps be considered as 'near synchronous' rather than synchronous.

11.4 DETECTING DECEPTION

People are typically poor at detecting lies – even those trained to detect lies, such as police officers (Vrij, 2008). Therefore, it should come as no surprise that psychologists have been interested in detecting deception since long before there was an Internet. It is, of course, interesting to detect deception in people's everyday lives, but it is also useful to help discern whether a suspect is guilty or innocent. Cognitive psychologists have considered how to improve detection in verbal accounts by increasing the cognitive load in narrating. Vrij et al. (2008), for example, found that detection of deception was improved when truth tellers and liars were asked to report their stories in reverse order.

Lies told by serious offenders might be even harder to detect given that these people are likely to have developed more accomplished strategies to deceive. In fact, research has found that offenders outperform nonoffenders in detecting lies. Moreover, the same researchers found that 94% of nonoffenders believed that lying required more mental effort than telling the truth, while only 60% of criminal offenders reported this opinion (Hartwig, Granhag, Stromwall & Anderson, 2004). Given the difficulties in detecting when a potential offender might be deceiving, there has been much research on how to improve interviewer techniques in order to catch out a liar (e.g., Dando, Bull, Ormerod & Sandham, 2015). One such strategy is to increase the cognitive load when questioning someone to determine whether they are a deceiver. Researchers in the UK have developed a security screening method that they refer to as 'controlled cognitive engagement' (CCE). This is a method security agents can apply to control an interview so that a passenger provides information that can be tested for veracity (Dando, 2014; Ormerod & Dando, 2015). According to Ormerod and Dando (2015), CCE 'embodies each of the six techniques shown in laboratory studies to improve deception detection rates: use of evidence; tests of expected knowledge; effective questioning styles; observation of verbal manoeuvring; asymmetric cognitive loading; and changes in verbal behaviour' (p. 78). This type of interviewing tests for expected knowledge, so that truth tellers experience a friendly, informal conversation while deceivers have their cognitive load increased given they have to ensure they are consistent and factual with their responses. The researchers have found this method to be highly successful in experimental studies testing for deception in aviation security screening.

In nonoffender populations, detecting deception is said to be slightly easier, although still challenging. Deceivers tend to exhibit overcontrolled behaviour, using fewer 'illustrators', such as body movements and gestures, to consciously covey information (Granhag & Strömwall, 2002). Nonoffender liars often consciously reduce their rate of speech (Vrij, 2008). Moreover, because deception might elicit feelings of guilt and fear, when individuals lie, they often show an increase in signs of stress cues, such as nervous smiles, speech hesitations and disturbances, and an increase in fidgeting (DePaulo et al., 2003; Vrij, Edwards & Bull, 2001). Although nonverbal cues might be useful in detecting deception, the problem is that in real life people are not always recorded when they deceive. We have already learnt in this chapter that people often avoid recordable forms of media when they lie. Nonetheless, some lies are told on recordable media, and, when people attempt to deceive using these media, there is a record that could be examined to help detect any potential deception.

The Internet has, therefore, opened up new opportunities to detect deception – especially in criminal cases, where one can potentially collect recorded material for the purposes of collating forensic evidence from around the time when a crime was believed to have taken place. Computer scientists and behavioural scientists have combined knowledge and skills in innovative research to detect deception in online environments. Research by Rashid et al. (2013) can detect criminals who hide behind multiple identities (or so-called digital personas). Their work examines word frequencies as well as key grammatical categories and semantic fields to establish a 'stylistic language fingerprint' for an author. Applying their methods, these researchers are able to establish, with a large amount of confidence, the age and gender of the 'real' person behind the digital persona, which would help to elucidate whether someone is creating an online person that varies substantially from whom they really are. This work can be applied to help in the online detection of criminals, such as child sex offenders, romance scam criminals and those involved in the radicalization of youth.

11.5 CONCLUSIONS

The Internet has opened up new opportunities to lie as well as increased the likelihood of the occurrence of identity–message deception (e.g., changing one's age, gender or physical description). Counterintuitively, however, researchers have found that people are more likely to lie on the telephone than via other media (e.g., face to face, email). The feature-based model was developed to account for the reasons why individuals might lie more on the telephone but, as is pointed out in this chapter, there is room to develop this model, considering the complexity of lies (the type of lie, the person being lied to, etc.).

As discussed in this chapter, not all people who tell lies do so with the intention to cause harm. Nonetheless, there are many reasons why researchers as well as others (e.g., law enforcement, security, industry) might want to learn where people are more likely to lie and how to detect deception. Although the Internet has provided new opportunities to lie, it has, in turn, also opened up new opportunities to detect deception. This chapter elucidates the benefits of working in interdisciplinary research teams to develop more effective methods in the detection of deception. Moreover, when considering detecting deception, researchers point out that methods need to make a distinction between noncrinimals and individuals who engage in criminal activities and have more reasons to lie and more practice at deception. There are specific types of deception that criminals engage in that academics and nonacademics have been especially interested in detecting. We examine some of these in Chapter 12, which examines online scams, phishing and illegal downloads.

DISCUSSION QUESTIONS

1. Should lying in all circumstances be considered as immoral? If not, when is it okay to lie and why?
2. Where do you think you might be more likely to get away with a lie? Why do you think that is? Is your line of thinking supported by any of the theoretical models on deception?
3. Are you more likely to lie to people closer to you or to strangers? Do you use different media to lie to those close to you versus strangers? Why do you think that might be?
4. Consider Hancock's feature-based model. Do you think there are other features that could be considered in this model to predict where people are more likely to deceive?
5. In addition to what has been summarized in this chapter, what other methods might be employed using digital media to detect deception? How would you go about testing the effectiveness of the methods you have proposed?

SUGGESTED READINGS

Galanxhi, H. & Nah, F. F.-H. (2007). Deception in cyberspace: A comparison of text-only vs. avatar-supported medium. *International Journal of Human–Computer Studies, 65*(9), 770–783.

Guillory, J. & Hancock, J. T. (2012). The effect of LinkedIn on deception in resumes. *Cyberpsychology, Behaviour, and Social Networking, 15*(3), 135–140.

Hancock, J. T., Thom-Santelli, J. & Ritchie, T. (2004). Deception and design: The impact of communication technologies on lying behavior. In *Proceedings of the SIGCHI Conference on Human Factors in Computing Systems* (pp. 129–134). New York, NY: Association for Computing Machinery.

Ormerod, T. C. & Dando, C. J. (2015). Finding a needle in a haystack: Veracity testing outperforms behaviour observation for aviation security screening. *Journal of Experimental Psychology: General, 144,* 76–84.

Rashid, A., Baron, A., Rayson, P., May-Chahal, C., Greenwood, P. & Walkerdine, J. (2013). Who am I? Analysing Digital personas in cybercrime investigations. *Computer, 46*(4), 54–61.

Vrij, A. (2008). *Detecting lies and deceit: Pitfalls and opportunities* (2nd ed.). Chichester, UK: John Wiley & Sons.

12 Online Crimes: Scams, Fraud and Illegal Downloads

I am writing you this mail from my father's home at … London believing that you will be of tremendous help in my effort to save the last of my family legacy. I choose to reach you through this medium because it is the fastest and most reliable way of communication, as I wish to solicit for your unflinching support and cooperation.

My name is Mr. West Alamieyeseigha, the heir to the Alamieyeseigha's family. My family's ordeal started sometime last year when my father, then the Governor of Bayelsa state in Southern Nigeria was at loggerhead with the Federal Government following his campaign against the insensitivity of the government to the plight of the Niger delta region, the region that produces the country crude oil – the major foreign exchange earner of my country. Shortly before his arrest in London UK, my father had series of meeting with the federal authorities part of which was aimed at getting him drop his campaign for true federalism and resource control but he turned down all the juicy promises that was offered him hence the plan to get him set up. He was arrested and detained in London last year. Somewhere along the line, he escaped to his State Bayelsa but not without the collaboration of the UK authorities who claimed he jumped bail. My ill mother of 50, Mrs. Margaret Alamieyeseigha was also humiliated in London and charged for money laundry offences.

I am certain you know much about this case however, you can make further enquiries. However, my reason for contacting you is to solicit your support and collaboration in securing my family legacy. I am contacting you on the instructions of my mother who asked me to seek for a reliable foreigner who will help us invest some of the undetected fund belonging to my father kept in private safes worth over $20,000,000.00. I shall provide you with details of how to access the money if you provide me with investment information in your country. For this Information and your collaboration, 30% of the entire money will be your reward for your assistance.

I shall detail you further when you indicate interest to help us. Meanwhile you may reach me on …

(Example of a Nigerian email scam; Whitty & Joinson, 2009, p. 57–58)

In Chapter 11 we looked at online deception, focusing predominantly on everyday deception while pointing out the importance of distinguishing between lies told in everyday conversation and those told for the purpose of engaging in criminal

---

Cyberpsychology: The Study of Individuals, Society and Digital Technologies, First Edition.
Monica Therese Whitty and Garry Young.
© 2017 John Wiley & Sons, Ltd. Published 2017 by John Wiley & Sons, Ltd.

activities. This chapter focuses on deception that criminals engage in online as well as the reasons why some people are tricked by this deception. In particular, we will focus on phishing, MMF and illegal downloads of online material, such as music and videos.

12.1 PHISHING

Phishing is the use of social engineering and technical subterfuge to trick individuals into giving up personal and financial information in order to fraudulently access a person's real account. This usually begins with an email message purportedly from a well-known and trustworthy organization (e.g., PayPal, eBay, a well-known bank) that requests the user to validate their information by logging on to the organization's website. However, the link provided does not lead to the official website – instead it directs the user to a mock-up. Similar messages can also appear on social media, such as Facebook. Technical subterfuge schemes plant crimeware onto users' computers to steal credentials from the user's system, by intercepting the user's online account usernames and passwords or by corrupting local navigational infrastructures to misdirect consumers to counterfeit websites (Anti-Phishing Working Group, 2014). Given that these attacks are sent out en masse, the term 'phishing' has been employed to describe this type of attack, as it is like a fishing expedition where the criminal puts a lure out hoping to fool at least a few of the prey that encounter the bait. An example of what a phishing email might look like can be seen in Figure 12.1. As the illustration shows, if the user examines the weblink, they will realize that the real website address reads nothing like a Nationwide authentic website.

The Anti-Phishing Working Group identified 17,320 unique phishing websites in December 2014. It also identified that 300 brands were targeted by phishing campaigns in December 2014. Examining a breakdown of the most-targeted industry sectors in December 2014, it found that retail services were the highest targeted industry (29.4%) followed by payment services (25.1%) and financial services (20.8%). Due to improved detection techniques, about half of phishing sites are shut down within a day (Rao, 2015). Nonetheless, the numbers that are in existence on a daily basis illustrate that these sites are still a problem that requires improved methods to detect and prevent. Moreover, their existence demonstrates that criminals, at least, perceive them as a successful method of defrauding victims.

In addition to phishing, readers might be aware of 'spear phishing', which is similar to phishing but, instead of a random hack, there is a specific target. As with phishing, spear phishing messages appear to come from a trusted source. However, unlike phishing, spear phishing attacks use specific knowledge about individuals and organizations. Hong (2012) gives the example of an attack on military personnel, which might contain an invitation to a general's retirement party, asking the recipient to click on a link to confirm that they can attend. Therefore, individuals might be more likely to respond to a spear phishing attack compared with an ordinary phishing attack, given that it appears to come from a known source.

> **Nationwide** proud to be different
>
> **Dear Customer,**
>
> Nationwide's Internet Banking, is here by announcing the New Security Upgrade. We've upgraded our new SSL servers to serve our customers for a better and secure banking service, against any fraudulent activities. Due to this recent upgrade, you are requested to update your account information by following the reference below.
>
> http://www.nationwide.co.uk/update.asp?ID=3b89db2a6001ec93328d21e59a011b0a 25a
>
> [http://www.drinkrezepte.de/shakes/index.html]
>
> **Regards**
> Rafiq Miah
> Customer Advisor
> Nationwide Direct
>
> Nationwide Building Society

Figure 12.1 *Example of a phishing email*

12.2 VISHING

Individuals continue to be confronted by new scams, and criminals persist in finding new ways to use media to convince potential victims that they are genuine. Vishing, for instance, is the use of the telephone by criminals in an attempt to scam users into disclosing private information that will be used in identity theft. The scammer typically pretends to be a legitimate business (e.g., a bank) and tricks the victim into believing that they are requesting personal information for legitimate reasons. In other versions, the criminal asks the victim to enter personal details into a website or convinces the victim to transfer their money into another account, persuading them that it is to protect their finances when, in reality, these are the accounts of money mules.

12.2.1 Number of victims

Despite the number of awareness campaigns and training workshops that organizations make available to end users, many individuals fall victim to phishing attacks. In a report conducted in 2015, Get Cyber Safe, which is sponsored by the Canadian government, estimates that about 10% of Canadians who click on a phishing link fall for the scam, which is about 800,000 individuals (Get Cyber Safe, 2015). A report compiled by Verizon in the UK claims that in 2014 about 25% of employees were likely to open a phishing email (BBC News, 2015).

> **SUGGESTED ACTIVITY**
>
> Read through some of the phishing emails you have received. What makes them appear authentic? What features helped you to detect that they were phishing emails?

12.3 WHY ARE PEOPLE TRICKED BY PHISHING?

Some researchers have examined the reasons why victims believe phishing emails are genuine. In research conducted by Wang, Herath, Chen, Vishwanath and Rao (2012), participants were presented with an image of a 'real' phishing email with the subject title 'UPGRADE YOUR EMAIL ACCOUNT NOW'. The email asked recipients for their username, their password, their date of birth, a security question and an answer. Recipients were also told that they would lose their email accounts if they did not send the requested information within seven days. Participants were not informed that this was a phishing email but were asked how likely they were to respond to the email and were asked a series of questions devised to help the researchers develop a theoretical model to predict which users are more likely to respond to phishing emails. They found that attention to visceral triggers, such as stressing the urgency to respond, increased the likelihood of responses, while attention to phishing deception indicators (such as grammar errors and the sender's address) decreased the likelihood of responses. Interestingly, these researchers found that the cognitive effort expended in processing the phishing email was not significantly related to the likelihood of responding to the email.

Alsharnouby, Alaca and Chiasson (2015) carried out experimental research asking participants to consider a series of websites (14 phishing and 11 genuine) to help understand why users are tricked by phishing scams. Participants were required to view each of the websites and were asked to determine whether each website was legitimate or fraudulent, their level of certainty, and how they arrived at their decision. In addition, participants were required to wear an eye-tracker device, which recorded their eye gaze data while they viewed the websites. These researchers found that the longer the participants spent looking at the security indicators in the browser Chrome, the more likely they were to notice the security indicators – although they note that this was not a strong effect.

In some noteworthy research carried out by Vishwanath (2015a), the relationships between Facebook use and vulnerability to phishing attacks was examined. Vishwanath points out that attempted phishing attacks that take place via social media, such as Facebook, are much more likely to be successful compared with email phishing attacks. He also argues that the reason for this success rate is that social media's interfaces, functionalities and user protections are constantly changing, making it difficult for users to achieve a degree of mastery over the use of the platform. Phishing attacks via social media take place in two stages. The first stage requires the user to accept a friend request that, when accepted, has the potential to provide the criminal with a wealth of data about the user. In the second stage of the attack, the criminal can use the messaging aspect of social media (such as Facebook's Messenger) to request information directly from the user. Vishwanath gives the example that the knowledge that someone is a dog lover could be used to then request a donation to a dog charity via Messenger, when in reality the victim is clicking on a link with hidden scripts and viruses that could infect the device used to access the message. The message from this study was that habitual Facebook use (including frequency of using Facebook and maintaining a large social network) and being unable to regulate these behaviours were the biggest predictors of individual victimization in social media attacks.

Although Vishwanath (2015b) acknowledges that social media phishing is more likely to be successful at scamming victims than email phishing, he has nonetheless been interested in learning more about the sort of person who tends to be susceptible to email phishing attacks. In this particular study (Vishwanath, 2015a), he sent a sample of students (200 out of 400, with 192 valid responses) enrolled in an undergraduate degree a phishing email, which contained a warning about email account closure and a tight deadline to click on a hyperlink to prevent the closure of the email account. The hyperlink was hidden using a shortened URL. Those who had not clicked on the link were sent a reminder a week later. Overall, 83% of the participants (n = 159) clicked on the hyperlink. Vishwanath argued that the joint influence of email habit strength (i.e., whether individuals automatically respond to receiving an email) and of cognitive processing predict susceptibility to phishing attacks. He also hypothesized that the personality traits of conscientiousness and neuroticism influence email habits. As predicted, it was found that those who scored high on conscientiousness and high on neuroticism were more likely to report safe email habits. Vishwanath found that individuals who checked their emails more habitually had increased chances of victimization. He also found that heuristic processing, also referred to as 'cognitive shortcuts', significantly increased the chances of victimization (e.g., the email might appear to come from a credible source, such as the student's university) and that systematic processing (a detailed assessment of the content of the communication) significantly decreased the chances of victimization. Email habits, however, were found to be the strongest predictors of victimization, suggesting that prevention needs to focus on changing habits in order to reduce susceptibility.

SUGGESTED ACTIVITY

Consider your own email habits. Do you think they need to change in light of the research discussed here? Consider how you might devise a training package to change email habits and how this might be implemented.

12.4 IMPROVING DETECTION

Understandably, detection software as well as training programmes to help the user recognize phishing emails have been developed to help reduce the number of people who fall victim to phishing emails, as well as to help protect organizations from the harm caused by employees who click on such emails. Jansson and von Solms (2013), for instance, have provided training to individuals who in the past responded to a solicited phishing email to determine whether their training programme was effective. After participants clicked on a link from a phishing email, their computers showed a red warning screen, alerting them to their 'insecure' behaviour, together with an email message making them aware of their 'insecure' behaviour. In addition, the email provided a hyperlink inviting them to participate in an online training programme. After engaging with the programme, the participant's likelihood of being attacked again was evaluated via a short set of questions asking about their understanding of security. The researchers argue that their findings show that being exposed to simulating phishing attacks, together with embedded training, can increase resilience in responding to phishing attacks; notably, however, this study did not employ randomized control groups.

In an earlier study, Davinson and Sillence (2010) developed a training programme that informed users about the common types of phishing attacks and how to identify them. In this study, participants were randomly assigned to one of four conditions: group 1 were told they were at low risk and did not complete training; group 2 were told they were at low risk and received training; group 3 were told they were at high risk and received no training; and group 4 were told they were at high risk and received training. The training programme involved an interactive game that trained the user to defend themselves against phishing attacks. They found that an apparently tailored risk message increased participants' intentions to act in a secure manner regardless of whether they were told they were at high or low risk. Raising awareness of risk, however, did not appear to increase secure behaviour. In addition, the researchers found that the training programme did not influence secure behaviour seven days after the training. The research stresses the importance of evaluating training programmes and highlights the need to develop more effective training programmes.

12.5 MASS-MARKETING FRAUD

Fraud can be broadly defined as trickery used to gain a dishonest advantage, which is often financial, over another person or organization. Mass-marketing fraud is a type of fraud that exploits mass communication techniques (e.g., email, instant messaging, bulk mailing, SNSs) to con people out of money. It is believed that the money criminals acquire from this crime is often used for more sinister crimes (e.g., drug trafficking, terrorism).

This chapter began by presenting an example of a Nigerian email scam, a MMF presumably known by most readers. This scam is also known as the 'advance fee fraud' or the '419 scam' (so named because of the section number of Nigerian criminal law that applies to it) and actually began as a postal mail scam. In most cases, the mail appears to be sent from an African country and/or an individual who is typically Nigerian, although others are sent from other African countries and in recent years from Asia and Eastern European countries. Advance fee frauds often refer to a large amount of funds that are trapped or frozen for a variety of reasons (e.g., unclaimed estate, corrupt executive, dying samaritan). In each case the sender offers the recipient rich rewards for simply helping government officials or family members out of an embarrassing or legal problem. Those who respond to such emails (and surprisingly there have been a number of people conned) then gradually experience problems with the financial transaction. Initially, the paperwork is said to be delayed, then excuses are given for why more money is needed – for example, to bribe officials. The money asked seems insignificant in light of the huge windfall the recipient will ultimately gain. Delays continue and more financial support is asked of the recipient. It becomes more difficult for them to refuse, given that they have already invested a significant amount of their own money into the deal. The scam only ends when the victim has learnt and accepted that they have been conned, and that it is highly unlikely that they will ever see their money again or that the criminal will be caught and arrested.

The Internet has opened up the floodgates to MMF given that criminals can use it to target many more potential victims with very marginal effort, to trick them into making electronic and even crypto-currency transfers on the basis of mistaken charity, investment or love. This crime can also have an impact on the digital economy, as citizens start to mistrust particular online sites that criminals use to target individuals. Banks and money transfer organizations have the problem of dealing with fraudulent transactions affecting not only their own trade but also the lives of their customers, to some extent irrespective of whether the customers were actually negligent or complicit.

Some MMFs are low-value, one-off scams of a large number of victims, while others involve developing a relationship (e.g., romantic, business, friendship) where money is defrauded over time, again with multiple simultaneous or sequential victims. Examples of MMF include:

- *Boiler room scam/investment scam*: This scam, like the classic 419 scam, cons victims into believing they will make large sums of money, very quickly. The criminal contacts the victim, offering worthless, overpriced or non-existent shares. The motivation for the victim is to make a large profit.
- *Online dating romance scam*: In this crime, criminals pretend to initiate a romantic relationship through online dating sites and then defraud their victims, often of large sums of money. The motivation of this scam for victims is to develop a long-term committed relationship. Since about June 2012, the scam has moved on to include another variation, whereby victims who meet the criminal on an adult dating website (set up to cheat on their partner) are videoed performing sexual acts and later blackmailed (a threat is made to send the video to loved ones and places of work).

- *Charity scam*: The charity scam involves a criminal scamming money for what appears to be a genuine charity. Scammers either pose as agents of legitimate, well-known charities or create their own charity name. Criminals set up false websites to look similar to those operated by real charities. These scams do not necessarily involve one-off payments and can con victims over a long period of time. The motivation of this scam for victims is to give money to others, rather than a hope to gain profits for themselves.
- *Emergency scam*: In this scam, real details about a person have been garnered from the Internet (e.g., through Facebook) and one or more of the people on an individual's contact list is contacted to say that the individual is in trouble and needs money immediately (e.g., has been in a car accident or is in trouble in a foreign country). Unlike the boiler room and the romance scams, this scam works rapidly. The motivation is to help a loved one in need.
- *Inheritance scam*: In this scam, a criminal posing as a lawyer tells victims that a rich person who shares the victim's family name or a name very similar has died and that, unless the lawyer can identify any of the person's relatives, the money will go to the government. The lawyer imposter suggests that, given the victim shares a similar name, the lawyer could pay the money to the victim and split the money, rather than handing it over to the government. Like other advance fee frauds, victims are asked to pay fees, such as taxes and legal fees, in order to release the funds. This can be a difficult scam to detect because legitimate companies do exist that make a living from tracking down heirs. Some victims of this crime may believe that they are not entirely acting within the law.

Reports suggest that significant proportions of individuals have been affected by MMF – either as victims themselves or as the loved one of a victim. The National Fraud Authority (2012) in the UK has estimated that fraud costs in the UK equate to over £78 billion a year, with £3.5 billion lost to MMF alone in 2011. The National Fraud Authority conducted a nationally representative study of more than 4,000 UK adults and found that, in 2011, 1 million UK adults (just under 2%) sent money in reply to unsolicited communications, with just under half of them being defrauded as a result. They also found that three quarters of UK adults (37 million people) received unsolicited communications in 2011 (the majority by email). Similarly, in a representative sample of 2,000 UK adults, Whitty (2013a) found that in 2012 approximately 800,000 adults were defrauded by MMF in the UK. In 2010, the UK Office of Fair Trading reported that 'just under half of UK adults are targeted by scams, and eight per cent will be a victim at least once in their lifetime' (p. 1). Whitty and Buchanan (2012) found from a representative UK sample that at least 230,000 individuals had been scammed by the online dating romance scam. As these statistics indicate, the financial costs of MMF are serious. The financial costs are not just to victims, their family and friends but also include the costs to law enforcement as well as those to social and health support services.

Mass-marketing frauds are believed to be underreported, due to the embarrassment and shame experienced by victims, the lack of hope that criminals will be caught and the fear that law enforcement will not treat the crime with the seriousness it warrants. Reporting bodies in the UK, such as Action Fraud, estimate that less than 10% of victims actually report this type of crime. In the US, according to the Internet Crime Complaint Center (IC3) in 2014, 123,684 victims reported to that body financial losses as a result of Internet crimes, many of which were MMFs. It is estimated that only 10% of victims report the crime to IC3. In Australia, just over AUS$94 million was reported lost by victims of MMF in 2012 (Australian Competition & Consumer Commission, 2012).

Victims of MMF suffer both financial loses and psychological impacts, with psychological effects sometimes outweighing the financial impact, even when large sums of money are lost (Button, Lewis & Tapley, 2014; Lea, Fischer & Evans, 2009a; Levi & Burrows, 2008; Whitty, 2015; Whitty & Buchanan, 2016). Psychological harm can include shame, guilt, embarrassment, depression, feeling suicidal, grief, anxiety and loss of trust. Moreover, victims often lack the support offered to victims of other types of crime (e.g., family, friends) due to a lack of understanding of the crime and because victims are often blamed for their situation. Some victims have been known to move on to commit criminal acts, such as working as 'money mules' for fraudsters, sometimes unwittingly and sometimes to recoup their losses.

Catching and prosecuting MMF criminals is a difficult task. This is the case for three main reasons: (1) the criminals often live in a different country from the victims, (2) the methods the criminals use make them difficult to trace, and (3) prosecution is very time consuming, owing to the large amounts of online data that need to be analysed to establish evidence against the criminals and gain intelligence about their whereabouts and operating tactics. Given these factors, novel strategies are needed to prevent and detect this crime. Dating sites, for instance, have been asked to share known fake profiles in order to help reduce the number of criminal profiles (created for the romance scam). Facebook has attempted to take down known fake profiles (which criminals create to enable a number of different types of MMFs). Anti-money-laundering regulations increase the identifiability of transactions and recipients when money is transferred via money transfer companies, such as Western Union and MoneyGram.

12.6 AWARENESS CAMPAIGNS

Similar to prevention strategies for phishing scams, various awareness campaigns have been devised to help prevent MMF. There are numerous websites and phone apps available that attempt to educate users about scams in an attempt to prevent victimization arising from MMF. These campaigns typically suggest basic rules such as never click on a link in an email; never respond to an email asking for confirmation of your banking details; and never send any money to strangers you meet online. As demonstrated earlier in this chapter when discussing training programmes developed to prevent phishing scams, warnings about online security often focus exclusively on idealized individual behaviour and assume that people fall for scams because they lack knowledge. One of the problems with this approach, at least for MMFs, is that many victims of MMF have heard of these scams prior to becoming defrauded. Lea et al. (2009a) have argued that detailed knowledge of a scam increases vulnerability, as these individuals often develop an 'illusion of invulnerability'. It has been found that, even when authority figures (e.g., police, law enforcement, bank managers) attempt to alert a person to the fact that they have become a victim of a romance scam, the victim often has difficulty believing them. Moreover, even when the victim questions the criminal about their authenticity, the criminal will employ persuasive techniques to convince the victim (Whitty, 2015). The number of repeat victims also suggests that this is a difficult population to help to recognize scams. Given that knowledge about a scam, therefore, may not be enough to prevent individuals from becoming defrauded, other types of interventions are needed. In order to help devise effective campaigns to prevent individuals from becoming defrauded as a result of MMFs, it is important to understand the reasons why individuals are tricked. As a way of assisting with prevention and detection, researchers have, for example, examined how individuals cognitively process information when presented with a scam, the sorts of individuals who are more likely to be conned and the stages involved in scams.

12.7 COGNITIVE AND MOTIVATIONAL ERRORS

It has been argued that 'falling for a scam comes down to errors in decision-making' and that 'scammers create situations (with their scam offers) that increase the likelihood of poor decision-making' (Lea et al., 2009a, p. 35). Cognitive (e.g., overconfidence in a specific topic) and motivational (e.g., the scam triggers positive emotions) processes also explain the psychological reasons why people respond to scams. The main reasons include 'appeals to trust and authority' (i.e., the use of people or institutions of authority to make the scam appear legitimate) and 'visceral triggers' (triggers

Table 12.1 *Errors in decision-making with respect to scams (identified by Lea et al. 2009a, p. 24)*

Motivational	Cognitive
Visceral influences	Reduced cognitive abilities
Reduced motivation for information processing	Positive illusions
	Background knowledge and overconfidence
Preference for confirmation	Norm activation
Lack of self-control	Authority
Mood regulation and phantom fixation	Social proof
Sensation seeking	Altercasting
Liking and similarity	
Reciprocation	
Commitment and consistency	

employed to make potential victims focus on huge prizes and imagined positive future emotional states). Another error victims frequently make is the belief that they are acting according to the social norm. Norms 'can be seen as rules of thumb based on social knowledge: they tell us how we "ought" to choose, and furthermore how people are likely to choose' (Lea, Fischer & Evans, 2009b, p. 25). A comprehensive list of the common errors Lea et al. (2009a) believe victims of MMF fall for is summarized in Table 12.1.

12.8 WHAT TYPE OF PERSON TENDS TO BE SUSCEPTIBLE TO MMF?

In addition to considering cognitive processes, researchers have examined the types of individuals who tend to be susceptible to MMFs. Furnell (2005) argued that greedy and naive individuals are more likely to be conned. Lee and Soberon-Ferrer (2005) found that victims of fraud tend to be older, poorer, less educated and single. Holtfreter, Reisig and Pratt (2008) looked broadly at 'consumer fraud' victimization and found that fraud victims were more likely to have low self-control. Buchanan and Whitty (2014), in contrast, found that those high in sensation seeking were not more likely to be scammed by the online dating romance scam. Instead, they found that high scores on the romantic belief of 'idealization' were associated with the likelihood of being a victim. There may be a generic typology for scam victims; however, given the distinctive nature of some of these scams (e.g., the emergency scam requires an immediate response; the romance scam usually takes several months before victims are defrauded), there might be specific risk factors depending on the type of scam. Understanding the sorts of people who are susceptible to online MMFs and the sorts of scams certain individuals are more susceptible to could be advantageous for prevention, as knowing who is more likely to be a victim of these crimes can help with tailoring the right message to the relevant people.

12.8.1 *The role of the Internet*

Very few studies have considered the role the Internet might play in persuading individuals to part with their money. Given that the Internet usually plays a role in the initiation or implementation of MMFs, an examination of the potential influence of communication via this medium could help to elucidate new ways to prevent these crimes. In Chapter 3 we summarized Walther's hyperpersonal theory. This theory has been further drawn upon by Whitty (2013b) to examine the online dating romance scam. She argues that in this particular scam a one-sided, 'hyperpersonal' relationship develops between the victim and the scammer. According to Whitty, victims idealize the fake persona, believing they have found the perfect romantic partner. Whitty elaborates on the role the Internet has to play in this scam in her stage model (described in the next section). Further research might focus more on how certain features of media might be used by criminals to scam victims of MMF.

12.9 STAGES INVOLVED IN THE ONLINE DATING ROMANCE SCAM

Considering scams as a series of stages might provide a useful method to enable individuals to gain insights into the anatomy of these scams. Research has found that the online dating romance scam progresses over a number of stages and that various media are used by criminals to persuade victims to part with their money (Whitty, 2013b). The stages identified are as follows:

- *Stage 1*: potential victims need to be motivated to find the 'ideal partner'.
- *Stage 2*: potential victims are presented with an ideal profile and given the promise of exclusivity by the scammer.
- *Stage 3*: potential victims are groomed by the criminal to gain trust and love and the criminal tests the waters to gauge whether the potential victim might be ready and willing to part with their money.
- *Stage 4*: the criminal employs techniques to persuade the potential victim to send money (e.g., a narrative about a crisis where money is urgently needed or the 'foot-in-the-door' technique).
- *Stage 5*: the criminal employs further techniques to keep the scam alive (e.g., inventing a further crisis or employing the 'door-in-the-face' technique).
- *Stage 6*: some victims may believe the scam is over but subsequently be revictimized (e.g., the criminal admits to the victim that they have been scamming them but has nevertheless fallen in love with them; the scammer then asks the victim for more money).

12.10 ILLEGAL DOWNLOADS

Major music labels are suing filesharing application Aurous for 'wilful and egregious copyright infringement' just days after its earliest alpha version launched.

US industry body the RIAA has filed a lawsuit on behalf of labels including Universal Music, Sony Music and Warner Music subsidiaries Warner Bros, Atlantic and Capitol seeking an injunction against the software as well as damages.

The Spotify-style application enables its users to search for songs to stream and download, and while its developer has said it intends to become an aggregator for music and licensed streaming services, the RIAA's lawsuit claims its sources are piracy sites. (Dredge, 2015)

The activities described so far in this chapter are clearly criminal; however, there are some activities conducted online that the user might not know to be illegal or might believe to be such common practice as to not be treated as crimes. Such activities include the practice of downloading copyrighted material illegally from the Internet (e.g., music, videos, books). Studies have shown that users have few ethical concerns about unauthorized downloading (Siegfried, 2004). Hardy, Krawczyk and Tyrowicz (2013) argue that, 'as a matter of fact, mere popularity of file sharing services seems to suggest that either millions of people are morally rotten or strongly object to equating online "piracy" with traditional theft'.

Given that many question whether engaging in such activities is morally wrong, prevention of this form of cybercrime might require a nontraditional approach. A large amount of money has, in fact, been invested in raising awareness and in educational campaigns in the hope of reducing online file sharing or 'piracy'. These campaigns, however, have been for the most part unsuccessful – doing little to change opinions or behaviour (D'Astous, Colbert & Montpetit, 2005). In fact, the number of end users engaging in online piracy appears to be continuing to rise (Cesareo & Pastore, 2014). Many of these campaigns equate traditional offline acts of theft with online theft. They also typically focus on the negative personal consequences associated with online piracy, such as fines and imprisonment. In 2012, the Serious Organised Crime Agency in the UK (now known as the National Crime Agency) took down the music site RnBXclusive, leaving a warning on the website that users could receive up to 10 years' imprisonment and an unlimited fine. This effort was in part successful, given that at least one other site, as a consequence, took itself offline voluntarily. However, the action did not appear to change end users' attitudes, with some calling this a bullying tactic and scaremongering (Geere, 2012; Moody, 2012). More recently, the City of London police have started placing banner advertisements on websites believed to be offering pirated content illegally; however, to date, there has been no follow-up research to investigate the effectiveness of this latest strategy.

Some of the problems with the previous strategies are the lack of insight into the psychology of changed behaviour as well as the personal ethics individuals hold regarding such acts. Fear campaigns have often had little success, given that campaigns that induce too much fear are often ignored by viewers in order to avoid feeling too much anxiety from paying attention to the message (see Bada & Sasse, 2014). Online security and stop smoking campaigns are good examples of advertisements that instilled too much fear and had little impact in changing behaviours. Researchers have argued that users have a different ethical stance regarding online piracy compared to traditional theft (see, e.g., Blythe & Wright, 2008; Moores & Chang, 2006). Moreover, as the theory of planned behaviour predicts, if individuals believe that something is the social norm and, in particular, if their peers are engaging in the activity, they are also likely to engage in that behaviour. Interestingly, Hardy et al. (2013) found that, even when an individual's ethical views are just as strict for online as for traditional appropriations, when people perceive the social norm is 'lax', they are more likely to engage in piracy.

Online piracy, therefore, is an interesting crime that might need new approaches to help reduce it. It might even mean developing new business models with respect to paying for online material. For example, Magnatune is a record label, started in 2003, that gives half its profits to artists and offers a sliding scale for purchases via PayPal. Some researchers believe that this approach might prevent illegal downloads. In a study on consumers' attitudes towards Magnatune, Regner (2015) concludes:

> the success of voluntary payment-based models, documented in a series of studies, is intriguing and it is important to improve our understanding of PWYW. Various underlying motivations have been identified as a determinant for voluntary payments. Based on this evidence it appears plausible that a combination of fairness, reciprocal concerns, self-image concerns, norm conformity and strategic concerns drives behaviour in PWYW settings. (p. 212)

The example of Magnatune might be the way forward; however, industry and researchers may well consider other approaches that draw from theories in psychology to help predict their success.

SUGGESTED ACTIVITY

Think of some new approaches to paying for online material. Do you think your approach(es) might help to prevent illegal downloads? Why, or why not?

12.11 CONCLUSIONS

This chapter focused on two types of online criminal behaviours: scamming and illegal downloads. The types of scams focused on here included phishing, the various subsets of phishing (e.g., spear phishing and vishing) and MMFs. The catching and prosecution of these criminals is challenging and time consuming, which is why other approaches, such as educational and awareness programmes, have been developed to help in the prevention of these crimes. The discipline of psychology has much to offer these programmes, in helping developers to understand how to change individuals' behaviour, the psychological characteristics of those vulnerable to scams, and the cognitive and motivational errors victims make when approached by a scammer.

DISCUSSION QUESTIONS

1. Given the evidence as a whole, what sorts of users are more likely to be scammed by a phishing attack? What are the limitations and strengths of the currently available research?
2. Consider some of the studies on training programmes to prevent phishing attacks. What are some of the critiques (including strengths and weaknesses) you might make of these programmes?
3. Have you known anyone who has been scammed by an MMF? Why do you think they were tricked?
4. What are your views about downloading music and/or videos illegally? Do you think it is morally wrong to do this? Why, or why not?

SUGGESTED READINGS

Alsharnouby, M., Alaca, F. & Chiasson, S. (2015). Why phishing still works: User strategies for combating phishing attacks. *International Journal of Human–Computer Studies*, 82, 69–82.

Cesareo, L. & Pastore, A. (2014). Consumers' attitude and behaviour towards online music piracy and subscription-based services. *Journal of Consumer Marketing*, 31(6/7), 515–525.

Davinson, N. & Sillence, E. (2010). It won't happen to me: Promoting secure behaviour among internet users. *Computers in Human Behavior*, 26, 1739–1747.

Lea, S., Fischer, P. & Evans, K. (2009). The psychology of scams: Provoking and committing errors of judgement. Office of Fair Trading. Retrieved 7 April 2016 from http://webarchive.national archives.gov.uk/20140402142426/http://www.oft.gov.uk/shared_oft/reports/consumer_protection/oft1070.pdf

Vishwanath, A. (2015). Examining the distinct antecedents of e-mail habits and its influence on the outcomes of a phishing attack. *Journal of Computer-Mediated Communication*, 20, 570–584.

Wang, J., Herath, T., Chen, R., Vishwanath, A. & Rao, R. (2012). Phishing susceptibility: An investigation into the processing of a targeted spear phishing email. *IEEE Transactions on Professional Communication*, 55(4), 345–362.

Whitty, M. T. (2013). The scammers persuasive techniques model: Development of a stage model to explain the online dating romance scam. *British Journal of Criminology*, 53(4), 665–684.

Whitty, M. T. (2015). Mass-marketing fraud: A growing concern. *IEEE Security & Privacy*, 13(4), 84–87.

13 Online Crimes: Cyberharassment, Hate Crimes and Cyberwarfare

Chapter 12 focused on financially related online crimes. This chapter focuses on crimes against individuals, organizations and society more generally. Such crimes – including cyberharassment and cyberattacks – are often motivated by hate. New legislation has been developed in the UK and many other countries to combat these crimes, but the psychological harm experienced by victims is only recently being better understood. Victims of these crimes can experience incredibly detrimental effects. In addition, for some, the fear of becoming a victim of these crimes can be debilitating. Although these crimes can and often do take place in the physical world, this chapter focuses predominately on their online equivalents. Moreover, we will touch upon the controversies over employing surveillance as a method to detect and prevent these crimes.

13.1 ONLINE HARASSMENT AND STALKING

When Newark optometrist David Matusiewicz and his former wife Christine Belford divorced in 2006 after having three children, their custody dispute seemed pretty typical.

Today their story is strewn with charges and counter charges, lies, kidnapping, spying, a hacked Facebook account, vitriolic postings on social media, and the murders of Belford and her friend Laura 'Beth' Mulford, both gunned down by David's father, Thomas Matusiewicz, in the New Castle County Courthouse lobby while walking into a child support hearing in 2013.

David Matusiewicz, his sister Amy Gonzalez and his mother Lenore Matusiewicz are the first defendants in America charged with cyberstalking resulting in death – a crime that, if jurors find was connected to Belford's death, could lead to life in prison.

(Reyes & Spencer, 2015)

Cyberpsychology: The Study of Individuals, Society and Digital Technologies, First Edition.
Monica Therese Whitty and Garry Young.
© 2017 John Wiley & Sons, Ltd. Published 2017 by John Wiley & Sons, Ltd.

> **SUGGESTED ACTIVITY**
>
> Read through any newspaper articles that you can find on cyberstalking. In your view, what type of psychological harm might this crime cause its victims?

Harassment is a term typically used in a legal sense to refer to behaviours that are considered to be threatening or disturbing. Making unwanted and persistent sexual advances in the workplace is an example of sexual harassment. Electronic communication can be used to harass both in similar and new ways to physical harassment. Cyberharassment might occur as a consequence of a romantic relationship gone wrong, or from unwanted romantic and/or sexual attention. It can occur within the workplace or between organizations. As with the offline world, various forms of harassment take place online, including but not limited to sexual and racial harassment. Barak (2005) points out three types of sexual harassment that can take place in cyberspace: gender harassment, unwanted sexual attention and sexual coercion. In addition to the forms of sexual harassment that Barak (2005) discusses, individuals might cyberharass by gaining access to an individual's computer, monitoring individuals' keystrokes, sending viruses or destroying an individual's reputation.

Researchers have noted that cyberharassment is also evident in online spaces where alternative physical identities are adopted, such as *Second Life* and other virtual worlds (Behm-Morawitz & Schipper, 2015). In Behm-Morawitz and Schipper's research, cyberharassment was operationalized as 'computer-mediated obscene comments, sexual harassment, and generally harassing behaviors aimed at debasing and/or driving out a virtual world user'. These authors created a questionnaire that was answered by 216 *Second Life* users, providing information about their avatars' appearance and virtual world experiences. Behm-Morawitz and Schipper found that cyberharassment was fairly common in *Second Life*, with about two thirds of their sample reporting some experience of cyberharassment. Women were significantly more likely to report feeling cyberharassed compared to men, and this was, in the main, due to avatar sexualization.

Stalking is understood to be a more severe form of harassment, although often the academic literature mixes up the terms (most likely this is because there is no agreed-upon definition among scholars). From a legal perspective, stalking is a relatively new crime that was not, in fact, recognized as an illegal behaviour until the 1990s. For example, in 1990, California saw the first law passed that specifically made stalking a crime. This was in response to the stalking and eventual murder of the actor Rebecca Schaeffer. Although this is a relatively new crime, researchers note that this type of activity dates back to antiquity, and that obsessive pursuit of another for the purposes of revenge has long been evident in literature (Spitzberg, 2002).

As highlighted in the extract at the start of this section, the Internet has afforded new opportunities to stalk individuals and organizations. Data garnered from online sources can be used to locate a person in the physical world in order to stalk them; however, individuals might be stalked solely online – which can cause harm of equal, or in some cases greater, severity compared with physical stalking. In an attempt to operationalize the term, McGrath and Casey (2002) have argued that:

> Stalking is the repeated uninvited monitoring and/or intrusion into the life and activities of a victim that is usually, but not always, undertaken for the purpose of frightening or intimidating the victim or those around the victim ... Cyberstalking is merely stalking that uses the Internet for information gathering, monitoring, and/or victim contact. (p. 88–89)

Bocij's (2004) definition of cyberstalking is more comprehensive, and includes groups and organizations as well as individuals:

> [Cyberstalking is] a group of behaviors in which an individual, group of individuals, or organization uses information and communications technology to harasses another individual, group of individuals, or organization. Such behaviors may include, but are not limited to, the transmission of threats and false accusations, identity theft, damage to data or equipment, computer monitoring, solicitation of minors for sexual purposes, and any form of aggression. Harassment is defined as a course of actions that a reasonable person, in possession of the same information, would think causes another reasonable person to suffer emotional distress. (p. 14)

Cyberstalking, of course, does not necessarily remain online. Cyberstalking behaviour can potentially be initiated online but progress to offline methods of stalking, including all traditional offline stalking behaviours, such as use of the phone, following the target, sending letters and so forth. It can also take place in conjunction with traditional stalking behaviours. In addition, the potential victim might simply be identified online and then stalked offline.

13.2 CYBERSTALKING AND THE LAW

Some legislation on stalking has been rewritten to include cyberstalking. For example, in South Australia the legislation defines cyberstalking as:

> Where stalkers take advantage of information technology either to cause physical or mental harm to the victim, or to cause the victim to feel serious apprehension or fear. Cyberstalking occurs when a person on at least two separate occasions with an intent to cause serious harm, uses the Internet or some other form of electronic communication to publish or transmit offensive material, or communicates with the person, or to others about that person in a manner that could reasonably be expected to arouse apprehension or fear.
>
> (SA Crimes Act 1990)

In a US Attorney General (1999) report, cyberstalking was defined as 'the use of the Internet, e-mail, or other electronic communications devices to stalk another person'. Interestingly, the England and Wales Protection from Harassment Act 1997 includes neither cyberstalking nor, specifically, stalking in its definition of harassing behaviour. Instead, it

> rules that a person must not pursue a course of conduct which amounts to the harassment of another person. No intent is required: instead the 'reasonable person' test is used, qualified in the Act by the words 'in possession of the same information'. The offence of causing harassment is unusual in that it is not always necessary to prove that a person actually knew the conduct amounted to harassment. The mental element in harassment is established on proof that the suspect knew or ought to have known that the conduct amounted to harassment (section1(1)). Its effects upon the victim determine whether a course of conduct amounts to 'harassment'. The advantage to this is that any persistent, unwanted behaviour can amount to harassment – permitting police to intervene before behaviour escalates to violence.
>
> (Metropolitan Police Service, 1997)

13.3 PSYCHOLOGICALLY PROFILING CRIMINALS AND VICTIMS

Given the dearth of research available on cyberstalking, it is difficult to conclude whether the Internet has provided another space and means for stalkers to harass their victims or whether cyberstalking is a distinct social problem. Theoretically, given that research (already discussed in this book) has found that individuals can feel more disinhibited in some spaces online, which consequently promotes greater risk-taking and asocial behaviour, it might be reasonable to predict that some people who would never have participated in traditional stalking might engage in cyberstalking behaviours. Some studies, however, have attempted to distinguish both the perpetrators and victims of stalking compared with those of cyberstalking.

There is some literature available on the profile of a person who is more likely to stalk as well as on those who cyberstalk. Fisher, Cullen and Turner (2002) contend that it is easier to collect data on individuals who engage in this criminal behaviour compared with other types of crimes given there is a high rate of self-identified stalkers (although there is potential bias between those who openly admit the behaviour and those who engage in the behaviour but deny their engagement). The research on offline stalking finds that stalkers are more likely to be men who experienced traumatic childhoods, are insecurely attached and have personality problems (Dye & Davis, 2003; Dutton & Winstead, 2006; Spitzberg & Cupach, 2003; Spitzberg & Veksler, 2007). Drug and alcohol problems are more common in violent stalkers (Rosenfeld, 2004). With regard to cyberstalking, Menard and Pincus (2012) found that stalkers and cyberstalkers were more likely to experience childhood sexual maltreatment than nonstalkers. They also found that, for men, narcissistic vulnerability and its interaction with sexual abuse predicted both stalking and cyberstalking behaviours and, for women, insecure attachment and alcohol expectancies predicted stalking and cyberstalking behaviours. Alexy, Burgess, Baker and Smoyak (2005) found that cyberstalkers were more likely to threaten to hurt themselves than overt stalkers.

It has been found that women are more likely to be the victims of stalking than men (Basile, Swahn, Chen & Saltzman, 2006). In contrast, research on cyberstalking has found that victims are more likely to be men (Alexy et al., 2005). More research with representative samples, however, is needed to confirm this difference. Victims of stalking experiences changes in their social and employment spheres as a consequences of being stalked, whereas victims of cyberstalking are more likely to experience a loss of family and friends (Sheridan & Grant, 2007). Notably, Sheridan and Grant found that psychological, social and financial variables did not significantly differ for victims of stalking compared with cyberstalked victims.

13.4 HATE CRIMES

Hate crimes are broadly understood to be criminal actions motivated by negative attitudes of culturally delimited groups of people (Brax & Munthe, 2015). Some cyberharassment, cyberstalking and even terrorism crimes can also be understood as hate crimes. Hate crimes, however, are difficult to operationalize. As Brax and Munthe point out:

> In hate crime debates, we thus find different views on what, more precisely, makes a crime into a hate crime. This is no mere verbal matter but has an impact on what concrete offenses are thought to be suitable targets of legal and policy measures. Such conceptual differences exist between countries, between authorities within single countries, and between different sectors of public policy. Conceptual differences also exist between and within academic disciplines addressing hate crime as a research topic. (p. 1688)

As with cyberharassment, the criminals might act out their hate crimes on the Internet or they might use the Internet to find out information about someone in order to cause them harm offline. The research in psychology on hate crimes, in particular those that involve the Internet, is fairly scant. This is perhaps because these crimes are not clearly defined and overlap with other more clearly defined crimes. Following is an example of a hate crime that took place in the UK:

> It was perhaps, therefore, dispiritingly inevitable that Mumsnet – 'a largely female space' – would be attacked too. As its popularity grew so did the insults, and it came to be targeted by what Roberts [the owner of Mumsnet], 48, describes as 'all kinds of weird protests' over the years – including, she says, the posting of underpants to the staff by campaign group Fathers 4 Justice. Twitter has meanwhile been awash with comments of the 'get back to the kitchen sink, know your place' variety.
>
> Then, one night in August [2015], the insults and assaults escalated in a way Roberts could never have predicted. The police received an anonymous phone call from someone

reporting she had been murdered and her four children taken hostage by a gunman. Eight police officers were duly scrambled in the middle of the night and dispatched to her London home, five armed with machine guns, accompanied by police dogs.

The family was in fact away on holiday, and all were safe. Only their 21-year-old Spanish au pair was at home to face the commotion.

I was what is known as a swatting attack – the false report of a crime that brings a swat team of officers to the victim's door. A phenomenon seen in the US, this was thought to be the first incident of its kind in Britain.

Around the same time, messages threatening Mumsnet appeared online and a denial of service hacking attack, apparently by a group calling itself @DadSecurity, where servers are flooded with data, temporarily brought the site down. Users' details were scammed in a phishing exercise and two Mumsnet members who were vocal about the attack on Twitter were also swatted.

The incident hit Roberts hard. 'It was incredibly stressful and for a period I was waking up pretty much every night thinking there was an armed gunman in my house – irrationally, because obviously I knew it was a hoax, but it was a very anxious time,' she says. 'I felt incredibly responsible for the welfare of our users and employees.'

(Silverman, 2015)

SUGGESTED ACTIVITY

Read through any newspaper articles that you can find on hate crimes involving the Internet. In your view, do these overlap with other crimes? What is the psychological harm caused by the crimes that you have read?

Far-right groups, also known as right-wing extremist groups, are clearly evident online. The Ku Klux Klan, Islamist extremist groups, the British National Party and National Action (UK) are but a few examples of such groups that have a Web presence – often set up to recruit new members. Hale (2012) has examined how these types of groups use online media to attract young people. In his paper, he points out that being able to quickly download hate materials facilitates recruitment, given that it helps users to feel safe and less at risk of being caught out and having unwanted attention directed towards them. Hale also notes that these groups attempt to recruit members by trawling through posts on online chat forums, and they track website user demographics in order to locate potential members by sending them training manuals and propaganda. Hale believes that custom-made SNSs, such as Stormfront, are useful recruitment tools, given they not only post information and messages but also encourage interaction with their members, thereby developing strong communities. Although Hale's presents some important points for researchers to consider regarding recruitment for hate groups, much more research is needed in order to find more effective ways to detect and deter these groups (see Chapter 7 for a more detailed discussion of online radicalization).

13.5 CYBERWARFARE

Hackers breaking into official U.S. networks are not just using Chinese systems as a launch pad, but are based in China, sources tell TIME. Their story: Sometime on November 1st, 2004, hackers sat down at computers in southern China and set off once again on their daily hunt for U.S. secrets. Since 2003 the group had been conducting wide-ranging assaults on U.S. government targets to steal sensitive information, part of a massive cyberespionage ring that U.S. investigators have codenamed Titan Rain. On this particular night, the hackers' quarry was military data, and they were armed with a new weapon to reach out across cyberspace and get it.

This was a scanner program that 'primed the pump,' according to a former government network analyst who has helped track Titan Rain, by searching vast military networks for single computers with vulnerabilities that the attackers could exploit later. As with many of their tools, this was a simple program, but one that had been cleverly modified to fit their needs, and then used with ruthless efficiency against a vast array of U.S. networks. After performing the scans, the source says, it's a virtual certainty that the attackers returned within a day or two and, as they had on dozens of military networks, broke into the computers to steal away as much data as possible without being detected.
(Thornburgh, 2005)

Cyberwarfare essentially consists of actions carried out by a nation state to penetrate another nation's networks for the purposes of causing harm, such as damage or disruption. The above extract is an example of a well-known cyberattack that took place in 2004, referred to as 'Titan Rain'. The harm can range from causing an effect on the national infrastructure to financial harm or theft, any of which can lead to physical harm.

The rules of war have changed over time as new technologies have been developed; however, new inventions and technologies have meant that we have had to rewrite the rules of war at an ever increasing pace (Singer, 2009). The international community, however, has yet to codify and sanction a body of norms to govern state action in cyberspace (Beidleman, 2009). Scholars, such as Singer, have asked why questions around ethics and technology are so difficult, especially in the realm of war. He quotes from a speech given by General Omar Bradley in November 1948: 'The world has achieved brilliance without wisdom, power without conscience. Ours is a world of nuclear giants and ethical infants. We know more about war than we know about peace, more about killing than we know about living' (cited in Singer, 2010, p. 300). An important point made by Singer is that there is a disconnection between the social sciences, humanities and physical sciences, whereby many new technologies that might be used in warfare are developed without any consideration of ethical issues. As touched upon throughout this book, interdisciplinary research can provide richer findings and potential solutions to problems. Cyberwarfare is a good example of an area where experts from a variety of disciplines need to join together to find the best solutions.

Cyberwarfare has a number of features that set it apart from the use of traditional weapons: it is often difficult to determine the source of cyberattacks, creating an attribution problem, and many cyberattacks are not directly lethal and will not result in permanent damage to physical objects (Dipert, 2010). Moreover, engaging in an act of cyberwarfare is arguably a different psychological experience from engaging in physical warfare.

Cyber-technology has also changed the nature of war. It has been argued, for instance, that the use of drones in war makes killing easy, given the distance the operator is from the target, suggesting that the more physical distance there is between the killer and their target, the more moral distance is created. A shorter distance between the target and the attacker creates emotional and empathic obstacles to killing (Coeckelbergh, 2013).

As discussed in several of the chapters in this book (see especially Chapter 3), psychologists have noted that in cyberspace there is a disinhibition effect. As a reminder, Suler (2004) has described this effect as a double-edged sword. Whereas some people reveal secret emotions, fears and wishes or show unusual acts of kindness and generosity, which Suler refers to as 'benign disinhibition', at other times people are ruder, more critical, angrier or more threatening than they typically are face to face. This Suler calls 'toxic disinhibition'. Cyberharassment, described earlier in this chapter, is an example of this type of toxic disinhibition. The disinhibition effect has been used to explain why some cybercriminals carry out their crimes. It can decrease the likelihood of feeling responsibility for committing a crime as well as of feeling negative emotions, such as shame (as there is no perceived audience to witness the crime) (Guitton, 2012). However, it might be equally important to consider the disinhibition effect with regard to how intelligence and government respond to a cyberattack or when they might themselves decide to initiate an attack. They might feel less inclined to retaliate, or retaliate with less harm, if they were confronted with the enemy in the physical world, for instance.

The ethics regarding the use of drones has been questioned by a number of scholars. They have asked whether physical distance during war has led individuals to make decisions to harm that they would not have made if the enemy were in closer proximity. Coeckelbergh (2013) writes: 'although it may be true that remote fighting implies a less embodied, social and engaged way of being-in-the-world (to use Heidegger's term), drone pilots are still embodied, social, meaning-giving beings, and also experience their fighting and killing in an embodied way' (p. 94). According to Coeckelbergh, the more practical empirical question is to learn more about what embodied experience these pilots experience. Moreover, he contends that these pilots need to do close-up surveillance of their targets – often for long periods of time – meaning they do see the 'faces' of their targets and might spend time constructing narratives about their targets' lives, making the moral distance closer rather than further away and potentially making killing more difficult. Coeckelbergh has focused on drones and surveillance methods that allow the person to see (up close) their target; however, this is not necessarily the case for all methods of attack/defence in cyberwarfare (e.g., denial-of-service attacks, where the person or group of people is likely to remain anonymous). It might be interesting to learn how disembodied analysts and other actors in war feel when monitoring or planning an attack, or engaging in an attack on cybercriminals.

13.5.1 Hacktivists

Some individuals or groups who engage in cyberwarfare are referred to as hacktivists. Hacktivists, however, can do much more than just engage in cyberwarfare. Moreover, some hacktivists do not break laws. Essentially, hacktivists gain unauthorized access to computer files or networks, typically to further social or political ends. Distinctions are often made between white-hat and black-hat hackers. White-hat hackers are understood to be ethical hackers and are sanctioned by their clients (e.g., breaking into a system to discover its vulnerabilities and reporting to the owner on the system's weaknesses so that security can be improved). Black-hat hackers, on the other hand, are cybercriminals who intend to cause harm.

Some hacktivists are not clearly black or white hats, given that they vacillate between malicious illegal harm and ethical actions. These individuals or groups are commonly referred to as 'grey hats'. A well-known grey hat group call itself 'Anonymous'. It essentially consists of an international network of activities with a loose and decentralized command structure. It is known for conducting DDoS (distributed denial-of-service) attacks (which are attempts to make a machine or network service unavailable to its intended users) on government, religious and corporate websites. They have, for example, declared cyberwar against militant Islamists. In 2015, they turned their attention to hate groups, such as the Ku Klux Klan, as reported in *The Guardian*:

> The hacking collective Anonymous has begun its promised leak of the identities of members of the Ku Klux Klan with a data dump of the names of more than 350 alleged members along with links to social media accounts. Many of the identities are already in the public domain.
>
> Only one of the names listed in the file, on the anonymous sharing site Pastebin, had a phone number attached. Fewer than five had email addresses. None returned requests for comment.
>
> Many in the release are already in the public eye, at least on social media. The Twitter biography of one such Klan member, James Pratt, reads: 'A veteran, a daddy, a Klansman of the Traditionalist American Knights of the Ku Klux Klan.'
>
> Frank Ancona, whose name was included in the release as an imperial wizard of the KKK's Traditionalist American Knights (TAK), has made TV appearances as a representative of the group. Former leader David Duke is listed in the release; so is Don Black, the founder of the white supremacist site Stormfront.
>
> (Woolf, 2015).

13.6 SURVEILLANCE AND MONITORING

Given the volume of crimes that take place online, the utility of the Internet in enabling offline crimes and the harms these crimes might cause, governments believe strong and effective measures are needed to prevent and detect these crimes as well as to catch the criminals behind them. One measure has been the surveillance and monitoring of Internet data. One of the problems with surveillance, however, is that, although it might be employed to prevent and detect criminal behaviour, the surveillance will undoubtedly lead to the monitoring of innocent people's personal lives. As a consequence, there have been many debates (both nationally and internationally) over how much monitoring is ethical and socially acceptable and who should be privy to this intelligence.

Concerns about surveillance have increased after Edward Snowden leaked the surveillance practices of governments in the US and other countries. This leak has led governments to consider whether transparency is needed regarding surveillance and whether legislation needs to be reworked. The 'snooper's charter' (the Draft Communications Data Bill) in the UK is an example of how governments have reconsidered their positions on surveillance. However, this new charter has caused much upset:

> I never thought I'd say it, but George Orwell lacked vision. The spies have gone further than he could have imagined, creating in secret and without democratic authorisation the ultimate panopticon. Now they hope the British public will make it legitimate.
>
> This bill is characterized by a clear anti-democratic attitude. Those in power are deemed to be good, and are therefore given the benefit of the doubt. 'Conduct is lawful for all purposes if ...' and 'A person (whether or not the person so authorised or required) is not to be subject to any civil liability in respect of conduct that ...': these are sections granting immunity to the spies and cops.
>
> The spies' surveillance activities are also exempt from legal due process. No questions can be asked that might indicate in any legal proceeding that surveillance or interception has occurred. This is to ensure the general public never learn how real people are affected by surveillance. The cost of this exemption is great. It means British prosecutors can't prosecute terrorists on the best evidence available – the intercepts – which are a key part of any prosecution in serious crime cases worldwide.
>
> Those without power – eg citizens (or the more accurately named subjects) – are potentially bad, and therefore must be watched and monitored closely and constantly. The safeguards mentioned in the bill are there to benefit the state not the citizen. The criminal sanctions aren't so much to stop spies or police abusing their powers, but rather to silence critics or potential whistleblowers. That's clear because there is no public interest exemption in the sweeping gagging orders littered throughout the bill. The safeguards for keeping secure the massive troves of personal data aren't there so much to protect the public but to stop anyone finding out exactly how big or invasive

these troves are or how they were acquired. Again, we know this because there is no public interest exemption.

> While the concerns of the state dominate, those of the citizen are nowhere to be seen. There is almost no mention in the bill of the privacy and democratic costs of mass surveillance, nor of seriously holding the state to account for the use and abuse of its sweeping powers.
>
> (Brooke, 2015)

There are a number of issues that need to be considered regarding individuals' online privacy. Sparck-Jones (2003) labelled a number of specific properties of the information collected that have consequences for privacy:

- *Permanence*: Once recorded, information rarely disappears. As such, fine-grained, searchable, persistent data exists on individuals and there are sophisticated, cheap data-mining devices that can also be used to analyse this information.
- *Volume*: The ease with which information is now recorded using technology results in huge datasets. Furthermore, storage is cheap, so large volumes of information can exist indefinitely.
- *Invisibility*: All information collected seems to exist within an opaque system and so any information collected may not be 'visible' to the person to whom it relates. Even if information collected is available to a person, that person may not be able to interpret it due to the use of incomprehensible coding.
- *Neutrality*: The ease with which information can be collected means that any qualifying information may be lost. Thus, information may be absorbed regardless of its metadata; that is, there are no distinctions between intimate, sensitive information and nonsensitive information.
- *Accessibility*: There are a number of tools for accessing information, meaning that any information collected may be read by any number of people. The ease with which information can be copied, transferred, integrated and multiplied electronically further increases this accessibility.
- *Assembly*: There are many effective tools for searching for, assembling and reorganizing information from many quite separate sources.
- *Remoteness*: Information collected is usually both physically and logically remote from the users to whom it refers. However, this information can be accessed and used by people whom the user does not know.

As Whitty and Joinson (2009) have argued, each of the above features affects privacy uniquely and in combination with other threats. Although massive data collection and storage are possible in many environments, the very structure of the Internet and its additional feature of connectivity further exacerbate the online privacy problem. The Internet allows for interactive two-way communication and is woven into people's lives in a more intimate way than some other media, as it connects people with places and people with people. Accordingly, it poses unique threats to information privacy.

One of the more recent issues regarding online privacy is how 'Big Data' can be recombined to provide insights about a person that the user might not be aware of and/or might never have guessed could be made using their data. Organizations, for example, have used Big Data to predict pregnancy, and, although this might not be an objective of government surveillance, this example does demonstrate that personal data might well be used in ways that the public did not imagine. This story is summed up in an extract below:

> As the marketers explained to Pole – and as Pole later explained to me, back when we were still speaking and before Target told him to stop – new parents are a retailer's holy grail. Most shoppers don't buy everything they need at one store. Instead, they buy groceries at the grocery store and toys at the toy store, and they visit Target only when they need certain items they associate with Target – cleaning supplies, say, or new socks or a six-month supply of toilet paper. But Target sells everything from milk to stuffed animals to lawn furniture to electronics, so one of the company's primary goals is convincing customers that the only store they need is Target. But it's a tough message to get across, even with the most ingenious ad campaigns, because once consumers' shopping habits are ingrained, it's incredibly difficult to change them.
>
> There are, however, some brief periods in a person's life when old routines fall apart and buying habits are suddenly in flux. One of those moments – *the* moment, really – is right around the birth of a child, when parents are exhausted and overwhelmed and their shopping patterns and brand loyalties are up for grabs. But as Target's marketers explained to Pole, timing is everything. Because birth records are usually public, the moment a couple have a new baby, they are almost instantaneously barraged with offers and incentives and advertisements from all sorts of companies. Which means that the key is to reach them earlier, before any other retailers know a baby is on the way. Specifically, the marketers said they wanted to send specially designed ads to women in their second trimester, which is when most expectant mothers begin buying all sorts of new things, like prenatal vitamins and maternity clothing. 'Can you give us a list?' the marketers asked.
>
> 'We knew that if we could identify them in their second trimester, there's a good chance we could capture them for years,' Pole told me. 'As soon as we get them buying diapers from us, they're going to start buying everything else too. If you're rushing through the store, looking for bottles, and you pass orange juice, you'll grab a carton. Oh, and there's that new DVD I want. Soon, you'll be buying cereal and paper towels from us, and keep coming back.' …
>
> Andrew Pole['s] … assignment was to analyze all the cue-routine-reward loops among shoppers and help the company figure out how to exploit them. Much of his department's work was straightforward: find the customers who have children and send them catalogs that feature toys before Christmas. Look for shoppers who habitually purchase swimsuits in April and send them coupons for sunscreen in July and diet books in December. But Pole's most important assignment was to identify those unique moments in consumers' lives when their shopping habits become particularly flexible and the right advertisement or coupon would cause them to begin spending in new ways …
>
> But when some customers were going through a major life event, like graduating from college or getting a new job or moving to a new town, their shopping habits became flexible in ways that were both predictable and potential gold mines for retailers.

The study found that when someone marries, he or she is more likely to start buying a new type of coffee. When a couple move into a new house, they're more apt to purchase a different kind of cereal. When they divorce, there's an increased chance they'll start buying different brands of beer ...

As Pole's computers crawled through the data, he was able to identify about 25 products that, when analyzed together, allowed him to assign each shopper a 'pregnancy prediction' score. More important, he could also estimate her due date to within a small window, so Target could send coupons timed to very specific stages of her pregnancy.

(Duhigg, 2012)

The use of surveillance to prevent and detect cybercrimes, even ones as serious as terrorism, will be an ongoing debate, and one that requires an interdisciplinary approach. Psychology can contribute by furthering our knowledge on identity in the physical and cyber realms, and on citizens' attitudes towards how their personal identity is watched and used by others.

13.7 CONCLUSIONS

This chapter focused on a number of cyberenabled crimes, all of which can potentially cause great harm to an individual, organization and/or society. To some extent, legislation has been reworked to recognize these crimes, but often this legislation is inconsistent across nations (making it especially difficult to deal with crimes that cross borders). As scholars, we are also yet to clearly operationalize these crimes (hate crime is a good example of a crime that has not been clearly defined). In the quest to prevent and detect these crimes, governments have reworked legislation on surveillance methods; however, these methods have met strong opposition from the public, given they potentially threaten individuals' privacy. In Chapter 14 we consider another form of crime that has become a bigger problem since the advent of the Internet: child pornography and paedophilia.

DISCUSSION QUESTIONS

1. Where should one draw the line between cyberstalking and watching someone's activities online?
2. What are some of the current limitations with regard to research on cyberharassment and cyberstalking?
3. In your view, what strategies might be implemented to prevent hate crimes?

4. What contributions do you see psychologists making to the area of cyberwarfare (e.g., with regard to prevention and decisions on retaliation, deterrence and detection)?
5. Are drones ethical weapons and/or means of surveillance? Why, or why not?
6. What is your view on the use of surveillance of online personal data to detect and prevent crimes? How might this best be conducted and who ought to be privy (if anyone) to individuals' personal data?

SUGGESTED READINGS

Barak, A. (2005). Sexual harassment on the Internet. *Social Science Computer Review, 23*(1), 77–92.

Behm-Morawitz, E. & Schipper, S. (2015). Sexing the avatar: Gender, sexualisation and cyber-harassment in a virtual world. *Journal of Media Psychology.* doi: 10.1027/1864–1105/a000152

Guitton, C. (2012). Criminals and cyber attacks: The missing link between attribution and deterrence. International *Journal of Cyber Criminology, 6*(2), 1030–1043.

Hale, W. C. (2012). Extremism on the World Wide Web: A research review. *Criminal Justice Studies, 25*(4), 343–356.

Sheridan, L. P. & Grant, T. (2007). Is cyberstalking different? *Psychology, Crime & Law, 13*(6), 1477–2744.

Singer, P. W. (2009). Military robots and the laws of war. *New Atlantis, 23*(winter), 28–47.

Sparck-Jones, K. (2003). Privacy: What's different now? *Interdisciplinary Science Reviews, 28,* 287–292.

14 Online Crimes: Child Pornography and Paedophilia

This chapter again focuses on online crimes. This time the focus is on (1) those who access and/or trade child pornography images but who have no history or seeming motivation to engage in hands-on sexual abuse with children and (2) those who access and trade child pornography and use the Internet to facilitate hands-on sexual contact with children through grooming. We will consider the relationship between child pornography and hands-on child sexual abuse in relation to those in category (2) and also the likelihood of those in category (1) exhibiting the offender behaviour characteristic of (2) as a result of their interest in viewing child pornography. In addition, we will consider theories that seek to explain why individuals are motivated to view child pornography, what helps to maintain this motivation and the potential for escalation to hands-on sexual abuse. We begin by examining the legal understanding of child pornography and issues relating to defining terms, and the problems with assessing the extent to which putatively pornographic material can be shown to have violated child pornography law. The question of pseudo-photographs and virtual child pornography, and their status under the law, is also discussed. A summary of offender typology is presented in this chapter, with an emphasis on the pathology underlying sexual voyeurism and the offender as a collector of child pornography, as well as other classifications and characteristics relating to child pornography and paedophilic behaviour. We also discuss the relationships between accessing child pornography on the Internet, the proliferation of Internet child pornography among contact offenders, and hands-on offending behaviour. Finally, an overview of the current psychological understanding regarding offending behaviour is presented followed by a brief discussion on the use of technology to detect child pornography use and other Internet offences involving minors, such as sexual solicitation.

Before moving on to discuss these issues, however, first a point of clarification. The perpetrators of child sexual abuse are often referred to in the popular press as 'paedophiles'. The clinical use of the term 'paedophile' is reserved for those who have a sexual interest in prepubescent children (Berlin & Sawyer, 2012). Child pornography law, at least in the UK and the US, includes the sexual abuse of (post)pubescent children (in short, anyone under the age of 18). Individuals with a sexual interest in pubescent and prepubescent children are known as a 'hebephiles' (Neutze, Seto,

Cyberpsychology: The Study of Individuals, Society and Digital Technologies, First Edition.
Monica Therese Whitty and Garry Young.
© 2017 John Wiley & Sons, Ltd. Published 2017 by John Wiley & Sons, Ltd.

Schaefer, Mundt & Beier, 2011). Based on this clinical definition, someone can be convicted of violating child pornography law who is not a paedophile (because their sexual interest is in pubescent children). This distinction will be reflected in the language used throughout this chapter.

14.1 THE INTERNET AND THE INCREASE IN CHILD PORNOGRAPHY

The advent of the Internet has ushered in a new era in the production, transmission and accessibility of pornography, including child pornography (Lee, Li, Lamade, Schuler & Prentky, 2012; Motivans & Kyckelhahn, 2007; Tsaliki, 2011), which has grown exponentially (Taylor & Quayle, 2003) to become one of the fastest growing Internet industries (Bell & Kennedy, 2000; Jenkins, 2009). The ease of access to the Internet has given rise to 'cyber-paedocriminality' (Webb, Craissati & Keen, 2007), which describes a new form of criminal behaviour consisting of the *online* display, exchange, sale and purchase of files containing child pornography. In the US, for example, crimes involving Internet child pornography *only* (that is, in the absence of additional sex crimes such as child molestation) increased significantly between 2000 (935 cases) and 2006 (2,417 cases), and then again in 2009 (3,719 cases) (Wolak, Finkelhor & Mitchell, 2012). Indeed, Internet child pornography (hereafter, child pornography) offences now represent the largest portion of sexual exploitation cases prosecuted by federal attorneys in the US (Lam, Mitchell & Seto, 2010). To combat this increase in child pornography, international police operations (Genesis in 2001, Falcon in 2004 and Koala in 2006) have identified many cyber-paedocriminals (Niveau, 2010). Moreover, by 2008, the international policing agency Interpol's Child Abuse Image Database had gathered over half a million images of child abuse, which were used to identify nearly 700 victims worldwide (Elliot & Beech, 2009). Elliot and Beech (2009) also reported the 2008 findings of the UK Internet Watch Foundation's analysis of recovered images from websites containing child pornography. Of those images, 80% were found to be of children of 10 years of age or under (10% aged 2 or under, 33% between 3 and 6, and 37% between 7 and 10). The vast majority of these images (79%) were also found to be of girls; in fact, the most common child pornographic image is that of a prepubescent girl (Seto, 2010).

The Triple A Engine, mentioned in Chapter 5, has been applied to explain the volume of child pornography, in terms of its increased accessibility, affordability and anonymity (Cooper et al., 2000). Added to this, Quayle, Erooga, Wright, Taylor and Harbinson (2006) note how digitized pornographic material is much easier to store than nondigital material and requires little effort to keep hidden. The Internet also provides a medium through which offenders can initiate contact with potential sex abuse victims, as well as others who share a predilection for child abuse both in terms of sexualized images and hands-on offending (McCarthy, 2010). Given the prevalence of child pornography consumption, an issue of practical importance is the extent to which the consumer of child pornography is likely also to engage in contact sex offences or risk doing so in the future (Endrass et al., 2009).

14.2 CHILD PORNOGRAPHY AND THE LAW

It was not until the late 1970s that laws were enacted in the UK and US to prohibit *child* pornography specifically: these laws recognized child pornography as a distinct classification of prohibited activity (here, of course, 'child pornography' refers to pre-Internet material). Prior to this, there occurred no differentiation between adult and child pornography, the regulation of each was based on the same obscenity laws (Gillespie, 2010). In fact, only in 1982 did the Supreme Court of the US expel child pornography – defined as material 'that visually depict[s] sexual conduct by children below a specified age' – from protection under the First Amendment (regarding freedom of expression) because it 'is intrinsically related to the sexual abuse of children' (New York v. Ferber, 1982, p. 764, cited in Ray, Kimonis, Donoghue, 2010, p. 85). Related to this point, it is worth noting that the UK Child Exploitation and Online Protection Centre, as a matter of course, sends out notes for editors to the effect that the phrase 'child pornography' should be replaced with 'child abuse' or 'images of child abuse'. Use of 'child pornography' incorrectly suggests legitimacy and compliance, rather than the actual abuse that has taken place (Adams, 2010; see also Edwards, 2000; Tate, 1992, Taylor & Quayle, 2003). This position is echoed by Williams (1991), who states: 'Child pornography is no less than a visual record of child abuse. Each video or photograph records a criminal offence against a child' (p. 88). Moreover, in addition to the abuse itself, the representation of this abuse (as a permanent record) amounts to the revictimization of the child (Beech, Elliot, Birgden & Findlater, 2008; Taylor & Quayle, 2003). While recognizing the validity of this point, we shall nevertheless continue to use the term 'child pornography' for convenience, given that the term is used extensively within the relevant literature.

14.2.1 Objective and functional aspects of child pornography content

Material that constitutes child pornography under the law and material used by those who have a sexual interest in children do not necessarily match. It may be that images of children used to elicit sexual arousal in an individual do not depict sexual abuse;

they may not even contain images of children partially or completely nude. In and of themselves, then, as images of children, they may be quite innocuous and not violate child pornography law (Tate, 1990). As Howitt (1995) points out, sexual stimulation may not be based on explicit sexual content but on the fantasy occurring in the mind of the offender. Taylor, Holland and Quayle (2001) thus distinguish between child pornography (which depicts explicit sexual abuse) and child erotica (which reflects more the use to which the image is put: to elicit sexual arousal).

It is more often the case, of course, that those with a sexual interest in children do possess, or are motivated to possess or at least view, images of children that do violate child pornography law and therefore do constitute images of child abuse. Nevertheless, Taylor and Quayle's point regarding the independence of some form of objective measure of content from the use to which the image is put (the purpose it serves for the viewer) is a pertinent one.

14.2.2 Varying legal interpretations

How child pornography is defined legally varies from country to country, as does the interpretation of terms such as 'child'. Given the worldwide variation in how child pornography is defined and regulated, our focus will be on UK and US legal definitions, as these tend to occupy a prominent place in the relevant literature. In the UK, Section 6A.1 of the 2003 Sexual Offences Act amends both the 1978 Child Protection Act and the Criminal Justice Act of 1988 such that it is 'a crime to take, make, permit to take, distribute, show, possess, possess with intent to distribute, or to advertise indecent photographs or pseudo-photographs of any person below the age of 18'. What constitutes 'indecent' is to be determined by a jury based on recognized standards of propriety. The level of sentencing for those found guilty of violating section 6A.1 must reflect the seriousness of the offence, ranging from level 1 (images depicting erotic posing with no sexual activity) to level 5 (involving sadism or penetration of, or by, an animal; see COPINE scale below).

In the US, the Department of Justice guide to Federal Law, under the child exploitation and obscenity section, states that:

> Section 2256 of Title 18, United States Code, defines child pornography as any visual depiction of sexually explicit conduct involving a minor (someone under 18 years of age). Visual depictions include photographs, videos, digital or computer generated images indistinguishable from an actual minor, and images created, adapted, or modified, but appear [sic] to depict an identifiable, actual minor.

In addition:

> The legal definition of sexually explicit conduct does not require that an image depict a child engaging in sexual activity. A picture of a naked child may constitute illegal child pornography if it is sufficiently sexually suggestive.
>
> (US Department of Justice, 2015)

14.2.3 Child pornography and the age of consent

Within the UK and the US definitions of child pornography, a child is anyone under the age of 18. This age is also stipulated in international law with regard to child pornography (Gillespie, 2010; see Article 1a of the UN Convention on the Rights of a Child; see also the Council of Europe's Convention on Cybercrime and the Council of Europe's Convention on Sexual Exploitation). As such, if the image is of a person under the age of 18, then, in relation to child pornography legislation, the image is of a child. In a number of countries, this age differs from the age of consent whereby one may legally engage in sexual intercourse. In the UK, for example, the age is 16 (but this can also depend on whether a vulnerable individual is involved and/or there is a power imbalance, as in the case of a pupil and teacher). In the US, the age of consent varies between 16 and 18, depending on which state you are in. Worldwide the range is 12–20 (in the case of consent at 12, the partner must be under 18 years of age).

Given this discrepancy, even between the UK and certain US states, if one is over the age of consent but under 18, one could engage in legal sexual intercourse with another over the age of consent yet not legally be allowed to possess sexually explicit images of one's partner or send such images of oneself to one's partner (see Berlin & Sawyer, 2012).

As mentioned in Chapter 5, sexting is a predominantly adolescent practice of sending or posting text messages and/or images of a sexually suggestive nature, including nude or seminude photographs, via one's mobile phone or over the Internet (Levick & Moon, 2010). The creation of such images of minors, by minors (even where the minor is over 16 years of age), meets statutory definitions of child pornography (Walsh, Wolak & Finkelhor, 2013; see also Mitchell, Finkelhor, Jones & Wolak, 2012). Yet, according to Levick and Moon (2010), prosecuting minors in sexting cases is a gross misapplication of child pornography law, given that such practice is merely a new expression of normative adolescent sexual development (see also Comartin, Kernsmith & Kernsmith, 2013). In the US, the prosecution of sexting occurs only in cases of:

- malicious intent, bullying, coercion or harassment (in cases where photographs are sent to someone and then distributed for the reasons noted);
- distribution (continued sexting after an intervention and/or the sending of images to people the images were not originally intended for in the absence of victim consent);
- a large age difference between the people involved;
- graphic representation (very sexually explicit and/or sexually violent images). (Adapted from Walsh et al., 2013)

Sexting is therefore a new social problem (as discussed in Chapter 5) that legislation has yet to come to grips with.

14.3 PSEUDO-PHOTOGRAPHS

The digital era has brought with it its own problems and challenges for those legislating against child pornography. Pseudo-photographs of child pornography involve the manipulation of actual photographs, or digital representations of persons/children that are then altered. This may involve manipulating the image of a nude adult such that it appears to be of a child, or the manipulation of a nonpornographic image of a child such that it appears to be pornographic. In the latter case, an image of a child originally depicted licking an ice-cream (for example) may be manipulated so that the child appears to be engaged in an act of fellatio on an adult (Gillespie, 2010).

In the case of actual child pornography, where the image is of a sexualized child or of child abuse, the photograph or video constitutes a record of the event. In the case of pseudo-photographs, however, what is produced is an event that is not real but that is presented *as if* it were real (Oswell, 2006). For Williams (2003), although such 'photoshopped' images are very unpleasant, they are in effect no more 'true' than paintings. Nevertheless, even though it is accepted that, in the context of child pornography, the indecent photograph and the indecent pseudo-photograph are not equivalent, with regard to UK legislation (see the 2003 Sexual Offences Act and the 2009 Coroners and Justice Act) they are treated *as if* identical (Oswell, 2006). As such, pseudo-photographs of the kind described above, even though they do not depict abuse per se, are held to be exploitative and therefore 'a crime not only against a *particular* child, but against *all* children' (Oswell, 2006, p. 252, emphasis in original).

Legislation in the US, for its part, sought to take account of the digital era with its 1996 Child Pornography Prevention Act (as noted above), whereby the definition of child pornography included not only that which actually depicts the sexual abuse of a minor but also that which *appears* to depict a minor engaging in sexual activity. Under this definition, creators and possessors of pseudo-photographs or even digitally created images involving no actual images of children could be prosecuted under the law (Samenow, 2012).

In 2002, however, a ruling was made in the case of *Ashcroft versus Free Speech Coalition* (525 U.S. 234), which set out to challenge the 1996 Child Pornography Prevention Act (18 U.S.C.§ 2251) (see Kosse, 2004). In contrast to UK legislation, the US Supreme Court ruled that whilst 'it remains illegal to make, show or possess sexually explicit pictures of children ... [there is] no compelling reason to prohibit the manufacture or exhibition of pictures which merely *appear* to be of children' (Levy, 2002, p. 319). Moreover, with regard to images of a purely digital origin – that do not involve any actual minors and therefore do not record a crime (namely, virtual child pornography) – the Supreme Court ruled that, as the US child pornography laws were implemented to prevent the victimization of children and as there was no victim in cases of virtual child pornography, there was no compelling reason to restrict such freedom of expression.

When Paul and Linz (2008) exposed adults to 'barely legal' pornography in order to test an assumption made by the US government in defence of the 1996 Child Pornography Protection Act – 'that virtual child pornography stimulates and whets adults' appetites for sex with children and that such content can result in the sexual abuse or exploitation of minors becoming acceptable to and even preferred by the viewer' (p. 35) – they found that, although those who viewed the material were more likely to cognitively associate sexual activity with nonsexual images of minors (based on response latency), there was no evidence that exposure caused the participants to be more accepting of child pornography or paedophilia. (Barely legal pornography uses models who are over 18 years of age but who are depicted as being under or just over the legal age of consent.) The Paul and Linz finding challenges the US government's assertion that child pornography leads to actual instances of child abuse and, instead, supports the 2002 Supreme Court's view that, at present, there is no evidence indicating that a causal link is anything other than contingent and indirect.

Importantly, and by way of clarification, the 2002 ruling of the Supreme Court did not affect the continued prohibition of 'morphed' images, which integrate images of real children in order to create child pornography. In 2003, however, the PROTECT Act was introduced; this limits the permissibility of virtual child pornography by prohibiting obscene material (obscenity is based on accepted contemporary community standards). Specifically, the law criminalizes:

> a visual depiction of any kind, including a 'drawing, cartoon, sculpture or painting' that 'depicts a minor engaging in sexually explicit conduct and is obscene' or 'depicts an image that is, or appears to be, of a minor engaging in ... sexual intercourse ... and lacks serious literary, artistic, political, or scientific value. (18 USC §1466A)
>
> (Samenow, 2012, p. 19)

With regard to virtual child pornography – which, in the US at least, is not illegal unless it contravenes obscenity law – the US Supreme Court decided that:

- Virtual child pornography is not intrinsically related to child sexual abuse in the way actual child pornography is and so cannot be linked to any actual crime.
- Any connection with actual child sexual abuse is indirect and contingent and so cannot be said necessarily to be connected to any future child abuse.
- Prohibition of virtual child pornography cannot be based on the *possibility* that it will cause harm to some children.

14.4 TYPES OF CHILD PORNOGRAPHY OFFENDERS

In this section, we consider how child pornography offenders can be categorized. Berlin and Sawyer (2012), for example, divide child pornography offenders into the following subcategories:

1. *Sexual molesters*: those who, in addition to viewing child pornography, have an interest in (and sometimes a past history of) actually approaching a child sexually (face to face).
2. *Sexual solicitors*: those who, in addition to viewing child pornography, engage in sexualized 'chats' with children without being motivated to meet face to face. (Some perpetrators may initiate contact in this way first, of course, as a means of achieving contact characteristic of subcategory 1).

3. *Sexual voyeurs*: those with no documented history of ever having attempted to approach a child sexually (and with no evidence of an interest in wanting to actually do so) but who nevertheless manifest a pattern of viewing child pornography (sometimes compulsively).

14.4.1 *Paraphilic disorder not otherwise specified*

When the computers of subcategory 3 offenders are confiscated, no evidence is found of sexually inappropriate 'chats' with children characteristic of subcategory 2 (Berlin & Sawyer, 2012). Following publicity after their arrest, there are no reports of children coming forward accusing them of any form of inappropriate contact akin to subcategory 1. In fact, as Berlin and Sawyer (2012) go on to note, many in subcategory 3 have children of their own who likewise do not report inappropriate sexual contact from their parent. Given this, Berlin and Sawyer (2012) conclude:

> Some individuals appear to be experiencing compulsive urges to voyeuristically view such images [of child pornography], devoid of any motivation to actually approach a child sexually. In other words, in such instances, the act of voyeuristically, and often compulsively, viewing such imagery over the Internet would appear to be an end in and of itself; rather than a means to some other end – such as actual sexual contact. (pp. 31–32)

Nevertheless, based on DSM-IV-TR, the voyeuristic viewing of child pornography, in the manner just described, is classified as a 'paraphilic disorder not otherwise specified'. This refers to individuals classified as having a compulsive desire to repeatedly view sexually explicit images of *prepubescent* children; the primary components of their paraphilic disorder are voyeurism and paedophilia (Berlin & Sawyer, 2012). The paedophilic aspect of this disorder is restricted to voyeurism over the Internet and, as such, should be distinguished from paedophilia per se, whereby an individual is motivated to *engage* in a sexual act with a prepubescent child (characteristic of direct victimization) and not simply view images of young children with sexualized content. In support of this clinical distinction, Galbreath, Berlin and Sawyer (2002) found in a study of 39 Internet child pornography offenders that 23% were diagnosed with paedophilia while 49% were diagnosed with a paraphilic disorder not otherwise specified.

The Internet has a number of characteristics (unique features) likely to appeal to cyber-paedocriminals, especially those who engage in high levels of sexual fantasy yet retain a strong inhibition from acting on their fantasies (Niveau, 2010). According to Niveau (2010), these characteristics are:

- relative, or at least perceived, anonymity;
- ease of access;
- affordability;
- unlimited market;

- a blurring of the border between consumer and producer (every consumer has the potential to be a producer by an exchange of files);
- unlimited opportunities for fantasy experiences.

14.4.2 Collectors

Many child pornographers go beyond merely viewing or even acquiring images of children or child abuse; more than this, they *collect* these images, cataloguing and indexing them as part of their collection: what Taylor (1999) refers to as the 'collector syndrome'. Svedin and Back (1996; cited in Oswell, 2006) describe different 'collectors' thus:

- The *closet collector* is someone who views images but has no direct sexual contact with children.
- The *isolated collector* is someone who, in addition to viewing images, engages in child sexual abuse.
- The *cottage collector* differs from the isolated collector in as much as they share their collection with others and are involved with others in hands-on abuse.
- The *commercial collector* is someone who profits from the distribution of the child pornography they produce. The commercial collector is compatible with Elliot and Beech's (2009) reference to 'commercial exploitation', which involves those who produce and trade child pornography for financial gain, perhaps as part of wider illegal activities, and who therefore may have no specific interest in child sexual contact.

The motivation to become a collector is seen as symptomatic of the underlying pathology and, in the case of the cottage collector, a binding feature of the social relationship the offender has with others who are similarly motivated (Oswell, 2006). Taylor et al. (2001) also argue that the collections themselves are not arbitrary; therefore their selective content reveals something about the 'mind' of the collector, such that even images that themselves would not fall foul of UK and US legal definitions of child pornography are abusive in virtue of their place within the collection, given what motivates that collection. Taylor et al. (2001) provide a typology of images based on the 10-point COPINE scale (COPINE stands for Combating Paedophile Information Networks in Europe). This scale range is as follows: (1) indicative, (2) nudist, (3) erotica, (4) posing, (5) erotic posing, (6) explicit erotic posing, (7) explicit sexual activity, (8) assault, (9) gross assault, (10) sadistic/bestiality. Thus, even images classified at the lowest point on the scale (nonerotic and nonsexualized images of children in everyday situations), when present within a collection (as described above), are indicative of the deliberate sexual victimization of children. For Taylor et al. (2001), then, whether a collector fits Svedin and Back's (1996; cited in Oswell, 2006) closet typology or whether a collector perpetrates actual hands-on child abuse makes no difference with regard to the pathology of the offender. To view images of children, especially within a collection put together to elicit sexual arousal, even at the lowest level of the COPINE scale, amounts to child victimization. The pathology of the offender is therefore not just restricted to, or solely characterized by, the hands-on sexual abuse of children but also evidenced through the images that form part of the collection of even a closet collector.

14.5 CHARACTERISTICS OF CHILD PORNOGRAPHY OFFENDERS

We now turn our attention to the characteristics of child pornography offenders. Galbreath et al. (2002) claim that those who access child pornography are overwhelmingly male (see, however, Seigfried-Spellar & Rogers, 2010, for a study on females) but, apart from that, come from a variety of backgrounds. Reijnen, Bulten and Nijman (2009), based on a Dutch sample, likewise state that child pornography offenders share much of the same heterogeneity found in the nonoffending population (see also Nielssen et al., 2011). In fact, McCarthy (2010) holds that, at present, a profile of a *typical* child pornography offender does not exist. Nevertheless, some studies have indicated differences.

Based on US findings, many are relatively well educated (O'Brien & Webster, 2007). Wolak, Finkelhor and Mitchell (2005) found that, from a sample of 1,713 individuals convicted of child pornography offences, 37% had gone to college and/or obtained a college diploma and an additional 4% had PhDs. According to Burke, Sowerbutts, Blundell and Sherry (2002), who used an Australian sample, offenders tend to be between the ages of 25 and 50. Web et al. (2007) reported that their sample of Internet offenders (n = 90) had a mean age of 38, which was lower than hands-on sexual offenders; they also tended to have fewer live-in relationships than hands-on sexual offenders.

Middleton, Elliot, Mandeville-Norden and Beech (2006) found that Internet offenders diagnosed with psychological deficits tended to be socially isolated or have intimacy problems. Henry, Mandeville-Norden, Hayes and Egan (2010), in turn, reported evidence of emotional inadequacy and high deviancy in a sample of 422 child pornography offenders. Internet use was also seen as a way of easing emotional stress. It is important to note, however, that almost half of the offenders in Henry et al.'s study did not exhibit any psychological deficits. In fact, Neutze et al. (2011) found no evidence of an emotional deficit at all in their sample. In addition, when comparing child pornography offenders with non-Internet sexual offenders, Reijnen et al. (2009) found child pornography offenders tended to be younger, to live alone, to be single and to have no children. Reijnen et al. thus concluded that child pornography offenders were more socially isolated. These findings are in line with those of Middleton et al. (2006) and Web et al. (2007) noted above. Reijnen et al. also speculated over whether social isolation (owing to, say, problems with intimacy) might act as a trigger for offenders' Internet behaviour or whether their paedophilic disposition has a detrimental effect on any attempt to engage in intimate adult relationships.

14.6 THE RELATIONSHIP BETWEEN CHILD PORNOGRAPHY AND HANDS-ON OFFENDING

Most contemporary child pornography offenders commit their offences over the Internet (Ray et al., 2010). As mentioned earlier in this chapter, among these offenders is a distinct category of individuals who restrict their offending behaviour to the voyeuristic pursuit of child abuse images. Given the dual potential of the Internet, however, for those with a sexual preference for minors – both in terms of viewing images and soliciting more direct contact (e.g., the direct victimization typology) – one is left to consider the relationship between child pornography and hands-on child sexual abuse. For, although a demarcation based on those who engage in hands-on child abuse and those who only view it may be legitimate in some cases, it nevertheless remains evident that those charged with child solicitation and/or molestation are often caught in possession of child pornography (Kingston, Fedoroff, Firestone, Curry & Bradford, 2008; Riegel, 2004).

There is also the matter of escalation, whereby the offender's deviant sexual excitation could prompt them to seek out increasingly shocking depictions (Niveau, 2010) and/or engage in hands-on child abuse (Seto & Eke, 2005). Quayle and Taylor (2002) and Sullivan and Beech (2003) argue that a proclivity for child pornography increases the likelihood of committing a contact offence against a minor in the form of either sexual molestation or sexual solicitation (Seto, Wood, Babchishin & Flynn, 2012). One is left to consider, then, the extent to which an active interest in child pornography leads perpetrators to contact offend or, instead, to remain content with viewing sexualized images of children.

In a study by Bourke and Hernandez (2009), based on a sample of 155 child pornography offenders, 85% admitted to abusing a child on at least one occasion. Wolak et al. (2005) reported that, from a sample of 1,713 child pornography offenders, 40% were dual offenders – meaning they also committed hands-on child sexual abuse – and, of these, 39% met their victims on the Internet. Seto, Hanson and Babchishin (2011) found that one in eight child pornography offenders had an official history of contact offending. Seto and Eke (2005) noted that child pornography offenders with a history of hands-on sexual abuse were more likely to reoffend, whereas those guilty only of child pornography violations did not go on to contact offend (at least during the study's follow-up period; see Eke, Seto & Williams, 2011, for a further follow-up study). Webb et al. (2007), in turn, found that, although there was evidence of reoffending among those convicted of child pornography offences (but who were not also child molesters), their reoffending was confined to the accessing of child pornography; there was no evidence that they went on to contact offend. In fact, McCarthy (2010) considers the lack of contact offending (including Internet grooming) to be a factor instrumental in distinguishing between these two deviant groups. To illustrate further, among a sample (n = 290) of child pornography offenders with a sexual preference for boys, Riegel (2004) found that 84% reported that the image acted as a substitute for an actual child, with 84.5% stating that viewing such imagery did not increase their desire to engage in hands-on abuse with boys.

Lee et al. (2012) found that child pornography offenders recorded high scores for Internet preoccupation and low scores for traits associated with antisocial personality disorder (what they call 'antisociality') compared to dual offenders who scored high on both measures. Lee et al. conjecture that the low or high measure on antisociality, in relation to high Internet preoccupation, might provide a useful predictor of dual offending and therefore who among those with a child pornography conviction might engage in (or have engaged in) hands-on child sexual contact.

14.7 THEORETICAL APPROACHES TO CHILD PORNOGRAPHY OFFENDING

This section outlines some of the psychological theories that have been proposed to explain why some people become paedophiles.

14.7.1 Courtship disorder theory

Courtship disorder theory (Freund & Blanchard, 1986; Freund, Scher & Hucker, 1983) posits that normal sexual interactions progress through four discrete stages. The first involves locating a potential partner. Contact is then made though looking and talking (known as pretactile interaction). Next, the courtship progresses towards tactile interactions such as caressing and kissing, before culminating in genital union. A pathological disturbance in this progression is typically characterized by a distortion – likely in the form of intensification – in one of the stages of normal courtship.

Earlier in this chapter, we saw how some child pornography offenders were found to be socially isolated, to have intimacy problems or to be emotionally inadequate (Henry et al., 2010; Middleton et al., 2006; Web et al., 2007). Jung, Ennis and Malesky (2012), following Elliot, Beech, Mandeville-Norden and Hayes (2009), suggest that the behaviour of child pornography offenders should be understood as part of a process of achieving a kind of pseudo-intimacy that compensates, without the risk of rejection, for any lack of intimacy in real life. Recall how those perpetrators diagnosed with a paraphilic disorder (not otherwise specified) exhibited a strong voyeuristic component to their pathology. Thus, Jung et al. (2012) conjecture, the 'compulsive use of the Internet to obtain illegal pornographic material may be conceptually similar to the pathological distortion of the first stage of locating and appraising a potential partner' (p. 662).

In response to the question of whether child pornography offending will escalate to either sexual solicitation or molestation, if the fixation on a minor by the individual with a paraphilic disorder (not otherwise specified) is part of a disordered courtship, then such an individual 'may not be confined to maintain non-contact with potential victims, but rather may be inclined to engage in the subsequent phases of human sexual interaction, progressing to pretactile interactions and onwards to engaging in genital union' (Jung et al., 2012, p. 662).

The explanation of courtship disorder theory is couched within an evolutionary approach to mate selection. This, however, has little to say about the social and/or situational influences on offending behaviour, particularly as they arise through the Internet (e.g., Wortley & Smallbone, 2006).

14.7.2 Social learning theory

As a reminder, social learning theory (Bandura, 1977) advocates learning through observation and modelling. If one observes a behaviour that is rewarded, one is more likely to model and therefore engage in that behaviour. The Internet's enhanced communication capabilities increase in scope the types of behaviours one can observe and therefore model, including sexually abusive behaviour towards children. Within an environment where it is possible to observe and/or interact with others engaged in child sexual abuse, observers will be able to learn and potentially model behaviours characteristic of abuse. It is also possible that in such an environment – within an online pro-paedophile group – individuals may experience a sense of community, where the virtues of child abuse are extolled and [individuals'] sexual interest in minors validated (Malesky & Ennis, 2004). Recall how, for cottage collectors, the sharing of child pornography images and even the joint organization of hands-on sexual abuse are binding features of the social relation the offender has with others who are similarly motivated.

Internet exposure of this kind may produce a cognitive shift in observers such that they adopt a more accepting stance towards offending behaviours and so become more inclined to relax the inhibitions that previously prevented them from engaging in sexual abuse (Jung et al., 2012). This sense of community and validation can be seen in the following quote, taken from a pro-paedophile website: 'Because of this newsgroup, I realized only one and a half months ago that I am a boy lover. I laugh, I cried, and shared all your beautiful, sad, and funny posting. It was the first time in my life that someone showed feelings which seemed to be mine' (Durkin, 1996, p. 108; cited in Jung et al., 2012, p. 658).

According to Jung et al. (2012), to an unprecedented degree, the Internet enables the dissemination and acquisition of beliefs that support child-offending behaviours. Pro-paedophilic views are available in the absence of censure and, importantly, a dissenting voice declaring that what offenders are doing is harmful. As such, the relative ease with which it is possible to access and/or trade child pornography on the Internet – seemingly with impunity – could, for the proponents of social learning theory, indirectly encourage others to engage in the same abusive behaviour.

14.7.3 Finkelhor's precondition model

Courtship disorder theory and social learning theory are by no means incompatible. Child pornographers may acquire a distorted sense of pseudo-intimacy through the observation of child sexualized images and learn (through modelling) more sophisticated offence behaviours; they may also feel vindicated in this through Internet communication with other like-minded individuals, which then acts to reinforce what they do. As part of courtship disorder theory's courtship progression and through further social learning theory practices, the Internet offender may 'progress' from Internet viewing of pornography to child sexual solicitation and/or molestation.

According to Finkelhor (1984), four preconditions must be satisfied before hands-on child sexual abuse can occur (adapted from Elliot & Beech, 2009). Perpetrators must:

1. be *motivated to offend* because (a) they believe that sex with children would be emotionally satisfying and/or (b) they are sexually aroused by children and/or (c) normal sexual outlets (with adults) are blocked and/or (d) they are disinhibited in ways others are not normally disinhibited;
2. be able to *overcome internal inhibitors*, perhaps through (a) cognitive distortions (of the kind described in 1a) and/or (b) impulsivity and/or (c) substance abuse;
3. be able to *overcome external inhibitors* (the normal barriers that would block access to children), perhaps through (a) grooming and/or (b) a caregiver or professional organization, if either has access to children;
4. be able to *overcome the resistance of the child*, perhaps through threats or gifts (including the giving and withholding of privileges) and/or desensitization and normalization through exposure (of the child) to child pornography.

14.7.4 The pathways model and the integrated theory of sexual offending

Ward and Siegert (2002) argue that child sexual abuse is the culmination of a number of different factors – or different pathways to abuse – one of which will exert a primary causal influence, the others only secondary (which pathway is considered primary and which are secondary will vary from offender to offender, of course). The pathways model posits that a number of different pathways could *lead* to the sexual abuse of a child; it does not, however, proffer an account of why child molestation may *continue*. Ward and Siegert (2002) identify four distinct and interacting psychological mechanisms within their causal account of child molestation. These present as deficits in intimacy and social skills, distorted sexual scripts, emotional dysregulation and cognitive distortions. In addition, as part of their integrated theory of sexual offending (ITSO), Ward and Beech (2006) introduce the idea of an 'ecological niche', which refers to the interaction of a person's biology with their sociocultural as well as physical environment (their social learning). ITSO also focuses on three neuropsychological systems that are said to express an individual's ecological niche – and, in the case of perpetrators of child sexual abuse, are suggested to be partly or wholly dysfunctional. Disruption in these neuropsychological systems is said to result in problems with adult sexual intimacy, behavioural self-regulation and maladaptive beliefs. Elliot and Beech (2009) integrate the pathways model and the ITSO and apply them to the perpetrators of child pornography. The key aspects of this integration are presented below.

14.7.4.1 Self-regulatory control problems

Child pornography offenders report viewing child sexualized imagery on the Internet as a means of escaping from some (perceived) unpleasant aspect of their lives (Quayle & Taylor, 2002); they shut themselves off from (unpleasant) personal circumstances. Viewing child pornography is therefore understood to be instrumental in dealing with difficult emotional states, particularly as the immediate reward of sexual gratification (achieved through viewing these images while masturbating) can be highly reinforcing (Gifford, 2002).

14.7.4.2 Social/intimacy problems

Previously, we discussed studies suggesting that some viewers of child pornography had problems initiating and/or maintaining intimate relationships with adults. As a result, the online sexual behaviour of these offenders takes on a more significant role given their problems with adult face-to-face sexual contact. This may lead to perpetrators accessing Internet child pornography (in the case of the periodically prurient group) and/or more actively seeking it out and trading it (in the case of the fantasy-only group) owing to the less threatening nature of this sexual behaviour compared to face-to-face sexual contact with adults (Middleton et al., 2006; see also section on courtship disorder theory above).

14.7.4.3 Antisocial thinking patterns

Ward (2000) argues that there are five beliefs characteristic of the distorted thinking patterns of child sex abusers:

1. Children are sexual beings insofar as they need/desire sexual contact with adults and are able to consent to this.
2. Sexual activity with children is not harmful.
3. The offender is superior to the child and is therefore deserving of special treatment.
4. The world is a dangerous place full of untrustworthy people.
5. The offender is not fully in control of their own actions.

Howitt and Sheldon (2007) found differences in the beliefs of child pornography offenders and child molesters with regard to (1), with the former group having a stronger belief to this effect than the latter. Elliot and Beech (2009) conjecture that this may be because pornography offenders – particularly from the fantasy-only group – typically view idealized sexualized images of children that appear to confirm belief (1), unlike child molesters, who experience the reality of the situation, which contradicts this belief.

Elliot and Beech (2009; following Taylor & Quayle, 2003) also describe how child sex pornography offenders engage in 'moral disengagement' (Bandura, 1986), which is a further feature of their distorted thinking patterns. They will often try to justify their behaviour and its relative harmlessness (as they construe it) in terms of it 'only involving pictures', and in terms of the images simply forming part of a collection. Normalization also occurs through the claim that they are not alone in their actions: 'others do it too'. The perception of images as objects is also characteristic of the process of dehumanization, which is a further feature of moral disengagement. Diffusion of responsibility is also evident when offenders talk about the Internet 'being to blame' owing to the prevalence of these images and their ease of access. Deviant sexual interest in children, according to Elliot and Beech (2009), is therefore the result of problems with the self-regulation of one's mood states, sexual desire and desire for sexual control in relation to distorted sex-related beliefs about children – all of which creates deviant sexual fantasies and an inappropriate sexual preoccupation.

14.8 CONCLUSIONS

The Internet has brought with it increased access to pornographic material involving children (images of child abuse) and facilitated its distribution. It has also provided increased opportunities for paedophiles to make contact with children. In this chapter we have offered reasons for this increase and, importantly, provided a summary of legislation around child pornography in the UK and the US, including some of the differences in this legislation. We have also look at the ways in which child pornography offenders have been categorized and considered their characteristics, recognizing, perhaps, that there is no typical child pornography offender. The relationship between those who view child pornography and hands-on offending has also been discussed, particularly in relation to the concern that viewing child pornography will lead to an escalation in offending behaviour (a kind of slippery-slope argument). We finished the chapter by examining theoretical models that have been applied or developed specifically to explain and therefore help us understand the mechanisms and processes that contribute to someone becoming a paedophile. The diversity of explanations is most likely an expression of the multiple factors that contribute to child pornography offending, which, far from being created with the inception of the Internet, has simply transcended spaces from the offline realm to the virtual.

DISCUSSION QUESTIONS

1. Do you think that sexting is merely a new expression of normal adolescent sexual development? Do you think that minors in sexting cases should be prosecuted or do you think that such prosecutions would amount to a gross misapplication of child pornography law?
2. In your opinion, how should the law treat sexualized pseudo-photographs? Should sexualized pseudo-photographs and sexualized images created in the absence of an image of an actual child (e.g., a computer-generated avatar of a child) be treated in the same way under the law as real images of children?
3. Evidence suggests that there exists a specific group of child pornography offenders who access child pornography without seeking to make contact with children online (for the purpose of solicitation and molestation). To what extent do you think such behaviour will inevitably escalate? That is, would you endorse a slippery slope argument in which it is held that this initial behaviour will or is likely to lead to the solicitation and molestation of children?
4. In relation to the question above, do you think that it would be morally and legally acceptable for child pornography offenders who have never engaged in solicitation or molestation of children to access sexualized images of virtual children (that is, digitally created representations of children)?

SUGGESTED READINGS

Berlin, F. S. & Sawyer, D. (2012). Potential consequences of accessing child pornography over the Internet and who is accessing it. *Sexual Addiction & Compulsivity, 19*(1–2), 30–40.

Quayle, E. & Ribisl, K. M. (2012). *Understanding and preventing online sexual exploitation of children.* London, UK: Routledge.

Seto, M. C. (2010). Child pornography use and Internet solicitation in the diagnosis of pedophilia. *Archives of Sexual Behavior, 39,* 591–593.

Taylor, M., Holland, G. & Quayle, E. (2001). Typology of paedophile picture collections. *Police Journal, 74*(2), 97–107.

Wortley, R. K. & Smallbone, S. (2012). *Internet child pornography: Causes, investigations and preventions.* Santa Barbara, CA: Praeger.

15 Online Support and Health Care

The aim of this chapter is to consider the impact of the Internet and related technologies on health care, in terms of the availability of health-related information, support and treatment. We begin by examining the types of people who are more likely to search for online health information and why they do so, as well as the potential negative impact of this on the individual, in the form of 'cyberchondria'. Following this, we look at online forums as places of knowledge and support for those with health-related issues. Use of the Internet for therapy has been around since the early days and so, importantly, we discuss online therapy (or e-therapy) and evaluate its effectiveness. Finally, we present examples of the ways in which immersive virtual environments are being used as treatments for a number of health-related conditions.

15.1 THE INTERNET AND HEALTH

The Internet has changed our relationship with health-related information, for, although research typically shows that health-care professionals continue to be the preferred contact point for the majority of people with health concerns (Berle et al., 2015; Fox, 2011), online resources such as health searches and forums (where one can seek advice from peers and/or 'informed others') have nevertheless become a significant source of health information, particularly in the US (Fox, 2011). It is therefore no exaggeration to state that 'the Internet is bringing about a structural transformation of the cultural practices and organization of health systems' (Rossi, 2006, p. 9). In support of this claim, in 2003, Eysenbach and Kohler reported that up to 6.75 million health-related Internet searches were made every day worldwide on Google. In addition, Rossi (citing the Pew Internet & American Life Project) reported that, at the turn of the twenty-first century, 55% of people in the US with Internet access (equating to 52 million people) had used the Internet to obtain health-related information or had used online health services (the average across European countries at that time was lower: around 23%). Of these, 92% reported finding the information useful. By 2008, the proportion of Americans searching for online health information had risen

Cyberpsychology: The Study of Individuals, Society and Digital Technologies, First Edition.
Monica Therese Whitty and Garry Young.
© 2017 John Wiley & Sons, Ltd. Published 2017 by John Wiley & Sons, Ltd.

to an estimated 75–80% of those with Internet access (Fox, 2008). More recently, Lauckner and Hsieh (2013) reported that Google had announced that general-health-related sites had an estimated combined unique monthly visitor tally of around 117.8 million and that WebMD had likewise claimed to receive 111.8 million unique monthly visitors.

As part of this changing relationship to health-related information, Powell (2011) makes the point that young people who have grown up with the Internet – sometimes referred to as 'digital natives' – are fundamentally different from previous generations in terms of how they communicate, seek information and generally interact and entertain themselves because of their familiarity with, and reliance on, digital technology (as discussed in Chapter 7). As such, they have 'expectations that public services such as healthcare will be digital' (Powell, 2011, p. 368; see also Owens et al., 2012). In response, social media is now being incorporated into health-care settings by providing, for example, emergency alerts, as well as by helping to monitor patient care. The World Health Organization likewise uses social media (Twitter and YouTube, among others) as a means of keeping the population up to date with the latest health-related news (Catford, 2011). The Internet should therefore be considered a source of health-related benefit to patients and health professionals alike (Wright, 2012).

15.2 CHARACTERISTICS AND MOTIVATIONS

Who is more likely to engage in online searches and what motivates this activity? According to Lee and Hawkins (2010), those with health problems tend to look for information to help them understand their diagnosis, prognosis and treatment; but, equally, those who consider themselves to be healthy also look for health-related information in order to learn more about their physical well-being (we will consider psychological/mental well-being in more detail later when discussing e-therapy). Similarly, Rice (2006), after analysing a number of US databases, concluded that those most likely to search for health-related information via the Internet are individuals who have just been diagnosed with a medical condition or who are seeking to help others cope with their medical problems (e.g., a friend or parent, or some other family carer, caring for a child who has a chronic illness). Rice also found that employed women are among those most likely to seek out health-related information online. In short, based on the growth of health-related websites and the findings of a number of studies carried out across Europe and North America (e.g., Health on the Net Foundation, 2001; Skinner, Biscope, Poland & Goldberg, 2003), what all of this means is that the Internet is used by large numbers of people to obtain information on illnesses, treatments and support (Horgan & Sweeney, 2010; Ybarra & Suman, 2006).

15.3 ONLINE HEALTH SEARCHING AND CYBERCHONDRIA

Those seeking health-related information online may begin simply by typing key words into a search engine, or perhaps directly consult the websites of professional health organizations (e.g., NHS Choices in the UK). In conjunction with consultations with health-care professionals, research has shown that such a relatively simple strategy can make one feel more at ease with the information received from professionals (Parker et al., 1999; Ybarra & Suman, 2008). Similarly, seeking online health content in this way has been shown to have a positive effect on one's adherence to medication (Samal et al., 2011) and one's ability to make informed decisions about health care (Seckin, 2010). Importantly, though, while there are clearly benefits associated with this kind of information seeking, such an approach is not without its problems. Helft, Eckles, Johnson-Calley and Daugherty (2005) report that cancer patients taking part in their study had a negative experience of reading online cancer information: one third felt more confused, and nearly a quarter more nervous, anxious or upset.

> **SUGGESTED ACTIVITY**
>
> Try searching for medical information online – say, something fairly innocuous like 'chicken pox'. What online search strategy did you use? How easy was it to locate information? What did you find and how informative was it? Do you trust the source of this information?

More generally, a common motivation for online medical searches is to gain reassurance that there is nothing medically wrong, or at least nothing seriously wrong (Baumgartner & Hartmann, 2011; Muse, McManus, Leung, Meghreblian & Williams, 2012). Reducing the discomfort caused by uncertainty is therefore a major reason people engage in Internet searches for health-related information. Yet online medical searches have been associated with increased depression in the general population (Bessière, Pressman, Kiesler & Kraut, 2010) and, as Fergus (2013) notes, they can often result in multiple medical possibilities, some more threatening than others. White and Horvitz (2009) found that those using general search engines (e.g., Google) to try to self-diagnose were disproportionately exposed to information about serious illnesses. Specifically, about 70% of those who used general search engines to self-diagnose common and innocuous symptoms ended up searching for rarer, more serious conditions (McManus, Leung, Muse & Williams,

2014). Such behaviour, which often leads to increased uncertainty rather than reassuring the person concerned, can exacerbate the situation, thereby increasing health-related anxiety, particularly if the individual has an intolerance for uncertainty (Fergus, 2013; Norr, Albanese, Oglesby, Allan & Schmidt, 2015). Increased anxiety as a result of Internet searches for health-related information has come to be known as 'cyberchondria', which is construed not only as a form of reassurance seeking but also as a manifestation of health anxiety and hypochondriasis (Starcevic & Berle, 2013).

McManus et al. (2014) argue that expressions of cyberchondria are consistent with cognitive behavioural models of health anxiety. As noted, repetitively checking sources of medical information online acts as a form of reassurance seeking; unfortunately, this activity is a factor in *maintaining* individuals' health anxiety, not reducing it. McManus et al. cite a number of studies (e.g., Haviland, Pincus & Dial, 2003; Lemire, Paré, Sicotte & Harvey, 2008; Muse et al., 2012) that report that those who are more health anxious search for health information online more often but, importantly, add that searching for health information more frequently has the potential to increase their health anxiety. Presumably, this increases the frequency with which they seek to be further reassured and search for online health information, and so the anxiety-provoking cycle continues.

Cyberchondria has been measured using the multidimensional Cyberchondria Severity Scale (McElroy & Shevlin, 2014; see also Fergus, 2014; Norr, Allan, Boffa, Raines & Schmidt, 2015, for reviews of the scale). Items on the scale are designed to assess levels of compulsion, distress, excessiveness, reassurance and mistrust of medical professionals. These factors are measured using a five-point Likert scale indicating frequency (1: never; 2: rarely; 3: sometimes; 4: often; and 5: always), which participants use in response to 33 statements, such as (adapted from McElroy & Shevlin, 2014):

- Researching symptoms or perceived medical conditions online interrupts my offline social activities (measuring level of compulsion).
- I have trouble relaxing after researching symptoms or perceived medical conditions online (measuring level of distress).
- I enter the same symptoms into a Web search on more than one occasion (measuring level of excessiveness).
- I discuss my online medical findings with my GP or health professional (measuring level of reassurance).
- I take the opinion of my GP or medical professional more seriously than my online medical research (measuring level of trust or mistrust of medical professionals).

When seeking out health-related information, in addition to more general Internet searching, more and more people are making use of health-related discussion forums (Tanis, 2008). In the age of the Internet, such virtual communities are growing into an ever more common form of health communication. Let us therefore consider this type of online activity further.

15.4 SOCIAL MEDIA, GROUP FORUMS AND SUPPORT SITES

Liang and Scammon (2011) note how, in today's health-care environment, it is not always easy, or indeed possible, for patients to obtain all the information and support they need through face-to-face communication with their doctor in what tends to be a relatively short consultation. As a consequence, since the turn of the century, SNSs have started to emerge in the form of virtual communities – sometimes referred to as self-help or social support groups – consisting of 'friends' or those more informed (perhaps through first-hand experience) about a particular health-related matter, which may be anything from irritable bowel syndrome (Coulson, 2005) to infertility (Malik & Coulson, 2008) to miscarriage (Gold, Boggs, Mugisha & Palladino, 2012) to depression (Griffiths et al., 2012) to HIV/AIDS (Mo & Coulson, 2008), and so on. Within these forums, people can ask for help and advice (Sillence, 2013). This often develops into a thread consisting of a series of responses to the initial question and/or discussion around these responses. It may also involve someone recounting a relevant anecdote that is informative or that at the very least conveys the message that there are others available – 'experiential experts' – who have an empathic understanding based on prior experience of what the particular individual is going through (Donelle & Hoffman-Goetz, 2009), which is perhaps more than can be said for others in the person's offline social network. In addition, Tanis (2008) describes how these forums can be good places to pick up useful information on treatments or coping strategies, or can simply be a place for encouragement and support that provides a sense of belonging. This may help an individual to feel more in control of, or at least less uncertain about, their condition, particularly if recently diagnosed. It may also be a place where they can feel more at ease discussing issues relating to what they are going through – compared to, say, being in the presence of colleagues or even friends and family – especially if they feel embarrassed or fear being stigmatized (Berger, Wagner & Baker, 2005; Webb, Burns & Collin, 2008). The potential and likely diversity of the forum members also means that there could be a rich vein of diverse information available that would be less accessible offline. Such diversity may go some way to help cater for different individuals' needs, for, as Liang and Scammon (2011) note, research on health communication supports the view that the most effective health communication is tailored health communication. Health-related information and communication should therefore be tailored to meet an individual's needs and characteristics, skill set and abilities (e.g., reading and comprehension, computer literacy), and motivation.

The usefulness of online forums in meeting the aim of tailored communication must be tempered, of course, with the fact that information may not always be reliable or medically sound (Owens et al., 2012). After all, such forums are not necessarily, or in any way required to be, frequented by medical experts. Horgan and Sweeney (2010) report concerns over the quality of health-related information obtained via the

Internet. In support of this claim, they cite Eysenbach, Powell, Kuss and Sa's (2002) review of 79 research studies that evaluated the quality of health information online. While there is concern over the quality of some of these original studies (and therefore their findings), Eysenbach et al. nevertheless report that 70% concluded that there was a problem with the standard of health-related information available online.

That said, a number of studies looking at the impact of health-related forums on their users have reported positive effects. Kramer et al. (2015), for example, researched online peer-support forums for those bereaved by suicide, many of whom presented with depressive symptoms and issues relating to well-being. They described how two thirds of those who took part in the study found the forums beneficial, particularly in terms of social support. They also found that, in general, there was a small to medium improvement in the participants' depressive symptoms and sense of well-being one year later (although some were still struggling with their mental health). Jones et al. (2011), as part of their survey focusing on an online forum for those who self-harm, found that participants valued being able to communicate anonymously with strangers about their self-harm issues. They found disclosure in this way easier to do than talking to someone in person or on the telephone. The participants also reported learning more about their condition from the forum than from online information sites, and felt they had benefitted from interacting with others who had similar feelings to them. Kirk and Milnes (2015) looked at the effectiveness of online support forums for young people with cystic fibrosis and their parents. Those with cystic fibrosis said that the online community meant they had a safe place in which to share experiences, exchange experientially derived advice and views on how to manage their treatment as well as their lives more generally, including their emotions, their relationships, their identities and the support they received from health services. The parents of children with cystic fibrosis, for their part, sought and received advice on managing their child's health, including specific therapies. Kirk and Milnes also described how the forums were able to supplement professional support and help parents and children to develop the expertise to empower themselves when interacting with health-care professionals.

Owens et al. (2012) were interested in the possible benefits of inviting health-care professionals to join in with discussions on online forums supporting young people who self-harm. They reported initial interest during the recruitment of those health professionals who agreed to take part, but this was followed by a reluctance to actively engage with the forums. Some of the reasons suggested for this were a lack of confidence on the part of the professionals in engaging in this type of exchange, issues relating to private–professional boundaries, and the need for role clarity given the implications for duty of care and accountability. What Owens et al.'s failed attempt at inviting health-care professions into the informal and anonymous world of online support-group discussion highlights is the issue (perhaps problem) of integrating these two mechanisms of information and support into a workable whole.

In concluding this section, it should be evident that 'the mechanisms within an online support group are the same as those created within a traditional group (mutual problem solving, swapping of information, expressing of experiences, catharsis, mutual help and assistance, empathy, etc.)' (Rossi, 2006, p. 11). Online forums have the advantage, however, of being much more accessible to those individuals who have difficulty accessing offline support groups, perhaps owing to some form of physical disability or other practical difficulty (e.g., time/distance) – difficulties that also feature in making e-therapies a more attractive option for some people.

> **SUGGESTED ACTIVITY**
>
> Think of an illness, disease or ailment and see whether you can locate an online forum. How easy was it to find? How many did you find (a few, many)? Try repeating the task with a different example.

15.5 E-THERAPY

The term 'e-therapy' refers to any form of psychological therapy that takes place online as opposed to face to face (Skinner & Latchford, 2006). More specifically, e-therapy has been defined as:

> a licensed mental health-care professional providing mental health services via e-mail, video conferencing, virtual reality technology, chat technology, or any combination of these.
> (Manhal-Baugus, 2001, p. 552)

Or, more recently, it has been said to constitute:

> a new therapeutic modality aimed at assisting clients to resolve life and relationship issues through electronic means, synchronous or asynchronous. [It is] a process of interacting with a therapist online in ongoing conversations over time when the client and counselor are in separate or remote locations and utilize electronic means to communicate with each other.
> (Olasupo & Atiri, 2013, p. 408)

Of course, the phenomenon of therapy over distance is not new. During the seventeenth and eighteenth centuries, for example, physicians would often form diagnoses based on patients' written descriptions of their symptoms, rather than physical examinations (Spielberg, 1999). Moreover, in the nineteenth century, Freud engaged in therapeutic practices via letter (Brabant, Falzeder & Giampieri-Deutsch, 1993). E-therapies, however, began to emerge as a delivery method within the practice of counselling psychology in the 1980s (Alleman, 2002; Oravec, 2000; Skinner & Zack, 2004). They incorporate a variety of electronic media compatible with the Internet and should be thought of as a form of therapy *delivery* rather than as a form of therapy per se (Sucala, Schnur, Brackman, Constantino & Montgomery, 2013).

Text-based sessions, for example, may involve email, chat rooms and text messaging (Andersson, Sarkohi, Karlsson, Bjärehed & Hesser, 2013; Hucker & McCabe, 2014).

Non-text-based therapy may involve voice-only communication or video conferencing (Dunstan & Tooth, 2012; Nelson & Lillis, 2013; Santhiveeran, 2005). Each of these can be synchronous (occurring in real time, thus providing immediate feedback) or nonsynchronous (involving a time delay and so a lack of immediate response). At the turn of the century, only about 10% of therapists reported using some form of online media to communicate with their patients/clients (VandenBos & Williams, 2000; Wright, 2002). This was found to have increased to 45% in a more recent study carried out in Norway (Wangberg, Gammon & Spitznogle, 2007).

Depending on the precise medium used, in addition to confidentiality, e-therapy affords a higher level of anonymity compared with face-to-face treatment. For some, this may provide additional appeal (Hucker & McCabe, 2014; Qian & Scott, 2007; Rains, 2014; Tanis, 2008). Moreover, Prabhakar (2013) informs us that research has been shown to support the view that 'clients are more honest and cooperative in online sessions than face-to-face therapy, and tend to explore deeper concerns in a shorter time period' (p. 213; although see discussion below on potential risks by way of a caveat to this claim). Further advantages of e-therapy include (adapted from Olasupo & Atiri, 2013):

- negating or reducing the inconvenience of geographical boundaries, including distance and therefore travel;
- being more convenient for those with time constraints or other responsibilities (e.g., child care), or who feel socially isolated;
- being able to receive therapy in the comfort of one's own home;
- serving as a genuine alternative for those who would seek to avoid face-to-face therapy out of embarrassment or fear of stigma;
- producing a written record (in the case of text-based e-therapy) of therapeutic sessions, which can act as a computerized patient record.

According to Recupero and Rainey (2005), patient preference may be one of the clearest indicators of the benefit of e-therapy. Postel, de Jong and de Haan (2005), for example, after carrying out research in the Netherlands, found that e-therapy was considered a more attractive means of treating alcohol problems by those who were reluctant to engage in offline (face-to-face) therapy. The ability to traverse otherwise difficult distances is also a benefit. E-therapy has been used, for example, to treat military personnel in remote areas (Jerome et al., 2000). Some patients may also perceive e-therapy as affording them increased privacy, although, as we will see below, this may not always be the case, as online therapy is not immune to risks relating to confidentiality. Recupero and Rainey also note that, for some, the removal of a face-to-face interaction may facilitate self-disclosure and honesty (again, see below for a discussion on potential risks based on increased inhibition). For Skinner and Latchford (2006), the ubiquity and convenience of the Internet, alongside the increased opportunity for anonymity, make it an ideal medium for counselling. That said, e-therapy is not without its disadvantages, which include (adapted from Olasupo & Atiri, 2013):

- being dependent on a reliable Internet connection or on having the appropriate hardware and software required for communication, or on possessing the technical

skill to use this equipment (all of which may exclude lower-income clients and the undereducated);
- the risk of encountering deceptive e-therapists;
- the risk to confidentiality: private correspondence may be hacked online and, even if not, copies of emails (should this be the chosen method of correspondence) are left in the majority of servers they pass through;
- a lack of nonverbal cues in text-based communication, which may lead to misunderstanding and so hamper clear communication and treatment, and there is also a lack of direct observation, which, again, may hamper the e-therapist's assessment of the effectiveness of the treatment;
- the risk of inconsistency with the treatment, with sessions not occurring at regular intervals, either because of technical difficulties or a lack of motivation on the part of the client;
- the fact that it is difficult for e-therapy to provide an emergency service.

Potential disadvantages of e-therapy are often seen as synonymous with new ethical concerns. In response to the increased presence and utility of e-therapy, and in recognition of some of the additional ethical challenges specific to this medium, the American Psychological Association's (2002) ethical guidelines were modified so as to be more inclusive of Internet therapy. In addition, the International Society of Mental Health Online (2009) provides a useful accompaniment to the American Psychological Association's guidelines. Together, they provide insight into the ethical nuances faced by e-therapists (Lee, 2010), some of which are discussed below.

One of the potential risks inherent within most forms of e-therapy is the lack of facial expression cues. Consequently, text-based communication may lower an individual's inhibitions (known as the disinhibition effect; Suler, 2004; see also Chapter 3). Given the increased likelihood of inhibition, according to Recupero and Rainey (2005), 'a shy patient may be more likely to disclose suicidal ideation in a chat room than in a therapist's office [meaning that] the e-therapist must now be concerned with the safety of a patient who may be far away' (p. 322). To help safeguard against such an eventuality and so improve the chance of offline crisis intervention, the e-therapist may decide to restrict online treatment to local patients. In fact, Recupero and Rainey (2006) report that some websites render ineligible certain prospective clients/patients (e.g., those with 'suicidality'). There is also the risk of misdiagnosis, especially given the fact that psychotherapists traditionally rely on nonverbal cues when making their diagnoses. Videoconferencing may reduce the chance of this, of course, but, as Santhiveeran and Grant (2006) found after surveying 73 e-therapy websites, the majority of treatment on these sites occurred in the form of email correspondence, with very few e-therapists offering videoconferencing. Recupero and Rainey (2005) also note how the lack of visual cues may mean that any harmful side effects of medication may go unnoticed by the e-therapist. As a result, some therapists will not prescribe medication online. Moreover, after studying 44 e-therapy websites, Heinlen, Welfel, Richmond and O'Donnell (2003) concluded that 'the number of psychologists offering e-therapy is small, their services are diverse, and their compliance with established ethical principles is uneven' (p. 112).

15.6 ASSESSING THE EFFECTIVENESS OF E-THERAPIES

Evidence is available to support the effectiveness of e-therapies for a variety of psychosocial problems (Barak, Hen, Boniel-Nissim & Shapira, 2008; Rochlen, Zack & Speyer, 2004), but extensive research on its effectiveness is limited and findings can be mixed. Studies by Aardoom, Dingemans, Spinhoven and Van Furth (2013) and Dölemeyer, Tietjen, Kersting and Wagner (2013), for example, drew positive conclusions on the effectiveness of e-therapy for the treatment of eating disorders. In contrast, Loucas et al.'s (2014) findings, based on a meta-analysis of 20 studies, led them to conclude that the effectiveness of e-therapy for eating disorders cannot be described as 'promising', nor is there any firm basis for the claim that e-therapy is an effective alternative to face-to-face treatment, at least as far as eating disorders are concerned.

An issue to be resolved in the study of e-therapy effectiveness is how to operationalize 'adherence', so that one can measure the relationship between adherence to the treatment programme and treatment outcomes with a greater degree of confidence. Donkin et al. (2011) performed a systematic review of various e-therapy interventions. They noted a large variation in the reporting of adherence and its association to outcomes, which could have contributed to the variation in research findings. Donkin et al. therefore suggest using a composite measure of adherence that encompasses time online, activity completion and active engagements with the intervention.

In addition, Sucala et al. (2013) have raised the issue of 'therapeutic alliance' and the potential difficulty that exists when trying to develop this within an online environment. Therapeutic alliance is defined as 'the nature of the working relationship between patient and therapist' (Sucala et al., 2013. p. 283). In face-to-face sessions, Sulcala et al. tell us, research indicates a robust positive correlation between therapeutic alliance and treatment outcome (see, e.g., Horvath, Del Re, Fluckiger & Symonds, 2011; Lambert & Barley, 2001). There is little research on this relationship in the context of e-therapy, however. What little work has been done (e.g., a systematic review of the literature by Sucala et al. in 2012) indicates that, while no firm conclusions can yet be drawn on the nature of the therapeutic alliance in e-therapy – owing to the paucity of research – there nevertheless does seem to be some indication that it is at least equivalent to face-to-face therapy. Sucala et al. (2013) were also interested in clinicians' perceptions of the importance of therapeutic alliance in an e-therapy context. They found that:

> Clinicians' ratings of the importance of alliance in face-to-face therapy were higher than their ratings of the importance of alliance in E-therapy, a result which might indicate that clinicians are less aware of the potentially important role of the therapeutic alliance in E-therapy. (p. 290)

From this, they conclude:

> This result seems to reflect the current state of E-therapy literature, in which the therapeutic relationship has been very rarely studied ... It is possible that clinicians'

perceptions of the importance of the alliance in E-therapy will change if the E-therapy literature catches up to and begins to mirror the general psychotherapy literature in terms of recognizing the role that therapeutic alliance plays in the therapeutic process. (p. 290)

In concluding this section, the view of Castelnuovo, Gaggioli, Mantovani and Riva (2003) seems pertinent. For these authors, the introduction of new online technologies should not be thought of as signalling a new theoretical approach to psychotherapy, nor as an alternative treatment. Instead, this technology should be treated simply as a resource that complements the traditional psychotherapeutic approach. As they state:

E-therapy could represent a useful integration between technological tools and traditional clinical techniques and protocols in order to improve the effectiveness and efficiency of therapeutic process ... [Yet,] to enhance the diffusion of e-therapy, further research is needed. More evaluation is required of clinical outcomes, organizational effects, benefits to health-care providers and users, and quality assurance. To date, the empirical research is not strong enough to objectively evaluate all the benefits and limits of e-therapy. (pp. 380–81)

In fact, based on the level of research presently available on the effectiveness of e-therapies, Loucas et al. (2014) perhaps best sum up the current situation, both in terms of e-therapy's inevitable development and the need for safeguards:

The treatment of mental health problems is likely to change markedly over the next 10–20 years, as a result of the widespread availability of the Internet and of mobile-device applications (apps), and their ability to deliver direct to the user certain psychological treatments. This change will greatly increase the availability of these treatments, but it will be associated with risks, a major one being the promulgation of ineffective or even harmful interventions. Clinicians and the public alike will therefore need access to authoritative and up-to-date guidance regarding the empirical status and clinical utility of the many online and app based interventions. (p. 122)

15.7 IMMERSIVE VIRTUAL ENVIRONMENTS AS AIDS TO TREATMENT

To end, it is worth noting that digital technologies in the form of 'immersive virtual environments' are being employed more and more as tools for the treatment of various psychological problems. Such immersive environments are capable of simulating numerous real-world situations, thereby allowing the patient to *experience* them in a real way but from within the relative safety and control of a digital simulation.

To illustrate: major cognitive and subsequent behavioural impairment can often follow traumatic brain injury and stroke. As part of their rehabilitation, patients need to be assessed on how well they are able to engage with the activities of daily life. Lee et al. (2003) designed an immersive virtual environment in the form of a supermarket to help assess patients' level of rehabilitation (assessing the extent to which patients navigate around the virtual supermarket, picking up items and opening or closing doors, etc.). Cárdenas, Munōz, González and Uribarren (2006) likewise reported the usefulness of immersive virtual environments for the treatment of agoraphobia (see also Alcañiz et al., 2003; Martin, Botella, Garcıá-Palarios & Osma, 2007). As part of the treatment, the patient can be exposed (virtually) to the feared situation (a simulation of an open space, in this case). Freeman (2008), for his part, found such immersive technology useful as a means of controlling schizophrenic patients' social environment (having to interact with virtual characters on a tube train): a major step, Freeman claimed, in the understanding of psychosis, including paranoid fear (see also Freeman et al., 2008; Ku et al., 2007). Immersive virtual environments have also been used to aid in the treatment of (among other things) spider phobia (Carlin, Hoffman & Weghorst, 1997), tobacco dependence (Culbertson, Shulenberger, De La Garza, Newton & Brody, 2012), the control of pain in a dental surgery (Hoffman et al., 2001), social phobia (Roy et al., 2003) and pain reduction in those experiencing phantom limbs (Murray, Patchick, Pettifer, Caillette & Howard, 2006). Immersive virtual environments have also been used to aid prolonged exposure therapy, whereby a patient suffering from post-traumatic stress disorder (PTSD) is required to re-experience the traumatic event (rather than seeking to avoid it). In the case of war veterans suffering from PTSD as a result of combat, patients are required to experience battlefield simulations, including exploding mines, being ambushed and having to treat casualties.

15.8 CONCLUSIONS

The Internet is proving to be a useful supplement to traditional care and support for patients. The full implications and scope of the Internet and related virtual technologies on health and health education are not fully known, however, nor have they been fully tested. What the Internet does offer is the possibility of increased user access to medical knowledge and support, thereby enabling increased collaboration and care.

DISCUSSION QUESTIONS

1. What are the benefits of being able to access medical information (e.g., disease symptoms and treatments) via the Internet? Might there be any potential problems or even dangers associated with this?

2. What type of support (if any) might a forum be able to offer a patient that more traditional social and/or medical support may not?
3. Why might medical professionals be reluctant or even unwilling to engage with online medical forums?
4. What are the advantages and disadvantages of e-therapy?
5. What advantage(s) might there be to treating patients within an immersive virtual environment, or even training doctors (including surgeons) in such environments?

SUGGESTED READINGS

Barak, A., Hen, L., Boniel-Nissim, M. & Shapira, N. (2008). A comprehensive review and a metaanalysis of the effectiveness of Internet-based psychotherapeutic interventions. *Journal of Technology in Human Services*, 26, 109–160.

Berle, D., Starcevic, V., Milicevic, D., Hannan, A., Dale, E., Brakoulias, V. & Viswasam, K. (2015). Do patients prefer face-to-face or Internet-based therapy? *Psychotherapy and Psychosomatics*, 84(1), 61–62.

DeJong, S. M. (2014). Blogs and tweets, texting and friending: Social media and online professionalism in health care. San Diego, CA: Elsevier Academic Press.

Fergus, T. A. (2013). Cyberchondria and intolerance of uncertainty: Examining when individuals experience health anxiety in response to Internet searches for medical information. *CyberPsychology, Behavior, and Social Networking*, 16, 735–739.

Hsiung, R. C. (2002). *E-therapy: Case studies, guiding principles, and the clinical potential of the Internet*. London, UK: W. W. Norton.

16 Concluding Thoughts

BY 2050 THERE will be 9 billion people to feed, clothe, transport, employ and educate. We're committed to a growth-driven world economy that must inflate for centuries, supplying limitless consumption to everyone. With new tech, could we add a digital world that helps everyone succeed and prosper while working together? Could we become a successful world where greatness is normal?

(Abelow, 2014)

The Internet was devised with the intention to connect computers rather than people. Nonetheless, people started to find social uses for this technology. Individuals were soon writing personal messages in the form of emails and online communities started sprouting up to connect people across the globe. Romantic relationships and friendships started to be initiated and to develop via digital technology – with onlookers finding it difficult to fathom that individuals could develop 'strong ties' with those they had not met in the physical world. As the above quote suggests, digital technologies will continue to develop and change well into the future – how the Internet will grow is yet to be determined. The 'Internet of things' is an example of how the world is changing as physical objects become connected, providing new opportunities for people to connect as well as live their lives. Connecting objects could potentially make life easier for us, relieving us of mundane tasks, but of course this new technology is not without its problems (e.g., security and privacy concerns).

In this book we have attempted to outline some of these changes in technology, as well as to highlight new theories that have been developed to explain the new relationships people have with technology. Researchers are not all in agreement with the potential and actual effects of digital technologies. As is evident in this book, for example, some scholars take strong positions for and against the potential psychological benefits that digital technologies afford individuals. Early on, in the field of cyberpsychology, some researchers made a distinction between the 'real world' and the 'cyber world' (often suggesting that what takes place via digital technologies is not real or is 'nearly real'). Readers will note this distinction is made in many of the theories and studies presented in this book. This categorization, however, is becoming less useful (and some have argued that it was never an accurate description) now that much of what we do involves digital technologies. What we do in cyberspace arguably *is* real, and the boundaries between the physical and cyber worlds are becoming less obvious. What is perhaps more important to recognize, and research in more detail, is how our realities and lives have changed as a consequence of digital technology.

Cyberpsychology: The Study of Individuals, Society and Digital Technologies, First Edition.
Monica Therese Whitty and Garry Young.
© 2017 John Wiley & Sons, Ltd. Published 2017 by John Wiley & Sons, Ltd.

This book has attempted to provide a comprehensive examination of the topics and research covered in the area of cyberpsychology. Although the book is grounded in psychology, the topics are also relevant to those interested in media and communications, philosophy, sociology, criminology and security studies (disciplines that often incorporate psychology in their curriculums). As elucidated in this book, cyberpsychology spans a large range of topics, some of which are arguably absent in this book. We have, however, attempted to present many of the well-researched topics as well as areas that have relevance to individuals and society at large. Where we can, we have presented real-life examples and examined how psychology might be applied to explain specific behaviours and events that have taken place online (e.g., online radicalization, DDoS attacks, the hacker attack on Ashley Madison). In almost every chapter we have also included suggested activities and discussion questions that we hope will engage readers and class groups. Many ask readers to consider their own lives in light of the theories and empirical research presented in the book and we hope this has provided new insights into people's lives. Moreover, we hope that these activities and questions have helped readers to take a critical stance on the current literature and helped them identify the gaps in research that require further investigation.

We began the book by presenting some of the key theories about the self and identity that were developed before there was an Internet, and proceeded to examine how these theories are relevant and/or have been adapted to explain identities in the cyber realm. In addition, we provided a critical overview of some of the new theories that have been developed about the self and identities, which have been used to explain the new opportunities cyberspace affords to re-create the 'self'. These theories were revisited in a number of chapters throughout the book (e.g., to explain relationship formation in online environments, children and teens' use of digital technologies, gaming in virtual environments and various forms of online crime). Other theories that have been developed exclusively in order to explain behaviours that take place in the cyber realms have been examined throughout the book. The 'disinhibition effect', for example (whereby people feel less inhibited because of the nature of cyberspace), which is given attention in various sections of the book, is used to explain why people carry out some behaviours in cyberspace that they are far less likely to engage in when in the physical world.

We have attempted to cover the social and psychological benefits as well as the problems and drawbacks cyberspace has thus far had to offer. Examples of positives include new opportunities for education, meeting new people and developing relationships, and improved methods for social support and health. Nonetheless, new problems have emerged as a consequence of digital technologies; for example, the new wave of crimes, which researchers have yet to find effective strategies to prevent and deter. However, some problems have emerged simply because we have yet to gain a better understanding of how people interact with technology. Once we do, digital technologies will potentially afford even more opportunities (e.g., in the areas of education and health).

We hope the reader enjoys engaging with the book as much as we did writing it. It has been a journey for us, and writing the book has helped us to think about our own work and important areas that require further examination. We also hope it opens up new paths for you, the reader, to explore, whether in your personal lives or in your research. Cyberpsychology is a new and exciting field and one where there is ample opportunity for others to contribute to the discipline – whether in the form of students' dissertations, academics' research projects or more generally in people's working and home lives.

References

Aardoom, J. J., Dingemans, A. E., Spinhoven, P. & Van Furth, E. F. (2013). Treating eating disorders over the Internet: A systematic review and future research directions. *International Journal of Eating Disorders, 46*, 539–552.

Abelow, D. (2014). If our future is digital, how will it change the world? *Wired*. Retrieved 7 April 2016 from http://www.wired.com/insights/2014/04/future-digital-will-change-world

Allen, I. E. & Seaman, J. (2013). *Changing course: Ten years of tracking online education in the United States*. Boston, MA: Babson Survey Research Group.

Allen, I. E. & Seaman, J. (2014). *Grade change: Tracking online education in the United States*. Boston, MA: Babson Survey Research Group.

Abrams, D. & Hogg, M. A. (1988). Comments on the motivational status of self-esteem in social identity and intergroup discrimination. *European Journal of Social Psychology, 18*, 317–334.

Australian Competition & Consumer Commission. (2012). *Targeting scams: Report of the ACCC on scam activity 2012*. Retrieved 7 April 2016 from https://www.accc.gov.au/system/files/Targeting scams 2012.pdf

Adams, A. A. (2010). Virtual sex with child avatars. In C. Wankel & S. Malleck (Eds.), *Emerging issues in virtual worlds* (pp. 55–72). Charlotte, NC: Information Age Publishing.

Adams, M., Oye, J. & Parker, T. (2003). Sexuality of older adults and the Internet: From sex education to cybersex. *Sexual and Relationship Therapy, 18*(3), 405–415.

Aggarwal, A. K. & Bento, R. (2000). Web-based education. In A. Aggarwal (Ed.), *Web-based learning and teaching technologies: Opportunities and challenges* (pp. 2–16). Hershey, PA: Idea Group.

Ahuvia, A. C. & Adelman, M. B. (1992). Formal intermediaries in the marriage market: A typology and review. *Journal of Marriage and the Family, 54*, 452–463.

Albright, J. M. (2007). How do I love thee and thee and thee: Self-presentation, deception, and multiple relationships online. In M. T. Whitty, A. J., Baker, J. A., Inman (Eds.), *Online matchmaking* (pp. 81–93). New York, NY: Palgrave Macmillan.

Alcañiz, M., Botella, C., Baños, R., Perpiñá, C., Rey, B., Lozano, … Gil, J. A. (2003). Internet-based telehealth system for the treatment of agoraphobia. *CyberPsychology & Behavior, 6*(4), 355–358.

Alexy, E. M., Burgess, A. W., Baker, T. & Smoyak, S. A. (2005). Perceptions of cyber stalking among college students. *Brief Treatment and Crisis Intervention, 5*, 279–289.

Allen, I. E. & Seaman, J. (2007). *Online nation: Five years of growth in online learning*. Needham, MA: Sloan Consortium.

Alleman, J. R. (2002). Online counseling: The Internet and mental health treatment. *Psychotherapy: Theory, Research, Practice, Training, 39*, 199–209.

Cyberpsychology: The Study of Individuals, Society and Digital Technologies, First Edition.
Monica Therese Whitty and Garry Young.
© 2017 John Wiley & Sons, Ltd. Published 2017 by John Wiley & Sons, Ltd.

Alsharnouby, M., Alaca, F. & Chiasson, S. (2015). Why phishing still works: User strategies for combating phishing attacks. *International Journal of Human–Computer Studies, 82*, 69–82.

Altman, I. & Taylor, D. A. (1973). *Social penetration: The development of interpersonal relationships.* New York, NY: Holt, Rinehart and Winston.

Alvarez, A. R. G. (2012). 'IH8U': Confronting cyberbullying and exploring the use of *cybertools* in teen dating relationships. *Journal of Clinical Psychology: In Session, 68*(11), 1205–1215.

American Psychological Association. (2002). *Ethical principles of psychologists and code of conduct.* Washington, DC: American Psychological Association.

Amosun, P. A. & Ige, O. A. (2009). Internet crime: A new breed of crime among in-school ages children in Nigeria. *African Symposium, 9*(2), 90–98.

Amato, P. R. & Previti, D. (2003). People's reasons for divorcing: Gender, social class, the life course, and adjustment. *Journal of Family Issues, 24*(5), 602–626.

An, Y.-J. & Frick, T. (2006). Student perceptions of asynchronous computer-mediated communication in face-to-face courses. *Journal of Computer-Mediated Communication, 11*, 485–499.

Anderson, B. (2008). The social impact of broadband household Internet access. *Information, Communication & Society, 11*(1), 5–24.

Anderson, C. A. (1997). Effects of violent movies and trait irritability on hostile feelings and aggressive thoughts. *Journal of Personality and Social Psychology, 45*, 293–305.

Anderson, C. A. (2004). An update on the effects of violent video games. *Journal of Adolescence, 27*, 113–122.

Anderson, C. A., Berkowitz, L., Donnerstein, E., Huesmann, R. L., Johnson, J., Linz, D., Malamuth, N. & Wartella, E. (2003). The influence of media violence on youth. *Psychological Science in the Public Interest, 4*, 81–110.

Anderson, C. A. & Bushman, B. J. (2002). Human aggression. *Annual Review of Psychology, 53*, 27–51.

Anderson, C. A. & Dill, K. E. (2000). Video games and aggressive thoughts, feelings, and behavior in the laboratory and in life. *Journal of Personality and Social Psychology, 78*, 772–790.

Anderson, C. A. & Ford, C. M. (1986). Affect of the game player: Short-term effects of highly and mildly aggressive video games. *Personality and Social Psychology Bulletin, 12*, 390–402.

Andersson, G., Sarkohi, A., Karlsson, J., Bjärehed, J. & Hesser, H. (2013). Effects of two forms of Internet-delivered cognitive behaviour therapy for depression on future thinking. *Cognitive Therapy and Research, 37*, 29–34.

Antheunis, M. L., Valkenburg, P. M. & Peter, J. (2010). Getting acquainted through social network sites: Testing a model of online uncertainty reduction and social attraction. *Computers in Human Behavior, 26*, 100–109.

Anti-Phishing Working Group. (2014). *Phishing activity trends report: 4th quarter 2014.* Retrieved 7 April 2016 from http://docs.apwg.org/reports/apwg_trends_report_q4_2014.pdf

Bada, M. & Sasse, A. (2014). *Cyber security awareness campaigns: Why do they fail to change behaviour?* (draft working paper). Global Cyber Security Capacity Centre. Retrieved 7 April 2016 from http://www.sbs.ox.ac.uk/cybersecurity-capacity/system/files/Awareness%20Campaigns%20Final%20July-1.pdf

Bandura, A. (1973). *Aggression: A social learning analysis.* Englewood Cliffs, NJ: Prentice-Hall.

Bandura, A. (1977). *Social learning theory.* Englewood Cliffs, NJ: Cognitive Prentice-Hall.

Bandura, A. (1986). *Social foundations of thought and action: A social cognitive theory.* Englewood Cliffs, NJ: Prentice-Hall.

Bandura, A., Ross, D. & Ross, S. A. (1963). Imitation of film-mediated aggressive models. *Journal of Abnormal and Social Psychology, 66*(1), 3–11.

Barab, S. A., Thomas, M. K. & Merrill, H. (2001). Online learning: From information dissemination to fostering collaboration. *Journal of Interactive Learning Research*, *12*(1), 105–143.

Barak, A. (2005). Sexual harassment on the Internet. *Social Science Computer Review*, *23*(1), 77–92.

Barak, A., Hen, L., Boniel-Nissim, M. & Shapira, N. (2008). A comprehensive review and a metaanalysis of the effectiveness of Internet-based psychotherapeutic interventions. *Journal of Technology in Human Services*, *26*, 109–160.

Barak, A., Boniel-Nissim, M. & Suler, J. (2008). Fostering empowerment in online support groups. *Computers in Human Behavior*, *24*, 1867–1883.

Bargh, J. A., McKenna, K. Y. A. & Fitzsimons, G. M. (2002). Can you see the Real Me? Activation and expression of the 'true self' on the Internet. *Journal of Social Issues*, *58*, 33–48.

Bartscha, R. A. & Cobern, K. M. (2003). Effectiveness of PowerPoint presentations in lectures. *Computers & Education*, *41*, 77–86.

Bartlett, C. P. & Gentile, D. A. (2012). Attacking others online: The formation of cyberbullying in late adolescence. *Psychology of Popular Media Culture*, *1*(2), 123–135.

Basile, K. C., Swahn, M. H., Chen, J. & Saltzman, L. E. (2006). Stalking in the United States: Recent national prevalence estimates. *American Journal of Preventive Medicine*, *31*, 172–175.

Baumgartner, S. E. & Hartmann, T. (2011). The role of health anxiety in online health information search. *Cyberpsychology, Behavior, and Social Networking*, *14*, 613–618.

Baumgartner, S. E., Valkenburg, P. M. & Peter, J. (2010). Unwanted online sexual solicitation and risky sexual online behaviour across the lifespan. *Journal of Applied Developmental Psychology*, *31*(6), 439–447.

Baumgartner, S. E., Valkenburg, P. M. & Peter, J. (2011). The influence of descriptive and injunctive peer norms on adolescents' risky sexual online behaviour. *Cyberpsychology, Behavior, and Social Networking*, *14*(12), 753–758.

BBC News. (2015). Phishing catches victims 'in minutes'. Retrieved 7 April 2016 from http://www.bbc.co.uk/news/technology-32285433

Beech, A. R., Elliot, I. A., Birgden, A. & Findlater, D. (2008). The Internet and child sexual offending: A criminological review. *Aggression and Violent Behaviour*, *13*, 216–228.

Behm-Morawitz, E. & Schipper, S. (2015). Sexing the avatar: Gender, sexualisation and cyber-harassment in a virtual world. *Journal of Media Psychology*. doi: 10.1027/1864-1105/a000152

Beidleman, S. W. (2009). *Defining and deterring cyber war*. Army War College, Carlisle Barracks, PA. Retrieved 7 April 2016 from http://oai.dtic.mil/oai/oai?verb=getRecord&metadataPrefix=html&identifier=ADA500795

Belenko, S., Dugosh, K. L., Lynch, K., Mericle, A. A., Pich, M. & Forman, R. F. (2009). Online illegal drug use information: An exploratory analysis of drug-related website viewing by adolescents. *Journal of Health Communication: International Perspectives*, *14*(7), 612–630.

Bell, D. & Kennedy, B. M. (2000). *The cybercultures reader*. London, UK: Routledge.

Bennett, D. C., Guran, E. L., Ramos, M. C. & Margolin, G. (2011). College students' electronic victimization in friendships and dating relationships: Anticipated distress and associations with risky behaviors. *Violence and Victims*, *26*, 410–430.

Berge, Z. L. & Collins, M. (1993). Computer conferencing and online education. *Arachnet Electronic Journal on Virtual Culture*, *1*(3). Retrieved 3 July 2016 from http://www.kovacs.com/ejvc/berge.htm

Berger, A. A. (2006). *Media and society: A critical perspective*. Lanham, MD: Rowman & Littlefield.

Berger, M., Wagner, T. & Baker, L. (2005). Internet use and stigmatized illness. *Social Science & Medicine*, *61*, 1821–1827.

Berkowitz, L. (1984). Some effects of thoughts on anti- and prosocial media events: A cognitive neoassociation analysis. *Psychological Bulletin*, *95*, 410–427.

Berkowitz, L. (1990). On the formation and regulation of anger and aggression. *American Psychologist, 45*, 494–503.

Berle, D., Starcevic, V., Milicevic, D., Hannan, A., Dale, E., Brakoulias, V. & Viswasam, K. (2015). Do patients prefer face-to-face or Internet-based therapy? *Psychotherapy and Psychosomatics, 84*(1), 61–62.

Berlin, F. S. & Sawyer, D. (2012). Potential consequences of accessing child pornography over the Internet and who is accessing it. *Sexual Addiction & Compulsivity, 19*(1/2), 30–40.

Bernard, R. M., Abrami, P. C., Lou, Y., Borokhovski, E., Wade, A., Wozney, L., ... Huang, B. (2004). How does distance education compare with classroom instruction? A meta-analysis of the empirical literature. *Review of Educational Research, 74*, 379–439.

Bessière, K., Seay, F. & Kiesler, S. (2007). The ideal elf: Identity exploration in *World of Warcraft*. *CyberPsychology & Behavior, 10*(4), 530–535.

Bessiere, K., Pressman, S., Kiesler, S. & Kraut, R. (2010). Effects of Internet use on health and depression: A longitudinal study. *Journal of Medical Internet Research, 12*(1), e6.

Bilton, N. (2010, 20 February). The surreal world of Chatroulette. *New York Times*. Retrieved 18 September 2010 from http://www.nytimes.com/2010/02/21/weekinreview/21bilton.html

Blythe, M. & Wright, P. (2008). Technology scruples: Why intimidation will not save the recording industry and how enchantment might. *Personal and Ubiquitous Computing, 12*(5), 411–420.

Bocij, P. (2004). *Cyberstalking: Harassment in the Internet age and how to protect your family*. Westport, CT: Praeger.

Bok, S. (1989). *Lying: Moral choice in public and private life*. New York, NY: Vintage.

Bond, B. J., Hefner, V. & Drogos, K. L. (2009). Information-seeking practices during the sexual development of lesbian, gay, and bisexual individuals: The influence and effects of coming out in a mediated environment. *Sexuality & Culture, 13*, 32–50.

Bonner, S. & Higgins, E. (2010). Music piracy: Ethical perspectives. *Management Decision, 48*(9), 1341–1354.

Borden, R. J. (1975). Witnessed aggression: Influence of an observer's sex and values on aggressive responding. *Journal of Personality and Social Psychology, 31*, 567–573.

Boudreau, K. & Consalvo, M. (2014). Families and social network games. *Information, Communication & Society, 17*(9), 1118–1130.

Bourke, M. L. & Hernandez, A. E. (2009). The 'Butner Study' redux: A report of the incidence of hands-on child victimization by child pornography offenders. *Journal of Family Violence, 24*, 183–191.

Bowker, N. & Tuffin, K. (2003). Dicing with deception: People with disabilities' strategies for managing safety and identity online. *Journal of Computer-Mediated Communication, 8*(2). doi: 10.1111/j.1083–6101.2003.tb00209.x

Boxall, M. (2012, 8 August). MOOCs: A massive opportunity for higher education, or digital hype? *The Guardian*. Retrieved 20 February 2013 from http://www.guardian.co.uk/higher-education-network/blog/2012/aug/08/mooc-coursera-higher-education-investment

boyd, D. M. & Ellison, N. B. (2007). Social network sites: Definition, history, and scholarship. *Journal of Computer-Mediated Communication, 13*(1), art. 11.

Brabant, E., Falzeder, E. & Giampieri-Deutsch, P. (Eds.). (1993). *The correspondence of Sigmund Freud and Sandor Ferenczi: 1908–1914 (Trans. P. Hoffer)*. Cambridge, MA: Harvard University Press.

Brand, M., Laier, C., Pawlikowski, M., Schachtle, U., Scholer, T. & Alstotter-Gleich, C. (2011). Watching pornographic pictures on the Internet: Role of sexual arousal ratings and psychological-psychiatric symptoms for using sex sites excessively. *Cyberpsychology, Behavior, and Social Networking, 14*(6), 371–377.

Brax, D. & Munthe, C. (2015). The philosophical aspects of hate crime and hate crime legislation: Introducing the special section on the philosophy of hate crime. *Journal of Interpersonal Violence, 30*(10), 1687–1695.

Bregha, F. J. (1985). Leisure and freedom re-examined. In T. A. Goodale & P. A. Witt (Eds.), *Recreation and leisure: Issues in an era of change* (2nd ed., pp. 35–43). State College, PA: Venture.

Brodie, M., Flournoy, R. E., Altman, D. E., Blendon, R. J. M., Benson, J. M. & Rosenbaum, M. D. (2000). Health information, the Internet, and the digital divide. *Health Affairs, 19*(6), 255–265.

Brooke, H. (2015, 8 November). This snooper's charter makes George Orwell look lacking in vision. *The Guardian*. Retrieved 7 April 2016 from http://www.theguardian.com/commentisfree/2015/nov/08/surveillance-bill-snoopers-charter-george-orwell

Brown, A. (2006). Learning from a distance. *Journal of Property Management, 71*(4), 42–45.

Brown, D. J., McHugh, D., Standen, P., Evett, L., Shopland, N. & Battersby, S. (2011). Designing location-based learning experiences for people with intellectual disabilities and additional sensory impairments. *Computers & Education, 56*(1), 11–20.

Brown, G., Maycock, B. & Burns, S. (2005). Your picture is your bait: Use and meaning of cyberspace among gay men. *Journal of Sex Research, 42*, 63–73.

Brown, J. J., Jr. (2008). From Friday to Sunday: the hacker ethic and shifting notions of labour, leisure and intellectual property. *Leisure Studies, 27*(4), 395–409.

Buchanan, T. & Whitty, M. T. (2014). The online dating romance scam: Causes and consequences of victimhood. *Psychology, Crime & Law, 20*(3), 261–283.

Buller, D. B. & Burgoon, J. K. (1996). Interpersonal deception theory. *Communication Theory, 6*, 203–242.

Burgstahler, S. (2000). Web-based instruction and people with disabilities. In F. Cole (Ed.), *Issues in web-based pedagogy: A critical primer* (pp. 389–396). Westport, CT: Greenwood Press.

Burke, A., Sowerbutts, S., Blundell, B. & Sherry, M. (2002). Child pornography and the Internet: Policing and treatment issues. *Psychiatry, Psychology and Law, 9*(1), 79–84.

Bushman, B. J. (1995). Moderating role of trait aggressiveness in the effects of violent media on aggression. *Journal of Personality and Social Psychology, 69*(5), 950–960.

Bushman, B. J. (1996). Individual differences in the extent and development of aggressive cognitive-associative networks. *Journal of Personality and Social Psychology Bulletin, 22*, 811–819.

Bushman, B. J. & Anderson, C. A. (2001). Is it time to pull the plug on the hostile versus instrumental aggression dichotomy? *Psychological Review, 108*, 273–279.

Buss, D. M. (1987). Selection, evocation, and manipulation. *Journal of Personality and Social Psychology, 53*(6), 1214–1331.

Buss, D. M. (2000). Desires in human mating. *Annals New York Academy of Sciences, 907*, 39–49.

Buss, D. M. & Barnes, M. (1986). Preferences in human mate selection. *Journal of Personality and Social Psychology, 50*, 559–570.

Buss, D. M. & Shackelford, T. K. (1997). Susceptibility to infidelity in the first year of marriage. *Journal of Research in Personality, 31*, 193–221.

Button, M., Lewis, C. & Tapley, J. (2014). Not a victimless crime: The Impact of fraud on individual victims and their families. *Security Journal, 27*, 36–54.

Brym, R. J. & Lenton, R. L. (2001). *Love at first byte: Internet dating in Canada*. Retrieved 25 March 2005 from http://www.societyinquestion4e.nelson.com/Chapter33Online.pdf

Calenda, D. & Meijer, A. (2015). Young people, the Internet and political participation: Findings of a web survey in Italy, Spain and the Netherlands. *Information, Communication & Society, 12*(6), 879–898.

Cameron, C., Oskamp, S. & Sparks, W. (1977). Courtship American style: Newspaper ads. *Family Coordinator*, 26(1), 27–30.

Cárdenas, G., Munõz, S., González, M. & Uribarren, G. (2006). Virtual reality applications to agoraphobia: A protocol. *CyberPsychology & Behavior*, 9(2), 248–250.

Carlin, A. S., Hoffman, H. G. & Weghorst, S. (1997). Virtual reality and tactile augmentation in the treatment of spider phobia: A case report. *Behaviour Research and Therapy*, 35(2), 153–158.

Caspi, A. & Gorsky, P. (2005). Instructional media choice: Factors affecting the preference of distance education coordinators. *Journal of Educational Multimedia and Hypermedia*, 14(2), 169–198.

Castelnuovo, G., Gaggioli, A., Mantovani, F. & Riva, G. (2003). From psychotherapy to e-therapy: The integration of traditional techniques and new communication tools in clinical settings. *CyberPsychology & Behavior*, 6(4), 375–382.

Cate, R. & Lloyd, S. (1992). *Courtship*. Newbury Park, CA: Sage.

Catford, J. (2011). The new social learning: Connect better for better health. *Health Promotion International*, 26(2), 133–135.

Cattell, R. B. (1946). *Description and measurement of personality*. Oxford, UK: World Book Company.

Cesareo, L. & Pastore, A. (2014). Consumers' attitude and behaviour towards online music piracy and subscription-based services. *Journal of Consumer Marketing*, 31(6/7), 515–525.

Cha, J. (2013). Do online video platforms cannibalize television? How viewers are moving from old screens to new ones. *Journal of Advertising Research*, 53(1), 71–82.

Chen, Y.-L., Chen, S.-H. & Gau, S. S.-F. (2015). ADHD and autistic traits, family function, parenting style, and social adjustment for Internet addiction among children and adolescents in Taiwan: A longitudinal study. *Research in Developmental Disabilities*, 39, 20–31.

Cheong, D. (2010). The effects of practice teaching sessions in *Second Life* on the change in pre-service teachers' teaching efficacy. *Computers & Education*, 55(2), 868–880.

Chickering, A. W. & Ehrmann, S. C. (1996). Implementing the seven principles of good practice in undergraduate education: Technology as lever. *Accounting Education News*, 49, 9–10.

Childs, M. (2010). A conceptual framework for mediated environments. *Educational Research*, 52(2), 197–213.

Childress, M. D. & Braswell, R. (2006). Using massively multiplayer online role-playing games for online learning. *Distance Education*, 27(2), 187–196.

Childwise. (2010). *Digital Lives 2010*. Retrieved 8 August 2011 from http://www.childwise.co.uk/reports.html

Clark, J. M. (1997). A cybernautical perspective on impulsivity and addiction. In C. Webster & M. Jackson (Eds.), *Impulsivity: Theory assessment and treatment* (pp. 82–91). New York, NY: Guilford Press.

Clark, R. E. (1994). Media will never influence learning. *Educational Technology Research and Development*, 42(2), 21–29.

Coeckelbergh, M. (2013). Drones, information technology, and distance: Mapping the moral epistemology of remote fighting. *Ethics and Information Technology*, 15, 87–98.

Cole, J., Suman, M., Schramm, P., Lunn, R., Coget, J., Firth, D., ... Lebo, H. (2001). *The UCLA Internet report 2001: Surveying the digital future*. Los Angeles, CA: University of California, Center for Communication Policy.

Coleman, E., Horvath, K. J., Miner, M., Ross, M. W., Oakes, M. & Rosser, S. B. R. (2010). Compulsive sexual behaviour and risk for unsafe sex among Internet using men who have sex with men. *Archives of Sexual Behavior*, 39(5), 1045–1053.

Collins, A. M. & Loftus, E. F. (1975). A spreading activation theory of semantic processing. *Psychological Review*, 82, 407–428.

Comartin, E., Kernsmith, R. & Kernsmith, P. (2013). 'Sexting' and sex offender registration: Do age, gender and sexual orientation matter? *Deviant Behavior, 34*(1), 38–52.

Comstock, G. & Scharrer, E. (2007). *Media and the American child.* San Diego, CA: Elsevier.

Connolly, T. M., Boyle, E. A., MacArthur, E., Hainey, T. & Boyle, J. M. (2012). A systematic literature review of empirical evidence on computer games and serious games. *Computers & Education, 59*(2), 661–686.

Cooley, C. H. (1902). *Human nature and the social order.* New York, NY: Charles Scribner's Sons.

Cooper, A. (1998). Sexuality and the Internet: Surfing into the new millennium. *CyberPsychology & Behavior, 1*, 181–187.

Cooper, A. (2002). *Sex & the Internet: A guidebook for clinicians.* New York, NY: Brunner-Routledge.

Cooper, A., Delmonico, D. L. & Burg, R. (2000). Cybersex users, abusers, and compulsives: New findings and implications. *Sexual Addiction & Compulsivity, 7*, 5–29.

Cooper, A., Scherer, C. & Marcus, I. D. (2002). Harnessing the power of the Internet to improve sexual relationships. In A. Cooper (Ed.), *Sex & the Internet: A guidebook for clinicians* (pp. 209–230). New York, NY: Brunner-Routledge.

Corley, M. D. & Hook, J. N. (2012). Women, female sex and love addicts, and use of the Internet. *Sexual Addiction & Compulsivity, 19*(1/2), 53–76.

Cornwell, B. & Lundgren, D. C. (2001). Love on the Internet: Involvement and misrepresentation in romantic relationships in cyberspace vs. realspace. *Computers in Human Behavior, 17*, 197–211.

Coulson, N. S. (2005). Receiving social support online: An analysis of a computer-mediated support group for individuals living with irritable bowel syndrome. *CyberPsychology & Behavior, 8*, 580–584.

Coyne, S. M., Stockdale, L., Busby, D., Iverson, B. & Grant, D. M. (2011). 'I luv u :)!': A descriptive study of the media use of individuals in romantic relationships. *Family Relations, 60*, 150–162.

Cress, U. (2005). Ambivalent effect of member portraits in virtual groups. *Journal of Computer Assisted Learning, 21*, 281–291.

Culbertson, C. S., Shulenberger, S., De La Garza, R., Newton, T. F. & Brody, A. L. (2012). Virtual reality cue exposure therapy for the treatment of tobacco dependence. *Journal of CyberTherapy & Rehabilitation, 5*(1), 57–64.

Cumberbatch, G. (2010). Effects. In D. Albertazzi & P. Cobley (Eds.), *The media: An introduction* (3rd ed., pp. 354–368). Harlow, UK: Pearson.

Cumberbatch, G., Jones, I. & Lee, M. (1988). Measuring violence on television. *Current Psychology, 7*(1), 1046–1310.

Daft, R. L. & Lengel, R. H. (1986). Organizational information requirements, media richness and structural design. *Management Science, 32*(5), 554–571.

Daft, R. L., Lengel, R. H. & Trevino, L. K. (1987). Message equivocality, media selection, and manager performance: Implications for information systems. *MIS Quarterly, 11*(3), 355–366.

Dando, C. J. (2014, November). Airport security measures aren't good enough – here's a fix. *Conversation.* Retrieved 7 April 2016 from http://theconversation.com/airport-security-measures-arent-good-enough-heres-a-fix-34456

Dando, C. J., Bull, R., Ormerod, T. C. & Sandham, A. L. (2015). Helping to sort the liars from the truth-tellers: The gradual revelation of information during investigative interviews. *Legal and Criminological Psychology, 20*, 114–128.

Daneback, K., Ross, M. K. & Månsson, S.-A. (2006). Characteristics and behaviors of sexual compulsives who use the Internet for sexual purposes. *Sexual Addiction & Compulsivity, 13*(1), 53–67.

D'Astous, A., Colbert, F. & Montpetit, D. (2005). Music piracy on the Web: How effective are anti-piracy arguments? Evidence from the theory of planned behaviour. *Journal of Consumer Policy*, 28, 289–310.

Davinson, N. & Sillence, E. (2010). It won't happen to me: Promoting secure behaviour among Internet users. *Computers in Human Behavior*, 26, 1739–1747.

Dawson, B. L. & McIntosh, W. D. (2006). Sexual strategies theory and Internet personal advertisements. *CyberPsychology & Behavior*, 9(5), 614–617.

De Andrea, D. C. & Walther, J. B. (2011). Attributions for inconsistences between online and offline self-presentations. *Communication Research*, 38(6), 805–825.

Dede, C. (1996). Emerging technologies and distributed learning. *American Journal of Distance Education*, 10(2), 4–36.

de Freitas, S. & Neumann, T. (2009). Pedagogic strategies supporting the use of synchronous audiographic conferencing: A review of the literature. *British Journal of Education Technology*, 40(6), 980–998.

Delwiche, A. (2006). Massively multiplayer online games (MMOs) in the new media classroom. *Educational Technology & Society*, 9(3), 160–172.

Dennis, A. R. & Kinney, S. T. (1998). Testing media richness theory in the new media: The effects of cues, feedback, and task equivocality. *Information Systems Research*, 9(3), 256–274.

DePaulo, B. M., Lindsay, J. J., Malone, B. E., Muhlenburck, L., Charlton, K. & Cooper, H. (2003). Cues to deception. *Psychological Bulletin*, 129, 74–118.

DePaulo, B. M., Wetzel, C., Sternglanz, W. R. & Wilson, M. J. W. (2003). Verbal and nonverbal dynamics of privacy, secrecy, and deceit. *Journal of Social Issues*, 59(2), 391–410.

DeSmet, M., Van Keer, H. & Valcke, M. (2008). Blending asynchronous discussion groups and peer tutoring in higher education: An exploratory study of online peer tutoring behaviour. *Computers & Education*, 50, 207–223.

DeSteno, D., Bartlett, M. Y., Braverman, J. & Salovey, P. (2002). Sex differences in jealousy: Evolutionary mechanism or artifact of measurement? *Journal of Personality and Social Psychology*, 83(5), 1103–1116.

DeSteno, D. & Salovey, P. (1996). Evolutionary origins of sex differences in jealousy? Questioning the 'fitness' of the model. *Psychological Science*, 7, 367–371.

Dickey, M. D. (2003). Teaching in 3D: Pedagogical affordances and constraints of 3D virtual worlds for synchronous distance learning. *Distance Education*, 24(1), 105–121.

Dimmick, J., Kline, S. & Stafford, L. (2000). The gratification niches of personal email and the telephone. *Communication Research*, 27(2), 227–248.

Dipert, R. R. (2010). The ethics of cyberwarfare. *Journal of Military Ethics*, 9(4), 384–410.

Doherty, A. M. & Sheehan, J. D. (2010). Munchausen's syndrome: More common than we realise? *Irish Medical Journal*, 103(6), 179–181.

Dölemeyer, R., Tietjen, A., Kersting, A. & Wagner, B. (2013). Internet-based interventions for eating disorders in adults: A systematic review. *BMC Psychiatry*, 13, 207.

Dollard, J., Doob, L., Miller, N., Mowrer, O. & Sears, R. (1939). *Frustration and aggression*. New Haven, CT: Yale University Press.

Donelle, L. & Hoffman-Goetz, L. (2009). Functional health literacy and cancer care conversations in online forums for retired persons. *Informatics for Health & Social Care*, 34(1), 59–72.

Donkin, L., Christensen, H., Naismith, S. L., Neal, B., Hickie, I. B. & Glozier, N. (2011). A systematic review of the impact of adherence on the effectiveness of e-therapies. *Journal of Medical Internet Research*, 13(3), 81–92.

Dredge, S. (2015, 14 October). Music labels sue Aurous filesharing app for 'copyright theft on a massive scale'. *The Guardian*. Retrieved 7 April 2016 from http://www.theguardian.com/technology/2015/oct/14/music-labels-sue-aurous-filesharing-copyright-theft

Duhigg, C. (2012, 16 February). How companies learn your secrets. *New York Times Magazine*. Retrieved 7 April 2016 from http://www.nytimes.com/2012/02/19/magazine/shopping-habits.html?pagewanted=all&_r=1

Dunstan, D. A. & Tooth, S. M. (2012). Treatment via videoconferencing: A pilot study of delivery by clinical psychology trainees. *Australian Journal of Rural Health*, 20, 88–94.

Dutton, W. H. & Blank, G. (2011). *Next generation users: The Internet in Britain*. Oxford Internet Surveys. Retrieved 7 April 2016 from http://www.oii.ox.ac.uk/publications/oxis2011_report.pdf

Dutton, W. H., Helsper, E. J., Whitty, M. T., Buckwalter, G. & Lee, E. (2008). *Mate selection in the network society: The role of the Internet in reconfiguring marriages in Australia, the United Kingdom and United States* (working paper). Social Science Research Network. Retrieved 7 April 2016 from http://papers.ssrn.com/sol3/papers.cfm?abstract_id=1275810

Dutton, L. B. & Winstead, B. A. (2006). Predicting unwanted pursuit: Attachment, relationship satisfaction, relationship alternatives, and break-up distress. *Journal of Social and Personal Relationships*, 23, 565–586.

Dye, M. L. & Davis, K. E. (2003). Stalking and psychological abuse: Common factors and relationship-specific characteristics. *Violence and Victims*, 18, 163–180.

Edirisingha, P., Nie, M., Pluciennik, M. & Young, R. (2009). Socialisation for learning at a distance in a 3-D multi-user virtual environment. *British Journal of Educational Technology*, 40(3), 458–479.

Edwards, S. S. M. (2000). Prosecuting 'child pornography': Possession and taking of indecent photos of children. *Journal of Social Welfare and Family Law*, 22, 1–21.

Eke, A. W., Seto, M. C. & Williams, J. (2011). Examining the criminal history and future offending of child pornography offenders: An extended prospective follow-up study. *Law and Human Behavior*, 35, 466–478.

Elias, N. & Lemish, D. (2009). Spinning the web of identity: The roles of the Internet in the lives of immigrant adolescents. *New Media & Society*, 11(4), 533–551.

Elliott, I. A. & Beech, A. R. (2009). Understanding online child pornography use: Applying sexual offense theory to Internet offenders. *Aggression and Violent Behavior*, 14, 180–193.

Elliott, I. A., Beech, A. R., Mandeville-Norden, R. & Hayes, E. (2009). Psychological profiles of Internet sexual offenders: Comparisons with contact sexual offenders. *Sexual Abuse: A Journal of Research and Treatment*, 21, 76–92.

Ellison, N., Heino, R. & Gibbs, J. (2006). Managing impression online: Self-presentation processes in the online dating environment. *Journal of Computer-Mediated Communication*, 11(2), art. 2.

Ellison, N. B., Steinfield, C. & Lampe, C. (2007). The benefits of Facebook 'friends': Exploring the relationship between college students' use of online social networks and social capital. *Journal of Computer-Mediated Communication*, 12, 1143–1168.

Ellison, N. B., Steinfield, C. & Lampe, C. (2011). Connection strategies: Social capital implications of Facebook-enabled communication practices. *New Media & Society*, 13(6), 873–892.

Endrass, J., Urbaniok, F., Hammermeister, L. C., Benz, C., Elbert, T., Laubacher, A. & Rossegger, A. (2009). The consumption of Internet child pornography and violent and sex offending. *BMC Psychiatry*, 9, 43–49.

Erikson, E. H. (1950). *Childhood and society*. New York, NY: Norton.

Erikson, E. H. (1964). *Insight and responsibility*. New York, NY: Norton.

Erikson, E. H. (1968). *Identity, youth and crisis*. New York, NY: Norton.

Evett, L., Battersby, S., Ridley, A. & Brown, D. (2009). An interface to virtual environments for people who are blind using Wii technology: Mental models and navigation. *Journal of Assistive Technologies*, 3(2), 30–39.

Eysenbach, G. & Kohler, C. (2003). What is the prevalence of health related searches on the World Wide Web? Qualitative and quantitative analysis of search engine queries on the Internet. *AMIA Annual Symposium Proceedings Archive*, 225–229.

Eysenbach, G., Powell, J. & Kuss, O. & Sa, E. R. (2002). Empirical studies assessing the quality of health information for consumers on the World Wide Web: A systematic review. *Journal of the American Medical Association*, 287, 2691–2700.

Fallows, D. (2006). Browsing the Web for fun. *Pew Research Center*. Retrieved 21 September 2015 from http://www.pewinternet.org/2006/02/15/surfing-for-fun

Feldman, M. D. (2000). Munchausen by Internet: Detecting factitious illness and crisis on the Internet. *Southern Medical Journal*, 93, 669–672.

Fergus, T. A. (2013). Cyberchondria and intolerance of uncertainty: Examining when individuals experience health anxiety in response to Internet searches for medical information. *Cyberpsychology, Behavior, and Social Networking*, 16, 735–739.

Fergus, T. A. (2014). The Cyberchondria Severity Scale (CSS): An examination of structure and relations with health anxiety in a community sample. *Journal of Anxiety Disorders*, 28(6), 504–510.

Ferguson, C. J. (2007). The good, the bad and the ugly: A meta-analytic review of positive and negative effects of violent video games. *Psychiatry Quarterly*, 78, 309–316.

Ferguson, C. J. (2010). Blazing angels or resident evil? Can violent video games be a force for good? *Review of General Psychology*, 14(2), 68–81.

Ferguson, C. J. & Kilburn, J. (2009). The public health risks of media violence: A meta-analytic review. *Journal of Pediatrics*, 154(5), 759–763.

Ferguson, C. J. & Rueda, S. M. (2009). Examining the validity of the modified Taylor competitive reaction time test of aggression. *Journal of Experimental Criminology*, 5, 121–137.

Ferrell, O. C. & Ferrell, L. (2002). Assessing instructional technology in the classroom. *Marketing Education Review*, 12, 19–24.

Finkelhor, D. (1984). *Child sexual abuse: New theory and research*. New York, NY: Free Press.

Fitness, J. (2001). Betrayal, rejection, revenge and forgiveness: An interpersonal script approach. In M. Leary (Ed.), *Interpersonal rejection* (pp. 73–103). New York, NY: Oxford University Press.

Fisher, B. S., Cullen, F. T. & Turner, M. G. (2002). Being pursued: Stalking victimization in a national study of college women. *Criminology & Public Policy*, 1, 257–308.

Fox, S. (2004). Older Americans and the Internet. *Pew Research Center*. Retrieved 21 September 2015 from http://www.pewinternet.org/2004/03/28/older-americans-and-the-Internet

Fox, S. (2008). The engaged e-patient population. *Pew Research Center*. Retrieved 19 August 2015 from http://www.pewinternet.org/2008/08/26/the-engaged-e-patient-population

Fox, S. (2011). The social life of health information. *Pew Research Center*. Retrieved 20 August 2015 from http://www.pewinternet.org/2011/05/12/the-social-life-of-health-information-2011

Freeman, D. (2008). Studying and treating schizophrenia using virtual reality: A new paradigm. *Schizophrenia Bulletin*, 34, 605–610.

Freeman, D., Pugh, K., Antley, A., Slater, M., Bebbington, P., Gittins, M., …Garety, P. (2008). Virtual reality study of paranoid thinking in the general population. *British Journal of Psychiatry*, 192, 258–263.

Freund, K. & Blanchard, R. (1986). The concept of courtship disorder. *Journal of Sex & Marital Therapy*, 12, 79–92.

Freund, K., Scher, H. & Hucker, S. J. (1983). The courtship disorders. *Archives of Sexual Behavior*, 12, 769–779.

Furnell, S. (2005). Internet threats to end-users: Hunting easy prey. *Network Security*, 7, 5–9.

Gagnon, D. (2012, 14 December). Cyberbullying suspect appears in court for violating conditions of release, gets tougher conditions. *Bangor Daily News*. Retrieved 31 December 2012 from http://bangordailynews.com/2012/12/14/news/bangor/cyberbullying-suspect-appears-in-court-for-violating-conditions-of-release-gets-tougher-conditions/?ref=polbeat

Gaimster, J. (2008). Reflections on interactions in virtual worlds and their implication for learning art and design. *Art, Design & Communication in Higher Education*, 6(3), 187–199.

Gainsbury, S. M., Russell, A., Wood, R., Hing, N. & Blaszczynski, A. (2015). How risky is Internet gambling? A comparison of subgroups of Internet gamblers based on problem gambling status. *New Media & Society*, 17(6), 861–879.

Galanxhi, H. & Nah, F. F.-H. (2007). Deception in cyberspace: A comparison of text-only vs. avatar-supported medium. *International Journal of Human–Computer Studies*, 65(9), 770–783.

Galbreath, N., Berlin, F. & Sawyer, D. (2002). Paraphilias and the Internet. In A. Cooper (Ed.), *Sex and the Internet: A Guidebook for Clinicians* (pp. 187–205). Philadelphia, PA: Brunner-Routledge.

Gass, K., Hoff, C. C., Stephenson, R. & Sullivan, P. S. (2012). Sexual agreements in the partnerships of Internet-using men who have sex with men. *AIDS Care*, 34(10), 1255–1263.

Garrison, D. R., Anderson, T. & Archer, W. (2000). Critical inquiry in a text-based environment: Computer conferencing in higher education. *Internet and Higher Education*, 2(2/3), 87–105.

Garofalo, R., Harrick, A., Mustanski, B. S. & Donenberg, G. R. (2007). Tip of the iceberg: Young men who have sex with men, the Internet, and HIV risk. *American Journal of Public Health*, 97, 1–6.

Geere, D. (2012). Soca seizes music blog, make threats against its readers. *Wired*. Retrieved 7 April 2016 from http://www.wired.co.uk/news/archive/2012-02/15/soca-website-takedown

George, J., Marett K. & Tilly P. (2004). Deception detection under varying electronic media and warning conditions. In *Proceedings of the 37th Hawaii International Conference on System Sciences*. Manoa, HI: Computer Society Press. Retrieved 3 July 2016 from https://www.computer.org/csdl/proceedings/hicss/2004/2056/01/205610022b.pdf

Gergen, K. J. (1991). *The saturated self*. New York, NY: Basic Books.

Gergen, K. J. (2000). The self: Transfiguration by technology. In D. Fee (Ed.), *Pathology and the Postmodern: Mental Illness as Discourse and Experience* (pp. 100–115). Newbury Park, CA: Sage.

Gershuny, J. (2003). Web use and net nerds: A neo-functionalist analysis of the impact of information technology in the home. *Social Forces*, 82(1), 141–168.

Get Cyber Safe. (2015). Phishing: How many take the bait? Retrieved 11 July 2016 from http://www.getcybersafe.gc.ca/cnt/rsrcs/nfgrphcs/nfgrphcs-2012-10-11-en.aspx

Gifford, A. (2002). Emotion and self-control. *Journal of Economic Behavior & Organization*, 49, 113–130.

Gikandi, J. W., Morrow, D. & Davis, N. E. (2011). Online formative assessment in higher education: A review of the literature. *Computers & Education*, 57, 2333–2351.

Gilbert, R. L., Murphy, N. A. & Avalos, M. C. (2011). Realism, idealization, and potential negative impact of 3D virtual relationships. *Computers in Human Behavior*, 27(5), 2039–2046.

Giles, D. (2002). Parasocial interaction: A review of the literature and a model for future research. *Media Psychology*, 4, 279–305.

Gillani, B. B. & Relan, A. (1997). Incorporating interactivity and multimedia into Web-based instruction. In B. H. Khan (Ed.), *Web-based instruction* (pp. 231–237). Englewood Cliff, NJ: Educational Technology.

Gillespie, A. (2010). Legal definitions of child pornography. *Journal of Sexual Aggression*, 16(1), 19–31.

Givens, D. (1978). The nonverbal basis of attraction: Flirtation, courtship, and seduction. *Psychiatry*, 41, 346–359.

Goffman, E. (1959/1997). In the presentation of self in everyday life. In C. Lemert & A. Branaman (Eds.), *The Goffman reader* (pp. 21–26). Cambridge, MA: Blackwell.

Gold, K., Boggs, M., Mugisha, E. & Palladino, C. (2012). Internet message boards for pregnancy loss: Who's on-line and why? *Women's Health Issues*, 22(1), e67–e72.

Goldberg, L. R. (1990). An alternative 'description of personality': The big-five factor structure. *Journal of Personality and Social Psychology*, 59(6), 1216–1229.

Gonzales, M. H. & Meyers, S. A. (1993). 'Your mother would like me': Self-presentation in the personal ads of heterosexual and homosexual men and women. *Personality and Social Psychology Bulletin*, 19(2), 131–142.

Granhag, P. A. & Strömwall, I. A. (2002). Repeated interrogations: Verbal and nonverbal cues to deception. *Applied Cognitive Psychology*, 16, 243–257.

Grandoni, D. (2015, 20 July). Ashley Madison, a dating website, says hackers may have data on millions. *New York Times*. Retrieved 7 April 2016 from http://www.nytimes.com/2015/07/21/technology/hacker-attack-reported-on-ashley-madison-a-dating-service.html

Granovetter, M. S. (1973). The strength of weak ties. *American Journal of Sociology*, 78(6), 1360–80.

Green, S. K., Buchanan, D. & Heuer, S. (1984). Winners, losers, and choosers: A field investigation of dating initiation. *Personality and Social Psychology Bulletin*, 10, 502–511.

Greenless, I. A. & McGrew, W. C. (1994). Sex and age differences in preferences and tactics of mate attraction: Analysis of published advertisements. *Ethology and Sociobiology*, 15, 59–72.

Greenwood, D. N. (2013). Fame, Facebook, and Twitter: How attitudes about fame predict frequency and nature of social media use. *Psychology of Popular Media Culture*, 2(4), 222–236.

Griffiths, K. M., Mackinnon, A. J., Crisp, D. A., Christensen, H., Bennett, K. & Farrer, L. (2012). The effectiveness of an online support group for members of the community with depression: A randomized controlled trial. *PLoS ONE*, 7(12), 1–9.

Griffiths, M. (1998). Internet addiction: Does it really exist? In J. Gackenbach (Ed.), *Psychology and the Internet* (pp. 61–75). New York, NY: Academic Press.

Griffiths, M. (1999). Internet addiction: Fact or fiction. *Psychologist*, 12, 246–250.

Griffiths, M. (2000a). Excessive Internet use: Implications for sexual behaviour. *CyberPsychology & Behavior*, 3, 537–552.

Griffiths, M. (2000b). Internet addiction: Time to be taken seriously? *Addiction Research*, 8, 413–418.

Griffiths, M. (2001). Sex on the Internet: Observations and implications for Internet sex addiction. *Journal of Sex Research*, 38, 333–342.

Griffiths, M. (2003). Internet gambling: Issues, concerns, and recommendations. *CyberPsychology & Behavior*, 6(6), 557–568.

Grohol, J. (1998). Response to the HomeNet study. *PsychCentral*. Retrieved 27 October 2004 from http://psychcentral.com/homenet.htm

Guardian, The. (2015, 23 February). UK in 'ever-losing battle' over online radicalisation, says Lady Warsi. Retrieved 7 April 2016 from http://www.theguardian.com/uk-news/2015/feb/22/uk-in-ever-losing-battle-over-online-radicalisation-says-lady-warsi

Guitton, C. (2012). Criminals and cyber attacks: The missing link between attribution and deterrence. *International Journal of Cyber Criminology*, 6(2), 1030–1043.

Guillen-Nieto, V. & Aleson-Carbonell, M. (2012). Serious games and learning effectiveness: The case of It's a Deal! *Computers & Education*, 58(1), 435–448.

Guillory, J. & Hancock, J. T. (2012). The effect of LinkedIn on deception in resumes. *Cyberpsychology, Behavior, and Social Networking*, 15(3), 135–140.

Giumetti, G. W. & Markey, P. M. (2007). Violent video games and anger as predictors of aggression. *Journal of Research in Personality*, 41(6), 1234–1243.

Hale, W. C. (2012). Extremism on the World Wide Web: A research review. *Criminal Justice Studies*, 25(4), 343–356.

Hancock, J. (2007). Digital deception. In A. N. Joinson, K., McKenna, T., Postmes & U.-D. Reips (Eds.), *Oxford handbook of internet psychology* (pp. 289–301). Oxford, UK: Oxford University Press.

Hancock, J. T., Curry, L., Goorha, S. & Woodworth, M. (2005). An automated linguistic analysis of deceptive and truthful computer-mediated communication. In *Proceedings of the Hawaii International Conference on System Sciences*. Retrieved 3 July 2016 from http://ieeexplore.ieee.org/xpl/login.jsp?tp=&arnumber=1385275&url=http%3A%2F%2Fieeexplore.ieee.org%2Fxpls%2Fabs_all.jsp%3Farnumber%3D1385275

Hancock, J. T. & Dunham, P. J. (2001). Impression formation in computer-mediated communication revisited: An analysis of the breadth and intensity of impressions. *Communication Research*, 28, 325–347.

Hancock, J. T., Thom-Santelli, J. & Ritchie, T. (2004). Deception and design: The impact of communication technologies on lying behavior. In *Proceedings of the SIGCHI Conference on Human Factors in Computing Systems* (pp. 129–134). New York, NY: Association for Computing Machinery.

Hanlon, M. (2009, 24 April). The KissPhone for remote kissing. *Gizmag*. Retrieved 28 December 2012 from http://www.gizmag.com/the-kissphone-for-remote-kissing/11532

Harasim, L. (1990). Online education: An environment for collaboration and intellectual amplification. In L. Harasim (Ed.), *Online education: Perspectives on a new environment* (pp. 39–64). New York, NY: Praeger.

Haraway, D. (1991). *Symians, cyborgs and women: The reinvention of nature*. London, UK: Free Association.

Hardy, W., Krawczyk, M. & Tyrowicz, J. (2013). Why is online piracy ethically different from theft? A vignette experiment. Retrieved 7 April 2016 from http://www.webmeets.com/files/papers/IEA/2014/436/vignette_HKT.pdf

Hargittai, E. & Litt, E. (2011). The tweet smell of celebrity success: Explaining variation in Twitter adoption among a diverse group of young adults. *New Media & Society*, 13(5) 824–842.

Hartwig, M., Granhag, P. A., Stromwall, L. A. & Anderson, I. O. (2004). Suspicious minds: Criminals' ability to detect deception. *Psychology, Crime & Law*, 10, 83–95.

Harris, C. R. (2004). The evolution of jealousy: Did men and women, facing different selective pressures, evolve different 'brands' of jealousy? Recent evidence suggests not. *American Scientist*, 92, 62–71.

Harris, C. R. & Christenfeld, N. (1996). Gender, jealousy, and reason. *Psychological Science*, 7(6), 364–245.

Harris, D. (2005). *Key concepts in leisure studies*. London, UK: Sage.

Harrison, A. A. & Saeed, L. (1977). Let's make a deal: An analysis of revelations and stipulations in lonely hearts advertisements. *Journal of Personality and Social Psychology*, 35, 257–264.

Haviland, M. G., Pincus, H. A. & Dial, T. H. (2003). Datapoints: Type of illness and use of the Internet for health information. *Psychiatric Services, 54*, 1198.

Hay, L. & Pymm, B. (2011). Real learning in a virtual world: A case study of the school of information studies' learning centre in *Second Life. Education for Information, 28*, 187–202.

Haythornthwaite, C. & Wellman, B. (2002). The Internet in everyday life: An introduction. In B. Wellman & C. Haythornthwaite (Eds.), *The Internet in everyday life* (pp. 3–44). Oxford, UK: Blackwell.

Health on the Net Foundation. (2001). Evolution of Internet use for health purposes: Feb/March 2001. Retrieved 19 August 2015 from http://www.hon.ch/Survey/FebMar2001/survey.html

Heinlen, K. T., Welfel, E. R., Richmond, E. N. & O'Donnell, M. S. (2003). The nature, scope, and ethics of psychologists' e-therapy web sites: What consumers find when surfing the web. *Psychotherapy: Theory, Research, Practice, Training, 40*(1/2), 112–124.

Helft, P. R., Eckles, R. E., Johnson-Calley, C. S. & Daugherty, C. K. (2005). Use of the Internet to obtain cancer information among cancer patients at an urban county hospital. *Journal of Clinical Oncology, 23*, 4954–4962.

Hemmi, A., Bayne, S. & Land, R. (2009). The appropriation of social technologies in higher education. *Journal of Computer Assisted Learning, 25*(1), 19–30.

Henry, O., Mandeville-Norden, R., Hayes, E. & Egan, V. (2010). Do Internet-based sexual offenders reduce to normal, inadequate and deviant groups? *Journal of Sexual Aggression, 16*, 33–46.

Hertlein, K. M. & Piercy, F. P. (2008). Therapists' assessment and treatment of Internet infidelity cases. *Journal of Marital and Family Therapy, 34*(4), 481–497.

Higgins, E. T. (1987). Self-discrepancy: A theory relating self and affect. *Psychological Review, 94*, 319–340.

Higgins, E. T. (1989). Self-discrepancy theory: What patterns of self-beliefs cause people to suffer? In L. Berkowitz (Ed.), *Advances in experimental social psychology* (Vol. 22, pp. 93–136). San Diego, CA: Academic Press.

Hiltz, S., Johnson, M. & Turoff, M. (1986). Experiments in group decision making: Communication process and outcome in face-to-face versus computerized conferences. *Human Communication Research, 13*, 225–252.

Himmelweit, H. T., Oppenheim, A. N. & Vince, P. (1958). *Television and the child.* London, UK: Oxford University Press.

Hinduja, S. & Patchin, J. W. (2007). Offline consequences of online victimization: School violence and delinquency. *Journal of School Violence, 6*(3), 89–112.

Hirzalla, F. & Van Zoonen, L. (2011). Beyond the online/offline divide: How youth's online and offline civic activities converge. *Social Science Computer Review, 29*(4), 481–498.

Hoffman, H. G., Garcia-Palacios, A., Patterson, D. R., Jensen, M., Furness, T. & Ammons, W. F., Jr. (2001). The effectiveness of virtual reality for dental pain control: A case study. *CyberPsychology & Behavior, 4*(4), 527–535.

Holtfreter, K., Reisig, M. D. & Pratt, T. C. (2008). Low self-control, routine activities and fraud victimization. *Criminology, 46*(1), 189–220.

Holmberg, K. & Huvila, I. (2008). Learning together apart: Distance education in a virtual world. *First Monday, 13*(10). Retrieved 4 March 2013 from http://www.uic.edu/htbin/cgiwrap/bin/ojs/index.php/fm/article/view/2178/2033

Hong, J. (2012). The current state of phishing attacks. *Communications of the ACM, 55*(1), 74–81.

Hong, Y., Li, X., Fang, X., Lin, X. & Zhang, C. (2011). Internet use among female sex workers in China: Implications for HIV/STI prevention. *AIDS and Behavior, 15*(2), 273–282.

Hooper, S., Rosser, B. R., Horvath, K. J., Oakes, J. M. & Danilenko, G. (2008). An online needs assessment of a virtual community: What men who use the Internet to seek sex with men want in Internet-based HIV prevention. *AIDS and Behavior, 12*, 867–875.

Horgan, A. & Sweeney, J. (2010). Young students' use of the Internet for mental health information and support. *Journal of Psychiatric and Mental Health Nursing, 17*, 117–123.

Horton, D. & Wohl, R. R. (1956). Mass communication and para-social interaction. *Psychiatry, 19*, 215–229.

Horvath, A. O., Del Re, A. C., Fluckiger, C. & Symonds, D. (2011). Alliance in individual psychotherapy. *Psychotherapy, 48*, 9–16.

Howitt, D. (1995). Pornography and the paedophile: Is it criminogenic? *British Journal of Medical Psychology, 68*, 15–27.

Howitt, D. & Sheldon, K. (2007). The role of cognitive distortions in paedophilic offending: Internet and contact offenders compared. *Psychology, Crime & Law, 13*, 469–486.

Hrastinski, S. (2006). Introducing an informal synchronous medium in a distance learning course: How is participation affected? *Internet and Higher Education, 9*, 117–131.

Hrastinski, S. (2008). Asynchronous and synchronous e-learning. *EDUCAUSE Quarterly, 31*(4), 51–55.

Hucker, A. & McCabe, M. P. (2014). A qualitative evaluation of online chat groups for women completing a psychological intervention for female sexual dysfunction. *Journal of Sex & Marital Therapy, 40*(1), 58–68.

Huesmann, L. R. (1988). An information-processing model for the development of aggression. *Aggressive Behavior, 14*, 13–24.

Huizenga, J., Admiraal, W., Akkerman, S. & ten Dam, G. (2008). Learning history by playing a mobile city game. Paper presented at the 1st European Conference on Game-Based Learning (ECGBL), 16–17 October 2008, Barcelona, Spain.

Human, K. (2007). Study links computer denial to Columbine. *Denver Post*. Retrieved 7 April 2016 from http://www.denverpost.com/headlines/ci_6300370?source=infinite

International Society of Mental Health Online. (2009). Suggested principles for the online provision of mental health services. Retrieved 7 November 2015 from http://ismho.org/resources/archive/suggested-principles-for-the-online-provision-of-mental-health-services

Internet Crime Complaint Center. (2014). *Annual report*. Washington, DC: Internet Crime Complaint Center.

Jambon, M. M. & Semetana, J. G. (2012). College students' moral evaluations of illegal music downloading. *Journal of Applied Developmental Psychology, 33*(1), 31–39.

James, M. L., Wotring, C. E. & Forrest, E. J. (1995). An exploratory study of the perceived benefits of electronic bulletin board use and their impact on other communication activities. *Journal of Broadcasting & Electronic Media, 39*, 30–50.

James, W. (1892/1963). *Psychology*. Greenwich, CT: Fawcett.

Jansson, K. & von Solms, R. (2013). Phishing for phishing awareness. *Behaviour & Information Technology, 32*(6), 584–593.

Jarmon, L. & Sanchez, J. (2008). The educators coop experience in *Second Life*: A model for collaboration. *Journal of the Research Center for Educational Technology, 4*(2), 66–82.

Jarmon, L., Traphagan, T., Mayrath, M. & Trivedi, A. (2009). Virtual world teaching, experiential learning, and assessment: An interdisciplinary communication course in *Second Life*. *Computers & Education, 53*, 169–182.

Jenkins, P. (2009). Failure to launch: Why do some social issues fail to detonate moral panics? *British Journal of Criminology, 49*(1), 35–47.

Jerome, L. W., Deleon, P. H., James, L. C., Folen, R., Earles, J. & Gedney, J. J. (2000). The coming age of telecommunications in psychological research and practice. *American Psychologist, 55*, 407–421.

Jiang, L. C., Bazarova, N. N. & Hancock, J. T. (2013). From perception to behaviour: Disclosure reciprocity and the intensification of intimacy in computer-mediated communication. *Communication Research, 40*(1), 125–143.

Jin, S.-A. & Phua, J. (2014). Following celebrities' tweets about brands: The impact of Twitter-based electronic word-of-mouth on consumers' source credibility perception, buying intention, and social identification with celebrities. *Journal of Advertising, 43*(2), 181–195.

Jones, J. G., Morales, C. & Knezek, G. A. (2005). 3D online learning environments: Examining attitudes towards information technology between students in Internet-based and face-to-face classroom instruction. *Educational Media International, 42*(3), 219–236.

Johnson, D. W. & Johnson, R. T. (1996). Cooperation and the use of technology. In D. Jonassen (Ed.), *Handbook of research for educational communications and technology* (pp. 1017–1044). London, UK: Macmillan.

Joinson, A. N. (2001). Self-disclosure in computer-mediated communication: The role of self-awareness and visual anonymity. *European Journal of Social Psychology, 31*, 177–192.

Jones, R., Sharkey, S., Ford, T., Emmens, T., Hewis, E., Smithson, J., ... Owens, C. (2011). Online discussion forums for young people who self-harm: User views. *The Psychiatrist, 35*, 364–368.

Jung, S., Ennis, L. & Malesky, L. A. (2012). Child pornography offending seen through three theoretical lenses. *Deviant Behavior, 33*(8), 655–673.

Kakietek, J., Sullivan, P. S. & Heffelfinger, J. D. (2011). You've got male: Internet use, rural residence, and risky sex in men who have sex with men recruited in 12 US cities. *AIDS Education and Prevention, 23*(2), 118–127.

Kalyuga, S. (2007). Enhancing instructional efficiency of interactive e-learning environments: A cognitive load perspective. *Educational Psychology Review, 19*(3), 387–399.

Kayany, J. M. & Yelsma, P. (2000). Displacement effects of online media in socio-technical contexts of households. *Journal of Broadcasting & Electronic Media, 44*(2), 215–229.

Kenski, K. & Stroud, N. (2006). Connections between Internet use and political efficacy, knowledge, and participation. *Journal of Broadcasting & Electronic Media, 50*, 173–192.

Kenrick, D. T., Sadalla, E. K., Groth, G. & Trost, M. R. (1990). Evolution, traits, and the stages of human courtship: Qualifying the parental investment model. *Journal of Personality, 58*, 97–116.

Keskitalo, T., Pyykkö, E. & Ruokamo, H. (2011). Exploring the meaningful learning of students in *Second Life*. *Educational Technology & Society, 14*(1), 16–26.

Kiesler, S. J., Siegel, J. & McGuire, T. W. (1984). Social psychological aspects of computer-mediated communication. *American Psychologist, 39*, 1123–1134.

Kingston, D. A., Fedoroff, P., Firestone, P., Curry, S. & Bradford, J. M. (2008). Pornography use and sexual aggression: The impact of frequency and type of pornography use on recidivism among sexual offenders. *Aggressive Behavior, 34*(4), 341–351.

Kirk, S. & Milnes, L. (2015). An exploration of how young people and parents use online support in the context of living with cystic fibrosis. *Health Expectations, 19*(2), 309–321.

Kirriemuir, J. (2010). UK university and college technical support for *Second Life* developers and users. *Educational Research, 52*(2), 215–227.

Klein, M. (1986). *The selected works of Melanie Klein* (J. Mitchell, Ed.). London, UK: Penguin.

Klein, R. (1999). If I'm a cyborg rather than a goddess will patriarchy go away? In S. Hawthorne & R. Klein (Eds.), *Cyberfeminism: Connectivity, critique and creativity* (pp. 185–212). North Melbourne, Australia: Spinifex Press.

Klein, H. (2012). Anonymous sex and HIV risk practices among men using the Internet specifically to find male partners for unprotected sex. *Public Health*, 126(6), 471–481.

Knight, P. (2007). Promoting retention and successful completion on masters courses in education: A study comparing e-tuition using asynchronous conferencing software with face-to-face tuition. *Open Learning*, 22(1), 87–96.

Koestner, R. & Wheeler, L. (1988). Self-presentation in personal advertisements: The influence of implicit notions of attraction and role expectations. *Journal of Social and Personal Relationships*, 5, 149–160.

Kosse, S. H. (2004). Virtual child pornography: A United States update. *Communications Law*, 9(2), 39–46.

Koutsabasis, P., Stavrakis, M., Spyrou, T. & Darzentas, J. (2011). Perceived impact of asynchronous e-learning after long-term use: Implications for design and development. *International Journal of Human–Computer Interaction*, 27(2), 191–213.

Kozma, R. (1994). Will media influence learning? Reframing the debate. *Educational Technology Research and Development*, 42(2), 7–19.

Kramer, J., Boon, B., Schotanus-Dijkstra, M., Van Ballegooijen, W., Kerkhof, A. & Van der Poel, A. (2015). The mental health of visitors of Web-based support forums for bereaved by suicide. *Crisis*, 36(1), 38–45.

Kraut, R., Patterson, M., Lundmark, V., Kiesler, S., Mukophadhayay, T. & Scherlis, W. (1998). Internet paradox: A social technology that reduces social involvement and psychological well-being? *American Psychologist*, 53(9), 1017–1031.

Ku, J., Han, K., Lee, H. R., Jang, H. J., Kim, K. U., Park, S. H., … Kim, S. I. (2007). VR-based conversation training program for patients with schizophrenia: A preliminary clinical trial. *CyberPsychology & Behavior*, 10, 567–574.

Kubicek, K., Carpineto, J., McDavitt, B., Weiss, G. & Kipke, M. D. (2011). Use and perceptions of the Internet for sexual information and partners: A study of young men who have sex with men. *Archives of Sexual Behavior*, 40(4), 803–816.

Kuh, G. D. (2003). What we're learning about student engagement from NSSE. *Change*, 35, 24–31.

Lam, A., Mitchell, J. & Seto, M. C. (2010). Lay perceptions of child pornography offenders. *Canadian Journal of Criminology and Criminal Justice*, 52, 173–201.

Lam, L. T. (2014). Internet gaming addiction, problematic use of the Internet and sleep problems: A systematic review. *Current Psychiatry Reports*, 16, 1–9.

Lambert, M. J. & Barley, D. E. (2001). Research summary on the therapeutic relationship and psychotherapy outcome. *Psychotherapy*, 38, 357–361.

Lan, Y.-F. & Sie, Y.-S. (2010). Using RSS to support mobile learning based on media richness theory. *Computers & Education*, 55, 723–732.

Larreamendy-Joerns, J. & Leinhardt, G. (2006). Going the distance with online education. *Review of Educational Research*, 76(4), 567–605.

Lauckner, C. & Hsieh, G. (2013). The presentation of health-related search results and its impact on negative emotional outcomes. Paper presented at the SIGCHI Conference on Human Factors in Computing Systems, Paris, France, 27 April – 2 May. Retrieved 21 August 2015 from http://faculty.washington.edu/garyhs/docs/lauckner-chi2013-health.pdf

Laurillard, D. (1998). Multimedia and the learner's experience of narrative. *Computers & Education*, 31, 229–242.

Lea, M. & Spears, R. (1991). Computer-mediated communication, de-individuation and group decision-making. *International Journal of Man-Machine Studies*, 39, 283–301.

Lea, M. & Spears, R. (1995). Love at first byte? Building personal relationships over computer networks. In J. T. Wood & S. W. Duck (Eds.), *Understudied relationships: Off the beaten track* (pp. 197–233). Newbury Park, CA: Sage.

Lea, M., Spears, R. & de Groot, D. (2001). Knowing me, knowing you: Anonymity effects on social identity processes within groups. *Personality and Social Psychology Bulletin*, 27(5), 526–537.

Lea, S., Fischer, P. & Evans, K. (2009a). *The psychology of scams: Provoking and committing errors of judgement*. Office of Fair Trading. Retrieved 7 April 2016 from http://webarchive.national archives.gov.uk/20140402142426/http://www.oft.gov.uk/shared_oft/reports/consumer_protection/oft1070.pdf

Lea, S., Fisher, P. & Evans, K. M. (2009b). The economic psychology of scams. Paper presented at the conference of the International Association for Research in Economic Psychology and the Society for the Advancement of Behavioral Economics, Nova Scotia, Canada, July.

Leasure, A. R., Davis, L. & Thievon, S. L. (2000). Comparison of student outcomes and preferences in a traditional vs. World Wide Web-based baccalaureate nursing research course. *Journal of Nursing Education*, 39(4), 149–154.

Lee, A. F., Li, N.-C., Lamade, R., Schuler, A. & Prentky, R. A. (2012). Predicting hands-on child sexual offenses among possessors of Internet child pornography. *Psychology, Public Policy, and Law*, 18(4), 644–672.

Lee, J. & Soberon-Ferrer, H. (2005). Consumer vulnerability to fraud: Influencing factors. *Journal of Consumer Affairs*, 31(1), 70–89.

Lee, J. H., Ku, J., Cho, W., Hahn, W. Y., Kim, I. Y., Lee, S. M., … Kim, S. I. (2003). Virtual reality system for the assessment and rehabilitation of the activities of daily living. *CyberPsychology & Behavior*, 6(4), 383–388.

Lee, S. (2010). Contemporary issues of ethical e-therapy. *Journal of Ethics in Mental Health*, 5(1), 1–5.

Lee, S. S., Tam, D. K., Mak, D. W. & Wong, K. H. (2011). Use of the Internet for sex partnership in men who have sex with men before HIV infection. *Public Health*, 125(7), 433–435

Lee, S. Y. & Hawkins, R. (2010). Why do patients seek an alternative channel? The effects of unmet needs on patients' health-related Internet use. *Journal of Health Communication*, 15, 152–166.

Lee, W. & Kuo, E. C. Y. (2001). Internet and displacement effect: Children's media use and activities in Singapore. *Journal of Computer-Mediated Communication*, 7(2). doi: 10.1111/j.1083–6101.2002.tb00143.x

Lee, W., Tan, T. M. K. & Hameed, S. S. (2006). Polychronicity, the Internet, and the mass media: A Singapore study. *Journal of Computer-Mediated Communication*, 11, 300–316.

Lemire, M., Paré, G., Sicotte, C. & Harvey, C. (2008). Determinants of Internet use as a preferred source of information on personal health. *International Journal of Medical Informatics*, 77, 723–734.

Lenhart, A. (2009). Teens and sexting. *Pew Research Center*. Retrieved 8 August 2011 from http://www.pewinternet.org/Reports/2009/Teens-and-Sexting.aspx

Lenhart, A., Rainie, L. & Lewis, O. (2001). *Teenage life online: The rise of the instant-message generation and the Internet's impact on friendships and family relations*. Washington, DC: Pew Internet & American Life Project.

Levi, M. & Burrows, J. (2008). Measuring the impact of fraud in the UK: A conceptual and empirical journey. *British Journal of Criminology*, 48, 293–318.

Levick, M. & Moon, K. (2010). Prosecuting sexting as child pornography. *Valparaiso University Law Review*, 44(4), 1035–1054.

Levitin, D. J. (2015, 18 January). Why the modern world is bad for your brain. *The Guardian*. Retrieved 7 April 2016 from http://www.theguardian.com/science/2015/jan/18/modern-world-bad-for-brain-daniel-j-levitin-organized-mind-information-overload

Levy, N. (2002). Virtual child pornography: The eroticization of inequality. *Ethics in Information Technology, 4*, 319–323.

Li, C. & Bernoff, J. (2011). *Groundswell: Winning in a world transformed by social technologies*. Boston, MA: Harvard University Press.

Liang, B. & Scammon, D. L. (2011). E-word-of-mouth on health social networking sites: An opportunity for tailored health communication. *Journal of Consumer Behaviour, 10*, 322–331.

Liau, A., Millet, G. & Marks, G. (2006). Meta-analytic examination of online sex seeking and sexual risk behaviour among men who have sex with men. *Sexually Transmitted Diseases, 33*, 576–584.

Lin, C. A. (2001). Audience attributes, media supplementation and likely online service adoption. *Mass Communication and Society, 4*(1), 19–38.

Linder, K. E., Fontaine-Rainen, D. L. & Behling, K. (2015). Whose job is it? Key challenges and future directions for online accessibility in US institutions of higher education. *Open Learning, 30*(1), 21–34.

Lindley, L. L., Friedman, D. B. & Struble, C. (2012). Becoming visible: Assessing the availability of online sexual health information for lesbians. *Health Promotion Practice, 13*(4), 472–480.

Liu, S.-H., Liao, H.-L. & Pratt, J. A. (2009). Impact of media richness and flow on e-learning technology acceptance. *Computers & Education, 52*, 599–607.

Livingstone, S. (2006). *UK children go online: End of award report*. Retrieved 14 May 2008 from http://www.york.ac.uk/res/e-society/projects/1/EndofAwardReportUKChildrenGoOnlineSoniaLivingston.pdf

Livingstone, S. (2009). *Children and the Internet: Great expectations, challenging realities* (Cambridge: Polity).

Livingstone, S. & Helsper, E. (2007). Gradations in digital inclusion: Children, young people and the digital divide. *New Media & Society, 9*(4), 671–696.

Löfström, E. & Nevgi, A. (2007). From strategic planning to meaningful learning: Diverse perspectives on the development of web-based teaching and learning in higher education. *British Journal of Education Technology, 38*(2), 312–324.

Loges, W. & Jung, J. (2001). Exploring the digital divide: Internet connectedness and age. *Communication Research, 28*(4), 536–562.

Loucas, C. E., Fairburn, C. G., Whittington, C., Pennant, M. E., Stockton, S. & Kendall, T. (2014). E-therapy in the treatment and prevention of eating disorders: A systematic review and meta-analysis. *Behaviour Research and Therapy, 63*, 122–131.

MacDonald, K. (1998). Evolution, culture, and the five-factor model. *Journal of Cross-Cultural Psychology, 29*, 119–149.

Macafee, T. & de Simone, J. J. (2012). Killing the bill online? Pathways to young people's protect engagement via social media. *Cyberpsychology, Behavior, and Social Networking, 15*(11), 579–584.

MacKay, T.-L. & Hodgins, D. C. (2012). Cognitive distortions as a problem gambling risk factor in Internet gambling. *International Gambling Studies, 12*(2), 163–175.

Maheu, M. & Subotnik, R. (2001). *Infidelity on the Internet: Virtual relationships and real betrayal*. Naperville, IL: Sourcebooks.

Malesky, L. A. & Ennis, L. (2004). Supportive distortions: An analysis of postings on a pedophile Internet message board. *Journal of Addiction & Offender Counseling, 24*, 92–100.

Malik, S. H. & Coulson, N. S. (2008). Computer-mediated infertility support groups: An exploratory study of online experiences. *Patient Education and Counseling, 73*, 105–113.

Malu, M. K., Challenor, R., Theobald, N. & Barton, S. E. (2004). Seeking and engaging in Internet sex: A survey of patients attending genitourinary medicine clinics in Plymouth and in London. *International Journal of STD & AIDS*, 15(11), 720–724.

Manfredo, M. J., Driver, B. L. & Tarrant, M. A. (1996). Measuring leisure motivation: A meta-analysis of the recreation experience preference scales. *Journal of Leisure Research*, 28(3), 188–213.

Mangao, A. M., Graham, M. B., Greenfield, P. M. & Salimkhan, G. (2008). Self-presentation and gender on Myspace. *Journal of Applied Developmental Psychology*, 29, 446–458.

Manhal-Baugus, M. (2001). E-therapy: Practical, ethical, and legal issues. *CyberPsychology & Behavior*, 4, 551–563.

Marcia, J. E. (1966). Development and validation of ego identity status. *Journal of Personality and Social Psychology*, 3, 551–558.

Marcia, J. E. (1980). Identity in adolescence. In J. Adelson (Ed.), *Handbook of adolescent psychology* (pp. 159–187). New York, NY: John Wiley & Sons.

Marcia, J. E. (1991). Identity and self-development. In R. M. Lerner, A. C. Petersen & J. Brooks-Gunn (Eds.), *Encyclopedia of adolescence* (Vol. 1, pp. 529–533). New York, NY: Garland.

Markus, H. & Nurius, P. (1986). Possible selves. *American Psychologist*, 41, 954–969.

Markus, H. & Nurius, P. (1987). Possible selves: The interface between motivation and the self-concept. In K. Yardly & T. Honess (Eds.), *Self and identity: Psychosocial perspectives* (pp. 157–172). Chichester, UK: John Wiley & Sons.

Martin, H. V., Botella, C., Garciá-Palarios, A. & Osma, J. (2007). Virtual reality exposure in the treatment of panic disorder with agrophobia: A case study. *Cognitive and Behavioral Practice*, 14, 58–69.

Marwick, A. E. & boyd, d. (2010). I tweet honestly, I tweet passionately: Twitter users, context collapse, and the imagined audience. *New Media & Society*, 13(1) 114–133.

Marwick, A. E. & boyd, d. (2011). To see and be seen: Celebrity practice on Twitter. *Convergence*, 17, 139–158.

Matarazzo, G. & Sellen, A. (2000). The value of video in work at a distance: Addition or distraction. *Behaviour & Information Technology*, 19(5), 339–348.

Mathews, S., Andrews, L. & Luck, E. (2012). Developing a *Second Life* virtual field trip for university students: An action research approach. *Educational Research*, 54(1), 17–38.

Mayadas, A. F., Bourne, J. & Bacsich, P. (2009). Online education today. *Science*, 323, 85–89.

Mayrath, M., Sanchez, J., Traphagan, T., Heikes, J. & Trivedi, A. (2007). Using *Second Life* in an English course: Designing class activities to address learning objectives. In C. Montgomerie & J. Seale (Eds.), *Proceedings of the World Conference on Educational Multimedia, Hypermedia and Telecommunications* (pp. 4219–4224). Chesapeake, VA: Association for the Advancement of Computing in Education.

McAdams, D. P. (1993). *Stories we live by: Personal myths and the making of the self*. New York, NY: William Morrow.

McCarthy, J. A. (2010). Internet sexual activity: A comparison between contact and non-contact child pornography offenders. *Journal of Sexual Aggression*, 16(2), 181–195.

McCrae, R. R. (2000). Trait psychology and the revival of personality and culture studies. *American Behavioural Scientist*, 44, 10–31.

McGrath, M. G. & Casey, E. (2002). Forensic psychiatry and the Internet: Practical perspectives on sexual predators and obsessional harassers in cyberspace. *Journal of the American Academy of Psychiatry and the Law*, 20, 81–94.

McDaniel, B. T. & Coyne, S. M. (2014). 'Technoference': The interference of technology in couple relationships and implications for women's personal and relational well-being. *Psychology of Popular Media Culture*. doi: 10.1037/ppm0000065

McElroy, E. & Shevlin, M. (2014). The development and initial validation of the cyberchondria severity scale (CSS). *Journal of Anxiety Disorders*, 28(2), 259–265.

McManus, F., Leung, C., Muse, K. & Williams, J. M. G. (2014). Understanding 'cyberchondria': An interpretive phenomenological analysis of the purpose, methods and impact of seeking health information online for those with health anxiety. *Cognitive Behaviour Therapist*, 7, 1–13.

McKenna, K. Y. A. & Bargh, J. A. (1998). Coming out in the age of the Internet: Identity 'demarginalization' through virtual group participation. *Journal of Personality and Social Psychology*, 75(3), 681–694.

McKenna, K. Y. A. & Bargh, J. A. (2000). Plan 9 from cyberspace: The implications of the Internet for personality and social psychology. *Journal of Personality and Social Psychology*, 4, 57–75.

McKenna, K. Y. A., Green, A. S. & Gleason, M. E. J. (2002). Relationship formation on the Internet: What's the big attraction? *Journal of Social Issues*, 58, 9–31.

McKenna, K. Y. A., Green, A. S. & Smith, P. K. (2001). Demarginalizing the sexual self. *Journal of Sex Research*, 34(4), 302–311.

McQuail, D. (1994). *McQuail's mass communication theory*. London, UK: Sage.

Menard, K. S. & Pincus, A. L. (2012). Predicting overt and cyber stalking perpetration by male and female college students. *Journal of Interpersonal Violence*, 27(1), 2183–2207.

Metropolitan Police Service. (1997). *The Protection from Harassment Act 1997: A guide, version 2.0*. London: New Scotland Yard.

Middleton, D., Elliot, I. A., Mandeville-Norden, R. & Beech, A. R. (2006). An investigation into the applicability of the Ward and Siegert pathways model of child sexual abuse with Internet offenders. *Psychology, Crime & Law*, 12, 589–603.

Mileham, B. L. A. (2007). Online infidelity in Internet chat rooms: An ethnographic exploration. *Computers in Human Behavior*, 23(1), 11–21.

Miller, H. & Arnold, J. (2000). Gender and Web home pages. *Computers & Education*, 34, 335–339.

Mitchell, M., Finkelhor, D., Jones, L. & Wolak, W. (2012). Prevalence and characteristics of youth sexting. *Pediatrics*, 129(1), 13–20.

Mongeau, P. A., Hale, J. L., Johnson, K. L. & Hillis, J. D. (1993). Who's wooing whom? An Investigation of female initiated dating. In P. J. Kabfleisch (Ed.), *Interpersonal communication: Evolving interpersonal relationships* (pp. 51–68). Hillsdale, New Jersey: Lawrence Erlbaum Associates, Inc.

Mo, P. K. H. & Coulson, N. S. (2008). Exploring the communication of social support within virtual communities: a content analysis of messages posted to an online HIV/AIDS support group. *CyberPsychology & Behavior*, 11, 371–374.

Moody, G. (2012). SOCA's frightening new approach to music piracy. Computerworld UK. Retrieved 7 April 2016 from http://www.computerworlduk.com/blogs/open-enterprise/socas-frightening-new-approach-to-music-piracy-3569177/

Moores, T. & Chang, J. (2006). Ethical decision making in software piracy: Initial development and test of a four-component model. *MIS Quarterly*, 167–180.

Morris, S. (2008, November 13). *Second Life* affair leads to real life divorce. *Guardian.co.uk*. Retrieved 22 December 2009 from http://www.guardian.co.uk/technology/2008/nov/13/second-life-divorce

Morton, L., Alexander, J. & Altman, I. (1976). Communication and relationship definition. In G. R. Miller (Ed.), *Explorations in interpersonal communication* (pp. 105–125). Beverly Hills, CA: Sage.

Motivans, M. & Kyckelhahn, T. (2007). Federal prosecution of child sex exploitation offenders, 2006. *Bureau of Justice Statistics Bulletin*, December. Retrieved 3 July 2016 from http://www.bjs.gov/content/pub/pdf/fpcseo06.pdf Washington, DC: U.S. Department of Justice, Office of Justice Programs, Bureau of Justice Statistics.

Muise, A., Christofides, E. & Desmarais, S. (2009). More information that you ever wanted: Does Facebook bring out the green-eyed monster of jealousy? *CyberPsychology & Behavior, 12*(4), 441–444.

Murphy, E., Rodriquez-Manzanares, M. A. & Barbour. M. (2011). Asynchronous and synchronous online teaching: Perspectives of Canadian high school distance education teachers. *British Journal of Education Technology, 42*(4), 583–591.

Murray, C. D., Patchick, E., Pettifer, S., Caillette, F. & Howard, T. (2006). Immersive Virtual Reality as a Rehabilitative Technology for Phantom Limb Experience: A Protocol. *CyberPsychology & Behavior, 9*(2), 167–170.

Muse, K., McManus, F., Leung, C., Meghreblian, B. & Williams, J. M. G. (2012). Cyberchondrias: factor or fiction? A preliminary examination of the relationship between health anxiety and searching for health information on the Internet. *Journal of Anxiety Disorders, 26*, 189–196.

Murstein, B. (1974). *Love, sex and marriage through the ages.* New York, NY: Springer.

Mustanski, B., Lyons, T. & Garcia, S. C. (2011). Internet use and sexual health of young men who have sex with men: A mixed-methods study. *Archive of Sexual Behavior, 40*(2), 289–300.

Mutz, D. C., Roberts, D. F. & Van Vuuren, D. P. (1993). Reconsidering the displacement hypothesis: Television's influence on children's time use. *Communication Research, 20*(1), 51–75.

NAHDAP. (2004). National Survey of Parents and Youth (NSPY), 1998–2004: Restricted use files (ICPSR 27868). Retrieved 11 July 2016 from http://www.icpsr.umich.edu/icpsrweb/NAHDAP/studies/27868

Naquin, C. E., Kurtzberg, T. R. & Belkin, L. Y. (2010). The finer points of lying online: Email versus pen and paper. *Journal of Applied Psychology, 95*(2), 387–394.

National Fraud Authority (UK). (2012). *Annual fraud indicator.* (Website no longer exists.)

Nelson, E.-V. & Lillis, T. A. (2013). Managing real-time telepsychology practice. In G. P. Koocher, J. C. Norcross & B. A. Greene (Eds.), *Psychologists' Desk Reference* (pp. 690–694). Oxford, UK: Oxford University Press.

Neumann, P. R. (2013). Options and strategies for countering online racialization in the United States. *Studies in Conflict & Terrorism, 36*, 431–459.

Neuman, S. B. (1991). *Literacy in the television age: The myth of TV effect.* Norwood, NJ: Ablex.

Neville, A. J. (1999). The problem-based learning tutor: Teacher? Facilitator? Evaluator? *Medical Teacher, 21*, 393–401.

Nie, N. H. & Erbring, L. (2002). Internet and society: A preliminary report. *IT and Society, 1*(1), 275–283.

Nie, N. H. & Hillygus, D. S. (2002). The impact of Internet use on sociability: Time-diary findings. *IT and Society, 1*(1), 1–20.

Nielssen, O., O'Dea, J., Sullivan, D., Rodriguez, M., Bourget, D. & Large, L. (2011). Child pornography offenders detected by surveillance of the Internet and by other methods. *Criminal Behaviour and Mental Health, 21*, 215–224.

Nimrod, G. (2010). Seniors' online communities: A quantitative content analysis. *The Gerontologist, 50*(3), 382–392.

Nimrod, G. (2011). The fun culture in seniors' online communities. *The Gerontologist, 51*(2), 226–237.

Nimrod, G. (2014). The benefits of and constraints to participation in seniors' online communities. *Leisure Studies, 33*(3), 247–266.

Niveau, G. (2010). Cyber-pedocriminality: Characteristics of a sample of Internet child pornography offenders. *Child Abuse & Neglect, 34*, 570–575.

Neutze, J., Seto, M. C., Schaefer, G. A., Mundt, I. A. & Beier, K. M. (2011). Predictors of child pornography offenses and child sexual abuse in a community sample of pedophiles and hebephiles. *Sexual Abuse: A Journal of Research and Treatment, 23*(2), 212–242.

Norr, A. M., Albanese, B. J., Oglesby, M. E., Allan, N. P. & Schmidt, N. B. (2015). Anxiety sensitivity and intolerance of uncertainty as potential risk factors for cyberchondria. *Journal of Affective Disorders, 174*, 64–69.

Norr, A. M., Allan, N. P., Boffa, J. W., Raines, A. M. & Schmidt, N. B. (2015). Validation of the Cyberchondria Severity Scale (CSS): Replication and extension with bifactor modelling. *Journal of Anxiety Disorders, 31*, 58–64.

O'Brien, M. D. & Webster, S. D. (2007). The construction and preliminary validation of the Internet Behaviours and Attitudes Questionnaire (IBAQ). *Sex Abuse, 19*(3), 237–256.

Ofcom. (2014). *Adults' media use and attitude report 2014*. Retrieved 7 September 2015 from http://stakeholders.ofcom.org.uk/market-data-research/other/research-publications/adults/adults-media-lit-14

Office of Fair Trading (UK). (2010). *Helping people affected by scams: A toolkit for practitioners*. Retrieved 7 April 2016 from http://www.oft.gov.uk/shared_oft/reports/consumer_protection/400585_OFT_ScamsToolkit_ful1.pdf

Olason, D. T., Kristjansdottir, E., Einarsdottir, H., Haraldsson, H., Bjarnason, G. & Derevensky, J. L. (2010). Internet gambling and problem gambling among 13 to 18 year old adolescents in Iceland. *International Journal of Mental Health and Addiction, 9*(3), 257–263.

Olasupo, M. O. & Atiri, O. S. (2013). E-therapy: Contemporary tool in psychotherapy. *IFE Psychologia, 21*(3), 408–413.

Omale, N., Hung, W.-C., Luetkehans, L. & Cooke-Plagwitz, J. (2009). Learning in 3-D multi-user environments: Exploring the use of unique 3-D attributes for online problem-based learning. *British Journal of Educational Technology, 40*(3), 480–495.

Ondrejka, C. (2008). Education unleashed: Participatory culture, education, and innovation in Second Life. In K. Salen (Ed.), *The ecology of games: Connecting youth, games, and learning* (pp. 229–252). Cambridge, MA: MIT Press.

O'Neil, H. F., Wainess, R. & Baker, E. (2005). Classification of learning outcomes: Evidence from the computer games literature. *Curriculum Journal, 16*(4), 455–474.

Opalinski, L. (2001). Older adults and the digital divide: Assessing results of a Web-based survey. *Journal of Technology in Human Services, 18*(3/4), 203–221.

Oravec, J. (2000). Online counseling and the Internet: Perspectives for mental health care supervision and education. *Journal of Mental Health, 9*(2), 121–135.

Ormerod, T. C. & Dando, C. J. (2015). Finding a needle in a haystack: Veracity testing outperforms behaviour observation for aviation security screening. *Journal of Experimental Psychology: General, 144*, 76–84.

Oswell, D. (2006). When images matter: Internet child pornography, forms of observation and an ethics of the virtual. *Information, Communication & Society, 9*(2), 244–265.

Owens, T. (2006). Self and identity. In J. Delamater (Ed.), *Handbook of Social Psychology* (pp. 205–232). New York, NY: Springer.

Owens, C., Sharkey, S., Smithson, J., Hewis, E., Emmens, T., Ford, T. & Jones, R. (2012). Building an online community to promote communication and collaborative learning between health professionals and young people who self-harm: An exploratory study. *Health Expectations, 18*, 81–94.

Oxford Internet Institute. (2011). *Me, my spouse and the Internet: Meeting, dating and marriage in the digital age*. Retrieved 11 July 2016 from http://www.oii.ox.ac.uk/research/projects/?id=47

Palloff, R. M. & Pratt, K. (2001). *Lessons from cyberspace classroom*. San Francisco, CA: Jossey-Bass.

Parker, R. M., Williams, M. V., Weiss, B. D., Baker, D. W., Davis, T. C., Doak, C. C., ... Nurss, J. (1999). Health literacy: Report of the Council on Scientific Affairs. *Journal of the American Medical Association, 281*(6), 552–557.

Parker, C. (1997). *The joy of cybersex: Confessions of an Internet addict*. Kew, Australia: Reed Books.

Parker, T. S. & Wampler, K. S. (2003). How bad is it? Perceptions of the relationship impact of different types of Internet sexual activities. *Contemporary Family Therapy, 25*(4), 415–429.

Parks, M. R. & Floyd, K. (1996). Making friends in cyberspace. *Journal of Communication, 46*, 80–97.

Parks, M. R. & Roberts, L. D. (1998). 'Making MOOsic': The development of personal relationships online and a comparison to their off-line counterparts. *Journal of Social and Personal Relationships, 15*, 517–537.

Parris, L., Varjas, K., Meyers, J. & Cutts, H. (2012). High school students' perceptions of coping with cyberbullying. *Youth & Society, 44*(2), 284–306.

Parsons, J. T., Koken, J. A. & Bimbi, D. S. (2004). The use of the Internet by gay and bisexual male escorts: Sex workers as sex educators. *AIDS Care, 16*(8), 1021–1035.

Pasek, J., Kenski, K., Romer, D. & Jamieson, K. H. (2006). America's youth and community engagement: How use of mass media is related to civic activity and political awareness in 14- to 22-year-olds. *Communication Research, 33*, 115–135.

Paul, B. & Linz, D. G. (2008). The effects of exposure to virtual child pornography on viewer cognition and attitudes toward deviant sexual behavior. *Communication Research, 35*(1), 3–38.

Paul, L. & Galloway, J. (1994). Sexual jealousy: Gender differences in response to partner and rival. *Aggressive Behavior, 20*, 203–211.

Pempek, T. A., Yermolayeva, Y. A. & Calvert, S. L. (2009). College students' social networking experiences on Facebook. *Journal of Applied Developmental Psychology, 30*(3), 227–238.

Peter, J. & Valkenburg, P. M. (2006). Adolescents' exposure to sexually explicit online material and recreational attitudes toward sex. *Journal of Communication, 56*(4), 639–660.

Petrakou, A. (2010). Interacting through avatars: Virtual worlds as a context for online education. *Computers & Education, 54*, 1020–1027.

Pew Internet. (2009). *Demographics of teen Internet users*. Retrieved 15 November 2010 from http://pewinternet.org/Static-Pages/Trend-Data-for-Teens/Whos-Online.aspx

Pittinsky, M. S. (2003). *The wired tower: Perspectives on the impact of the Internet on higher education*. Upper Saddle River, NJ: Pearson Education.

Plant, S. (1992). *The most radical gesture: The situationist international in a postmodern age*. London, UK: Routledge.

Postel, M. G., de Jong, C. A. J. & de Haan, H. A. (2005). Does e-therapy for problem drinking reach hidden populations? *American Journal of Psychiatry, 162*(12), 2393.

Poley, M. E. M. & Luo, S. (2012). Social compensation or rich-get-richer? The role of social competence in college students' use of the Internet to find a partner. *Computers in Human Behavior, 28*, 414–419.

Potenza, M. N., Wareham, J. D., Steinberg, M. A., Rugle, L., Cavallo, A., Krishnan-Sarin, S. & Desai, R. A. (2011). Correlates of at-risk/problem Internet gambling in adolescents. *Journal of the American Academy of Child & Adolescent Psychiatry, 50*(2), 150–159.

Powell, J. (2011). Young people, self-harm and Internet forums. Commentary on 'Online discussion forums for young people who self-harm'. *The Psychiatrist, 35*, 368–370.

Prabhakar, E. (2013). E-therapy: Ethical considerations of a changing healthcare communication environment. *Pastoral Psychology, 62*, 211–218.

Pulman, A. & Taylor, J. (2012). Munchausen by Internet: Current research and future directions. *Journal of Medical Internet Research*, 14(4), e115.

Pyszczynski, T., Abdollahi, A., Solomon, S., Greenberg, J., Cohen, F. & Weise, D. (2006). Mortality salience, martyrdom, and military might: The great satan versus the axis of evil. *Personality and Social Psychology Bulletin*, 32(4), 525–537.

Qian, H. & Scott, C. R. (2007). Anonymity and self-disclosure on weblogs. *Journal of Computer-Mediated Communication*, 12, 1428–1451.

Quayle, E., Erooga, M., Wright, L., Taylor, M. & Harbinson, D. (2006). Collecting images. In E. Quayle, M. Erooga, L. Wright, M. Taylor & D. Harbinson (Eds.), *Only pictures? Therapeutic work with Internet sex offenders* (pp. 119–129). Lyme Regis, UK: Russell House.

Quayle, E. & Taylor, M. (2002). Child pornography and the Internet: perpetuating a cycle of abuse. *Deviant Behaviour*, 23(4), 331–362.

Raacke, J. & Bonds-Raacke, J. (2008). Myspace and Facebook: Applying the uses and gratifications theory to exploring friend-networking sites. *CyberPsychology & Behavior*, 11(2), 169–174.

Rains, S. A. (2014). The implications of stigma and anonymity for self-disclosure in health blogs. *Health Communication*, 29, 23–31.

RAND Europe. (2015). Radicalisation in the digital era. Retrieved 7 April 2016 from http://www.rand.org/pubs/research_reports/RR453.html

Rao, R. S. (2015). A computer vision technique to detect phishing attacks. In *Communication Systems and Network Technologies (CSNT), 2015 Fifth International Conference on Communication Systems and Network Technologies, 4–6 April* (pp. 596–601). Piscataway, NJ: Institute of Electrical and Electronics Engineers.

Rashid, A., Baron, A., Rayson, P., May-Chahal, C., Greenwood, P. & Walkerdine, J. (2013). Who am I? Analysing digital personas in cybercrime investigations. *Computer*, 46(4), 54–61.

Ray, V. R., Kimonis, E. R. & Donoghue, C. (2010). Legal, ethical, and methodological considerations in the Internet-based study of child pornography offenders. *Behavioral Sciences & the Law*, 28, 84–105.

Raskauskas, J. & Stoltz, A. (2007). Involvement in traditional and electronic bullying amount adolescents. *Developmental Psychology*, 43(3), 564–575.

Recupero, P. R. & Rainey, S. E. (2005). Informed consent to e-therapy. *American Journal of Psychotherapy*, 59(4), 319–331.

Recupero, P. R. & Rainey, S. E. (2006). Characteristics of e-therapy Web sites. *Journal of Clinical Psychiatry*, 67(9), 1435–1440.

Regner, T. (2015). Why consumers pay voluntarily: Evidence from online music. *Journal of Behavioral and Experimental Economics*, 57, 205–214.

Reicher, S. D. (1984). Social influences in the crowd: Attitudinal and behavioural effects of de-individuation in conditions of high and low group salience. *British Journal of Social Psychology*, 33, 145–163.

Reijnen, L., Bulten, E. & Nijman, H. (2009). Demographic and personality characteristics of Internet child pornography downloaders in comparison to other offenders. *Journal of Child Sexual Abuse*, 18(6), 611–622.

Reyes, J. M. & Spencer, S. H. (2015, 22 June). A national first: Cyberstalking resulting in death. *News Journal*. Retrieved 7 April 2016 from http://www.delawareonline.com/story/news/local/2015/06/13/national-first-cyberstalking-resulting-death/71176760

Rheingold, H. (1993). *The virtual community: Homesteading on the electronic frontier*. Reading, MA: Addison-Wesley.

Rice, F. P. (1996). *Intimate relationships, marriages, and families*. Mountain View, CA: Mayfield Publishing.

Rice R. (2006). Influences, usage, and outcomes of Internet health information searching: Multivariate results from the Pew surveys. *International Journal of Medical Informatics, 75*, 8–28.

Rideout, V. J., Foehr, U. G. & Roberts, D. F. (2010). *Generation M2: Media in the lives of 8- to 18-year-olds*. Retrieved 7 September 2015 from http://kff.org/other/poll-finding/report-generation-m2-media-in-the-lives

Rieber, L. P. (1996). Animation as a distractor to learning. *International Journal of Instructional Media, 23*, 53–57.

Riegel, D. L. (2004). Effects on boy-attracted pedosexual males of viewing boy erotica. *Archives of Sexual Behavior, 33*(4), 321–323.

Riggio, R. E. & Woll, S. B. (1984). The role of nonverbal cues and physical attractiveness in the selection of dating partners. *Journal of Social and Personal Relationships, 1*, 347–357.

Robinson, C. C. & Hullinger, H. (2008). New benchmarks in higher education: Student engagement in online learning. *Journal of Education for Business, 84*(2), 101–108.

Robinson, J. P. (1972). Television's impact on everyday life: Some cross-national evidence. In E. Rubinstein, G. Comstock & J. Murray (Eds.), *Television and social behavior* (Vol. 4, pp. 410–431). Washington, DC: Government Printing Office.

Robinson, J. P. (2011). IT use and leisure time displacement. *Information, Communication & Society, 14*(4), 495–509.

Robinson, J. P., Barth, K. & Kohut, A. (1997). Social impact research: Personal computers, mass media and use of time. *Social Science Computer Review, 15*(1), 65–82.

Robinson, J. P. & Kestnbaum, M. (1999). The personal computer, culture and other uses of free time. *Social Science Computer Review, 17*(2), 209–216.

Robinson, J. P., Kestnbaum, M., Neustadtl, A. & Alvarez, A. (2000). Mass media use and social life among Internet users. *Social Science Computer Review, 18*(4), 490–501.

Rochlen, A. B., Zack, J. S. & Speyer, C. (2004). Online therapy: Review of relevant definitions, debates and current empirical support. *Journal of Clinical Psychology, 60*, 269–283.

Rogers, C. R. (1951/2003). *Client-centered therapy*. London: Constable & Robinson.

Rogers, C. R. (1961/2004). *On becoming a person: A therapist's view of psychotherapy*. London, UK: Constable & Robinson.

Rojek, C. (1994). *Ways of escape: Modern transformations in leisure and travel*. Lanham, MD: Rowman & Littlefield.

Rollman, J., Krug, K. & Parente, F. (2000). The chat room phenomenon: Reciprocal communication in cyberspace. *CyberPsychology & Behavior, 3*, 161–166.

Rosenfeld, B. (2004). Violence risk factors in stalking and obsessional harassment: A review and preliminary meta-analysis. *Criminal Justice and Behavior, 31*, 9–36.

Roscoe, B., Cavanaugh, L. & Kennedy, D. (1988). Dating infidelity: Behaviors, reasons, and consequences. *Adolescence, 23*, 35–43.

Rossi, L. (2009). Breaking new ground: Innovation in games, play, practice and theory. In *Proceedings of DiGRA 2009*. Retrieved 25 September 2015 from http://www.digra.org/wp-content/uploads/digital-library/09287.20599.pdf

Rossi, P. (2006). Medicine in the Internet age: The rise of the network society. *Functional Neurology, 21*(1), 9–13.

Rowe, D. (2006). Leisure, mass communications and media. In C. Rojek, S. M. Shaw & A. J. Veal (Eds.), *A handbook of leisure studies* (pp. 317–331). New York, NY: Palgrave Macmillan.

Roy, S., Klinger, E., Légeron, P., Lauer, F., Chemin, I. & Nugues, P. (2003). Definition of a VR-based protocol to treat social phobia. *CyberPsychology & Behavior, 6*(4), 411–420.

Rubin, R. B. & McHugh, M. P. (1987). Development of parasocial interaction relationships. *Journal of Broadcasting & Electronic Media, 31*, 279–292.

Ryan, C. & Glendon, I. (1998). Application of leisure motivation scale to tourism. *Annals of Tourism Research, 25*(1), 169–184.

Sahin, M. (2012). The relationship between the cyberbullying/cybervictimization and loneliness among adolescents. *Children and Youth Services Review, 34*, 834–837.

Salmon, G. (2004). *E-moderating: The key to teaching and learning online*. London, UK: Routledge Falmer.

Salmon, G. (2009). The future for (second) life and learning. *British Journal of Educational Technology, 40*(3), 526–538.

Salmon, G., Nie, M. & Edirisingha, P. (2010). Developing a five-stage model of learning in *Second Life*. *Educational Research, 52*(2), 169–182.

Samal, L., Saha, S., Chander, G., Korthuis, P. T., Sharma, R. K., Sharp, V., … & Beach, M. C. (2011). Internet health information seeking behavior and antiretroviral adherence in persons living with HIV/AIDS. *AIDS Patient Care and STDs, 25*(7), 445–449.

Samenow, C. P. (2012). Child pornography and the law: A clinician's guide. *Sexual Addiction & Compulsivity, 19*(1/2), 16–29.

Santhiveeran, J. (2005). Use of communication tools and fee-setting in e-therapy: A Web site survey. *Social Work in Mental Health, 4*(2), 31–45.

Santhiveeran, J. & Grant, B. (2006). Use of communication tools and fee-setting in e-therapy. *Social Work in Mental Health, 4*(2), 31–45.

Savin-Baden, M. (2008). From cognitive capability to social reform? Shifting perceptions of learning in immersive virtual worlds. *ALT-J, 16*(3), 151–161.

Savin-Baden, M., Gourlay, L., Tombs, C., Steils, N., Tombs, G. & Mawer, M. (2010). Situating pedagogies, positions and practices in immersive virtual worlds. *Educational Research, 52*(2), 123–133.

Scharlott, B. W. & Christ, W. G. (1995). Overcoming relationship-initiation barriers: The impact of a computer-dating system on sex role, shyness, and appearance inhibitions. *Computers in Human Behavior, 11*(2), 191–204.

Schellens, T. & Valcke, M. (2006). Fostering knowledge construction in university students through asynchronous discussion groups. *Computers & Education, 46*, 349–370.

Scheufele, D. A. & Nisbet, M. C. (2002). Being a citizen online: New opportunities and dead ends. *International Journal of Press/Politics, 7*, 55–75.

Schneider, J. P. (2000). Effects of cybersex addiction on the family: Results of a survey. *Sexual Addiction & Compulsivity, 7*, 31–58.

Schneider, J. P., Weiss, R. & Samenow, C. (2012). Is it really cheating? Understanding the emotional reactions and clinical treatment of spouses and partners affected by cybersex infidelity. *Sexual Addiction & Compulsivity, 19*(1/2), 123–139.

Schramm, W., Lyle, J. & Parker, E. B. (1961). *Television in the lives of our children*. Stanford, CA: Stanford University Press.

Schwartz, H. (1990). *Narcissistic process and corporate decay: The theory of the organization ideal*. New York, NY: New York University.

Sears-Roberts Alterovitz, S. & Mendelsohn, G. A. (2011). Partner preferences across the life span: Online dating by older adults. *Psychology of Popular Media Culture, 1*(S), 89–95.

Seckin, G. (2010). Cyber patients surfing the medical Web: Computer-mediated medical knowledge and perceived benefits. *Computers in Human Behavior, 26*(6), 1694–1700.

Seigfried-Spellar, K. C. & Rogers, M. K. (2010). Low neuroticism and high hedonistic traits for female Internet child pornography consumers. *Cyberpsychology, Behavior, and Social Networking, 13*(6), 629–635.

Seto, M. C. (2010). Child pornography use and Internet solicitation in the diagnosis of pedophilia. *Archives of Sexual Behavior, 39*, 591–593.

Seto, M. C. & Eke, A. W. (2005). The criminal histories and later offending of child pornography offenders. *Sexual Abuse, 17*(2), 201–210.

Seto, M. C., Hanson, R. K. & Babchishin, K. M. (2011). Contact sexual offending men with online sexual offenses. *Sexual Abuse: A Journal of Research and Treatment, 23*, 124–145.

Seto, M. C., Wood, J. M., Babchishin, K. M. & Flynn, S. (2012). Online solicitation offenders are different from child pornography offenders and lower risk contact sexual offenders. *Law and Human Behavior, 36*(4), 320–330.

Seyal, A. H. & Pijpers, G. G. M. (2004). Senior government executives' use of the Internet: A Bruneian scenario. *Behaviour & Information Technology, 23*(3), 197–210.

Shackelford, T. & Buss, D. (1996). Betrayal in mateships, friendships, and coalitions. *Journal of Personality and Social Psychology, 22*, 1151–1164.

Sharpe, R., Benfield, G., Roberts, R. & Francis, R. (2006). *The undergraduate experience of blended e-learning: A review of UK literature and practice.* York, UK: Higher Education Academy.

Shaughnessy, K., Byers, S. & Thornton, S. J. (2011). What is cybersex? Heterosexual students' definitions. *International Journal of Sexual Health, 23*(2), 78–89.

Shaw, J. (1997). Treatment rationale for Internet infidelity. *Journal of Sex Education and Therapy, 22*(1), 29–34.

Shea, P. & Bidjerano, T. (2009). Community of inquiry as a theoretical framework to foster 'epistemic engagement' and 'cognitive presence' in online education. *Computers & Education, 52*, 543–553.

Sheridan, L. P. & Grant, T. (2007). Is cyberstalking different? *Psychology, Crime & Law, 13*(6), 1477–2744.

Sherry, J. (2001). The effects of violent video games on aggression: A meta-analysis. *Human Communication Research, 27*, 409–431.

Siegfried, R. M. (2004). Student attitudes on software piracy and related issues of computer ethics. *Ethics and Information Technology, 6*(4), 215–222.

Sillence, E. (2013). Giving and receiving peer advice in an online breast cancer support group. *Cyberpsychology, Behavior, and Social Networking, 16*(6), 480–485.

Silvern, S. B. & Williamson, P. A. (1987). The effects of video game play on young children's aggression, fantasy, and prosocial behavior. *Journal of Applied Developmental Psychology, 8*, 453–462.

Silverstone, R. (1991). From audiences to consumers: The household and the consumption of communication and information technologies. *European Journal of Communication, 6*(2), 135–154.

Singer, P. W. (2009). Military robots and the laws of war. *New Atlantis, 23*(winter), 28–47.

Singer, P. W. (2010). The ethics of killer applications: Why is it so hard to talk about morality when it comes to new military technology? *Journal of Military Ethics, 9*(4), 299–312.

Silverman, R. (2015, 8 November). Mumsnet's Justine Roberts: 'The police said what the hoaxers did was a victimless crime'. *The Telegraph.* Retrieved 7 April 2016 from http://www.telegraph.co.uk/women/womens-life/11980694/Mumsnets-Justine-Roberts-The-police-said-what-the-hoaxers-did-was-a-victimless-crime.html

Skinner, A. & Zack, J. S. (2004). Counseling and the Internet. *American Behavioral Scientist, 48,* 434–446.

Skinner, A. E. G. & Latchford, G. (2006). Attitudes to counselling via the Internet: A comparison between in-person counselling clients and Internet support group users. *Counselling & Psychotherapy Research, 6*(3), 158–163.

Skinner, H., Biscope, S., Poland, B. & Goldberg, E. (2003). How adolescents use technology for health information: Implications for health professionals from focus group studies. *Journal of Medical Internet Research, 5,* e32.

Slonje, R. & Smith, P. (2008). Cyberbullying: Another main type of bullying? *Scandinavian Journal of Psychology, 49,* 147–154.

Solis, B. (2011). *Engage: The complete guide for brands and businesses to build, cultivate, and measure success in the new Web.* New York, NY: John Wiley & Sons.

Sparck-Jones, K. (2003). Privacy: What's different now? *Interdisciplinary Science Reviews, 28,* 287–292.

Spielberg, A. R. (1999). Online without a net: Physician–patient communication by electronic mail. *American Journal of Law & Medicine, 25*(2/3), 267–295.

Spitzberg, B. H. (2002). The tactical topography of stalking victimization and management. *Trauma, Violence & Abuse, 3*(4), 261–288.

Spitzberg, B. H. & Cupach, W. R. (2003). What mad pursuit? Obsessive relational intrusion and stalking related phenomena. *Aggression and Violent Behavior, 8,* 345–375.

Spitzberg, B. H. & Veksler, A. E. (2007). The personality of pursuit: Personality attributions of unwanted pursuers and stalkers. *Violence and Victims, 22,* 275–289.

Starcevic, V. (2013). Is Internet addiction a useful concept? *Australian & New Zealand Journal of Psychiatry, 47*(1), 16–19.

Starcevic, V. & Berle, D. (2013). Cyberchondria: Towards a better understanding of excessive health-related Internet use. *Expert Review of Neurotherapeutics, 13,* 205–213.

Stebbins, R. A. (2007). *Serious leisure: A perspective for our time.* New Brunswick, NJ: Transaction.

Smith, R. (2010). The long history of gaming in military training. *Simulation & Gaming, 41*(1), 6–9.

Smith, J. E., Waldorf, V. A. & Trembath, D. L. (1990). Single white male looking for thin, very attractive… *Sex Roles, 23*(11/12), 675–685.

Spears, R. & Lea, M. (1994). Panacea or panopticon? The hidden power in computer-mediated communication. *Communication Research, 21,* 427–459.

Spears, R., Lea, M. & Lee, S. (1990). De-individuation and group polarization in computer-mediated communication. *British Journal of Social Psychology, 29,* 121–134.

Sproull, L. & Kiesler, S. (1986). Reducing social context cues: Electronic mail in organizational communication. *Management Science, 32,* 1492–1512.

Steinfield, C., Ellison, N. B. & Lampe, C. (2008). Social capital, self-esteem, and use of online social network sites: A longitudinal analysis. *Journal of Applied Developmental Psychology, 29,* 434–445.

Stern, S. R. (2004). Expressions of identity online: Prominent features and gender differences in adolescents' World Wide Web home pages. *Journal of Broadcasting & Electronic Media, 48,* 218–243.

Stever, G. S. & Lawson, K. (2013). Twitter as a way for celebrities to communicate with fans: Implications for the study of parasocial interaction. *North American Journal of Psychology, 15*(2), 339–354.

Stoll, C. (1995). *Silicon snake oil.* New York, NY: Doubleday.

Subrahmanyam, K. & Greenfield, P. M. (1994). Effect of video game practice on spatial skills in girls and boys. *Journal of Applied Developmental Psychology*, *15*, 13–32.

Subrahmanyam, K. & Greenfield, P. M. (2008). The future of children. *Online Communication and Adolescent Relationships*, *18*(1), 119–146.

Subrahmanyam, K., Reich, S. M., Waechter, N. & Espinoza, G. (2008). Online and offline social networks: Use of social networking sites by emerging adults. *Journal of Applied Developmental Psychology*, *29*(6), 420–433.

Subrahmanyam, K., Smahel, D. & Greenfield, P. (2006). Connecting development constructions to the Internet: Identity presentation and sexual exploration in online teen chat rooms. *Developmental Psychology*, *42*(3), 395–406.

Sucala, M., Schnur, J. B., Brackman, E. H., Constantino, M. J. & Montgomery, G. H. (2013). Clinicians' attitudes toward therapeutic alliance in e-therapy. *Journal of General Psychology*, *140*(4), 282–293.

Sucala, M., Schnur, J. B., Constantino, M. J., Miller, S. J., Brackman, E. H. & Montgomery, G. H. (2012). The therapeutic relationship in e-therapy for mental health: A systematic review. *Journal of Medical Internet Research*, *14*(4), 175–187.

Suler, J. (2004). The online disinhibition effect. *CyberPsychology & Behavior*, *7*, 321–326.

Sullivan, J. & Beech, A. R. (2003). Are collectors of child abuse images a risk to children? In A. MacVean & P. Spindler (Eds.), *Policing paedophiles on the Internet* (pp. 11–20). London, UK: New Police Bookshop.

Sun, P.-C. & Cheng, H. K. (2007). The design of instructional multimedia in e-learning: A media richness theory-based approach. *Computers & Education*, *49*, 662–676.

Sutton, L. A. (2001). The principle of vicarious interaction in computer-mediated communications. *International Journal of Educational Telecommunications*, *7*(3), 223–242.

Suzuki, L. K. & Calzo, J. P. (2004). The search for peer advice in cyberspace: An examination of online teen bulletin boards about health and sexuality. *Applied Developmental Psychology*, *25*, 685–698.

Tajfel, H. (1979). Individuals and groups in social psychology. *British Journal of Social and Clinical Psychology*, *18*, 183–190.

Tajfel, H. & Turner, J. (1979). An integrative theory of conflict. In W. G. Austin & S. Worchel (Eds.), *The social psychology of intergroup relations* (pp. 33–48). Monterey, CA: Brooks/Cole.

Tallent-Runnels, M. K., Thomas, J. A., Lan, W. Y., Cooper, S., Ahern, T. C., Shaw, S. M. & Liu, X. (2006). Teaching courses online: A review of the research. *Review of Educational Research*, *76*(1), 93–135.

Tamim, R. M., Bernard, R. M., Borokhovski, E., Abrami, P. C. & Schmid, R. F. (2011). What forty years of research says about the impact of technology on learning: A second-order meta-analysis and validation study. *Review of Educational Research*, *81*(1), 4–28.

Tanis, M. (2008). Health-related on-line forums: What's the big attraction? *Journal of Health Communication*, *13*, 698–714.

Tate, T. (1990). *Child pornography*. St Ives, UK: Methuen.

Tate, T. (1992). The child pornography industry: International trade in child sexual abuse. In C. Itzin (Ed.), *Pornography: Women, violence and civil liberties* (pp. 203–216). Oxford, UK: Oxford University Press.

Taylor, M. (1999). The nature and dimensions of child pornography on the Internet. Retrieved 13 February 2013 from http://www.ipce.info/library_3/files/nat_dims_kp.htm

Taylor, M., Holland, G. & Quayle, E. (2001). Typology of paedophile picture collections. *Police Journal*, *74*(2), 97–107.

Taylor, M. & Quayle, E. (2003). *Child pornography: An Internet crime.* Hove, UK: Routledge.

Thibaut, J. W. & Kelley, H. H. (1959). *The social psychology of groups.* New York, NY: John Wiley & Sons.

Thomson, R. & Murachver, T. (2001). Predicting gender from electronic discourse. *British Journal of Social Psychology, 40,* 193–208.

Thornburgh, N. (2005, 25 August). Inside the Chinese hack attack. *Time.* Retrieved 7 April 2016 from http://content.time.com/time/nation/article/0,8599,1098371,00.html

Toma, C. L. & Hancock, J. T. (2012). What lies beneath: The linguistic traces of deception in online dating profiles. *Journal of Communication, 62,* 78–97.

Tong, S. T., Van der Heide, B., Langwell, L. & Walther, J. B. (2008). Too much of a good thing? The relationship between number of friends and interpersonal impressions on Facebook. *Journal of Computer-Mediated Communication, 13,* 531–549.

Townsend, J. & Wasserman, T. (1997). The perception of sexual attractiveness: Sex differences in variability. *Archives of Sexual Behavior, 26,* 243–268.

Trevino, L. K., Lengel, R. K. & Daft, R. L. (1987). Media symbolism, media richness and media choice in organizations. *Communication Research, 14*(5), 553–574.

Tsaliki, L. (2011). Playing with porn: Greek children's explorations in pornography. *Sex Education, 11*(3), 293–302.

Tufekci, Z. (2008). Grooming, gossip, Facebook and Myspace. *Information, Communication & Society, 11*(4), 544–564.

Turkle, S. (1995). *Life on the screen: Identity in the age of the Internet.* London, UK: Weidenfeld & Nicolson.

Turkle, S. (2011). *Alone together: Why we expect more from technology and less from each other.* New York, NY: Basic Books.

Turner, J. C. (1975). Social comparison and social identity: Some prospects for intergroup behavior. *European Journal of Social Psychology, 5,* 5–34.

Twitter Counter. (2016). Twitter top 100: Most followers. Retrieved 27 May 2016 from http://twittercounter.com/pages/100

Twomey, R. (2011, 30 July). Xbox addict, 20, killed by blood clot after 12-hour gaming sessions. *MailOnline.* Retrieved 7 April 2016 from http://www.dailymail.co.uk/news/article-2020462/Xbox-addict-20-killed-blood-clot-12-hour-gaming-sessions.html

UK Safer Internet Centre. (2014). Online safety: Protecting our children from radicalisation and extremism. Retrieved 7 April 2016 from http://www.saferInternet.org.uk/Content/Childnet/SafterInternetCentre/downloads/Online_Safety_-_LSCB_bulletin_-_Radicalisation.pdf

US Attorney General. (1999). *Cyberstalking: A new challenge for law enforcement and industry.* Retrieved 11 July 2016 from http://www.harassmentlaw.co.uk/book/cyberep.htm

US Department of Justice. (2015). Citizen's guide to US federal law on child pornography. Retrieved 7 November 2015 from http://www.justice.gov/criminal/ceos/citizensguide/citizensguide_porn.html

Utz, S. (2000). Social information processing in MUDs: The development of friendships in virtual worlds. *Journal of Online Behavior, 1*(1). Retrieved 7 February 2005 from http://www.behavior.net/JOB/v1n1/utz.html

Utz, S. (2005). Types of deception and underlying motivation: What people think. *Social Science Computer Review, 23*(1), 49–56.

Utz, S. & Beukeboom, C. J. (2011). The role of social network sites in romantic relationships: Effects on jealousy and relationship happiness. *Journal of Computer-Mediated Communication, 16*(4), 511–527.

Valkenburg, P. M. & Peter, J. (2007). Who visits online dating sites? Exploring some characteristics of online daters. *CyberPsychology & Behavior, 10*(6), 849–852.

Valkenburg, P. M. & Peter, J. (2008). Adolescents' identity experiments on the Internet: Consequences for social competence and self-concept unity. *Communication Research, 35*(2), 208–231.

Valkenburg, P. M., Schouten, A. P. & Peter, J. (2005). Adolescents' identity experiments on the Internet. *New Media & Society, 7*, 383–402.

Valkyrie, Z. C. (2011). Cybersexuality in MMORPGs: Virtual sexual revolution untapped. *Men and Masculinities, 14*(1), 76–96.

VandenBos, G. R. & Williams, S. (2000). The Internet versus the telephone: What is telehealth, anyway? *Professional Psychology: Research and Practice, 31*, 490–492.

Van Gelder, L. (1991). The strange case of the electronic lover. In C. Dunlop and R. Kling (Eds.), *Computerization and controversy: Value conflicts and social choice* (pp. 364–375). Boston MA: Academic Press.

Vichuda, K., Ramamurthy, K. & Haseman, W. D. (2001). User attitude as a mediator of learning performance improvement in an interactive multimedia environment. *International Journal of Human–Computer Studies, 54*(4), 541–583.

Vishwanath, A. (2015a). Examining the distinct antecedents of e-mail habits and its influence on the outcomes of a phishing attack. *Journal of Computer-Mediated Communication, 20*, 570–584.

Vishwanath, A. (2015b). Habitual Facebook use and its impact on getting deceived on social media. *Journal of Computer-Mediated Communication, 20*, 83–98.

Vrasidas, C. & McIsaac, M. S. (2000). Principles of pedagogy and evaluation for web-based learning. *Educational Media International, 37*(2), 105–111.

Vrij, A. (2008). *Detecting lies and deceit: Pitfalls and opportunities* (2nd ed.). Chichester, UK: John Wiley & Sons.

Vrij, A., Edwards, K. & Bull, R. (2001). People's insights into their own behaviour and speech content while lying. *British Journal of Psychology, 92*, 373–389.

Vrij, A., Mann, S., Fisher, R. P., Leal, S., Milne, R. & Bull, R. (2008). Increasing cognitive load to facilitate lie detection: The benefit of recalling an event in reverse order. *Law and Human Behavior, 32*, 253–265.

Vyas, R. S., Singh, N. P. & Bhabhra, S. (2007). Media displacement effect: Investigating the impact of Internet on newspaper reading habits of consumers. *Journal of Business Perspective, 11*(2), 29–40.

Vygotsky, L. S. (1978). *Mind in society: The development of higher psychological processes*. Cambridge, MA: Harvard University Press.

Walsh, W., Wolak, J. & Finkelhor, D. (2013). *Sexting: When are state prosecutors deciding to prosecute? Third National Juvenile Online Victimization Study (NJOV-3)*. Retrieved 13 February 2013 from http://www.unh.edu/ccrc/pdf/CV294_Walsh_Sexting%20&%20prosecution_2-6-13.pdf

Walther, B., Morgenstern, M. & Hanewinkel, R. (2012). Co-occurrence of addictive behaviours: Personality factors related to substance use, gambling and computer gaming. *European Addiction Research, 18*, 167–174.

Walther, J. B. (1992). Interpersonal effects in computer-mediated interaction: A relational perspective. *Communication Research, 19*, 52–90.

Walther, J. B. (1995). Relational aspects of computer-mediated communication: Experimental observations over time. *Organizational Science, 6*, 186–203.

Walther, J. B. (1996). Computer-mediated communication: Impersonal, interpersonal and hyperpersonal interaction. *Communication Research, 23*, 3–43.

Walther, J. B. (2007). Selective self-presentation in computer-mediated communication: Hyperpersonal dimensions of technology, language, and cognition. *Computers in Human Behavior, 23*, 2538–2557.

Walther, J. B., Slovacek, C. & Tidwell, L. (2001). Is a picture worth a thousand words? Photographic images in long-term and short-term computer-mediated communication. *Communication Research, 28*, 105–134.

Wang, J., Herath, T., Chen, R., Vishwanath, A. & Rao, R. (2012). Phishing susceptibility: An investigation into the processing of a targeted spear phishing email. *IEEE Transactions on Professional Communication, 55*(4), 345–362.

Wang, J., Iannotti, R. J. & Nansel, T. R. (2009). School bullying among US adolescents: Physical, verbal, relational and cyber. *Journal of Adolescent Health, 45*(4), 368–375.

Wangberg, S. C., Gammon, D. & Spitznogle, K. (2007). In the eyes of the beholder: Exploring psychologists' attitudes towards and use of e-therapy in Norway. *CyberPsychology & Behavior, 10*(3), 418–423.

Warburton, S. (2009). Second in higher education: Assessing potential for and the barriers to deploying virtual worlds in learning and teaching. *British Journal of Educational Technology, 40*(3), 414–426.

Ward, T. (2000). Sexual offenders cognitive distortions as implicit theories. *Aggression and Violent Behavior, 5*, 491–507.

Ward, T. & Beech, A. R. (2006). An integrated theory of sexual offending. *Aggression and Violent Behavior, 11*, 44–63.

Ward, T. & Siegert, R. J. (2002). Toward and comprehensive theory of child sexual abuse: A theory knitting perspective. *Psychology, Crime & Law, 9*, 319–351.

Wardle, H., Moody, A., Griffiths, M., Orford, J. & Volberg, R. (2011). Defining the online gambler and patterns of behaviour integration: Evidence from the British Gambling Prevalence Survey 2010. *International Gambling Studies, 11*(3), 339–356.

Webb, L., Craissati, J. & Keen, S. (2007). Characteristics of Internet child pornography offenders: A comparison with child molesters. *Sexual Abuse, 19*, 449–465.

Webb, M., Burns, J. & Collin, P. (2008). Providing online support for young people with mental health difficulties: Challenges and opportunities explored. *Early Intervention in Psychiatry, 2*, 108–113.

Wei, L. & Hindman, D. B. (2011). Does the digital divide matter more? Comparing the effects of new media and old media use on the education-based knowledge gap. *Mass Communication and Society, 14*(2), 216–235.

Wei, X., Yang, J., Adamic, L. A., de Araújo, R. M. & Rekhi, M. (2010). Diffusion dynamics of games on online social networks. Retrieved 25 September 2015 from http://www-personal.umich.edu/~ladamic/papers/FBgames/FBgameDiffusion.pdf

Weinstein, A. & Weizman, A. (2012). Emerging association between addictive gaming and attention-deficit/hyperactivity disorder. *Current Psychiatry Reports, 14*, 590–597.

Weiss, W. (1969). Effects of mass media on communication. In G. Lindzey & E. Aronson (Eds.), *Handbook of social psychology* (pp. 77–195). Reading, MA: Addison-Wesley.

White, R. W. & Horvitz, E. (2009). Cyberchondria: Studies of the escalation of medical concerns in Web search. *ACM Transactions on Information Systems, 27*, 1–37.

White, D. & Le Cornu, A. (2010). Eventedness and disjuncture in virtual worlds. *Educational Research, 52*(2), 183–196.

Whitty, M. T. (2003a). Cyber-flirting: Playing at love on the Internet. *Theory & Psychology, 13*(3), 339–357.

Whitty, M. T. (2003b). Pushing the wrong buttons: Men's and women's attitudes towards online and offline infidelity. *CyberPsychology & Behavior, 6*(6), 569–579.

Whitty, M. T. (2005). The 'realness' of cyber-cheating: Men and women's representations of unfaithful Internet relationships. *Social Science Computer Review, 23*(1), 57–67.

Whitty, M. T. (2007a). Manipulation of self in cyberspace. In B. H. Spitzberg & W. R. Cupach (Eds.), *The dark side of interpersonal communication* (2nd ed., pp. 93–118). Mahwah, NJ: Lawrence Erlbaum Associates.

Whitty, M. T. (2007b). The art of selling one's self on an online dating site: The BAR approach. In M. T. Whitty, A. J. Baker & J. A. Inman (Eds.), *Online matchmaking* (pp. 57–69). Houndmills, UK: Palgrave Macmillan.

Whitty, M. T. (2008a). Revealing the 'real' me, searching for the 'actual' you: Presentations of self on an Internet dating site. *Computers in Human Behavior, 24*, 1707–1723.

Whitty, M. T. (2008b). The joys of online dating. In E. Konjin, T. Martin, S. Utz & A. Linden (Eds.), *Mediated interpersonal communication: How technology affects human interaction* (pp. 234–251). New York, NY: Taylor & Francis/Routledge.

Whitty, M. T. (2008c). eDating: The five phases of online dating. In C. Romm (Ed.), *Social networking and edating* (pp. 278–291). Hershey, PA: Information Science Reference.

Whitty, M. T. (2008d). Liberating or debilitating? An examination of romantic relationships, sexual relationships and friendships on the Net. *Computers in Human Behavior, 24*, 1837–1850.

Whitty, M. T. (2010). Internet infidelity: A 'real' problem. In K. Young (Ed.), *Internet addiction: A handbook for evaluation and treatment* (pp. 191–204). Chichesterm UK: John Wiley & Sons.

Whitty, M. T. (2011). Internet infidelity: A 'real' problem. In K. Young (Ed.), *Internet addiction: A handbook for evaluation and treatment* (pp. 191–204). Hoboken, NJ: John Wiley & Sons.

Whitty, M. T. (2013a). *Mass-marking fraud in the UK: 2013*. Unpublished report.

Whitty, M. T. (2013b). The scammers persuasive techniques model: Development of a stage model to explain the online dating romance scam. *British Journal of Criminology, 53*(4), 665–684.

Whitty, M. T. (2015). Mass-marketing fraud: A growing concern. *IEEE Security & Privacy, 13*(4), 84–87.

Whitty, M. T. & Buchanan, T. (2009). Looking for love in so many places: Characteristics of online daters and speed daters. *Interpersona, 3*(2), 63–86.

Whitty, M. T. & Buchanan, T. (2010). 'What's in a "screen name"?' Attractiveness of different types of screen names used by online daters. *International Journal of Internet Science, 5*(1), 5–19.

Whitty, M. T. & Buchanan, T. (2012). The online dating romance scam: A serious crime. *Cyberpsychology, Behavior, and Social Networking, 15*(3), 181–183.

Whitty, M. T. & Buchanan, T. (2016). The online dating romance scam: The psychological impact on victims – both financial and non-financial. *Criminology & Criminal Justice, 16*(2), 176–194.

Whitty, M. T., Buchanan, T., Joinson, A. N. & Meredith, A. (2012). Not all lies are spontaneous: An examination of deception across different modes of communication. *Journal of the American Society for Information Science and Technology, 63*(1), 208–216.

Whitty, M. T. & Carr, A. N. (2003). Cyberspace as potential space: Considering the web as a playground to cyber-flirt. *Human Relations, 56*(7), 861–891.

Whitty, M. T. & Carr, A. N. (2005). Taking the good with the bad: Applying Klein's work to further our understandings of cyber-cheating. *Journal of Couple & Relationship Therapy, 4*(2/3), 103–115.

Whitty, M. T. & Carr, A. N. (2006). *Cyberspace romance: The psychology of online relationships*. Basingstoke, UK: Palgrave Macmillan.

Whitty, M. T. & Carville, S. E. (2008). Would I lie to you? Self-serving lies and other-oriented lies told across different media. *Computers in Human Behavior, 24*, 1021–1031.

Whitty, M. T. & Gavin, J. (2001). Age/sex/location: Uncovering the social cues in the development of online relationships. *CyberPsychology & Behaviour, 4(5)*, 623–630.

Whitty, M. T. & Joinson, A. N. (2009). *Truth, lies, and trust on the Internet*. London, UK: Routledge/Psychology Press.

Whitty, M. T., Young, G. & Goodings, L. (2011). What I won't do in pixels: Examining the limits of taboo violation in MMORPGs. *Computers in Human Behavior, 27*, 268–275.

Whitty, M. T. & Quigley, L. (2008). Emotional and sexual infidelity offline and in cyberspace. *Journal of Marital and Family Therapy, 34(4)*, 461–468.

Wijers, M., Jonker, V. & Kerstens, K. (2008). MobileMath: The phone, the game, and the math. In *Proceedings of the 2nd European conference on games-based learning (ECGBI)* (pp. 507–516). Reading, UK: Academic Publishing.

Wilbur, S. (1998). Creating a community of learning using Web-based tools. In R. Hazemi, S. Hailes & S. Wilbur (Eds.), *The digital university: Reinventing the academy* (pp. 73–83). London, UK: Springer.

Williams, K. R. & Guerra, N. G. (2007). Prevalence and predictors of Internet bullying. *Journal of Adolescent Health, 41(6)*, S14–S21.

Williams, N. (1991). *False Images: Telling the Truth about Pornography*, London, UK: Kingsway Publications.

Williams, Z. (2003, 14 January). Panic on the screens. *The Guardian*. Retrieved 6 February 2013 from http://www.guardian.co.uk/media/2003/jan/14/newmedia.childrensservices

Wingrove, T., Korpas, A. L. & Weisz, V. (2011). Why were millions of people not obeying the law? Motivational influences on non-compliance with the law in the case of music piracy. *Psychology, Crime & Law, 17(3)*, 161–276.

Wolak, J., Finkelhor, D. & Mitchell, K. J. (2005). *Child-pornography possessors arrested in Internet-related crimes: Findings from the National Juvenile Online Victimization Study*. Alexandria: National Center for Missing & Exploited Children. Retrieved 13 February 2013 from http://www.unh.edu/ccrc/pdf/jvq/CV81.pdf

Wolak, J., Finkelhor, D. & Mitchell, K. J. (2012). *Trends in arrests for child pornography possession: The Third National Juvenile Online Victimization Study (NJOV-3)*. Retrieved 13 February 2013 from http://www.unh.edu/ccrc/pdf/CV269_Child%20Porn%20Possession%20Bulletin_4-13-12.pdf

Wolak, J., Mitchell, K. J. & Finkelhor, D. (2006). Online victimization of youth: Five years later. Retrieved 7 April 2016 from http://www.unh.edu/ccrc/pdf/CV138.pdf

Woll, S. B. & Young, P. (1989). Looking for Mr. or Ms. Right: Self-presentation in videodating. *Journal of Marriage and the Family, 51(2)*, 483–488.

Woolf, N. (2015, 6 November). Anonymous leaks identities of 350 alleged Klu Klux Klan members. *The Guardian*. Retrieved 7 April 2016 from http://www.theguardian.com/technology/2015/nov/06/anonymous-ku-klux-klan-name-leak

Wouters, P., Van der Spek, E. & Van Oosendorp, H. (2009). Current practices in serious game research: A review from a learning outcomes perspective. In T. M. Connolly, M. Stansfield & E. A. Boyle (Eds.), *Games-based learning: Techniques and effective practices*. Hershey, PA: Information Science Reference.

Wood, L. & Howley, A. (2012). Dividing at an early age: The hidden digital divide in Ohio elementary schools. *Learning, Media and Technology, 37(1)*, 20–39.

Wood, N. T., Solomon, M. R. & Allan, D. (2008). Welcome to the matrix: E-learning gets a *Second Life. Marketing Education Review, 18*(2), 47–53.
Wortley, R. K. & Smallbone, S. (2006). Applying situational principles to sexual offenses against children. In R. K. Wortley & S. Smallbone (Eds.), *Situational prevention of child sexual abuse* (pp. 7–36). Morsey, NY: Criminal Justice Press.
Wright, C. R. (1986). *Mass communication: A sociological perspective*, New York, NY: Random House.
Wright, J. (2002). Online counselling: Learning from writing therapy. *British Journal of Guidance & Counselling, 30*, 287–298.
Wright, M. (2008). Technology & terrorism: How the Internet facilitates radicalization. *Forensic Examiner, 17*(4), 14–20.
Wright, P. (2012). The Internet's potential for enhancing healthcare: *Gerontechnology, 11*(1), 35–44.
Wynn, E. & Katz, J. (1997). Hyperbole over cyberspace: Self-presentation and social boundaries in Internet home pages and discourse. *Information Society, 13*(4), 297–328.
Wysocki, D. K. (1998). Let your fingers to do the talking: Sex on an adult chat-line. *Sexualities, 1*, 425–452.
Wysocki, D. K. & Thalken, J. (2007). Whips and chains? Fact or fiction? Content analysis of sado-masochism in Internet personal advertisements. In M. T. Whitty, A. J. Baker & J. A. Inman (Eds.), *Online matchmaking* (pp. 178–196). Basingstoke: Palgrave Macmillan.
Yang, M. L. & Chiou, W. B. (2010). Looking online for the best romantic partner reduces decision quality: The moderating role of choice-making strategies. *Cyberpsychology, Behavior, and Social Networking, 13*(2), 207–210.
Yarab, P. E. & Allgeier, E. (1998). Don't even think about it: The role of sexual fantasies as perceived unfaithfulness in heterosexual dating relationships. *Journal of Sex Education and Therapy, 23*(3), 246–254.
Yarab, P. E., Sensibaugh, C. C. & Allgeier, E. (1998). More than just sex: Gender differences in the incidence of self-defined unfaithful behavior in heterosexual dating relationships. *Journal of Psychology & Human Sexuality, 10*(2), 45–57.
Ybarra, M. L. & Suman, M. (2006). Help seeking behavior and the Internet: A national survey. *International Journal of Medical Informatics, 75*(1), 29–41.
Ybarra, M. L. & Suman, M. (2008). Reasons, assessments and actions taken: Sex and age differences in uses of Internet health information. *Health Education Research, 23*(3), 512–521.
Yee, N. (2001). The Norrathian Scrolls. Retrieved 15 October 2008 from http://www.nickyee.com/eqt/home.html
Yee, N. (2006). The demographics, motivations and derived experiences of users of massively-multiuser online graphical environments. *PRESENCE: Teleoperators and Virtual Environments, 15*, 309–329.
Yen, J. Y. & Ko, C. H. (2014). The association between Internet gaming disorder and nicotine dependence: The mediating role of impulsivity. *Alcohol and Alcoholism, 49*(1), i69.
Yorke, M. (2004). Retention, persistence and success in on-campus higher education, and their enhancement in open and distance learning. *Open Learning, 19*(1), 19–32.
Young, G. & Whitty, M. T. (2012). *Transcending taboos: A moral and psychological examination of cyberspace*. Hove, UK: Routledge.
Young, G. & Whitty, M. T. (2011). Should gamespace be a taboo-free zone? Moral and psychological implications for single-player video games. *Theory and Psychology, 21*(6), 802–820.
Young, K. S. (1998). *Caught in the Net: How to recognize the signs of Internet addiction and a winning strategy for recovery*. New York, NY: John Wiley & Sons.

Young, K. S., Griffin-Shelley, E., Cooper, A., O'Mara, J. & Buchanan, J. (2000). Online infidelity: A new dimension in couple relationships with implications for evaluation and treatment. *Sexual Addiction & Compulsivity, 7*, 59–74.

Young, K. S., Pistner, M., O'Mara, J. & Buchanan J. (1999). Cyber disorders: The mental health concern for the new millennium. *CyberPsychology & Behavior, 2*(5), 475–479.

Zhao, S., Grasmuck, S. & Martin, J. (2008). Identity construction on Facebook: Digital empowerment in anchored relationships. *Computers in Human Behavior, 24*, 1816–1836.

Zhong, Z.-J. (2011). From access to usage: The divide of self-reported digital skills among adolescents. *Computers & Education, 56*, 736–746.

Zimbler, M. & Feldman, R. S. (2011). Liar, liar, hard drive on fire: How media content affects lying behaviour. *Journal of Applied Social Psychology, 41*(10), 2492–2507.

Zyda, M. (2005). From visual simulation to virtual reality to games. *Computer, 38*(9), 25–32.

Index

419 scam 141, 147
  see also mass-marketing fraud; Nigerian email scam
ACE model 115
activism 3, 76, 79, 81–82, 85
Adams, M. 53
addiction 4–5, 51, 53, 54–55, 60–61, 114–118, 126–127
  and cybersex compulsives 3, 53–55
  and gambling 4–5, 114, 116–117, 126–127
  and gaming 4–5, 114, 117–118, 126–127
ADHD 5, 118
advance fee fraud 6, 79, 133, 141, 146–152, 154–155
  see also mass-marketing fraud; Nigerian email scam
age of consent 174, 175
aggression 5, 28, 114, 118–124, 126–127, 136, 158
Alexy, E. M. 160
Allen, I. E. 87
Alsharnouby, M. 144, 155
Altman, I. 24
Amosun, P. A. 77
An, Y-J. 89, 91, 92, 93
Anderson, C. A. 121, 122, 123, 126
anonymity 2, 3, 5, 11, 13, 18–22, 29–30, 33, 37–38, 52–53, 55, 78–79, 84, 116, 130–132, 164, 171, 177, 192, 194
  and cyberbullying 78–79
  and deception 130–132
  and deindividuation 11, 19–22
  and expression of the self 2, 11, 13, 18–22, 29–30, 37–38, 52–53, 192, 194
  and privacy 5, 116, 194
  and self-disclosure 18–19, 29–30, 37–38
Antheunis, M. L. 35
anxiety 7, 10, 32, 41, 69, 118, 124, 130, 149, 153, 190, 199
asynchronous communication 4, 32, 45, 90–93, 95, 96, 97, 105, 108, 132, 193
attraction 11, 23 26, 33, 35, 36, 38–50, 65, 130, 136
avatars 3, 14, 31, 34, 62, 70–72, 88, 95–100, 130, 139, 157, 169, 186
  and cyberharassment 157, 169
  and virtual affairs 3, 62, 70–72
awareness campaigns 6, 143, 146, 149, 153, 154–155

Bada, M. 153
Bandura, A. 120, 121, 182, 185
BAR theory 44
Barak, A. 27, 157, 169, 196, 199
Bargh, J. A. 18, 19, 22, 29, 58, 61
Bartlett, C. P. 85
Baumgartner, S. E. 59, 61, 189
Behm-Morawitz, E. 157, 169
Bennett, D. C. 78
Berkowitz, L. 121
Berlin, F. S. 170, 174, 176, 177, 186
Bessière, K. 18, 22, 189
Blackboard 87
  see also virtual learning environments

Cyberpsychology: The Study of Individuals, Society and Digital Technologies, First Edition.
Monica Therese Whitty and Garry Young.
© 2017 John Wiley & Sons, Ltd. Published 2017 by John Wiley & Sons, Ltd.

blogs 15, 20, 33, 74, 78, 81, 83, 88, 90, 97, 105, 108, 110–113
Bocij, P. 158
boiler room scam 147, 148
    see also investment scam; mass-marketing fraud
Bok, S. 128, 129
Bond, B. J. 58
Boudreau, K. 103
Bowker, N. 130
boyd, D. M. 34, 110, 111
Brax, D. 160
Bregha, F. J. 101
Brown, A. 87
Brym, R. J. 40
Buchanan, T. 26, 31, 41, 47, 148, 149, 151
Buller, D. B. 128
bulletin boards 13, 30, 52, 58, 108
Bushman, B. J. 122, 123, 126
Buss, D. M. 24, 66, 67, 70

Calenda, D. 82
Cameron, C. 42, 44
Caspi, A. 92, 133
Castelnuovo, G. 197
Cattell, R. B. 9
charity scam 147, 148
    see also mass-marketing fraud
chat rooms 20, 31, 33, 58, 61, 63, 64, 88, 115, 132, 161, 193, 195
Chen, Y-L. 118
child pornography 7, 170–176, 180–186
child pornography offenders 176–186
Childs, M. 88
civic activities 76, 81, 85
    see also activism
Clark, R. E. 88
Coeckelbergh, M. 163
cognitive errors 6, 116, 150–151, 154, 183
cognitive load 137
cognitive neoassociation model 5, 121–122
cognitive presence 4, 91, 93
cognitive shortcuts *see* heuristic processing
Coleman, E. 56
collector 7, 170, 178–179, 182

consumer fraud 151
    see also mass-marketing fraud
controlled cognitive engagement 137
Cooley, C. H. 9
Cooper, A. 3, 52, 53, 55, 61, 63, 171
COPINE scale 173, 178, 179
coping 5, 7, 57, 79, 124, 188, 191–199
Corley, M. D. 55
courtship disorder theory 7, 181–182, 183
Cress, U. 20
criminal behaviour 6, 141–155, 156–169, 170–186
criminal profile 77, 138, 147, 159–162, 164, 169, 176–179, 181–186
    and cyberstalkers 159–160, 161–162, 169
    and stalkers 159–160
Cumberbatch, G. 120, 122
cyberaffairs *see* Internet infidelity
cyberattack 7, 162, 163
    see also DDoS attack
cyberbullying 76, 77–79, 84–85, 153, 174
cyberchondria 7, 187, 189–190, 199
cyberharassment 3, 6, 27, 53, 76–79, 155–160, 163, 168–169, 174
cybersex 2, 3, 51–61, 62, 64, 65, 68, 70–72, 115
cybersex compulsives 51, 53, 54–55, 60–61, 115
    see also addiction; Internet addiction
cyberstalking 6, 156–160, 168–169
cyberwarfare 6, 156, 162–164, 169

Daft, R. L. 93
Dando, C. J. 137
Daneback, K. 55
dating sites *see* online dating
Davinson, N. 146
DDoS attack 164, 201
    see also cyberattack
De Andrea, D. C. 36, 38
de Freitas, S. 91, 92, 96
deception 2, 5, 6, 44–45, 49–50, 128–140, 141–149, 152
    and attractiveness 2, 130–131, 152
    and category 130
    and definition 128–133
    and detection 5, 45, 137–140

deception (cont'd)
    identity-based 2, 5, 130–132, 138–140
    message-based 5, 132, 138–140
    and relationships 44–45, 49–50
    and self-presentations 2, 5, 131, 141–149, 152
DePaulo, B. M. 133, 138
depression 12, 18, 84, 105, 117, 123, 132, 149, 189, 191, 192
DeSteno, D. 67, 72
developmental theory 67
Diagnostic and Statistical Manual of Mental Disorders (DSM) 5, 115, 117, 126, 132, 177
Dickey, M. D. 96
digital divide 3, 73–75, 85
discussion groups 32, 93
    see also Usenet newsgroups
disembodiment 13, 15
disinhibition effect 2, 26, 27, 78, 84, 116, 132, 159, 163, 183, 195, 201
Dollard, J. 121
Donkin, L. 196
double-shot hypothesis 67–68
drug trafficking 146
Dutton, W. H. 33, 73

ecological niche 183, 184
education 4, 5, 76, 86–100, 125, 153–154, 198, 201
e-learning 4, 86–100
e-therapy 7, 186, 193–197, 199
Elias, N. 80
Elliot, I. A. 171, 172, 178, 179, 181, 183, 184, 185
Ellison, N. B. 34, 35, 38, 43, 45
emergency scam 149, 151
    see also mass-marketing fraud
emotional harm 3, 6, 60, 75–79, 114, 124, 126, 148–149, 152, 156–158, 160–162, 187, 189–190
emotional support 27, 57–58, 76, 79, 149, 191–199, 201
entertainment 4, 54, 76, 101–113, 125, 126
equity theory 2, 24–26
Erikson, E. H. 10, 57, 80

ethical concerns 153–154, 162–165, 169, 195
excessive online gaming 114–118, 126
exchange theory 2, 24–26, 43–45
extremist groups 6, 82–84, 161, 169
    British National Party 161
    Islamist extremist groups 161, 164
    Ku Klux Klan 161, 164
    National Action 161
    Stormfront 161, 164
eye-tracker 144
Eysenbach, G. 57, 186, 192

Facebook 17, 35, 36, 38, 81, 90, 103, 109, 110, 142, 144, 145, 148, 149, 156
    and identity 17, 35, 36, 38
    and relationships 35
    and scams 142, 144, 145, 148, 149
    see also social networking sites
feature-based model 134–139
Feldman, M. D. 132
Ferguson, C. J. 120, 122, 123, 125, 127
Finkelhor, D. 78, 171, 174, 179, 183
Finkelhor's precondition model 7, 183
Fox, S. 104, 186, 188
friendship 2, 16, 17, 19, 21, 24, 29, 31–38, 58–59, 65, 73, 76, 103, 109, 115, 117, 123, 128, 147–149, 160, 188, 191, 199, 200
frustration–aggression hypothesis 5, 121

Gainsbury, S. M. 116
Galanxhi, H. 130, 139
gambling 4–5, 76, 114–118, 126–127
    and addiction 4–5, 116–118, 126–127
    and demographic differences 116–117
    and health problems 5, 116, 118, 126–127
games 4–5, 18, 30–31, 33–34, 61, 63, 70, 71, 72, 76, 79, 80, 83, 84, 100, 103, 104, 106, 109, 112, 114–127
    and addiction 4–5, 114–118, 126–127
    and education 5, 125–126
Garofalo, R. 56
Garrison, D. R. 91, 96
gender switching 130
general aggression model 5, 122–123
George, J. 131

Gergen, K. J. 2, 12, 16, 21, 22
Gilbert, R. L. 34, 71, 72
Gillespie, A. 172, 174, 175
Giumetti, G. W. 122
Givens, D. 47, 48, 49
Goffman, E. 2, 12, 17, 21, 22, 45, 50
Gonzales, M. H. 42
Green, S. K. 43
Greenwood, D. N. 110, 111
Griffiths, M. 54, 115, 116, 127, 191
Grohol, J. 115
Guillory, J. 131, 139

hacking 161, 164
  and harassment 161
hacktivists 164
  black hat 164
  grey hat 164
  white hat 164
Hale, W. C. 161, 169
Hancock, J. T. 29, 45, 50, 129, 130, 131, 134, 135, 136, 139
harassment 3, 6, 27, 40, 53, 76, 76–79, 84, 156–160, 163, 168–169, 174
Haraway, D. 2, 15, 16, 17, 22
Hardy, W. 153, 154
Harris, C. R. 67, 102
hate crimes 6
Haythornthwaite, C. 81
health-related information 7, 187–192
heuristic processing 145, 156, 160–162, 168
Higgins, E. T. 11, 12, 18, 85
Hiltz, S. 27
Hirzalla, F. 81, 85
Hong, J. 142
Hong, Y. 57
Hooper, S. 57
Howitt, D. 173, 184
Huesmann, L. R. 120
hyperpersonal relationships 2, 26, 28–29, 37, 38, 39, 68, 69, 128, 151

idealization 69, 72, 151
identity 1, 2, 3, 9–22, 29–30, 32, 38, 43–44, 47, 57–58, 61, 73, 76, 79, 80–81, 84, 95, 99, 130–133, 138, 142–143, 158, 168, 201

  and postmodern self 1, 12–13, 15–17
  and Real Me 18–19, 22, 29–30, 32, 38
  and saturated self 16
  and social constructionist theory 1, 16–17, 43–44
  and social identity theory 1, 2, 10–11, 19–20, 22
  and theft 79, 142–143, 158
  and trait theory 1, 9–10, 18–19, 29, 32
  and young people 80–81, 84
illegal activities *see* criminal behaviour
illegal downloads 6, 139, 152–155
impression management 17
  see also self-presentation
inheritance scam 148
  see also mass-marketing fraud
instant messaging 6, 31, 33, 48, 80, 133–137, 146
integrated theory of sexual offending 7, 183–184
Internet child pornography *see* child pornography
Internet dating *see* online dating
Internet gaming disorder 5, 117–118, 126
Internet infidelity 3, 53, 63, 62–72
Internet of things 200
investment scam 147
  see also boiler room scam; mass-marketing fraud

Jambon, M. M. 77
James, W. 9
Jansson, K. 146
jealousy 3, 35, 66–67, 69–72
Jin, S.-A., A. 110, 111
Joinson, A. N. 26, 27, 31, 38, 128, 141, 166
Jung, S. 181, 182

Kayany, J. M. 105, 107, 108
Keskitalo, T.
Kirk, S. 192
Kirriemuir, J. 96
Klein, M. 15, 55, 69–70, 72
Koestner, R. 42
Kramer, J. 192
Kubicek, K. 56, 57

Lam, L. T. 118
Larreamendy-Joerns, J. 88
Lea, M. 11, 15, 19, 22
Lea, S. 149, 150, 151, 155
learning environments 4, 87, 89, 90, 92, 95, 97–99
    and 3-D 4, 97–99
learning performance 4, 88, 94
leisure 4, 101–113, 124–125
Lenhart, A. 59, 80
Liau, A. 55
linguistics 15, 45, 50
    and cues 15, 45
LinkedIn 35, 131, 139
    see also social networking sites
Liu, S.-H. 89, 90, 95
Livingstone, S. 73, 74, 75, 76, 85
loneliness 16, 58, 97
Loucas, C. E. 196, 197
lying see deception

Macafee, T. 81, 82
Maheu, M. 63
Malu, M. K. 55, 56
Manfredo, M. J. 102
Marcia, J. E. 10, 57, 80
Markus, H. 11
Marwick, A. E. 110, 111
mass-marketing fraud 6, 79, 133, 141, 146–152, 154–155
    see also scams
matchmaking sites see online dating
Mathews, S. 98
McDaniel, B. T. 104
McElroy, E. 190
McGrath, M. G. 158
McKenna, K. Y. A. 18, 19, 22, 29, 32, 38, 41, 58, 61
McManus, F. 189, 190
media richness 4, 93–95, 99, 134
Menard, K. S. 159
Mileham, B. L. A. 64
misrepresentation see deception
MMORPG 18, 33–34, 53, 70–71, 103, 124
    see also Second Life; virtual world

monitoring 7, 58, 117, 157–158, 164–169
    see also surveillance
MOO 13, 15, 30–31, 33–34
MOOC 87
motivational errors 154
MUD 13–15, 30–31, 33–34
Munchausen by Internet 5, 131–132
Mustanski, B. 56, 57, 58

near synchronous communication 31, 137
Neuman, S. B. 91, 92, 96, 107
Neumann, P. R. 83, 84, 85
newsgroup 19, 29, 32, 63, 102
Nigerian email scam 141, 147
Nimrod, G. 102, 103, 104
Niveau, G. 171, 177, 180
nonverbal communication 12, 27, 30, 31, 47–48, 138, 195
numbers game 45–46
    see also 419 scam; advance fee fraud; mass-marketing fraud

object relations 69–70
Olason, D. T. 116
Olasupo, M G. 193, 194
online counselling see e-therapy
online dating 2, 6, 17, 20, 26, 33, 37, 39–49, 62, 147–149, 151–152, 155
    and deception 6, 44–46, 49–50
online dating romance scam 6, 147–149, 151–152, 155
    see also mass-marketing fraud
online relationships 2, 3, 15, 16, 19, 21, 23, 25–32, 34–38, 39–50, 66, 68–70, 71, 78, 104, 115, 128, 133, 147, 151–152, 200–201
online sex see cybersex
online social support groups 7, 27, 191–193, 199
Ormerod, T. C. 137, 140
Oswell, D. 175, 178
Owens, T. 9, 188, 191, 192

paedophilia 7, 124, 126, 170, 175, 177
paranoid–schizoid position 69–70
paraphilic disorder 177, 181, 182
Parker, T. S. 53, 64, 68

Parks, M. R. 31, 32
Parris, L. 79
Parsons, J. T.
pathways model 7, 183, 184
Paul, B. 175
personal ads 25, 42–44, 47
personality 2, 6, 10, 18, 24, 26, 29, 39, 40, 41, 42, 44, 70, 145, 159, 181
Peter, J. 35, 41, 50, 59, 61, 80
Petrakou, A. 86, 91, 92, 96–97, 100
Pew Internet and American Life Project reports 73, 74, 187
phishing 6, 76, 139, 142–146, 149, 154, 155, 161
photographs 20, 21, 26, 31, 33, 39, 43, 47, 49, 59, 74, 78, 133, 170, 172–175, 186
Poley, M. E. M. 41, 50
politics 81, 82, 85, 104
pornography 115, 168, 170–185
possible selves 1, 2, 11–12, 18–19, 22, 29–30, 32, 38, 50
  and true selves 29, 30, 41
Potenza, M. N. 117, 127
presentations *see* self-presentation
privacy 5, 7, 17, 40, 76, 116, 131, 133, 166–169, 194, 195, 200
pseudo-photographs 170, 173–175
psychological harm 3, 6, 75–79, 124, 126, 149, 156–158, 160–161
  see also emotional harm
psychological well-being 18, 192
Pulman, A. 131, 132
Pyszczynski, T. 84

Quayle, E. 171–173, 180, 184–186

radicalization 3, 82–85, 138, 162, 201
Rashid, A. 138, 140
Recupero, P. R. 194, 195
Regner, T. 194, 195
Reijnen, L. 179
relationship transgressions 3, 62, 6–68, 70, 72
relationships 2–4, 16, 19, 23–25, 28, 32–34, 36, 37, 41, 52, 63–65, 67–68, 70, 97, 101, 111, 133, 178–179, 184
  see also online relationships
rich-get-richer hypothesis 41

Rideout, V. J. 105
Riggio, R. E. 43
risk 3, 5, 55–56, 58–61, 73, 75–77, 79, 83, 85, 116, 117, 131, 135, 146, 151, 159, 194–195
  and young people 73, 75–77, 79, 83, 85, 117
Robinson, C. C. 86, 89, 90
Robinson, J. P. 105, 107–109, 113
romantic beliefs 151
Roscoe, B. 65, 67, 72
rules of war 6, 162

Salmon, G. 95, 97–98
Salmon's stage model of e-learning 4, 95, 98
scaffolding 92
scams 3, 6, 76, 79, 138, 139, 141–152, 154–155, 161
Scharlott, B. W. 39
Schellens, T. 93
schemas 120
Schneider, J. P. 55, 64
script theory 5, 120
searching, matching, and interacting model (SMI model) 47
Sears-Roberts Alterovitz, S. 44
Second Life 3, 4, 70, 95–98, 157
  and virtual affairs 3, 71
  see also MMORPG; virtual world
self-disclosure 5, 24, 26, 29, 30, 36, 38, 48, 128, 194
self-esteem 12, 18, 35, 58, 102, 118
self-presentation 11, 36, 37, 42, 43, 69
self-regulatory control problems 184
serious games 125–126
Seto, M. C.
sexting 170, 171, 180, 186
sexual desire 30, 52, 65, 185
sexual harassment *see* harassment
sexual health 3, 56–58, 74
sexual molestation 171, 180, 182, 183
sexual solicitation 158, 170, 180, 182, 183
sexual voyeurism 170, 177
Shackelford, T. K. 66, 67, 70
Shaughnessy, K. 53
Shaw, J. 63
Sheridan, L. P. 160, 169
Sherry, J. 122

shyness 2, 30, 32, 39, 40, 41, 91, 118, 195, 198
Singer, P. W. 162, 169
slippery slope 3, 7, 76, 185
Smith, J. E. 42
social anxiety *see* shyness
social cognitive approach 3, 62, 67
social compensation hypothesis 41
social distance theory 134–136
social engineering 142
social evolutionary theory 2, 3, 24, 25–26, 44
social information processing theory 2, 28
social intimacy problems 184
social isolation 92, 179
social learning theory 5, 7, 120–121, 182–183
social networking sites 6, 17–18, 20, 33–35, 63, 74, 78–79, 109–110, 131, 135–136, 146, 161, 191
  and identity 17, 19–20, 33
  and relationships 33, 35–36, 110
  see also Facebook; LinkedIn; Twitter
social penetration theory 24, 26
social phobia *see* shyness
social presence 2, 4, 27–28, 91, 96–98, 136
social support 57–58, 191, 192, 201
Sociolotron 124
Sparck-Jones, K. 166, 169
spear phishing 6, 142–143, 154–155
Spears, R. 11, 15, 19, 22
Spitzberg, B. H. 157, 159
splitting 3, 69–70, 72
stalking 6, 156–160
  see also cyberstalking
Starcevic, V. 115, 116, 127, 190, 199
Stever, G. S. 110–113
stress 124, 138, 161, 179
Sucala, M. 193, 196
Sun, P.-C. 88, 93, 94
Suzuki, L. K. 58
Subrahmanyam, K. 33, 35, 57, 125
Suler, J. 27, 163, 195
support sites 191
surveillance 7, 82, 156, 163, 165–168
  see also monitoring
synchronous communication 4, 31, 52, 64, 90–98, 105, 135, 193, 194
systematic processing 145

taboos 5, 114, 123–124, 126
Tajfel, H. 10
Tamim, R. M. 86
Tanis, M. 190, 194
Tate, T. 172, 173
teaching presence 4, 91
teledildonics 51, 60
terrorism 83, 146, 160, 168
theory of planned behaviour 153
therapeutic alliance 196–197
Thibaut, J. W. 24, 25, 46
Titan Rain 162
Toma, C. L. 45, 50
Tong, S. T. 35, 38
training programmes 6, 146, 149
Triple A Engine 2, 52, 171
truth/lies paradox 128
Turkle, S. 1, 2, 13, 14, 15, 16, 17, 20, 22
Twitter 110–112, 160, 161, 164, 180
two-for-one hypothesis 67, 68

uncertainty reduction strategies 35, 36
Usenet newsgroups 32
  see also discussion groups
Utz, S. 31, 35, 130

Valkenburg, P. M. 35, 41, 50, 59, 61, 80
victim profile
  and cyberstalking 157, 159–160, 168–169
  and scams 79, 143–145, 148–152, 155
  and stalking 160
victimization 78, 79, 143–145, 148–152, 155, 160, 172, 175, 177–180
video dating 42–44, 47
videoconferencing 54, 195
virtual environments *see* virtual world
virtual learning environments 87–88, 98
  see also Blackboard; virtual world
virtual world 8, 13, 15, 34, 53, 69, 70, 91, 96–98, 119, 157, 187, 201
  and therapy 197–198
  see also MMORPG; *Second Life*
visceral triggers 6, 144, 150
vishing 143, 154
Vishwanath, A. 144–145, 155
visual anonymity 2, 11, 130

Vrij, A. 137–138, 140
Vygotsky, L. S. 92

Walther, B. 118
Walther, J. B. 28, 33, 35, 36, 38, 69, 129
Wang, J. 78, 144, 155
Ward, T. 183, 184
webcam 31, 54
Weinstein, A. 118
Wingrove, T. 77
Wolak, J. 78, 171, 174, 179, 180
Woll, S. B. 43
Wood, L. 75
Wood, N. T. 90
World of Warcraft 18, 34, 124

Wright, M. 83
Wysocki, D. K. 52, 61

Yahoo Boyz 77
Yang, M. L. 46, 50
Yarab, P. E. 65
Yee, N. 34
Yen, J. Y. 118
Young, G. 122, 123, 124, 127
Young, K. S. 63, 114–115
YouTube 90, 188

Zhong, Z.-J. 75
Zimbler, M. 113
zone of proximal development 92